'A riveting account of a remarkable Elizabethan whose experiences as a scholar, traveller, soldier, exile, outlaw, spy, traitor and compulsive letter-writer prepared him well for his greatest challenge: serving as King James's ambassador to Venice. Deeply researched, captivatingly told and richly rewarding for anyone interested in British history and diplomacy.'

James Shapiro, author of *1599: A Year in the Life of William Shakespeare*

'This is an enchanting book. And, for any lover of Shakespeare, an exhilarating one. With characteristic panache, Carol Chillington Rutter introduces another performer of the period, a diplomat, and a worthy addition to that great generation of writers, actors and thinkers.'

Simon Russell Beale, actor

'Carol Chillington Rutter communicates her rigorous scholarship in lucid, sparkling prose. More than a biography, this is a compelling study of a vital period in our history – and one of the best books about Venice that I have read. Entertaining, erudite and essential reading.'

Anna Beer, author of *Patriot or Traitor: The Life and Death of Sir Walter Ralegh*

'Combining political history with a life of high drama, Carol Chillington Rutter tells the story of Henry Wotton, whose career as English ambassador to Venice was both dramatic and highly impactful. Deeply researched and evocative, *Lying abroad* brings the man who was arguably the first modern diplomat back to life.'

Elizabeth Norton, author of *The Lives of Tudor Women*

'During the course of this exuberant narrative, Carol Chillington Rutter plunges readers into a world that is at once surpassingly strange yet jarringly familiar. In *Lying abroad*, Henry Wotton learns to survive perilous times and even thrive in a landscape of dangerous diplomacy. I read it with mounting excitement.'

Laurence Bergreen, author of *In Search of a Kingdom*

'I wanted to highlight the whole book. Carol Chillington Rutter gives us Henry Wotton's character and world in a style that embodies and illuminates the teeming intellectual, political, cultural and linguistic exuberance of the man and his age. *Lying abroad* is full of fascinating detail and it was a continual, stimulating delight to spend time in Wotton's and Rutter's company.'

Sarah Fraser, author of *The Prince Who Would Be King*

'As witty and entertaining as its subject – the brilliant, quirky dilettante, man of letters and diplomat Henry Wotton – this book distils formidable knowledge into a page-turner that brings to life a fascinating journey, from Shakespeare's London to Paolo Sarpi's Venice and back.'

Filippo de Vivo, author of *Information and Communication in Venice*

Lying abroad

Manchester University Press

Lying abroad

Henry Wotton and the invention of diplomacy

Carol Chillington Rutter

Manchester University Press

Copyright © Carol Chillington Rutter 2026

The right of Carol Chillington Rutter to be identified as the author of this work has been asserted in accordance with the Copyright, Designs and Patents Act 1988.

Published by Manchester University Press
Oxford Road, Manchester, M13 9PL

www.manchesteruniversitypress.co.uk

British Library Cataloguing-in-Publication Data
A catalogue record for this book is available from the British Library

ISBN 978 1 5261 7206 8 hardback

First published 2026

The publisher has no responsibility for the persistence or accuracy of URLs for any external or third-party internet websites referred to in this book, and does not guarantee that any content on such websites is, or will remain, accurate or appropriate.

EU authorised representative for GPSR:
Easy Access System Europe, Mustamäe tee 50, 10621 Tallinn, Estonia
gpsr.requests@easproject.com

Typeset
by Cheshire Typesetting Ltd, Cuddington, Cheshire
Printed in Great Britain
by Bell and Bain Ltd, Glasgow

Legatus est vir bonus peregre missus ad mentiendum Reipublicae causa.
(The ambassador is an honest man sent to lie abroad for the sake of his country.)
Henry Wotton, inscribed in a friend's album, Augsburg, 1604

Ben confessarò … che tutto quello che dicono li Ambasciatori non è l'evangelio. Il nostro cibo non è altro che la novità. Ci vengono portate delle cose alcune delle quali sono vere, ma qualche volta ci bisogna ingiottir delle mosche.
(To tell the truth … not everything Ambassadors say is gospel. Our food is nothing but news. Things come to us, some of it true, but sometimes we have to swallow flies.)
Henry Wotton in the Collegio, *Esposizioni Principi* XVII, 14 August 1608

Ambassadors are supposed to know what they're doing.
Retired ambassador commenting on expulsion of UK's ambassador to Syria, June 2012

For Anwen Mabli, Kasper Harry and Loken Joseph
who make 'a July's day short as December'

Contents

Author's note		*page* xi
Introduction		1
Prologue: 'chosen from among a thousand'		5

Part I: Furnishing a mind

1	Schooling an ambassador	13
2	Wit ballasted with learning	30
3	The useful library of travel	44
4	The wandering time of my life	59
5	A man well tumbled in the world	77

Part II: A world of business

6	Mr Secretary Wotton	99
7	Campaigning with Essex	116
8	This unsettled kingdom	132
9	An interlude: executions, exile and strange encounters	144

Part III: Sent to lie abroad

10	Commanded in embassy	157
11	Household stuff	177
12	Service in a turbulent time	195
13	Crossing the Rubicon	213
14	Some particular men	222
15	So many sheets of paper	240
16	Return into our sweet England	258

Epilogue: no longer Sisyphus   271

List of illustrations   274
Acknowledgements   277
Appendix   280
Sources   283
Index   297

Author's note

I do not reconcile the two calendars operating across Europe during Wotton's lifetime. By 1582, when Pope Gregory promulgated reforms, the Julian calendar dating from the time of Julius Caesar was ten days adrift of the tropical year. Reformation England, however, refused to adopt the 'papist' calendar. The ten-day discrepancy between the Julian calendar (in England) and Gregorian calendar (in Venice) matters to diplomatic correspondence and decision-making.

Over the period Wotton knew him, Robert Cecil's name changed four times as new titles were conferred upon him. To avoid confusion, I refer to him as 'Cecil' throughout. Young Wotton is 'Harry' until he reaches adulthood upon his twenty-eighth birthday, March 1596, when he becomes 'Wotton'. When he grovels before Cecil in May 1603, however, he's 'Harry'. After 1604, Venice knows him as 'Arrigo VVottoni'.

Introduction

Stare down into the waters of a Venetian canal and you begin to see faces. Maybe they're nothing more than shapes made by drifting seaweed, or reflections written on the water's surface. But maybe they're *ignoti* – unknowns – faces from the past who want to return to the light of day.

This book is about one of them.

Many of us know the definition of an ambassador as 'an honest man sent to lie abroad for the sake of his country', left in an autograph album in Austria in 1604. And many Shakespeareans (like me) know the story of the Globe playhouse burning to the ground during a performance of Shakespeare's *Henry VIII* in 1613. But almost no one could tell you who wrote the quip or reported the fire.

In both cases the *ignoto* is Henry Wotton.

Wotton is someone who turns up as a footnote in other men's lives. Nobody thinks of him as a serious diplomat. In 1907, his only modern biographer considered him 'of more interest to us as a writer of letters, full of wit and gossip, than as a statesman'. Under-valuations like that one rest on partial readings. Nobody until now has paid attention to Wotton's full dossier, his complete diplomatic bag compiled from archive sources that, when his audiences in Venice are interleaved with dispatches to London, show the evolution of his diplomacy and the sheer industry of the man. Certainly, nobody makes the bold claim, as I do here, that when a dispute between Venice and Rome ruptured Christendom in 1606, it was Wotton's diplomacy, his maverick diplomacy, that averted pan-European war.

This book aims to bring the *ignoto* back into the light. It places Henry Wotton among that extraordinary generation of Elizabethans born in the 1560s who defined the era as an age of gold: statesmen, scholars, soldiers, explorers, churchmen, playwrights and poets. Many of them appear in this book, for this book is not just about Wotton: it's about the world he inhabited, the people he knew and the tangles of their relationships, tangles that were enlivening but sometimes also deadly.

When King James sent him as the ambassador to Venice in 1604, Wotton was only thirty-six, too young for the job, and with no experience of diplomacy. His qualification was that he'd survived half a dozen previous lives lived on the edge, as a student, a traveller, a secretary, a soldier, a scoundrel and a spy. Plus, he was fluent in Italian. Sending him to Venice, the king handed him a blank slate, for while diplomacy was an art that had been refined in Italy across several centuries, and while the Italians in the mid-fifteenth century had invented the role of the resident ambassador, Venice hadn't seen an English ambassador for over fifty years.

In the 1540s Henry VIII paid an English wool merchant to act as a kind of nuncio and to inform him on Venetian matters; in 1550 Edward VI replaced the merchant with an accredited ambassador, but Queen Mary withdrew him three years later and left the post vacant. After Elizabeth became queen in 1558 and Pope Pio V excommunicated her as an Anglican heretic, the lapse in Anglo-Venetian relations looked permanent. But in any case, diplomacy wasn't high on Elizabeth's foreign policy agenda. In the last two decades of her reign, she emptied all her embassies across Europe, severing diplomatic ties from the Hague to Madrid.

It was this isolationist history that James I, styling himself the 'Rex Pacificus', aimed to reverse by launching his project of pan-European peacemaking, bundling off ambassadors to embassies as fast as he could appoint them. When he arrived in London from Edinburgh to claim the English throne in April 1603, he happened to find a secretary of the Venetian government waiting for him. Giovanni Carlo Scaramelli had come to protest about English piracy in the Mediterranean, but his presence may have been what prompted James to think beyond those vacant embassies in Paris and Madrid, and to imagine a new office in the Republic.

Scaramelli suggested (mischievously but, indeed, seriously) that someone from one of England's known 'recusant' Catholic families – Lord Crichton of Sanquhar, perhaps – be sent as ambassador to Venice, someone who would soft-pedal politics. What Venice got instead was a determined Protestant and hard-pedaller, but someone who, when faced with constructing Anglo-Venetian relations from the ground up, would prove himself devoted to Venetian interests, 'un vero Venetiano'.

Across the six years of his appointment, Wotton's devotion never wavered. If he despaired of the Republic's inability to make up its mind, he rarely reported that to London. For their part, the Venetians often found him perplexing. In audiences with the doge, the head of the Venetian state, his English responses were frequently tin-eared. He couldn't quite bring himself to stick to the established protocols. He genuinely seemed unable to grasp how decisions were reached in the Republic, that the doge wasn't an absolute monarch, as James was in England. This, of course, was the crucial difference that inflected Wotton's diplomacy like no other ambassador's in Europe. Other ambassadors faced executive monarchs; Henry Wotton faced committees, and rule by consensus.

But maybe Wotton deliberately played dumb. He regularly went off message to act uninstructed, to agitate and aggravate, to disconcert and enrage – and also to amuse, endlessly to amuse. For Henry Wotton was a charmer. Personally and in dispatches he delighted King James. In his audiences, he had the same effect on Doge Leonardo Donà (but not on Pope Paolo V, who called Wotton a 'viper'). Calculated or not, Wotton's unpredictability opened up a space for creative diplomatic improvisation. As an outsider, he challenged the Venetian state to interrogate its own reactionary instincts and its calcified habits. His improvisation was often productive, always entertaining, sometimes obstructive and on two occasions even explosive.

At university, before a career in diplomacy was ever on the cards, Wotton's tutor impressed upon him that the only materials a diplomat had to work with were 'words and opportunities'. Wotton turned out to have a gift for words. They survive in family letters, scrawled across envelopes, on a treaty, in thick files of state documents in London and in Venice, thousands upon thousands of words written, spoken, recorded, dispatched. Some of them are recognised in this book for the very first time as his.

The sheer abundance of these words shows Wotton's world to be very different from ours. He didn't report himself in soundbites. He wrote copiously. He quoted Cicero, Caesar, Tacitus. He enlivened observation with extended metaphors. He illustrated with allusion, piled high with more allusion. He was particularly addicted to the parenthetical remark.

It's by delving deeply into his words that this book comes to know Henry Wotton. We have no portrait of the young man. (His only surviving likenesses show him in his late fifties.) Instead, we listen to his written voice, thinking, arguing, feeling. He laughs. He mourns. His words give us the wide-eyed student, the cocky adventurer, the homesick brother, the exile on the run.

His words, too, let us see diplomacy in the making. They document the practice of diplomacy, the painstaking day-to-day work of a jobbing ambassador wading through tedious arguments about trade, taxes, piracy. But also chasing murderers, burying bodies at sea, exposing (and generating) fake news, pursuing Protestant English interests by planting intelligencers – in other words, spies – inside the Papal Curia in Rome. This world is different from ours, but also, sometimes, strikingly familiar.

It's a gift to the story I aim to tell here that Wotton's words survive. But it's as great a gift that Wotton's Venice survives. His embassy, in a modest palazzo at Cannaregio; the Jewish Ghetto and furniture magazzino; the Palazzo Ducale; the Sala del Collegio; the bench outside the door where he sat; the Basilica; the astonishing clock he passed under to walk through the Merceria to cross the just-completed Ponte Rialto; the canals where *ignoti* lurk: all of this we can actually see, a material world that invites our imaginations to embed the ambassador in the city known as La Serenissima, inventing diplomacy in ways that still inform international relations today.

When King James sent Henry Wotton to Venice, Robert Cecil, the secretary of state who would receive all of Wotton's dispatches, knew his backstory, his distinctly chequered past. Cecil didn't think much of Italy or Italians. For him, they were 'pantaloons'. Perhaps he imagined that by sending Wotton to Venice the king was moth-balling a loose cannon, for Cecil couldn't think that the English ambassador would have much to do there, 'the passages of affairs between us and that state' being 'very barren'. But that's not how things panned out.

Prologue: 'chosen from among a thousand'

1 October 1604. Shortly before daybreak Sir Henry Wotton rises to his *giorno d'audientia*. He's been in Venice for a week or so, unannounced, staying out of sight, unpacking, purging himself homeopathically after a long journey that's hard on a man's bowels. Today, Wotton goes public. Today, the English ambassador is summoned to his first audience with Doge Marino Grimani, the elected head of the Venetian state, and the twenty-odd senators who, with him, sit as the Collegio, their business to receive foreign ambassadors, listen to what they have to say in their esposizioni, and report them to the Senato. It's the Senato – the 'Signoria' – that makes decisions in Venice. Wotton is on his mettle: focused, determined. He's the first ambassador England has sent to the Republic in fifty years, quite a transformation for a man who so recently was an outlaw, living in exile.

By a marvellous coincidence, back in London, the man who sent him will shortly be settling down to watch *Othello*, a new play by William Shakespeare. Wotton can't know it, but as he's walking the pavements of Venice King James will be there with him. And when audiences see the tragedy of *the Moor of Venice* at the Globe that autumn, they too will be transported to a city almost mythical in England's cultural imagination.

Wotton is kitted out in his black velvet robes of office, white spider-web lace at cuffs and collar beneath a broad-brimmed hat, clothes that sit more easily on him than his title does. He was 'Sir-ed' only days before he left England to take up this post, more in honour of the king than of the king's subject. 'Sir Henry' is still 'Harry' to himself, 'Arrigo' here. Now in his thirty-sixth year the beard he first grew on campaign with the earl of Essex to Cadiz eight years back is showing flecks that match the grey in his eyes.

He steps into the covered gondola of his escort, 'the most illustrious' Cavaliere Vendramin, resplendent in a gold-embroidered stole, to be rowed up the Canal Grande under the gaze of the whole city who crowd bridges, windows, pavements. The oars cutting the water leave bubble trails like spools of Burano lace. Behind follows a flotilla of lesser gondolas carrying the suite of young gentlemen Wotton has brought to Venice to staff his embassy, along with every recruitable Englishman (traveller, merchant, pilgrim) who happens to be in the city plus a gaggle of English students brought over from the university at Padua to fill out the scene. On these occasions, Wotton knows, ostentation is important.

He disembarks at the quayside onto the piazetta emptying into Piazza San Marco under the shadow of the winged lion, the emblem of San Marco, that presides over the Republic from atop a column of Egyptian granite. Crowds of scarlet robes stretching the full length of the Palazzo Ducale part like the Red Sea to allow Wotton to cross the brick pavement to the Porta della Carta (the 'paper door', so called because notaries of old deposited their state papers there). As he goes, the faces of thirty-two lions in marble stare down at him from the palazzo façade. There's no missing the presence, the presidence of San Marco in this city.

Wotton passes through the entrance reserved for statesmen beneath its impressive architrave, an astonishing compilation of marble sculpture that builds to a baroque climax in the figure of Justice seated at the top. She holds a sword and scales. Her eyes are wide open. In Venice, Justice isn't blind. The sculpture that dominates the whole places a centuries-dead doge kneeling before another winged lion. The beast dwarfs the human – and ignores him, eyeballing instead whoever enters below. The lion's mane ruffles like white-caps on the lagoon. His massive paw rests on an open book. Spread across two pages is the city's motto, the message delivered to Mark in a dream from one of God's ambassadors, those angels who do His regular business conveying to mortal man what's on His eternal mind. Angels are the diplomatic 'originals' upon whom every subsequent ambassador models himself. The inscription reads: 'Pax Tibi Marce Evangelista Meus' (Peace unto you, Mark, my evangelist).

Henry Wotton takes in this rich iconography as he crosses the entrance. It's dramatic, theatrical: statecraft rendered in stone. Of course, unlike the youths in his suite, he's seen this façade before, but only from a distance, as a traveller taking in sights. Now passing below, it's as though he's loading the weight of these figures onto his own shoulders. They represent the ideas and ideals that structure Venetian politics, instruction in marble. He crosses the interior cortile and starts up the vast, white-scoured marble Scala dei Giganti. (These giants, Mars, Neptune, Jacopo Sansovino's work, figure the Republic's power on land

and sea and intentionally diminish whoever climbs their stairs.) He turns right, then left, up another staircase.

The Scala d'Oro, the golden staircase, speaks of a Venice different from the Venice of the monumental giants. Golden Venice dazzles. The fantasticated barrel ceiling that arches above is designed in stucco, marked out in gold-framed panels picturing highly wrought classical scenes. And plenty of naked putti. Wotton doesn't look. He's concentrating on what's coming. He pats his pocket, letters safely stowed.

Trailing behind him, though, his retinue gapes, 'bocca aperta', open-mouthed. They thought nothing could match yesterday's *entrata*, the ambassador's ceremonial entrance that had them rowed several miles across the lagoon to the island of Santo Spirito, the spiritual jewel of the lagoon, where they took in, goggle-eyed, Sansovino's restoration of the church there. It's just one of the master-builder's works that, across decades, have transformed Venice into a modern Renaissance city. And the ceiling! A contemporary artist, Titian, painted it: Abraham and Isaac, Cain and Abel, David and Goliath. Scenes of roiling bodies. Near naked. Knotted muscles strained in acts of violence seeming to plummet onto the upturned gaze of the puny mortals below – who today are being beckoned by winsome golden cherubs towards seduction.

One more flight up, the retinue passes through the Sala delle Quattro Porte. One of its four doors leads to the notorious room where the Consiglio di Dieci, the Council of Ten, presides over criminal cases. The condemned who exit through the door opposite find themselves crossing a flying bridge – a later, romantic century will name it 'The Bridge of Sighs' – that vomits them into the city's most fearsome prison.

Vendramin leads Wotton through a third door. Behind, the escort crowds into the small chamber known as the Sala di Anticollegio. It's lined with wooden benches. Time for a pause, giving old men a moment to catch their breaths. They need it. Venice is governed by a gerontocracy. Even the *giovani* – the faction of young men that challenges the *vecchi*, the oldies in the Senato – are mostly twice Wotton's age.

Wotton, too, needs a breather. Time to reflect. His life to date has been tumultuous. And not a little tarnished, veering between high adventure and low farce. He wonders whether, sending him to Venice, the king who'll soon be known as 'the wisest fool in Christendom' has given spectacular evidence of his foolishness. Wotton is walking into a diplomatic void. He has no experience of diplomacy. On top of which Venice has no experience of English diplomats. It's been fifty years since Mary Tudor withdrew England's last ambassador.

Still, what he does know is that he brings to his appointment a mental alignment with the Republic. Take yesterday's ritual, the rowing to and fro across the lagoon, arriving only to be carried back again, a long-winded and curiously redundant business if looked at pragmatically. But Wotton doesn't see it that way. Rather, he recognises its symbolism, that it performs a concise enactment of La Serenissima's self representation and demonstrates her command of the lagoon, which advertises her domination of the Adriatic and Mediterranean seas. Looking around at the sheer number of scarlet robes the Senato put on the water, Wotton had impressed upon him the magnitude and splendour of the *nobili* it assembled on a daily basis to manage the Republic's affairs. It reminded him – should his Protestant English eyes need reminding – that La Serenissima's power derives from 'Santo Spirito'. Then, too, it achieved its immediate objective of putting the new resident ambassador on display. And display, Wotton knows, on these occasions is important.

The door to the Collegio cracks open. Wotton checks his hat. He's taken particular instruction on hat etiquette. Renewing diplomatic relations between his state and Venice, he's determined to get things right. That means, heading a new delegation, he won't yield precedence to any rival ambassador, thereby unwittingly marking his king inferior to theirs. It's a tricky balancing act, deference v. precedence. Hats are involved. Or more precisely, when they're removed. A couple of days ago he pressed the Collegio secretary who was prepping him for his entrance to detail the drill. He's heard that the Spanish ambassador doesn't 'uncover' until he reaches his seat at the right hand of the doge. If that's so, the English ambassador can't possibly 'uncover' until he, too, is seated. The secretary says he's misinformed; corrects him. Today Wotton knows what to do.

Now the door swings wide. He straightens his hat. Like an actor making an entrance he steps onto the stage where, for the next six years, he's going to perform. He's concentrating too hard to take in the setting, the room so recently restored after the disastrous fire of 1577: not Tintoretto's sumptuous paintings celebrating Good Government; not the extraordinary twenty-four-hour clock whose numbers and single hand run backwards; not even, covering the whole wall behind the tribunal dais, Veronese's epic celebration of Venetian victory at the battle of Lepanto in 1571. He ignores the six red-robed Consiglieri representing the city's six municipal districts, the sestiere, who flank the doge, and the nineteen black-robed Savii, 'wisemen' advisors, seated like choristers in stalls facing each other below the dais. He doesn't notice Scaramelli – the secretary he consulted a couple of days ago – standing at a podium to the side, pen in hand, poised to record verbatim what's said in this audience for communicating onwards to the Senato.

Wotton's eyes are fixed on the doge. He knows Marino Grimani by reputation, a nobleman loved by the poor of Venice for his gifts of gold. In the flesh, swathed in his dogal robes, he looks to Wotton's eyes like an embodiment of his reputation, a mountain of gold, but, with hands resting lightly on his lap and lively brown eyes above rosy cheeks hung with a cat-sized white beard that looks like it's asleep on his chest, he's hardly intimidating. Wotton glances at the empty seat to the doge's right. His destination. He remembers to remove his hat. He bows. Marino Grimani rises, greets his new ambassador with terms of honour and affection. Gestures. Vendramin stands aside. Wotton climbs the five stairs to the tribunal. He replaces his hat. Sits. Begins.

His voice is low, a little unsteady. He digs from his pocket a letter. It's from King James. Accepting it, Doge Grimani hands it to Scaramelli who reads it aloud. (When it's entered in the record, its Latin will be translated. Venetians, to the contempt of high-brow Florentines, conduct their state business in Italian.)

That's all Wotton has to do today: hand over his credentials; speak some 'complimenti', 'prendere licentia', bow and leave.

But he doesn't. Off the cuff, 'senza premeditate et senza concetti' (that is, without forethought, and without flowery language) he decides to add some 'parole' (words) of his own. He tugs another letter from his pocket, personal greetings from ten-year-old Henry, prince of Wales, signed in the child's schoolboy hand. Wotton goes on. (The Consiglieri, disconcerted, shift in their seats.) He says more about the restoration of diplomatic relations, his ambitions to employ all his attention and spirit to serving Venice, the honour he feels to have been 'chosen' for this appointment 'from among a thousand' of quality, 'in spite of my little worth'. The doge responds graciously, glossing over the possibility that, registering humility, Wotton cack-handedly insults Venice. Why would they welcome an ambassador of little worth? He gives Wotton his exit line.

But Wotton doesn't exit. Caught up in the moment, he daffs aside protocol. He enters a heated appeal for a young Scotsman, arrested upon 'a youthful indiscretion' made in 'ignorance'. (Wotton is winging it. He has no idea of the lad's crime or why the Signoria is punishing it so severely. Indiscretion and ignorance come nowhere near covering the case.) He asks the doge to honour his arrival by investigating the allegations. (This is brash, not to say impudent. Appealing for a judicial review? Or is Wotton bidding to have the importance of the English embassy recognised?) The doge, bemused, deflects.

PROLOGUE

Wotton should give the young man's name to Secretary Scaramelli. Everything will be done to 'gratify' him.

Only then does the ambassador depart. As the door closes, we can imagine the Savii trading glances under raised eyebrows. Admitting this Italianate Englishman, what have they let themselves in for?

To begin answering that question we need to rewind to May 1603, to look over Harry's shoulder as he writes to Secretary of State Robert Cecil from, as it happens, Venice. His letter reads like an audition piece for diplomacy. Deciphering it sends us even further back, to the 1570s, to see in Part I of this book how the mind of a future ambassador was formed by education and expanded by travel. In Part II, we'll watch that mind being disciplined by service to Robert Devereux, earl of Essex, in his household as private secretary; later, soldiering alongside him on campaigns to raid Cadiz and subdue Ireland. After that, we'll know who it was on that October morning in 1604 who climbed the Scala d'Oro. In Part III, as the man King James called his 'honest dissembler' moves from exile to political insider, we'll see Henry Wotton making a career of lying abroad for the sake of his country – and changing the course of European history.

Part I
Furnishing a mind

I
Schooling an ambassador

First drafts

23 May 1603. Venice. Harry Wotton is writing the letter that will change his life, addressing it to Secretary of State Robert Cecil who, just now, is managing regime change in England. Elizabeth Tudor died on 23 March after reigning forty-seven years, longer than the whole lifetimes of 'Elizabethans' like Harry Wotton and William Shakespeare. In May, Scottish king James VI arrived in London from Edinburgh to claim the English throne as James I. That a peaceful transfer of power happens is largely down to Cecil, the man with the twisted back, Elizabeth's 'pygmy' or 'littil beagle', as the king will soon call him. It will take some kicking and prodding and some radical readjustments to initial high optimism and wild speculation, but Englishmen will soon enough morph into 'Jacobeans'.

Meanwhile, for the past two years Harry has been on the run in Italy, a self-proclaimed exile. He'd been secretary to Robert Devereux, earl of Essex, but left England around the time the shattering events of February 1601, the so-called Essex 'rebellion', ignited – then fizzled out. Perhaps someone tipped him off. Perhaps he read the grim writing on the wall by the candle of his own wit. While Cecil rounded up the earl's supporters and turned the screws of interrogation upon them, someone bundled Harry aboard a boat, handed him cash and shipped him off to the continent. Now, is someone again tipping him off? The old queen is dead. The new king is actively rehabilitating the earl's reputation and restoring his favourites. Is it time for the renegade to work his peace with Cecil – the most politick of the earl's opponents and instrumental in his downfall? Time for Harry to come home?

This letter of 23 May works his redemption – and then some. Within a year of his homecoming he's knighted and sent back to Venice, now Sir Henry, ambassador, tasked with restoring Anglo-Venetian relations lapsed since 1553. How does he do it, shed the ragged reputation of the outlaw to put on the gorgeous gown of political insider? This letter: how does he know what to write – or how to write it? One answer: he started drafting it twenty-three years ago, at school – where he also studied the metamorphic habits of the chameleon.

Mothered upon learning

There's a snapshot of the sixteenth-century grammar schoolboy's experience in Shakespeare's *The Merry Wives of Windsor* in an impromptu Latin lesson conducted on a Windsor street. A pushy mother is exasperated that the Eton boys have been given yet another holiday. Her lad is foot-dragging because he wants to be on holiday. The master she's buttonholed is exasperated that she's demanding a test of her son's learning (when he wants to be on holiday). But teacher and pupil go through the motions. First, there's a wobbly demonstration of that standard grammar school teaching method, double translation (made all the more rackety by the Welsh schoolmaster's pronunciation):

> EVANS: What is 'lapis', William?
> WILLIAM: A stone.
> EVANS: And what is 'a stone', William?
> WILLIAM: A pebble.
> EVANS: No, it is 'lapis': I pray you, remember in your prain.

Then there's a test of 'accidence':

> EVANS: What is he, William, that doth lend articles?
> WILLIAM: Articles are borrowed of the pronoun, and be thus declined, Singulariter, nominativo, hic, haec, hoc.

Which produces correction:

> EVANS: Nominativo, hig, hag, hog ...

Only to hit the brick wall of ignorance:

> EVANS: Show me now, William, some declensions of your pronouns.
> WILLIAM: Forsooth, I have forgot.

The scene is a spoof, but it shows in outline standard Tudor pedagogy: learning by rote, testing by question and answer, embedding basics by repetition, repetition, repetition, all aimed at installing Latin, the international European language of cultural, political and commercial exchange, in English boys' brains. The uncomprehending mother stands by watching the scene. Mrs Page doesn't have a clue what her son is saying – which reminds us that Elizabethan learning is gendered. 'In the grammar' it's boys who are learning the patriarchal discourse that will overpeer their mother tongue. The scene reminds us too of the gap between pedagogic theory and pedagogic achievement: 'Remember in your prain'; 'I have forgot'.

This is the education system Harry Wotton enters, a system expanded by the Tudor revolution in education that settled *de facto* a national curriculum based upon the large-minded humanist writings of Desiderius Erasmus (who, from the first decades of the sixteenth century, taught boys everything from how to write a letter to how to blow their noses). 'In the grammar', boys up and down England follow more or less the same syllabus, whether at Eton, Winchester or Shrewsbury, or at one of the free grammar schools established in the reign of Edward VI in market towns like Stratford-upon-Avon. Local lads of the middling sort like Will Shakespeare live only a few minutes' walk from the school they attend as day boys. Boys like Harry approach grammar school from a different direction.

Born in 1568, he's the child of his father's late middle age, a surprise litter from a second marriage, the youngest of four sons spread across twenty years. The Wottons are prominent Kentishmen and Crown servants seated at Bocton Malherbe. Like John Shakespeare, who's risen to alderman in Stratford, but operating at a much higher rank, the Wottons are recruits to that army of amateurs who manage the bulk of Tudor governance. (Something like 50,000 salaried officials run France. The Elizabethan state pays just 1,200.) They work through personal networks of overlapping duty and purpose whose currency is acquaintance coined into social capital. Harry's grandfather was sheriff of Kent, treasurer of Calais, executor of Henry VIII's will and counsellor to his heir. His great-uncle was dean of both York and Canterbury. His father, Thomas, was named sheriff of Kent six days after Elizabeth's accession.

Thomas calls himself 'an unlearned man' and feels his 'lack of learning' a 'great grief'. But his library contains a 1542 Chaucer folio, a ten-volume Erasmus printed at Basel in 1540 and Nicole Gilles's 1551 *Annales ... des ... Gaulles*. His letter-book shows his connections: Francis Walsingham (the queen's principal secretary and later master of intelligence-gathering), Henry Sidney (lord deputy of Ireland, Philip's father), Matthew Parker (archbishop of Canterbury), the earls of Warwick, Leicester and Sussex, William Cecil, lord Burghley (the queen's chief privy counsellor) – as well as his Kentish neighbours. No doubt it was the murderous throes of multiple regime-change across four Tudor monarchs that taught Thomas Wotton to shun ambition, to cherish instead his 'country recreations and retirement'. He declines all offers of Court appointment, even when Queen Elizabeth comes in person to Bocton Hall to make them: a two-day visit in August 1573 when Harry is five years old.

Thomas in his fifties is right to duck the latest political crossfire. Informants have written to Lord Burghley of the 'cankered faction' of Catholic recusants so recently hatching 'cockatrices eggs' of open rebellion: Thomas Percy, earl of Northumberland, leading the revolt of the northern earls, executed August 1572; Thomas Howard, duke of Norfolk, tangled in a cat's cradle of intrigue to marry the queen of Scots, a noose he escapes only to lose his head in another assassination plot, executed June 1572. On progress through the weald of Kent in the summer of 1573 Elizabeth may look like she's distributing grace and favour, dropping knighthoods on bowed heads. But she's also touting solidarity. Thomas Wotton, however, is not royal quarry to be flushed from cover.

For the child, though, what is there to cherish in his father's geriatric world of retirement? Throwing stones at rabbits? Kicking heels in summer grass? The family hall is an 'ancient and goodly structure' 'seated ... on the brow of such a hill' as gives 'the advantage of a large prospect'. In the late August of his fifth year Harry perhaps watches from that advantage as the queen on horseback makes her way up Bocton hill, her closest entourage in tow – Burghley grumbling of Kent's 'worss ground' and 'wondeross rockes and vallyes', the rest of the three hundred carts and welter of attendants that carry her around the country parked elsewhere.

Perhaps the lad is allowed to sit up late to watch the queen's entertainment. And somewhere in the shadows, to gawp. Is she wearing that Spanish gown of white satin made so recently by Walter Fyshe, its bodice embroidered with a guard of gold and silver? Or perhaps the plain black velvet French gown she'd worn when Nicholas Hilliard painted her miniature only months ago? Nearly forty, does she look to the child like a crone rattling jewels or like a porcelain-faced goddess, fresh roses late-blooming in the Hall garden pinned to her headtire? Could trees talk, the tree the queen planted that afternoon that still stands at the entrance to Bocton Hall might tell of a boy who, himself a sapling, watched ground broken to royal command. From this large prospect a child's dazzled imagination is surely beckoned to a world beyond.

Thanks to his ambition-shunning father, though, he'll never forget that golden bait dangles from hooks of lead. 'Princes', as he'll regularly observe, will 'do what they will'. Mere mortals have to 'love one [an]other' and try to survive.

From Bocton Hall Kentish countryside falls steeply away as far as the eye can see. There's little else to look at. The nearest market village is Lenham, three miles distant; the nearest grammar school, Maidstone, ten. There will be no daily commute, then, for young Harry; no 'creeping like snail' to school. When he finally does go to school, he'll leave home and family far behind.

That's some time in Harry's future. For now, he's 'mothered upon learning'. Eleanora is his 'tutoress', and his contemporary biographer, Izaak Walton, rhapsodises that her 'care and pains' were repaid 'each day with such visible signs of future perfection … as turned her employment into a pleasing-trouble'. That's impossibly saccharine. The likelier scenario is the one playing out in fictional Windsor, Mrs Page tugging her reluctant scholar by the ear towards the mysteries of learning. Eleanora – pleasingly troubled or not – teaches Harry to read and write, to draw and play music. (Later, his viol da gamba will travel back and forth to Venice with him.) These are the four basics that Richard Mulcaster, a decade later, will set out in his *Positions … Necessarie for the Training vp of Children* (1581), the first English treatise on early years education. We need reading because reading serves 'our memory' and hands on to us 'that which is bequeathed us by others'. Writing does 'the like thereby for others which others have done for us'. Writing, then, is an exercise in sociability. But it's also self-ish. Writing almost magically captures our essential 'self' by 'knitting' the 'articulate voice' to the page, thereby serving 'as interpreter to the mind'. Drawing teaches us to look. 'Music' – vocal and instrumental – develops 'the voice instruments within the body'. Music is recreation: literally seeming 'in some degree to be a medicine from heaven, against our sorrows upon earth'. Mulcaster's *Positions* offers insight not just into the syllabus on Harry's pedagogic plate. It sets the table on a world of mental feasting.

Above all, Eleanora teaches Harry from his cradle what Mulcaster says boys need to be taught first: English. Their mother tongue. English gives boys words to make sense of themselves and the world around them. It's the language 'we speak first' and 'care for … most'; the language 'most natural to our soil, and most proper to our faith'. Endorsing English in these terms, Mulcaster is making a bold and still controversial claim for a language called 'rude' as recently as 1570. He promotes English as liberating Englishmen. It's the language of the Protestant Reformation. 'Our religion', formerly 'restrained to the Latin', is now 'restored to liberty', inscribed in the English Book of Common Prayer. The language of 'our faith', 'our soil', our national identity: English is the language of our English self.

By the time he's seven, though, Harry starts his second language, Latin. That's the age when boys all over England are breeched, changed out of uni-sex petticoats into their first doublets and hose, a mini-codpiece advertising their masculinity. Latin-learning is a kind of linguistic breeching: it's men's talk. Harry is being prepped for Winchester school, a place, writes Izaak Walton, 'of strict discipline and order' where Harry's father intends his son to 'be moulded into a method of living by rule', 'to make the future part of his life, both happy to himself, and useful for the discharge of all business, whether public or private'. Thomas Wotton's aspirations produce a scheme of childhood education every bit as instrumentalist as Mulcaster's. Its object: personal happiness, but also usefulness, a self trained for business in the world.

These, then, are the educational foundations of Wotton's future diplomacy. Reading and writing will be the diplomat's stock-in-trade; words will be his work. As we'll see, Wotton's utterly charismatic writing will knit voice to page in lines of ink shuttled across paper that will discover a self that is quick, eager, furnished, quirky and constantly blurring lines he shouldn't cross. His reading will be wide, and his bookish habit of quoting whatever he happens to be reading will alternately charm and annoy Venetian greybeards. He'll write a sloping, instantly legible secretary hand, a gift to the over-worked secretary of state in London who reads his dispatches. Their witty, frequently irreverent content will delight the king, who tells him so himself. He'll draw, sketching out architecture. He'll admire, commission and collect Italian painting. To the end, he'll play his much-travelled viol da gamba. Furnished with these basics, the child Harry leaves Bocton in 1579 for school, 125 miles and four days' travel away. He'll return home only as a visitor. He's eleven years old.

Moulded for business

Harry goes up to Winchester College as a fee-paying commoner in a year group of boys selected from all over England and Wales: Banbury, Newbury, Oxford, Southampton, Denbigh, Swalcliffe, Stratford-upon-Avon, London. School fees are not inconsiderable: a £3 entrance fee (when the statutory national wage for a tradesman such as a dyer or mercer is £5 per year); 4 shillings per week for 'commons', that is, food and lodging; then tuition on top (a figure not recorded). For his commons only, then, Harry is paying twice a tradesman's annual wage to live in College.

His father hasn't educated any of his elder sons in public school. They're tutored at home, and none goes up to university. So it's worth speculating why he makes different provision for young Harry. Edward, the eldest brother, twenty years Harry's senior, is, before Harry finishes school, a travelled diplomat, multi-languaged; later, a member of Grey's Inn and a gentleman of Her Majesty's Privy Chamber; still later, knighted, appointed to the Privy Council and made comptroller of the Queen's Household (a post he'll retain under King James). Brother James is a soldier, one of 'the martial men of his age'. He'll be knighted by the earl of Essex at Cadiz in 1595. (Among the scrum of adventurers scrambling for a place on that voyage will be his little brother, Harry, serving the earl as his personal secretary.) Brother John, 'excellently accomplished, both by learning and travel', is another Wotton knight.

Given this pedigree of spectacular achievement outside formal education, why is Harry's progress different? Is Winchester his father's hedge against mortality? His first brood were born to him in his youth. Harry comes when he perhaps doubts he'll live long enough to exert the 'strict discipline and order' necessary to mould his son's childhood for usefulness. Or perhaps, having produced a courtier, an ambassador and a soldier, he hopes to raise a university man, one headed for ordination, like great-uncle Nicholas. (As we'll see, the natural capacities of this youngest child don't fit the ecclesiastical mould.)

Winchester is the 'feeder' school to New College, Oxford, and boys have the automatic option of matriculating, so perhaps Thomas wants for Harry what a university education offers. Recent Winchester boys are professors of Physic and Greek at Oxford; bishops of Oxford and Worcester; poets; barristers; civil servants. Or maybe something more hard-headed is motivating Thomas: the awareness that what was optional in the 1560s is mandatory in the 1570s. Formal grammar school education is now available to even glovers' sons like Will Shakespeare, and fathers of Harry's generation across the whole social spectrum are seeing grammar school as equipping their sons with the code language that will enable their public life, making them 'insiders', whether they work as printers, polemicists, playwrights, preachers, lawyers or ambassadors. Harry is a youngest son. With little hope of inheritance, he'll have to make his own way in the world. Grammar schooling gives him the toolkit.

Certainly, if 'strict discipline and order' is what Thomas wants for young Harry, Winchester is the place. He's in school every day of the week, including Sunday, across fifty-two weeks, his day beginning at 5am with a psalm and ending with another before bed at 8pm. He sits on a form in the single schoolroom wedged in among seventy scholars and a hundred or so commoners. The place is cramped, only 29 feet by 46 feet, and heaving, boys around him scratching on slates, sing-songing declensions, declaiming orations, standing up to catechism-style interrogation from the head and usher who manage this pedagogic circus. There's no fireplace. So many young bodies packed as tight as Cicero's rhetoric doubtless generate heat enough. Over his head he reads a painted board advertising three life choices, 'Aut disce': to learn, illustrated with a bishop's mitre; 'Aut discede': to leave, showing sword, pen and pounce-pot, signs of public life in trade or war; 'Manet sors tertia caedi', this last producing a bundle of dry sticks for 'caedi', thrashing. Beating boys, though, isn't school policy at Winchester. As Erasmus wrote fifty years back, thrashing doesn't teach boys anything, except, perhaps, to despise learning. And teachers.

So much for feeding Harry's mind. As far as his body goes, it's bread, small beer and mutton every day, except in Lent when fish replaces mutton. He exercises on St Catherine's Hill twice a week. On Friday nights he gets no supper; the school reads a bit of a Terence comedy.

It's the same regime boys have known at Winchester since 1531. The curriculum and teaching method haven't changed either, both laid down by Erasmus in 1512. Harry needs Greek and Latin quite simply, writes Erasmus, 'Because almost everything worth learning is set forth in these two languages'. Latin will connect him to men of learning across Europe in a common patriarchal discourse, no matter what their native mother tongue. But, more than giving him the keys to the storehouse of human knowledge, education will 'instruct' Harry 'to live well'. Education informs civil society. The 'arts', says one bold educationalist, 'are the only helps toward human perfection'.

Whether he plods or flies (we remember he's not a scholarship boy so not the brightest in his year), Harry makes his way through Winchester's graded curriculum. First step: memorising beginner's sentences like 'Cognosce teipsum / Know yourself' and moral aphorisms laid out as binaries of the ilk still current with Shakespeare's Polonius: 'Be gentle to all men; but be familiar only with the good'. He reads Aesop's *Fables* in Latin; Cicero's easiest letters; extracts from Ovid, Terence and Erasmus. Then he's set harder texts like *De amicitia* (Cicero's essay on friendship, learned, it seems, by every grammar schoolboy in England); Virgil's *Aeneid*; Ovid's *Metamorphoses*; Caesar's wars in Gaul; more plays by Terence and Plautus; more Erasmus.

These are the school texts that stuff Wotton's adult mind. His habits of quotation, of arguing *pro* and *contra*, of thinking in binaries, of working arguments towards rhetorical climaxes, and (a particular habit, graphically evident in his personal letters and ambassadorial dispatches) of constantly modifying assertions with parenthetical qualifiers, are all learned from these texts. He'll memorise some of them word for word 'without book', making them, as the educationalist writes, his 'own to use perpetually', 'the originals' 'imprinted' 'in his heart'. That's an apt metaphor in a culture that sees the child as 'a form in wax' to be 'imprinted' by patriarchal authority.

This is a system that depends on rote memorisation – which doesn't just sediment grammar into Harry's muscle memory but develops phenomenal habits of recall. (Later, like Hamlet remembering a speech about 'rugged Pyrrhus' from a play he's heard only once, Wotton in Venice will set down in twelve complex bullet points the substance of a document he's been allowed half an hour to scan.) It's also a system that depends on imitation: reading a Cicero letter, aping it, then writing something new. With Erasmus's 'how to' manual at his elbow, Harry studies strategies for writing forms of letters, a begging letter, a letter of advice, of apology, a tongue-in-cheek letter to the college dog. All this epistolary drilling: nothing equips him better for diplomacy than this, for the entire administration of Tudor government is conducted through the exchange of dispatches written as letters. Ink to an ambassador: it's like water to a fish.

While Harry's reading produces imitation that produces composition that feeds invention, it's also producing speaking. He delivers orations from his own compositions. He writes then speaks 'ethopoeia', literally 'a speech for a character', played in role, as an 'other', like Achilles mourning the body of Patroclus or Theseus crowing victory over the Amazons, or, boys linguistically cross-dressed to become women, Ariadne on a clifftop on Naxos watching a traitor's sails disappear, Philomela pleading with her rapist. Perhaps astonishingly to post-modern eyes, exercises that require boys to play the woman's part put emotional literacy on the Tudor school syllabus.

All this reading, writing and speaking is in Latin, the *lingua franca* at Winchester, both inside and outside the classroom. (We have to imagine boys at games shouting 'Calcitra pilam!': kick the ball!) Harry will leave the place bilingual. From now on, he'll always be thinking in two languages – and in Venice he'll start speaking his mind in Italian. It's a simple fact that no educated man in Elizabethan or Jacobean England is monolingual.

To a boy just reaching adolescence, school must seem an endless forced march of declensions stretching out like milestones on the road to doomsday. The saving grace at Winchester is that this school models itself on Erasmus as a 'ludus literarius'. The man from Rotterdam wanted 'the place that the Greeks call *schola* from the word for leisure and the Latins *ludus* from the word for play' to be 'a theatre' where the inscription over the entrance would be 'all learnt in play'. Winchester is that theatre. Harry is set word games. His vocabulary swells with puns. (As an adult he'll never lose his delight in the mischief of word-play, and it will be a pun he means in English but writes in Latin that nearly costs him his career.) He acts in the school plays that are a regular feature of the calendar, put there to teach boys performativity, the 'facial expressions' and 'gestures' to 'accompany the spoken word': how to express interiority; 'to raise or lower or change the tone of your voice'; 'to move properly without exhibitionism'. Harry laps it up (forgetting only the warning about 'exhibitionism'). He's a born performer. He'll astonish gaggles on the streets when he rides into Rome in disguise years hence and he'll bemuse Venetian statesmen with his theatrical flourishes, pulling concealed letters out of his sleeve. Indeed, he'll see diplomacy as a branch of theatre, himself acting on a political stage where gestures that astonish create profound effects.

But there's even more to this curriculum for a boy like Harry who wants to peer into things. Winchester instructs boys in scientific topics: latest theories about comets and acoustics, how toxic substances can be tested on mice, ideas about the origin of the world and why the sea is salty. A fascination with natural sciences seeded at school never leaves Harry: optics, homeopathy, pharmacology, astronomy. At university – and beyond – he'll occupy himself with extra-curricular experimentation. He'll investigate the physiology of eyesight as a subset of mindsight. In his travels he'll search out books on the science of ciphering, on alchemy, on munitions. In Venice, he'll do science at home in the embassy, and he'll get his hands on the ingenious new instrument that the 'mathematical professor' at Padua is using to investigate the stars. Along with his well-travelled viol da gamba, he'll leave in his will an illustrated edition of Dioscorides's encyclopaedia of herbal medicine.

Everything is grist to the mill of the future ambassador. Grammar school teaches Harry to do things with language: structures of thought and utterance he'll find on the tip of his tongue and pen. His mind is prodigiously trained in memory, in the art of recall and quotation. He's been taught to cultivate a sense of self, or rather selves, performing different roles to different audiences to calculated effects. Such habits of alterity are the habits of the chameleon. Finally, though, the rhetorical competence he learns schools him in the art and craft of persuasion. And persuasion is the entire point of diplomacy. Its tools are the tropes and figures he'll deploy, wielding them sometimes like scalpels, sometimes shovels, hammers, tuning forks, gunpowder. Grammar school is for Harry a daily theatre for Latin-learning. Latin-learning, though, equips him also for mighty business in his mother tongue.

Tumbled up and down

Now that we have seen how grammar school prepped Harry, we can return to the life-changing letter of May 1603 that opened this chapter, to see what it said, and how it said it, as our own prep for reading Wotton's diplomacy. For among much else, it's Harry's earliest attempt at a diplomatic dispatch. And given that the early modern state conducted its administrative business in transactions that look like personal letters, it's a template for all his future diplomatic correspondence.

We have to start with the backstory. Harry's no stranger to the man he's addressing. He dashed off a few lines to Robert Cecil in 1595 as he leaped aboard the ship *Due Repulse* to sail with Essex to raid Cadiz. Then, he was a cocky adventurer; five years later, an outlaw. What sent him into exile is recounted by Izaak Walton, a grubby story of the after-events of February 1601 whose details must have come from Harry himself. Wotton was then one of Essex's private secretaries, but not 'of that faction' that 'encouraged the Earl to those undertakings' – a euphemism for rebellion – 'which proved so fatal to him'. Once the 'undertakings' were undertaken, Wotton equivocated: 'knowing treason to be so comprehensive as to take in even circumstances', he 'thought prevention by absence out of England a better security than to stay in it, and there plead his innocency in prison'.

In short, Harry scarpered. 'So soon as the Earl was apprehended, very quickly, and as privately' he fled 'through Kent to Dover, without so much as looking toward his native and beloved Bocton; and was by help of favourable winds, and liberal payment of the mariners, within sixteen hours after his departure from London, set upon the French shore; where he heard shortly after, that the Earl was arraign'd, condemned, and beheaded'. Shabbiness is poised against self-preservation in this account. Even so, the Harry who 'prevents' rather than 'pleads' is little short of a scoundrel.

Two years later, Scottish James ascends the English throne and immediately makes decisions that appear stupendously counter-intuitive, keeping virtually intact Elizabeth's Privy Council and household but moving swiftly to restore Essex's supporters. Thus, he effectively puts the earl's opponents – the most powerful among them, Robert Cecil – on the back foot, keeping their jobs but unsteady of their futures.

Among other business, the new king enquires of his baffled household comptroller if Edward Wotton knows 'one Henry Wotton'? He commands Harry home. Edward sends a letter that doesn't survive, but we know some of its contents from Harry's to Cecil on 23 May. Harry is no doubt following protocol when he addresses himself not to the king but to the king's secretary of state. But he must be urged, too, by political circumspection. It appears Edward has instructed his little brother to work his reconciliation with the kingdom's chief minister. Edward has certainly read the writing on the wall that's legible to Giovanni Carlo Scaramelli, the secretary of the Venetian Senato, currently in London, who informs Venice that, despite 'early hopes among the nobility and people that some of the universally hated of the old Council would be unseated', instead 'these Englishmen – nothing less can be said – have enchanted the king'.

Cecil's footing now looks set in concrete. In the coming months factions will preen and jockey for position at Court and the king will bask in the afterglow of crowds cheering his arrival in London, but the hard, slogging daily work of administering the kingdom – indeed, *two* kingdoms in search of a union – will fall on the hunched back of the king's 'littil beagle'. If Harry wants a future in England, he'll have to repair his relationship with Mr. Secretary Cecil. His epistolary challenge in May 1603, then, is to write a letter of apology for a fault he can't admit, because to do so would make him an ingrate – or traitor.

Advice: how to read an early modern letter

1. *Look at the handwriting.* Wotton writes in a studiously crafted italic script, not his usual slouching secretary hand.
2. *Look at the layout.* Space is significant. 'Right Honorable' gets lots of room at the top. At the bottom, Harry's signature, crouching in the corner, sidles off the page. Note how many parentheses interrupt the writing. Here is a writer constantly gain-saying himself.
3. *Consider vocabulary.* Wotton chooses his words carefully. And shuffles their meanings.
4. *Consider structure.* Where does this letter begin? How does it proceed? Where does it end?
5. *Remember Erasmus (1).* You'll find this letter's prototype in Chapter 63 of *De conscribendis*. Letters of reconciliation 'admit obvious guilt *and yet* beg pardon'. Thus, they see-saw rhetorically. 'And yet' offers a space for strategic equivocation where guilt can be minimised and excused by youth or inexperience, and blame can be shifted onto someone else.

> 6 *Remember Erasmus (2)*. He tells you that letters are acts of performance that consciously script a self (in this case, an apologetic self) while simultaneously setting up a dialogue that imagines the person reading it (and insinuates *how* the person should be reading it). Letters are artful. Also crafty.
>
> 7 *Are you sitting comfortably?* We are going to plough through many, many words to get to the point of this letter. (But there are even *more* – as you'll see in the transcription of the complete letter that appears in the appendix. Below, I pull out the most important points, updating Wotton's original spelling.)

Harry opens with a little preamble on the subject of 'opinion', worried, it seems, about what Cecil thinks of him.

> The good opinion which it hath pleased your honour first to conceive in yourself of me, and then to deliver it unto my brother (who is in nature and in love the nearest unto me) doth assure me that how full of care soever the times are now at home (whereof I can easily understand the greatest weight next his Majesty to lie upon your wisdom) yet that you will pardon in me this troubling of you from abroad, and honourably interpret the offer of my poor service though it come both unseasonably and late.

Notice how he immediately loads the rhetorical dice, supposing that he already has Cecil's '*good* opinion', since that's what his brother reported to him. This, then, might excuse him writing in times 'full of care' (regime change in England is only two months old) to the man upon whose shoulders rests 'the greatest weight' in the kingdom, to add more weight. He's sorry for this 'troubling of you from abroad' but balances that with an offer of service, if apologetically rendered as 'poor' and coming 'both unseasonably and late.' Perhaps two years too late? Maybe, but a flurry of pronouns binding Harry to Edward to Cecil aims to insinuate alliance. Those pronouns say 'we're connected'. Still, we can hear Harry's anxiety in this preamble. Even interrupted twice with parentheticals, it doesn't pause for breath. It's one, single sentence. Whoosh.

Harry has to get down to business, to account for his unauthorised absence from England. But what's the story? Good question. 'Sir, I will gain your favour with plainness', he continues. But in the lines that follow he's anything but plain.

Allowing for syntax increasingly clotted and punctuation that ignores full stops, the letter's third sentence runs on for some 230 words (including five parentheticals) that tie the narrative in knots as Harry appears to argue, without ever saying so, that it was loyalty to Essex that impelled the actions he took.

1 From Henry Wotton, self-exiled in Venice, this letter to Secretary of State Robert Cecil dated May 1603 worked his pardon and rehabilitation.

He speaks of 'the death of our Master' (Essex) and of 'that unfortunate family' (men, like Wotton) who served him. He refers to the 'so public unkindness' between Cecil and Essex (a devastating understatement). And he struggles (remembering Erasmus's instruction) to minimise his deed. He couldn't have been involved in the 'knowledge and participation of ill', Harry writes, 'mine own person having been removed … (either of purpose or by accident)'. The parenthesis is a tell-tale. Was he passive in that removal? Was someone, Essex perhaps, sending him abroad on business? How does that square with Izaak Walton's story of Harry scrambling to safety in France? If Wotton was 'removed' 'of purpose', he would have travelled on a passport. Abroad when it happened, he'd be innocent of rebellion. He might have faced some sticky questions, but his passport would have licensed his return. So what explains his two-year absence? Why is he only now applying 'my self' to Cecil's 'service'?

Harry side-steps these difficulties to address another: the world's opinion. Uniquely of the earl's 'unfortunate family', he got off scot-free. Surely, that escape should have 'obliged' him to persist in loyalty, not to turn coat to serve his master's persecutor. (None of this is explicit: it has to be raked out of the undergrowth of Wotton's rhetorical thicket. We notice skulking there the word he never writes: treason.) Cecil might have known Essex 'worthy of opposition'. But 'the world' hero-worships Essex in death as in life. So what is the *world's* 'opinion' of Harry, the turncoat? Particularly if some 'corrupt instruments' have cast 'some little distrust' upon him, someone like the earl of Southampton, who's no longer languishing in the Tower and who might bear a grudge against one 'not worth the considering'. Such self-disparagement makes Harry out to be a target not worth the throw of a poisoned dart. In fact, he was one of those closest to Essex's daily life.

Is Harry an ingrate to be blamed? He tilts the see-saw back, from blamed to blamer as he gives a fleeting glimpse into the relationship between the earl and his secretary. As secretary Harry 'owed' – and paid – Essex a 'double duty' of fidelity and reverence. But Essex did not balance the accounts. Harry's parenthetical insertion 'I think I may justly say' takes some of the ugliness out of what comes next: 'he owed unto me in some respects more regard of me then I found about him'. That's an astonishing revelation. A bombshell. Such 'disestimation' is bitter. But, conveniently unprovable, it also, of course, licenses his new allegiance to Cecil.

Thus, Cecil (as Harry imagines him reading this letter) watches Wotton 'tumble' him 'self up and down strengthening and weakening the obligations of a servant'. His frankness is painful. Perhaps slightly comical. Or maybe it's the curtain raiser to the entrance of a new role-player, one who seeks service with Cecil, God's 'apparent ... instrument' in the 'great business' of James's peaceful accession. (Wotton can't resist an aside, noting that the apparent instrument is only keeping his position 'contrary to malicious imaginations'. Thus he dismisses the rumours Scaramelli heard while sliding in that he's heard them.)

We can deal with the second half of the letter briefly. It changes tone. The stuttering parentheticals drop out. Harry writes straightforwardly of practicalities. He provides information, a rehearsal for future service, perhaps as intelligencer to the Crown. He promises 'perpetual fidelity'. Indeed, he inscribes himself 'Your Honor's from the day above written to the end of my life'. From today, he'll 'fashion me unto your self', Cecil's man.

How does Cecil read this letter? Wotton's 'short accompt' of Venice tells him little he doesn't know, except perhaps about the city's horse-mad 'Clarissimi'. Cecil is well acquainted with Scaramelli (though Wotton clearly isn't: he gets his name wrong). A detail about Scaramelli's ability – one of the Republic's 'ablest instruments' – against his status – not a nobleman but only a *cittadino*, one of the state's second-class elite, therefore not qualified to serve as an ambassador – might interest the secretary of state. Undoubtedly more piquing is a line about the Republic's internal politics, 'A Signory that with long neutrality of state' is 'almost slipped into a neutrality of religion'. Does Cecil credit this report? Is he sceptical? Whichever, Harry's wittily turned opinion that doubles the Venetian state with Venetian Catholicism and sees them both as somehow 'neutral' (or better said, unaligned with Rome) will colour all his future diplomacy in the Republic. It will inform English policy towards the Signoria – explosively, three years hence.

But what about this letter as repair job? Cecil sees its devices writ large on its surface. And still he might spare some sympathy. Difficult letters litter Cecil's past. Like the one he wrote to James in Scotland while Elizabeth was still alive, agreeing to a secret correspondence. Then, it was he who had to 'tumble' him 'self up and down', professing himself entirely Elizabeth's 'creature' while simultaneously arguing that 'with strictest loyalty and soundest reason' faithful ministers might 'conceal sometimes both thoughts and actions from princes when they are persuaded it is for their own greater service'. Was he a man of conscience – or a traitor? Secret correspondence with James was one of the allegations Cecil used to condemn Essex to the block in 1601.

Looking at the studiously penned letter from Venice now lying on his desk, how might Cecil read it if he'd seen the passionate message Harry Wotton sent

2   Derived from a pattern taken by John de Critz the Elder, this portrait showing Cecil in his Garter robes was commissioned by Henry Wotton in 1609 to be produced in Venice in mosaic. Now at Hatfield House.

the Grand Duke of Tuscany in April 1601? In that earlier letter Harry told the duke he'd never return to England after Essex's execution and offered himself as 'servant and instrument' to inform on those things that 'touch upon' England and Scotland. The self who's now representing himself as a 'poor traveller' desiring 'service': will Cecil recall his own squirming and give Harry the benefit of the doubt? In the event, the king's will will be done, and the letter young Harry started drafting as a schoolboy will have done its work. For his part, however, Harry can't begin to imagine a future when he'll be England's ambassador to Venice – service that will mean he'll spend his life writing letters to Robert Cecil.

2

Wit ballasted with learning

Fathers, sons and 'ingenious studies'

September 1584. Winchester school is formative, but only a university education will lavish upon Harry the solid 'ornaments of learning' he'll need for any future in public service – as he applies himself to a curriculum that makes no concessions to idlers. He's sixteen when his father sends him up to Oxford. Whatever aspirations Thomas has for his boy's education, however, aren't fulfilled. He dies in January 1587, two months short of Harry's nineteenth birthday, so he doesn't live to see his son supplicate his Bachelor of Arts from Queen's College in June 1588. Within months, that son will collect the annuity his father bequeathed him, cash it in for French 'Crowns of the Sun' and set off for Italy. Would this turn of events have disappointed Harry's dad? A cryptic comment in Izaak Walton's 'Life' suggests so. Of the four years Harry spends at Oxford he writes, 'his stay there was not long', 'at least, not so long as his friends once intended'. 'Once intended'? We'll return to that.

When he arrives in Oxford Harry finds himself among a new breed of student. These are dizzying times, for the young men coming up to university in the past two decades have been changing what the university is, and what they want it to do for them. It's still ostensibly a 'society of clerics', its primary aim to educate the kingdom's priests and theologians. But these latest undergraduates have different futures in mind. They're the lads who sat under that 'aut' board at Winchester and set their hearts on 'aut discede', sword and pen beckoning them to a public world of action. They're well born and secular-minded, and they're at Oxford to get the higher humanist education that will equip them to govern the realm, not as priests, but as civil servants, secretaries of state, ambassadors, able to network across educated Europe via the books that all educated Europe reads in the language that all educated Europe shares: Latin.

If Thomas 'once intended' anything for Harry staying longer at Oxford, it was probably to proceed to MA and then to ordination, following in his great-uncle Nicholas's footsteps. If so, Harry isn't the first BA to kick over the traces. At Cambridge, Christopher Marlowe is currently taking a spectacular detour from what's mapped out for him by his Parker scholarship, dumping theology to write 'mighty lines' for that 'atheist' Tamburlaine to strut and bellow on the London stage. Some time later, John Donne, that restless poet of sex-hungry and oh-so-carnal verse, will, too, veer off the straight and narrow, only to be wrenched back, put into clericals by the king's command. Donne is Harry's fellow in college and life-long friend, writing him verse letters for decades, to Ireland, to Venice.

Oxford sets Harry the statutory Latin curriculum: two terms of grammar (using Virgil, Horace or Cicero's letters); four terms of rhetoric (taught from Cicero or Aristotle); five terms thereafter of dialectic; three terms of arithmetic, geometry and astronomy, including Copernicus and the revolutionary new cosmology (theorising the heliocentric universe as against the one inherited from Ptolemy that puts man at the centre of things), supplemented with a 'new' subject, geography. Two final terms cover the related science of music. This is not far off the 'course of learning and ingenious studies' Lucentio says he's going to 'institute' at the university in Padua in Shakespeare's *The Taming of the Shrew*, though ironically, it's his servant Tranio who has the firmer grasp of what's actually on the syllabus. Then too, Tranio has a shrewd idea of a parallel syllabus, one that balances 'profit' with 'pleasure', that relieves dusty Aristotle with goat-heeled Ovid; that studies 'virtue' and 'moral discipline' but doesn't turn students into 'stocks' and 'stoics'.

As we'll see, this alternative curriculum sounds more like what really interests Harry at Oxford. We don't have his book list. But if the titles in his father's library at Bocton are anything to go by, it's as eclectic as the one his contemporary at Cambridge, 'Mr Smith', copies out: Virgil, Ortelius, Suetonius ('in English') and Camden, but also Boccaccio, *The Faerie Queene*, a 'viol book', and *The Theoricke and practicke of modern wars*. Perhaps like undergraduates at Cambridge – as they've been reported, since it was published a year ago – freshman Harry sleeps with Shakespeare's steamy *Venus and Adonis* under his pillow.

The curriculum is important for what it teaches, but (if we're thinking about education as equipping a future ambassador) perhaps even more so for the way it teaches. Harry practices rhetoric through a programme of formal disputation. This means standing on his hind legs, facing an adversary and arguing some set question in Latin, applying to it all the skills of analysis, exposition, discrimination, deliberation and creative thinking he can muster. It's an exercise that's designed to hone his Latin. But as active learning, disputation prepares him to face challenge, to be cross-questioned, to think on his feet, to draw upon memory, to have quotation at his immediate disposal, and finally to triumph – 'Sic probo!' – when he beats his opponent into rhetorical pulp.

Laddish point-scoring and the ability to snap a witty riposte have their uses. But much more seriously, disputation for Oxford's future governors-in-waiting is politically implicated. Youths like Harry expect statesmen to give 'reasons' for their actions, what in Italy he'll encounter as *ragioni di stato*. They expect the powerful to listen to disagreement and answer objections. Reasons, objections, answers: these are expectations shaped under the pressure of disputation that will travel to Venice with young Harry Wotton. Of course, to 'dispute well', as Marlowe's university man Dr Faustus puts it, depends on Harry applying himself to dialectic. Its object: to teach him how to construct persuasive arguments, which will also teach a future ambassador how to anticipate objections to his diplomatic message – and how to gag them. Dialectic instils in Harry that most useful of skills, the logical analysis of texts, and teaches him to pay attention to how words work. Nothing will be more instrumental to his future than knowing how to work with words.

'Sleight imployment'

Like the book list we don't have for Harry's time in Oxford or the buttery bill for his meals in college, we don't have an inventory of his wardrobe to tell us what he looks like. He may dress 'rich, not gaudy', like 'Mr Smith', whose 'things' at Cambridge include a grey cloth suit, a satin suit, a pair of pearl colour silk stockings with garters and roses, a frieze jerkin, a gown, a cloak, a pair of boots and a pair of spurs, and a sword. Sartorially, Harry may put himself on display, like the youth who gazes out so steadily from the portrait dated 1585 that we take to be Christopher Marlowe at Corpus Christi, a youth who looks designed. His auburn mane swept voluptuously off his wide forehead picks up the orange in the silk we can see poking through the slashes in his black padded doublet, and both play off the glint of gold in buttons that, lining sleeves and chest, seem to catch the light in his eyes. Or is Harry more sober, like John Donne in his portrait, aged eighteen, in black doublet? (That portrait is, of course, a visual oxymoron, the sober suit sabotaged by the theatrical signs about him that blazon alternative lives, the cross-shaped 'Catholic' jewel hanging from his left ear, the dandy-ish hand resting on the decorative grip of a sword.)

Where does Harry fit on a scale between the ostentatious and the downplayed? He certainly has in his wardrobe his habitual academic attire, a statutory black gown. At Oxford as at Winchester, he's a fee-paying gentleman-commoner, not a scholar. Not, then, a lad who wins exhibitions. But that means he's marked from the scholarship boys by his dress, by the elaborate cut of his winged-sleeved gown whose shoulders and skirt are richly decorated with button-and-cord braiding. Since school he's grown tall. He wears his hair short, fringed far back from his forehead. He's smooth-cheeked. He won't grow a beard until his future employer does – the earl of Essex. For his person, he's known among friends for 'a loose humour', a wit who loves jokes and plays the fool. That's no great addition to his reputation. 'Youth's dross', Izaak Walton points out, is 'mirth and wit'. When twelve-year-old John Donne arrives in college he's besotted by the older boy. Perhaps no wonder. They're a pair. (That dour comment on 'youth's dross' is actually directed at Donne.)

Harry isn't an undergraduate who needs a college servant like Tranio to persuade him to shut his Aristotle and reach for Ovid. As Walton records, he spends plenty of time on the university's alternative curriculum – which in his case may turn out to be even more formative than the authorised syllabus. First, he makes a foray into playwriting. At Queen's, 'the chief of that College' (Walton records) 'persuasively' enjoins Harry 'to write a play for their private use'. He chooses 'the tragedy of Tancredo'. His source is Torquato Tasso's Italian epic, *La Gerusalemme liberata* (*Jerusalem Delivered*), which he adapts into Latin, his rendition so impressive, 'so interwoven with sentences' and so 'exact' in 'personating' 'humours, passions, and dispositions' that 'the gravest of that [college] society' declare that Harry has 'in a sleight imployment given an early, and a solid testimony of his future abilities'. At Winchester, the school play *as play* had been a pedagogic feature of life. Now, in Walton's oxymoronic puff – 'sleight imployment', 'solid testimony' – we hear its further public and personal instrumentalism in college *as play*. In its 'sentences' Harry's *Tancredi* displays Latin dexterity. In its 'exact personating' it studies 'becoming other'. It gives notice, then, of the theatrical turn Harry will always be aware of in diplomatic performances, a constitutional duplicity the ambassador shares with the actor.

Beyond its method, however, the subject of this play deserves attention for how it weighs on Harry's mind. Tancredi is one of the chivalric crusaders of Tasso's sprawling poem, but his progress through Tasso's twenty books (and 15,000 lines) splatters him with as much mud as glory. Interesting, then, that Harry is drawn to the drama of tarnished youth, that he hits on Tancredi for young college men to 'personate' instead of, say, the more unambiguously heroic Rinaldo.

In the epic's opening stanzas when 'il Padre eterno' surveys mankind, looking for someone to lead a crusade to oust 'the Painim' from the Holy City, He sees Christendom inert. Among the champions, 'Vede Tancredi haver la vita à sdegno: / Tanto un suo vano amor l'ange, e martira' (He sees Tancredi, careless of life: / So much a futile love torments and afflicts him). The Christians have no greater warrior except Rinaldo – but Tancredi is languishing, paralysed, besotted with Clorinda, the radiant-faced warrior woman who cross-dresses to fight alongside the 'pagans' who hold Jerusalem. They first meet in Book 3, hot from battle. 'O meraviglia'! 'Amor' new-born sends his heart soaring. She, though, straps on her helmet and squares up. They're interrupted. She flees. He pursues her phantom across the next nine books, finally meeting again in single combat. 'Tell me thy name', Tancredi challenges an unknown opponent. The answer is a boast: 'I am one of those … / Which late with kindled fire destroi'd the [Christians' siege] towre'. Enraged, he thrusts. She falls. Only then, pulling off her helmet, he releases her blond mane to the wind – and sees what he's killed. She dies in his arms. But not before she requests, and he performs, Christian baptism.

This doomed love story perhaps offers Harry as much as he needs for his adaptation. But Tancredi's story doesn't end there. With eight books to go, Harry finds plenty of brutal action ahead. Body parts pile up, blood pools in streets, enchantments are broken, wounds tented and miraculously cured – or not. Tancredi meets 'the fierce Circassian' who's vowed to avenge Clorinda, and, though himself near-fatally wounded, kills Argantes in a fight sequence that might have been scripted for cinema. In Book 19 'The town is won'. 'Liberation' erupts in Christian rampage, scenes appalling in their vividness. Now 'Rageth the sword, death murdreth great and small', 'Here runs the blood in ponds, there stands the gore, / And drowns the knights in whom it liu'd before'. A final showdown routs the Egyptian army. Christian banners drape the city's walls. Miraculous conversions occur. Tancredi lives. Jerusalem is delivered.

Racing through Tasso we can see what a gift he is to Harry as he devours the books, pen in hand: 'humours, passions, and dispositions'; matter for scripting into 'sentences', into vaunts and challenges, into rousing speeches to encourage heroics, but also perhaps into speeches of introspection, the delinquent soldier-turned-dotard cross-examining himself in soliloquy. Speeches of political negotiation, diplomatic attempts to end the bloodshed. Speeches that interrogate male violence.

There's also the sheer theatrical appeal of Tasso, when epic poetry is translated into live action on stage. The moment in performance when Clorinda's helmet comes off and her sex is revealed is sensational, and Harry immediately sees its theatrical impact. In the poem's narrative, the revelation is spoiled: gendered pronouns mean the reader always knows she's a girl. On Harry's all-male college stage, in one-to-one dialogue, the gender disguise is complete, and the revelation is double. The knight who turns out to be a girl is actually a twice cross-dressed undergraduate wearing women's clothes beneath 'his' armour. And who among the play's college spectators could see that discovery coming? For which of them would know anything about the *Liberata*? In 1586 the *Liberata* is virtually new to England. It first appeared in print only five years earlier in Ferrara, but there's no English translation. In England, it's read in the 1580s by the Italian-languaged elite: Queen Elizabeth, Philip Sidney, Edmund Spenser.

Taking up Tasso, then, Harry's 'sleight imployment' is working at the cutting edge of cultural exchange and, moving across Italian and Latin, at the deep end of language acquisition and translation. Coincidentally, 1586 is the year Scipione Gentili, a Protestant Italian refugee settled in Germany, employs John Wolfe, the English printer widely known for his Italian book list, to publish in London his Italian-language *Annotationi* glossing the *Liberata*, a crib Harry no doubt finds useful. And more coincidence: that same year Harry is being tutored in Italian by Scipione's big brother, Alberico, another Protestant refugee who's crossed Europe to get to England, where he's now in Oxford, incorporated into the University, and a year hence, 1587, elected Oxford regius professor of civil law.

The entrance of the Gentili brothers – both of them scholars and lawyers, both of them close readers of Tasso – puts a new spin on Harry's playwriting project. It suggests that under Alberico's supervision and guided by Scipione's commentary, he's reading Tasso not – or not just – for the action but for the politics, specifically the politics of diplomacy. For while the *Liberata* on the surface tells the (mythologised) story of the First Crusade of 1096–1099, the lens Scipione applies to Tasso in his *Annotationi* focuses on something else, a new understanding of the 'law of nations', the law that governs all international relations. Scipione is an original thinker, and he's trying to imagine new judicial principles to deal with religious war. In Tasso, religious war pits Christian versus Muslim in the Holy Land half a millennium earlier. Scipione reframes it: Catholic v. Protestant. In Western Europe. Now. That is, the war he's seeing is the one being fought across the confessional fault line that has divided Europe since 1517, when Luther nailed his 'Theses' to the church door in Wittenberg. What's at stake is nothing less than 'Truth', as defined by one side or the other. Harry will spend his whole life staring across that fault line. It will position his diplomacy in Venice from 1604, and in 1606, starting from a wrangle between Venice and Rome, he'll see it threatening Christendom with pan-European war.

For now, Harry must be knocked sideways by the question Scipione puts to European Christians. It's about the notion of 'pious arms'. Going to war, are only the Christians in the *Liberata* pious? Aren't the pagans, defending themselves, equally pious? That's an argument for the bilateral justice of war that shocks Christian cultural supremacism, an argument big brother Alberico will develop in his treatise *De iure belli* (*On the Law of War*, 1589). For the Gentili brothers, Tasso's deeply ambivalent epic isn't triumphalist. Christians rampaging in their victory are brutalists: Jersualem's streets are 'ponds' of 'gore'. Warriors drown in their own blood. Read politically, the *Liberata* urges new diplomatic practices leading to international laws governing war, a proto-Geneva Convention three hundred and fifty years *avant la lettre*.

In whatever way Harry's 'sleight imployment' brings him into contact with the Gentili brothers – whether on the page or in tutorials where their ideas take a sledgehammer to an undergraduate's received opinions – those encounters are among his most formative at Oxford. Perhaps Harry finds Tasso first, which leads him to Alberico Gentili. Perhaps Alberico introduces Harry to Tasso, using the *Liberata*'s Books and Scipione's *Annotationi* to tutor him in Italian and suggesting Tancredi and Clorinda as ripe for staging. Alberico champions academic drama. It will be he, across several months' back-and-forth pot-shotting in 1593, who defends college plays against the Puritan John Rainoldes's hectoring attack, published later as *Th'overthrow of Stage-Playes* (1599). Rainoldes is appointed fellow at Queen's in 1586 – perhaps just in time to see Harry's *Tancredi*. Twenty years earlier he'd cross-dressed in college to play the Amazon queen Hippolyta, but now fulminates against the 'vanitie and unlawfulnesse of Plaies and Enterludes' and brands 'players' who 'put on women's raiment' 'abominations'. Gentili has little time for such liverish rants, not being 'greatly influenced by [theologians like Rainoldes] in matters of morals or politics'. For him, poets – specifically, makers of comedy, tragedy and epic – have a civic function. Poets are 'the philosophers most especially suitable for the instruction of the state', 'doctors' who 'cure through the emotions'. This connection between poetry and statecraft is not lost on Harry Wotton. As for cross-dressing, writes Gentili, it 'cannot much harm actors'. This must come as good news for Harry's *Tancredi* – and the undergraduate who plays Clorinda.

Gentili's 'ocelli'

However it comes about, 'his dear Harry' (as Walton says Gentili called him) is 'taken into … a bosom friendship with the learned' Alberico, who endears him as 'Henrice mi ocelli', his little eye, after he hears the undergraduate declaim three lectures, *De oculo*, that surely draw on a Winchester schoolboy's fascination with science. Again, these lectures show the undergraduate busy beyond the statutory syllabus. In them he examines the physiology of the eye, perhaps while anatomising some bit of beast acquired from the college kitchens, but he also considers the fundamental 'Optique Question' that divides early modern theorists: how does seeing work? 'By the emission of the beams from within'? Or by 'reception of the species from without'? Crudely, is vision a sort of physiological ball game where the eye throws out 'certain beams' that smack up against the thing it sees, which wallops them back to the eye 'even as a hand-ball struck against a wall doth rebound back'? Or is vision more like hunting and gathering? Do objects produce 'species' that the watchful eye bags?

The science of this debate is informed by meticulous anatomy. But it's also moralised. Optics impacts theology. A decade hence, the optical instrument Galileo trains upon the night sky in Padua will produce a 'starry messenger' that will overthrow theology (and Harry will be in Venice, among the first to hear the messenger's news). For now, though, in an undergraduate lecture at Oxford, optics confirms theology. The eye (Walton quotes Harry) is the 'body's guide' to 'inform the soul'. It allows man to gaze upwards at 'the great light of the world' to 'discover the fabric of the heavens', or downwards, at the earth's flowers. They bloom, they wither. They show man an image of his human ephemerality and bid him 'silently moralize his own condition'. That's the stuff of conventional *respice finem* – look to your end – philosophising. Surely, in Harry's case, mere undergraduate posing. He's pious – but he's also loose-humoured, not one to turn gathering daisies into thoughts of tombs.

Soon enough, though, he'll see optics not just moralised but politicised. How we see, what we see, how we interpret what we derive from casting upon the material world 'the sense' that God has given us to use 'as spies': Harry will discover how all this feeds into questions of simulation, dissimulation and – ultimately – spying. For now, he's happy gazing up at the stars and down at the grass. Later, he'll look into other men's eyes, using his own eyes to search their faces, and behind their faces, to find out their minds.

One person listening to Harry's *De oculo* is smitten. Alberico Gentili is in the audience, and afterwards it's as if the mighty professor would adopt Harry his intellectual heir, would 'have breathed all his excellent knowledge, both of the mathematics and law into the breast of his dear Harry'. If we hear echoes of Old Testament Ezekiel in Walton's messianic turn of phrase, we're probably not wrong. As it is, Harry's 'connaturalness to the Italian language, and those studies, whereof Gentili' is 'a great master' ensures that their friendship 'did daily increase'. One of those studies is the history and theory of diplomacy.

It's here that the tutor makes his most indelible mark on Harry Wotton. In November 1584, shortly after the fresh-faced sixteen-year-old arrives in Oxford, Gentili is summoned to give Queen Elizabeth's Privy Council legal advice as one of Europe's foremost experts in international law. The Spanish ambassador resident in London, Bernardino de Mendoza, has been discovered in a plot to assassinate Elizabeth and place her Catholic cousin, Mary queen of Scots, on the throne. How to deal with the English conspirators is clear-cut: arrest, trial and execution by the usual method. They're hanged, drawn and quartered. But what about Mendoza? Can the ambassador, a subject of Spain, be arrested for treason? What satisfaction can an expert on the law of nations give a Privy Council baying for Mendoza's blood?

None. Gentili's advice is unequivocal. Ambassadors, even criminal ambassadors, are 'inviolable'. They're protected by the 'privilege of immunity', the 'right of embassy' 'defended by a rampart of human and divine authority'. So the Privy Council's only recourse is to order Mendoza recalled. Elizabeth's men follow Gentili's advice – grudgingly. When Mendoza ignores the order, he's unceremoniously bundled to Dover and shipped off to Calais.

Out of this case comes Gentili's definitive statement on diplomacy, published a year later in London as *De legationibus libri tres* (1585), a three-volume treatise that constitutes the first systematic work in the special field of the law of nations. These books: what a gift to any student who imagines himself a future governor of the realm. If Harry is reading Tasso with Gentili, perhaps his tutor extends his reading list with *De legationibus*. The epic poem teaches him Italian; the treatise on the law of nations tests his Latin; and both offer him what he can get nowhere else on his Oxford syllabus: instruction in the history, theory and politics of diplomacy. Later, *De legationibus* will become mandatory reading for anyone interested in the relationship between domestic and foreign policy. Now, it's hot off the press, and potentially glossed for the student by the author himself.

However, as a 'how to' manual it makes for odd reading today, because Gentili isn't really interested in the statecraft of diplomacy. Rather, he's concerned with what interests young Harry more: the qualities of the good ambassador, his capabilities, moral profile, duties, which Gentili lays out in miles of citations. Reading *De legationibus* is like wading through an Oxford stubble field in August: the text bristles with thousands of cracking quotations gleaned from authorities ancient and modern, Aesop to Aristotle; Plato to Plautus; Cicero, Caesar, Livy and Tacitus to Plutarch and Guicciardini; Machiavelli to Erasmus to Lipsius; not forgetting the Old Testament of the Bible, and Tasso, to whom Gentili regularly returns, regularly to disagree with him. Wotton knows stubble fields, and he also knows more and more of the books Gentili cites.

His tutor writes like a lawyer in *De legationibus*, carefully, laboriously, pedantically, but in compact chapters that set out bite-sized problems to chew over. Reading him as a handbook, Harry needs more than sunlight to penetrate the dark lumber rooms of Gentili's high-piled quotation. But he also comes upon utterances of such startling clarity that he's stopped in his tracks, fumbling for the commonplace book he's kept about him since school to write down some sentence or other to think about further, lines like the ambassador 'is not entitled to think beyond his instructions' and the ambassador 'is actually invested with the person of his prince'. So, what does Harry learn from Gentili?

First, that the original ambassadors were angels, appointed by God to deliver messages between heaven and earth, a scenario played out between Gabriel and the Virgin Mary in hundreds of *Annunciations* and between God and Gabriel in Tasso's opening books. Later, ambassadors are necessary for trade. Now (and ambassadors should never forget this) trace memories of both these histories shape diplomacy: angels rub shoulders (metaphorically) with merchants in contemporary practice, for on the one hand, embassy is bound by sacred codes and hedged in by divinity, but on the other, it conducts its business – trading information, delivering word-cargo – like a bustling factor tasked with managing his master's affairs.

Secondly, that the ambassador is a function of the state apparatus. He's a proxy, a stand-in; someone sent 'by the state', 'in the name of the state' and as 'the representative of the state', but 'without right to command'. That means that he has 'no jurisdiction'. He's not 'entitled to think beyond his instructions'. Very much like a player enacting a part, the ambassador speaks from a script but never makes up the words for himself. (These sentences should land in Harry's commonplace book. He'll need them in Venice.)

Thirdly, that the ambassador enjoys a 'privilege of immunity' underwritten by the law of nations. His person is 'inviolable', and so is his 'suite and paraphernalia'. His residence – the embassy – his goods, his *famiglia*: none may be arrested, searched or confiscated. And that includes 'the rabble' of 'attendants, followers, menials' and even 'slaves' who 'assist the ambassador', for they're just so many more of the ambassador's 'possessions'. These protocols will give legs to Harry's embassy in Venice, and, like invisible bodyguards, safeguard it, allowing him to sit inside a Protestant enclave on a backwater in Cannaregio, to celebrate Holy Communion according to the English Book of Common Prayer, to import boxes of books that the searchers may not open, to send and receive post through protected diplomatic channels (theoretically at least), and to evade the pope's Inquisition.

Finally, that the ambassador can depend on freedom of speech, but within limits. He is, after all, someone else's mouthpiece, a messenger who must freely deliver his prince's will, and 'What is it to be free', Gentili asks, 'if speech (especially in the case of an ambassador) is not free?' Free speech, however, doesn't excuse an 'insulting tongue'. But who's to say what's free and what's insulting – a question all the more vexed when the ambassador is working in a foreign language. Not just words but cultures need translating: Gentili notes the ambassador whose hat was nailed to his head for insulting a prince by failing to remove it at the proper moment of greeting. An extreme case (that Harry surely remembers: he's dogged on hat etiquette, prepping for his first audience in Venice). Normally, 'punishment is not exacted for words', and that's crucial, for ambassadors work in words. Indeed, 'the only things consigned' to them 'are words and opportunities'. So they need to take great care with them – as Harry will find to his terrible cost when his words go rogue in Venice and bring his diplomacy crashing down around his ears.

Following on from these bullet points (which he elaborates unsparingly across the first two books of *De legationibus*), Gentili uses his final book to write a description of the 'perfect' ambassador. A student who's been weeping with exhaustion as he labours to keep up with the lawyer who's so far been building his case upon pettifogging discriminations (herald v. messenger; legate v. orator) while piling up brain-fogging detail (whether fecial priests carried sacred herbs or flint stones; whether hogs were sacrificed or sows; what Cicero had to say and whether Caesar agreed) finally reaches the point of relevance. Book III talks *to him*, gives him a template for his own aspirations. 'Perfect' means not 'faultless' but 'complete'. So Book III is Gentili's diplomatic version of the International Highway Code. When we know what's in it, we know what's driving Henry Wotton in Venice.

Ambassadors don't need encyclopaedic knowledge, 'the whole science of medicine', for instance. But they must have 'certain external advantages': a 'comely appearance', 'nobility' – so no applications from plebs. But nobility isn't only inherited. It can be learned. It's essential, though, because the ambassador is a substitute for his prince. He needs to impress. Here, Gentili analogises the show the ambassador makes to an actor's show on stage and asks, 'If we would hiss off the boards an actor who, when playing the role of king, comes on the stage with a shabby retinue and in anything but royal attire, what is to be done to the ambassador, who is not merely taking part in a play for a few hours, but is actually invested with the person of his prince?'

That phrase, 'actually invested with the person of his prince', needs scrutinising because it's going to have profound application to Harry's business in Venice. Indeed, it sends us to the dictionary, coding as it does for early modernity both the literal and mystified contract that defines the ambassador's relationship to his role. Harry will be invested literally. He'll wear the vestments of his office, robes that recognise his function. But he'll be invested figuratively as well. Through an act of participation between clothes and office, he'll 'actually' become 'the dignity itself', a transfer real and performed, not just virtual. He'll become the 'person' of his prince, where we need to understand 'person' signifying in its early modern meaning, not a unique psychological identity but rather the social role (father, senator, husband) that a self performs, a role that can be enacted but also proxied. The situation Harry will occupy in his official capacity will be paradoxical, both 'self' and 'other', his 'other' being the prince-in-person. This actual investment is important to keep in mind, for it explains the fierce jealousy with which resident ambassadors argue the matter of precedence in foreign courts, petty squabbles about who visited whom first or who is offered the better seat at some ceremonial, squabbles that simmer for weeks then explode into huge diplomatic rows. Gentili, in an assertion that feels counter-intuitive to the largest purposes of embassy, insists that ambassadors are right to defend precedence, to 'refuse to tolerate the slightest infringement of their dignity'. It's instruction Harry in Venice will follow.

Harry sees the person he could become in Gentili's Book III. An ambassador has 'dexterity of intellect' at his command. He marshals wit and even jokes to turn difficult conversations around. He's never 'at a loss to reply, speak and act'. He excels in the chief 'art of ambassadors' – 'the art of winning friendships' – by speaking simply, 'without embellishment, figures or ornamentation', adopting the style 'Cicero somewhere calls popular rhetoric', and delivering messages 'with dispatch'. He's multi-languaged. He speaks 'the living languages of the countries where he is to serve' (not just 'dead' Latin). That's essential, for (as Gentili quotes Cicero), 'We are all deaf in languages which we do not understand'. He should acquire at least 'three'; 'and if he can, one or two more'.

That's not a 'very difficult undertaking', Gentili thinks, 'for men who have an abundance of leisure'. (Like undergraduates?)

There's more. Rhetorical skills. (Harry can tick that one off.) History (a subject not yet on the university syllabus), vital because 'knowledge of the present and prescience of the future are drawn from the past'. And not just ancient history. (Gentili is being radical here.) *Modern* history studied 'within the field of ... useful practical experience'. That word 'practical' comes up time and again: ambassadors should be men 'educated in practical politics'.

Finally, ambassadors must be ethically armour-plated, 'courageous' 'to perform ... duties fearlessly'; temperate, to impose 'a seemly limit on things'; superabundantly faithful, the whole weight of diplomatic mission 'intrusted to ... fidelity'. Here, Gentili offers Harry one of his stunningly memorable sentences: 'The ambassador of irreproachable fidelity practices a healing art' ('Legatus optima fidei medicinam facit'). Physician to the commonwealth, the ambassador holds surgeries in an international consulting room, binding up wounds, salving hurts, knitting broken limbs – or anatomising diplomatic corpses. As 'medicine man', he shares his civic function with the epic and dramatic poets, 'doctors', we remember Gentili calling them, who 'cure through the emotions'. Like theirs, the ambassador's word is 'an instrument of active civil philosophy'. But he needs yet another ethical quality, 'highest prudence', and that's because, as the Venetian Giucciardini makes him, the ambassador is his state's 'ears and eyes'. He needs to 'discern ... the truth of every situation'. Does that mean he should *spy* for his government? No. He should not 'pry into the secrets of a foreign kingdom'. And never, in the service of his king, 'diverge from his duty to God'; never perform any dishonest command.

This is rousing stuff – though the bit about plain speaking will be acquired by hard learning and the bit about spying ignored. When Harry closes Book III he must feel his tutor has armed him like some latter-day Tancredi to conquer diplomacy's strongholds. He should pause, though, over one caution. There is 'nothing more difficult', Gentili writes, than for an ambassador 'to combine two qualities so widely separated as affability and dignity'. Harry has affability in spades. But dignity? He'll need to work on that. For his own part, publishing *De legationibus* Gentili admits he's an idealist, 'depicting the ambassador, not as he generally is, but as he ought to be'. Still, he can identify one 'perfect ambassador'. Gentili dedicates his treatise to Philip Sidney, which surely thrills young Harry, for Sidney is practically family, and his diplomacy, a family affair: Harry's big brother Edward was the one who shepherded Sidney on the mission to Prague in 1577 that established his diplomatic credentials. Alas, within a year of Gentili's dedication Sidney is dead, an untimely waste of a golden life. But perhaps not altogether so. Gentili's dedication just might push an emulous youth to follow in Sidney's footsteps.

Harry leaves Oxford with a BA in hand and Gentili under his belt. His four-year residence has been absent of the 'luxuries' that attend aristocratic students, like, three years his elder, the earl of Essex, who paid to have his Cambridge windows glazed, shelves built, a table, settle, forms and a 'great desk' for 'books' moved in, locks fitted, a 'place for fuel' arranged, and yards and yards of painted cloths hung. Nothing so glamorous as painted cloths and glass in the windows has furnished Harry's Oxford room, and he certainly isn't waited on by servants like the two who go up to Cambridge with Essex. Living bare bones, though, has taught him fortitude, in unheated halls, starting the study day between four and five in the morning with Common Prayer in chapel; fed two meals a day, the fare substantial but monotonous (mutton, mutton, more mutton). He has learned the kinds of survival skills Thomas Cogan publishes in *The Haven of Health* ('chiefly gathered for the comfort of students') where (wishful) homeopathic recipes to fight contagions endemic to Oxford – malaria, typhus, plague and 'the sweating sickness' whose symptoms sound very much like those of modern-day influenza – are given alongside suggestive advice on young men's sexual health in all-male colleges (including 'the commodities which come by moderate evacuation', that is, masturbation).

Leaving the University in June 1588 Harry has added 'to his great wit' 'the ballast of learning and knowledge of the arts'. He is twenty years old. And the Invincible Armada, launched from Spain in May (but really as long ago as that spectacular failure of diplomacy that Gentili dealt with in Wotton's first year at Oxford, the Mendoza affair), is entering the English Channel.

3
The useful library of travel

'Look about you'

19 July 1588. The moment the coastguards stationed on Lizard Point see what's sailing towards Cornwall through the lowering sun on that long, late summer afternoon, they touch fire to the beacon they stand guarding. It roars into flame the height of four grown men, its pitch pot sending up plumes of greasy black smoke visible for miles. All along the southern coast race message-bearing beacon fires, like those that leaped from ancient Ilium to Argos to tell the fall of Troy – a precedent not lost on a nation that calls itself 'Troynovant'. These latest 'flame-a-phores' alert towns from Falmouth to Foy, Plymouth to Shotstone Point to Salcombe, Portsmouth to Dartmouth of what's coming. They run right the way round the Isle of Wight, all along Sussex via Hastings and Rye, up through Kent past Denge Ness and Romney Haven to Hythe, Folkestone, Dover. They signal across the strait to lookouts on the treacherous Goodwin Sands, carrying the news to Ramsgate, to Margate. Still more beacons set on church towers and hilltops flame the message up country: Salisbury to Newbury to Windsor to London; Bristol to Oxford to Coventry. By the following morning, York and Berwick-upon-Tweed have the news. The Spanish Armada, the 'Invincible', has entered the English Channel.

One hundred and thirty-eight ships are under sail. Galleons and galleasses, masts straining under miles of swelling canvas, tiers of gundecks capable of bristling with fire power. Galleys, low-slung in the water, powered, when the winds fail, by gangs of convicts. Hulks stuffed with salt biscuit, shovels, mules. Supply boats with 'artificers to attend' to running repairs. Hospital ships to pick up casualties. This is the 'greatest and strongest combination that was ever gathered in Christendom', John Hawkyns, commanding *Victory*, reports of its approach. Terrifying, it looks like a floating fortress on the surface of the sea. Solid. Because it sails in close-packed formation, its shape, a crescent, its forward curve an impregnable prow; its wings 'spreading out about the length of seven miles' to protect its core, daring attack from the rear. It approaches implacably as if in the slurred motion of a nightmare, 'sailing very slowly', writes the historian William Camden, 'though with full sails, the winds being as it were tired with carrying them, and the ocean groaning under the weight of them'.

But this Armada's mission isn't to engage the English in sea battle. It's to rendezvous at Dunkirk with the duke of Parma, currently waging the latest round of Spain's war in the Netherlands. There, it will collect up Parma's land troops and flotilla, a fleet of 'ships and many flat-bottomed boats, each of them big enough to carry 30 horse, with bridges fitted to them'. Combined, they'll skirt Margate, turn north then west to enter the Thames estuary to land within striking distance of London. Parma's men are issued 'bags of earth two foot long and half a yard wide' 'to make a present shelter' when they beach. He knows the English will put up a fight. Intelligence tells him of the English encampment at Tilbury near Thames-mouth where the earl of Leicester commands a land army of a thousand horse and twenty-two thousand foot. But once he's disposed of Leicester, he'll march straight to London, putting to the sword any who resist. Those are Parma's orders. Then he's to capture the 'heretic queen', proclaim the True Faith restored to an England misled by Reformation apostasy, and install a Catholic monarch, reducing England to Spain's puppet. England will get what she deserves: payback for the enormity her queen committed eighteen months earlier when Elizabeth ordered her cousin executed, Mary Stuart, one-time queen of Scots, former queen of France, Spain's elected (Catholic) heir-apparent to the English throne, currently dead pawn on the political chessboard of Europe.

Spain has more than little England in her imperialist sights. She exploits Mary's memory to reveal designs on France as well. In Paris, Spain is secretly fuelling the ultra-conservative Catholic League headed by the charismatic, fox-faced duke of Guise in opposition to Henri III, a king despised by his subjects as weak-kneed and religiously uncertain because his policy is to tolerate Protestant Huguenots. Launch of the Armada is timed to coincide with insurrection in Paris. Its aim: a popular uprising by the revolutionary Committee of Sixteen to bring onto the streets Parisians like themselves. The Sixteen count among their number a butcher, a tinsmith, an auctioneer, a couple of lawyers, a smattering of low-grade officials, a curé. Students from the Sorbonne can be depended upon to swell the citizen rabble. Their aristocratic frontman (though kept off stage on the day) is Guise. Failing a coup d'état, this action will at least paralyse the French monarchy as effectively as the stone-filled barrels rolled into barricades on the morning of 12 May paralyse the Paris streets. Beleaguered France will be in no position to resist Parma or aid England.

And who sits at the centre of Spain's international machiavellian operations, pulling the strings of intelligence and intrigue – and stuffing French pockets with New World gold? None other than Bernardino de Mendoza, the ambassador thrown out of England in 1584, detected in a conspiracy to assassinate Elizabeth. Now he's Spain's resident ambassador in Paris – and urging on the wild dogs of religious war. Once they've ripped each other's throats out, Spain will put on Henri's throne another puppet. For Mendoza, revenge on England is personal. Hustled aboard that ship that deposited him in Calais, he sent a message to London: 'Tell your mistress that Bernardino de Mendoza was born not to disturb kingdoms but to conquer them'.

In July 1588 continental Europe looks like one vast battlefield, but so far, England's moat, the channel, has kept the fighting 'over there'. Now, the thousands of grim-faced Englishmen who line their kingdom's coastal clifftops to watch the Armada's progress (some of them raw recruits, quick-marched up to make a show of force) must be wondering when they'll be invaded and hauled into the world war. We can imagine Harry Wotton among them, fresh from taking his degree in Oxford in June, returning to Kent to the family estate, and hearing the noise abroad, riding the twenty-seven miles from Bocton to Folkestone to watch Francis Drake harrying the Spanish towards Calais while dozens of plucky 'volunteers' dash out of channel ports to resupply 'il Draco' with shot and food. Eight miles further up the coast to Dover he'd see both navies drop anchor under Calais cliffs then witness the thrilling manoeuvre that dooms the Armada's rendezvous with Parma. In the dead of night, August 7, the English send 'down the wind' against the Spanish a flotilla of fireships, eight tall vessels volunteered for sacrifice, 'besmeared … with wild-fire, pitch and rosin', filled 'with brimstone and other combustible matter'. When the Spaniards see 'the whole sea glittering and shining with the flame' of this towering inferno, they 'cut their cables, and in a terrible panick … put to sea'.

The 'Great Enterprise', as Felipe II of Spain called it, never recovers. The Spanish sea monster stampedes, battling pell-mell into the North Sea, to spend the next two months limping around Scotland and down the west coast of Ireland, starved, sick, straggling back to Santander. When they reach port, there are hardly enough hands on some decks to weigh anchor. Ships run aground. The sleek-coated Spanish horses meant to carry the conquerors into

London are long since thrown overboard. Long since, too, the English gave up the chase. They let the wind, the tides, the battering weather finish their work for them.

Those beacon fires that fire the news across England fire 'all the youth of England' too. Twenty thousand young men are called up to defend the southern coasts. Thousands more are recruited to Leicester's army. The antiquarian John Stow says in his *Annales* that they march 'dancing and leaping' to Tilbury, and when they hear 'rumours' of the 'foe's approach' they are 'as joyful at such news as if lusty giants were to run a race'. So once the Spanish threat is drowned in the North Sea and wrecked upon the rocky outcrops of Donegal, what is England to do with her fired-up youth? That question occupies every eager lad who, like Harry Wotton, is coming of age in the last decade of Elizabeth's reign. It's argued – in fictional terms – in the opening lines of a play shortly to hit the London stage, Shakespeare's *The Two Gentlemen of Verona*. One of the gentlemen, off 'to see the wonders of the world abroad', fears the other is wasting his youth in idleness, 'dully sluggardis'd at home'. 'Home-keeping youths', Valentine warns Proteus, 'have ever homely wits'.

Their elders agree. Fathers are meant to 'Put forth their sons to seek preferment out': 'to the wars' or to voyages to 'discover islands far away'. So why is Proteus not 'put forth'? Youth is a resource. Fathers have a duty to bankroll it, and sons have a duty to spend it. But youth is a 'slippery' age, 'the most dangerous time of all a man's life', not just because 'youth' as Elizabethans calculate it lasts a full decade 'from seventeen to seven and twenty', but because in these years adolescents have 'the rein of all licence in their own hand'. What's to stop them galloping headlong into all manner of danger and disaster? Now that Spain is on the run – at least temporarily – and the queen's galleons are stood down, her recruits sent home to get the harvest in, where can sons 'seek preferment out' – and find best profit from their father's spending?

For young men like Harry Wotton whose pupil years were among books, there's one clear answer: travel. They've come down from university entitled by their degree to call themselves 'gentlemen' and entitled by the statute that regulates every Englishman's apparel to 'wear satin, damask, grogran and taffeta' in their 'hose and doublet'. Their status is legible at a glance. But how can it be tested? At school and university they've been equipped with a rhetorical toolkit to know the world. They're literate in Latin, which links them into pan-European communication networks. They've been taught to observe, record, report; to keep a commonplace book. They know how to weigh up and discriminate, and, as Englishmen of the Protestant Reformation, to recognise the truth of religion against the delusions of Catholic 'superstition'. (Harry doesn't doubt the existential threat Catholicism poses: that Armada in the channel is seared on his memory.) But the very seas that serve as England's defensive moat are a barrier to the experience his future needs. A Little Englander like Harry must widen his horizons. Travelling abroad, he'll discover difference in customs, clothes, food, political systems, cultural norms. He'll encounter challenges to what he takes for orthodoxy that will test his innate sense of superiority against other nations' sense of self. Travelling, he'll set learning against living, entering what his future employer, Essex, calls the 'useful library of travel' where he'll 'study men and actions' as before he was 'wont to do books'. In short, he'll be initiating 'a more general conversation with mankind'.

Harry's travel won't be recreational. It isn't for any Elizabethan. It's arduous, dangerous, expensive. It requires independent means. But it's also 'enabling'. In a Europe whose deadly political rivalries are mapped out in the factions that drove the failed invasion of England in 1588, the object of Harry's travel is political, to 'get knowledge' for 'the bettering' of himself 'and his country'. The whole point of going abroad is to return home, to bring back a self seasoned in the world, a knowledgeable self fit for service to Crown, Privy Council, aristocratic patron – and England. The crisis England so narrowly averts in July 1588 sets these ideas squarely in Harry's view.

'Self-eye-seeing experience'

He spends the next fifteen months arranging his future. If he has disappointed his father's ambitions by failing to stay on at Oxford, he is instead heading for vistas opened up by his surrogate father, his college tutor Alberico Gentili. Rather over-earnestly he tells his brother he aims to 'pass into Italy', and on the way, to search out the best minds in Europe to apply himself to their 'conversation'. His not inconsiderable ambition is to 'become the best Civilian in Basel' – that is, expert in Civil Law, or what the English term Roman Law. His eye already looks fixed on future preferment towards service. Knowledge of continental law is the necessary qualification of a diplomat.

Edward Wotton supports his little brother's projects. Twenty years earlier in his own youth he was a traveller and Crown agent, living in Naples so long that he spoke Spanish like a native (along with Italian and French), which he used as informant to Francis Walsingham, head of intelligence in Elizabeth's government. Later, as secretary to the English embassy in Vienna, he was the experienced senior who attended a still wet-behind-the-ears Philip Sidney when

Sidney arrived in the Holy Roman Emperor's court in 1577. That visit (and perhaps something of both the flourish and arrogance of youth) would be forever remembered in the decidedly oblique opening lines of Sidney's *Defence of Poesy*, where Sidney's eye seems to be not on poetry but cavalry: 'When the right virtuous Edward Wotton and I were at the Emperor's Court we gave ourselves to learn horsemanship of John Pietro Pugliano'.

Edward knows the value of networking. To be familiar with Sidney is to be connected to Sidney's uncle Robert Dudley, earl of Leicester, and to Leicester's stepson, Robert Devereux, earl of Essex, who will later marry Sidney's widow, the daughter of Walsingham, Edward's one-time employer. Such circles form the interlocking wheels that turn the machinery of Elizabethan politics. Edward's little brother needs to get on board. Edward will help. His own prospects are about to change, for in 1589 he's made Gentleman of Her Majesty's Privy Chamber, which gives him residence at Court. There, he'll be positioned to drop Harry's name into those permanently pricked-up ears that wait upon business in the anterooms of power. More immediately, however, Edward makes good his dying father's wish, a bequest not inscribed in Thomas's will, so evidently relying on verbal instructions – and Edward's good will to follow them. It gives Harry an annuity of £67, which likely matures on Harry's twenty-first birthday, 30 March 1589. From beyond the grave, then, Thomas is able to 'put forth' his youngest son 'to seek preferment out'.

That summer the brothers will pore over maps, marking destinations, planning routes – then revising them. Much of Europe is off limits, or becoming so. There'll be no travel into Spain or Spain's client territories, Portugal, Naples. Even now, rumours are circulating that Spanish shipwrights are knocking up a new Armada to sail next year. The quickest cross-channel route, Dover to Calais, is barred to all except the musters the Crown is sending over to shore up the Protestant cause. France, once again, is an inferno of civil war. After the day of the barricades a year back, and after the defeat of the Spanish invasion of England, Henri III's pusillanimity in the face of Guise's pretensions curdles into toxic watchfulness. At the end of the year, Henri acts. On the morning of 23 December, so insolent that he scrawls 'He would not dare' across a message warning him that the king is plotting his assassination, Guise walks open-eyed into the ambush that cuts him down at the door of the king's cabinet. He is thirty-seven. If the line attributed to Henri is accurate – 'At last I am king' – he's not so for long. In August a fanatical monk plunges a dagger into his belly. He is thirty-seven. The king's cousin, Henri of Navarre, a Protestant who's been fighting the Huguenot cause in France for years, takes the throne – whereupon

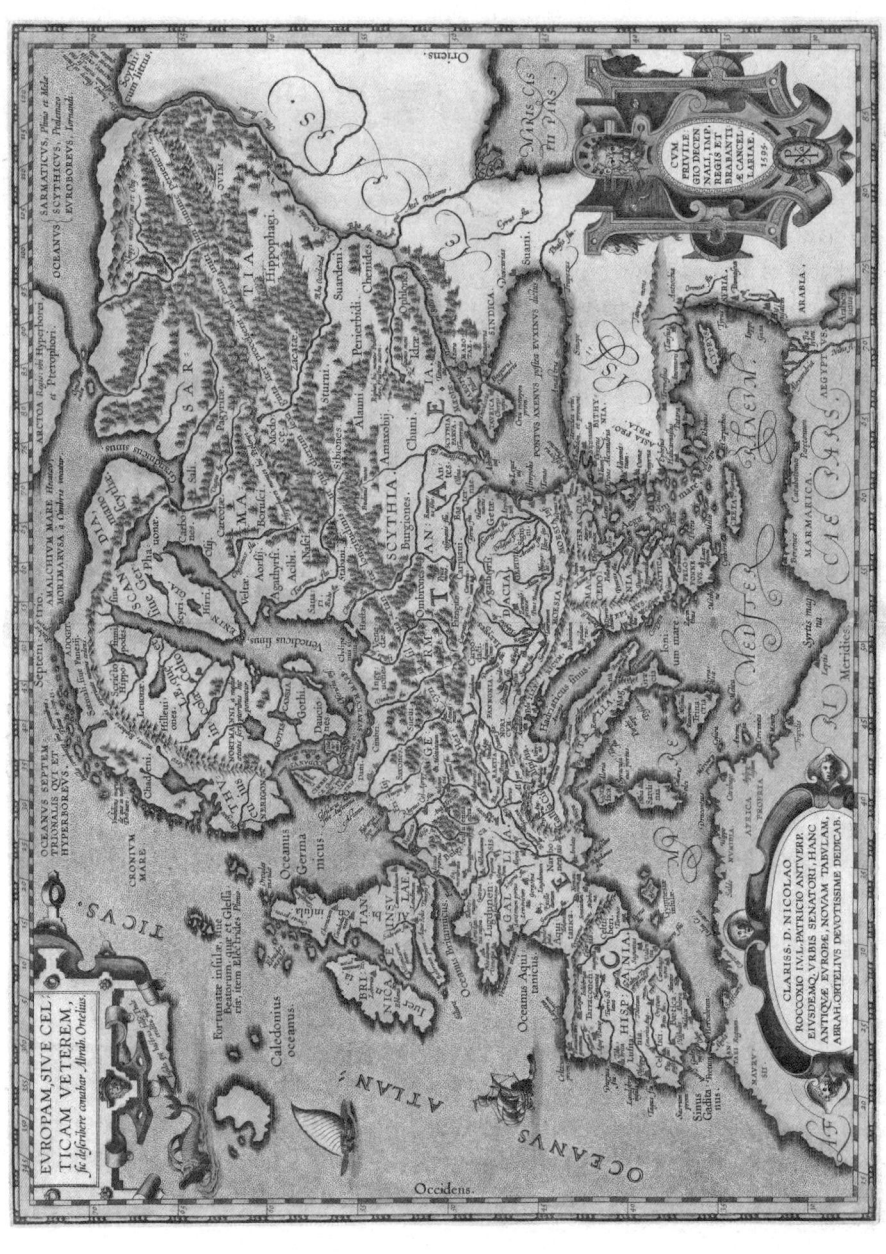

3 Abraham Ortelius map of Europe, 1595.

France rushes headlong into the next suicidal cycle of religious war. Is it the sixth – or seventh – since that Bartholomew's Day in 1572 when Parisian gutters ran with Huguenot blood? In 1591 the English queen will 'forbid all manner of persons to resort to any towns held by the French King's rebels, or to traffic with any of them, upon pain to be punished as traitors'.

The straightest high roads into Europe blocked, Harry maps his route to Italy via Basel through Germany. Still, that's no bad thing for someone 'first setting forth'. He'll pick his way from one Protestant-aligned town to the next, skirting Catholic enclaves, but he'll also learn German self-sufficiency. The trouble with us Englishmen, observes one seasoned traveller, is that we're stoutly chauvinist on the one hand and comically hapless on the other. We 'despise the company of mean people at bed or board'. But we're 'scarcely' able to 'make our selves ready', that is, dress ourselves, because we 'use too much the help of our servants'. They do things differently in Germany. In Germany, anyone who 'comes into a shoemaker's shop must find out the shoes' that 'will fit him and put them on himself'. In Germany, 'we' Englishmen have to 'learn to serve our selves'; at meals, 'to admit the company of mean men', and at bedtime, to allow 'poor fellows, yea, very coachmen' 'to be our bedfellows', even 'when they are drunk'. Germany will be an education for young Harry.

No traveller of Harry's age travels blind. If travel is purposeful, it's also informed. First, by Her Majesty's Privy Council. Anyone who leaves the kingdom needs to secure a licence stating his business in going abroad, frequently given as a desire 'to travel into foreign lands to learn languages and gain experience'. This passport specifies the length of time permitted overseas and how much money can be carried out of the kingdom (by law, a maximum of £20, which is still four times the annual wage of a grocer or brewer). It tells the bearer he can be summoned home at any time – and must comply. It stipulates what servants and horses (if any) will attend the traveller, and with what 'bags, baggages and necessaries' he may travel. It might impose restrictions: forbidding any to venture into a war zone. Categorically, the traveller may not 'haunt or keep company' with any unlicensed English exile – specifically, any recusant Englishman who's fled abroad. Anyone 'unlicensed' is an outlaw.

Harry might read any number of travel writers that summer. Letters, precepts, treatises, reports of voyages, itineraries, schedules circulating both in manuscript and print: Thomas Elyot in *The Boke Named the Governour* (1531), Roger Ascham in *The Scholemaster* (1570), Richard Hakluyt's *Divers Voyages* (1583) and his just-published *Principal Navigations* (1589), Philip Sidney's letter to his brother Robert (printed before 1587). These authors are humanist-trained men writing to like-minded men, men who affect 'the knowledge of state affairs, histories, cosmography'. Their advice wades deep in classical precedents, citing the great 'travellers' Ulysses and Aeneas and the heroes of modern European epics. Harry understands the genre. He reads Tasso, and what is *Gerusalemme Liberata* if not travel literature?

Ascham and the rest write philosophically about travel. What Erasmus claimed for humanist scholars reading in schools in the 1480s is now claimed for humanist travellers reading the world. Travel opens the door to all human knowledge. Without the 'industry of travellers', the world-travelling Fynes Moryson asks in one of his four volumes of *Itineraries*, 'Who would have taught us geography?' How 'should we have learned all other arts?' Or 'discovered new worlds?' Indeed, without those early travellers, Christ's disciples, how should we have attained 'knowledge of the holy Gospel'? Philip Sidney tells his brother to read Aristotle's *Ethics* and to travel thoughtfully, not like himself and his callow fellows, who 'never thought in our selves why we went, but a certain tickling humour to do as other men had done'. Essex says travellers must look beyond the mere 'ornaments' of travel like sight-seeing 'to attain to knowledge, which is not only the excellentest thing in man, but the very excellency of man'. Much loftier ambitions, then, than 'tickling' curiosity.

Such writing puts fire in young Harry's belly. It reads like poetry, figuring travel in metaphors, like Moryson calling 'this world' first a 'theatre' where 'the Almighty Maker hath manifested his unspeakable glory' then 'a stately palace of a great king'. Who, he wonders, would be 'happy' to be 'led only into the kitchen?' The traveller needs to thrust himself into every chamber and closet. But he must not get stuck there. Travellers who affect 'endless meanderings abroad' are like 'rude stage players' who 'spend more time in putting on their apparel than acting their comedy'. Travel, then, is merely the *rehearsal* for life. The real performance is to be made back at home to that expectant audience who awaits 'proof' that he'll 'act' his 'affairs in the world' – not 'lie by the fire' like some notional 'sluggardis'd' gentleman of Verona.

It's obvious to Harry that Moryson's global theatre isn't like those playhouses that are springing up just now across London. It is God's Theatrum Mundi. This makes travel tantamount to worship, a way of knowing 'the incomprehensible majesty of God'. Travellers aren't just 'citizens of the whole world' or 'this world'. They're citizens of that world 'to come'. 'All our life is a pilgrimage', Moryson tells travellers – as if they needed reminding. Its itinerary and final destination are marked from birth by God who, 'for his only begotten son's sake (the true Mercury of travellers)' will 'bring us that are here strangers into our true country'. Such thoughts are empowering. Harry's classically trained mind would note the crossover between Mercury, patron of travellers in the ancient world, and Christ, sure guide to Christian pilgrims. No matter what happens to Harry's physical body on the dangerous road he's setting himself, he knows that the material world is only the transitory, mortal world he occupies as a 'stranger'. His 'real' self is his soul. He'll end his 'pilgrimage' when Death takes him home to eternity. On earth, he should travel with that destination in mind – and mindful of any distractions, any mis-directions that might lose him his way.

Writing thus, writing philosophically, writing metaphorically, travel writers aren't saying anything that hadn't been said before and wouldn't be said again, usually at much greater length. Certainly, they aren't saying anything that isn't impressed upon young Harry by his big brother. It's the very fact that such 'discourses' state the conventional that makes them so important, not least in alerting us to what strikes our contemporary ears as most distant to our own behaviours, the language of faith that frames and everywhere informs the Elizabethan practice of travel. Every travel writer enjoins the traveller to daily prayer, and not casually 'while he slumbers in bed' but 'in private, withdrawn from company, either kneeling as before his father' (every Elizabethan son kneels in his father's company) 'or standing as before his Master and Lord'. Prayer is the cornerstone of devotion for Protestant Englishmen, and Harry is solidly Protestant.

His daily exercise will fortify him spiritually – but also *essentially*. It's a kind of armour. Crossing Europe Harry will be moving through Catholic territories where he'll be considered a heretic, where 'snares' will be laid to capture him for conversion, where the papal Inquisition will arrest him for interrogation. He 'must have great care to preserve his health', not just for the good of his short-lived mortal body, but for the ultimate and real good of his eternal soul. 'Our countrymen in Italy', Moryson warns, 'run high dangers'. As long as they're healthy, they can 'discreetly shun the snares of the Inquisition'. But that changes when they fall ill. For then Catholic priests 'thrust upon them' rites that Protestants consider heretical, rites like 'Confession' and 'Extreme Unction'. Men 'ready to die', writes Moryson laconically, 'can ill dissemble'. If, therefore, the 'sick man' by refusing Catholic rites exposes that he is 'of the Reformed Religion', medical care is instantly withdrawn: 'the Physician and the Apothecary are forbidden to help him, and very kitchen physic is denied him by the Priest's command'. If the man recovers, he'll 'be sure to be brought into the Inquisition'. If he dies, 'his body shall be buried in the high-way' – or worse, buried as a Catholic and claimed by the papal propaganda machine as a convert. Harry Wotton is well aware that in daily prayer he defends his faith and reminds himself who he is while 'estranged' abroad.

But reading them in the summer of 1589 he might observe how, in these authors, a philosophy of travel is shading into practical advice – like Moryson advising travellers before they leave home to make their will. In bygone days their grandfathers wrote wills before travelling from York to London. How much more necessary is this insurance today for youths travelling so many 'leagues beyond man's life'? Thomas Coryat tells them to carry a personal medical kit: no telling when such supplies will come in handy. In Moryson's kit there's a stinking ointment he uses for dressing scabs. On one occasion, it serves a secondary 'medical' purpose. His gold is wrapped in a packet soaked in the stuff. When ruffians attack and ransack his saddlebags, ripping open his padded doublet, they find the money sewn in its lining – but turn up their noses at the noisome mess that conceals his real treasure.

Writers give Harry advice that he'll follow, like arranging a dependable London agent to forward letters of credit and bills of exchange that brokers or merchants in Brussels, Frankfurt or Venice will convert into ready cash. Maintaining a steady correspondence with home is essential, not least so his family knows he lives. But this involves some trouble and expense. There's no regular postal service in England. The delivery of letters depends on casual 'carriers', and even on the continent where a much more sophisticated system is in place, getting messages home is a fraught business that relies on packets handed from courier to courier, regularly lost, regularly left forgotten on some merchant's shelf. Even dating letters is a tricky business. When he crosses the channel, Harry leaves the English time zone, a difference he'll have to calculate not in hours but *days*, for Europe runs to Pope Gregory's 'new' calendar, introduced only seven years earlier, while England keeps stubbornly to Julius Caesar's. These calendars are out of sync by ten days: 1 August in London is 10 August in Venice, a quirk Harry will mark (and we'll need to observe) by dating his letters from Europe 'style of the place', and from England 'OS', old style. No matter how urgently he writes, he'll have to make his youthful self a Job waiting reply: a letter from Venice encountering no mishap (or appalling weather in the Channel) only arrives in London twenty-one days later. And the return? Another twenty-one days. That timeframe might test even Job.

Again, following the literature's advice, travelling alone – no money for a servant – he plans to travel light, packing only the 'most necessary things'. In Italy, carriers take a traveller 'not to his inn but only to the water side, or to the gates of the city' – and charge extra for baggage. After that, he'll have to shoulder his stuff himself. He'll learn to 'enquire after the best inns', to avoid 'frauds and injuries of knaves', to carry money safely: to wit, Moryson's stinking swaddling. Most importantly, he'll learn how 'to behave in foreign parts'. In sum, say the travel writers, 'Paese dove vai, usa comme truovi': 'Wherever you go, take the country as you find it'. Or, 'When in Rome …'.

Harry's preparation is as much mental as practical. He understands that England's expanding participation in European affairs needs his generation to grow into men whose private selves will be located in the public, political sphere, men who can move in European Court and cultural circles, skilled diplomats, knowledgeable in people, places, governments, and canny in acquiring that knowledge. It needs public servants who understand modernity: modern history, modern languages, and the political and social institutions of foreign countries – including international banking systems and the movement of money. Tutored by Gentili, Harry knows some of this theoretically. Travelling, he'll learn it in his bones. Books like Thomas Palmer's *An Essay of the Meanes how to make our Trauailes, into forraine Countries, the more profitable and honourable* offer instruction. It doesn't matter that Palmer isn't published until 1606. His conspicuously titled *Essay* is just as conspicuously derivative. The 'six general heads' he sets out in a schematic diagram (usefully for us) gives us the same check-list of knowledge acquisition that Harry finds elsewhere.

Of the things he'll need to learn, top of the list comes 'the tongue' – language. That's obvious, because, as Harry knows from Gentili quoting Cicero, we're 'deaf in languages we do not understand'. Moryson goes one further. We're not just 'deaf'. We're 'deaf and dumb'. It's good diplomacy to learn the vernacular, and the shortest way to winning friends. The traveller who speaks 'the language where he stays', says Moryson, will 'catch' the 'loves' of the locals 'as it were with a fish-hook'. More crucially, no matter what the educationalist Richard Mulcaster says in praise of English, the Englishman knows his native tongue simply doesn't travel. In John Florio's teach-yourself-Italian manual, composed as a series of direct-method dialogues, an exchange between an Englishman and an Italian states the humiliating truth. What, asks the Englishman, does the Italian think of English? The Italian replies:

> È un lingua che vi fara bene in Inghilterra,
> ma passate Dover, la non val niente.

That is, it's a language that serves well in England, but past Dover, it's worth nothing. The Englishman blunders on: 'Dunque, non è practicata fori in altri paesi?' (So, it's not used abroad?). The reply is crushing: 'Signor no, con chi volete che parlino?' (No sir. Who would they talk to?) According to Florio's Italian, not even English merchants speak English abroad.

Across Europe, Latin is still the international language of scholarship and learning; of the Catholic church; of royal epistolary exchange. But daily life is conducted in the vernacular. In Venice, as Harry will see, Mass is sung in Latin, public preaching is in Italian, and fish is sold in Veneziano. When a letter in Latin signed by Queen Elizabeth of England reaches the Venetian Republic, it's translated into Italian before being read to the Senato. In 1608 Thomas Coryat can make his way from Somerset on foot across France, Germany and Italy to Venice speaking only Latin, but his lack of any 'vulgar' tongue means he travels 'deaf and dumb' with respect to ordinary people. So when he's curious about the *popolani*, he has to rely on some elite's interpretation of them. In the English Court language skills aren't considered 'ornation'. They're 'necessary'. Elizabeth converses with ambassadors in Italian, French and Latin; King James hears Venetian ambassadors in Italian but answers in French. Most of Her Majesty's civil service and privy counsellors – Walsingham, Burghley, Essex, Robert Cecil – have second and third languages. Harry is already proficient in Latin and fluent in Italian. Gentili has seen to that. In Germany he'll acquire 'high Dutch'.

Words, as Harry already knows, aren't neutral, and acquiring new ones might put a target on his back. For just as foreign fashion might 'turn' him into a monster of apparel – or religious conversion might 'turn' him 'Turk' – so 'far-fetched' words (or what mockers back home *think* are 'far-fetched') might 'turn' him into an 'ape' of foreign 'form', his language a 'fantastical banquet' of 'strange dishes'. And that wouldn't be dangerous just to his outward form. Learning new words is inevitably to learn new practices, practices that start at the level of language, on the tip of the tongue, but then manifest themselves in behaviour. (Fast forward: we'll see Harry in Venice having to learn to behave around that diplomatically loaded, untranslatable but deeply un-English word 'conveniente'.) That said, there's no escaping the fact that anywhere Harry goes, until he knows the local language, he's 'a mere stranger', and 'likely to know no more than *res gestas*', that is, yesterday's news, stuff to wrap up fish in the market but not to bother sending home as 'intelligence'.

Given the imperative to put foreign tongues into English mouths, it's no wonder travel licences so frequently give language-learning as the reason for going abroad. But learning a foreign language isn't an end in itself; rather, it's the means to accessing the other 'general heads' Palmer tells travellers they must investigate. First, 'the people', whether they live in 'civility or barbarousness', 'freedom or servileness', 'religiousness or profaneness'. Then, 'the country', its name, situation and 'populousness'; its 'commodities', both 'natural' and 'artificial' (soil, rivers, ports, 'baths and medicinable things'; 'buildings and fortifications'). Next, its 'laws and customs'. Who governs? A 'monarch'? 'Nobles'? Or 'the Popularitie'? Finally, its state 'secrets', the 'ordinary strength of the state', its 'commodities' and 'treasure'; the 'persons governing' and the 'persons governed'. Are the plebs jumped-up upstarts prone to sedition? How are they 'affected in rumours'? Gentili in *De legationibus* tells ambassadors categorically they're not spies; Palmer makes intelligencers of every traveller who steps off the boat in Calais.

As Harry realises, this sort of intelligence-gathering requires first-person witness. Anyone who thinks 'the best travailing' – we should note the Elizabethan coincidence between 'travel' and 'travail' – is 'in maps and good authors' is simply wrong. A 'sedentary traveller' (writes Moryson) might pass for 'a wise man' as long as he converses 'either with dead men by reading' or 'by writing, with men absent'. But let him 'once enter on the stage of public employment', he'll be helpless. Travel sets Harry to study men, here and now. Its stage is action, and Harry, since that scene on Dover clifftops, wants to be in the thick of things. So he won't hover like some gadfly on the surface of the landscape. He'll stage direct encounters with the foreign, drilling down into geographical, political, civic and cultural difference. The Elizabethan state needs 'experts', not 'novellanties' who hang around 'marts' picking up scraps of 'news' like picked-over fish bones. He'll keep his eyes and ears open, and report what he finds. He'll make himself an informant, recording his journey, dispatching 'advertisements' of its progress, finally rendering an account on his return. As Moryson advises, he'll 'make a book of paper' – like the commonplace book he first kept at school – to write up 'all things occurrant'. But Moryson warns him, and his brother underscores: writing is perilous. Harry is a Protestant travelling in mainly Catholic Europe. So:

> Great caution must be had … how he carry about him … papers, the subject whereof cannot but in many places be offensive and perhaps dangerous, if once upon suspicion he chance to be searched. … And for abundant caution, lest any thing he notes by the way, should in any place upon mischance prejudice him, he shall do well to write such things in ciphers and unknown characters, being also ready to give a feigned interpretation of them to any magistrate, if need be.

Harry will be subject to search. European towns and cities are walled. Guards keep their gates. Strangers are stopped, and papers they carry sometimes sent for further investigation by local authorities. He'll have to be careful. But when he's advised to write in 'ciphers and unknown characters' and how to 'feign' before the 'magistrate', the 'informant' starts to sound like an 'intelligencer', first cousin to the Venetian *confidenti*, the spy. When he's told (as Essex's agent in Venice is told) to 'seek ... acquaintance', 'to win' into his confidence persons 'from whence the greatest news can come' and to 'assure' those who will 'advertize' such news that they will receive 'good allowance to the value of their wares' – that is, they'll get cash for information – words like 'seek', 'win', 'advertize', 'allowance', 'wares' seem to locate this business if not at the same address as cloak-and-dagger practice (otherwise, espionage), then surely just around the corner from it. As we'll shortly see, travelling in Italy, Wotton will regularly knock on the back door of this shady address before shoving papers through its letter box.

For now though, setting out to talk his way across Europe, Harry goes equipped with cultural superiority, like every Englishman who knows himself better than others. He knows the proverb that calculates the cultural exchange rate: 'Three Moors to a Portuguese; three Portuguese to an Englishman'. But Harry also knows his inferiority, what Florio tells him about his language. Travelling, he'll encounter difference. Difference that contests his national prejudices. Difference that confirms them. (In the Venetian Ghetto in 1608, meeting 'some few' 'goodly and proper' 'elegant' Jews, Thomas Coryat amazedly discovers that the 'English proverb: To look like a Jew, whereby is meant sometimes a weather beaten warp-faced fellow' simply is 'not true'. He attempts to convert those 'goodly and proper' Jews anyway.) Travelling, sometimes what Harry knows will have to be concealed. The surest way to avoid suspicion, to evade any brush with authority, is to learn to keep his mouth shut. Fynes Moryson offers him 'two good Italian Proverbs':

> In bocca serrata mai non entrò mosca.
> La lingua non ha osso; ma fa rompere il dosso.
> [A fly never entered a locked mouth.
> The tongue has no bone, but can still break your back.]

For a young man just setting out, a young man like Harry Wotton of Bocton Malherbe, this is splendid advice.

4
The wandering time of my life

'From Redcross Street'

October 1589. The long months of speculation are over. Michaelmas is past. Kent's apple orchards are stripped of their harvest. The days are shortening when Harry Wotton writes to his brother in Kent from Redcross Street in London. He's in the city to arrange his affairs, a young man preparing for a journey. He hasn't written his will, as Fynes Moryson tells travellers to do before setting out, but he's done something just as legally significant, and he gives his brother a 'little history' of these 'matters', telling him he's 'consulted with Graisen in the never-erring form of law' and 'taken such order as the half-blood shall be no hurt at all to the whole name'.

'Graisen' is a private joke. Only last year Edward Wotton was admitted to Gray's Inn, one of the four Inns of Court that constitute the so-called 'third university' of the realm where young gentlemen train as barristers – or acquire enough working knowledge of the law to manage country estates. The jest sets the tone of this letter between brothers and helps tease out Harry's opaque comment about the law. Harry is always respectful of Edward's status. He's not just Edward's younger brother. He's Edward's half-brother, the runt of his father's second litter, thus, 'the half-blood'. By English Common Law, his claims to inheritance are limited. In Kent, however, the custom of gavelkind still obtains, even where – as his grandfather had done a generation back – testators petitioned Parliament to alter its terms. By gavelkind all male children of the deceased, not just the eldest son, inherit equally. Consulting 'Graisen', Harry appears to be making legally clear as he leaves England that he's binding himself to the unwritten terms of his father's will, accepting in full satisfaction of his inheritance the annuity that's funding his travel. Thus, 'the half-blood' is protecting his brother's 'whole name', affirming Edward's Common Law title by primogeniture to the family estate. He's also settling himself to mortality. He may not live to return from his travels. If he does, his brother may not live to welcome him home.

On Redcross Street Harry perhaps lodges in one of the new buildings halfway up this narrow thoroughfare that runs north just outside Cripplegate to end abruptly where a cross marks the street turning into Golding Lane, a far less salubrious passage pestered on both sides with crowded tenements. He's not a Londoner. This city is as foreign to him as to any visitor from abroad. So if he's been soaking up travel literature over the past summer, he's prepped to look with the eyes of a stranger on London's huddle and sprawl, her fashionable new frontages sitting cheek by jowl with ruinous dereliction; her former religious premises turned into carpenters' yards, saw pits, abattoirs, stables; her crowds, markets; even the mire festering in her gutters. Essex's 'Look about you' is as much a motto for home as abroad. And here's a chance to survey London the way he'll survey cities from Basel to Rome.

While he blows his nails waiting for Graisen to dispose his affairs, he occupies his eager interests in government, law, theology, architecture, medicine. Around him, there's so much to see, so much to store up for comparison with cities abroad. Eight churches stand in the ward, all of them packed with monuments, as well as several of London's forty-eight livery companies, the ancient trade guilds that now essentially run the city – and show how a city should be run. The Brewers are on Addle Street; the Curriers, around the corner on Little Wood Street. Opposite the Bowyers on Monkswell Street stands Barbers' Hall, home to the Barber-surgeons, medieval England's dentists, therapeutic bloodletters, bone-setters and surgeons. Now, though, anatomy has transformed surgery. Huddles of gentlemen in furred gowns, ruffs and satin doublets watch dissections in the hall while specialists like John Banister deliver lectures over opened corpses. Given his interest in optics at Oxford, Harry may well step into Barbers' Hall to observe a dissection – unwitting preparation he'll dredge up a decade hence in Venice. Remembering advice to travellers to carry a medical kit on their journeys, he'll walk in the company's garden – it's been growing there since at least 1555 – noting the homeopathic properties of plants and which of them to stuff in his pack.

Once he's finished with the lawyers, Harry tells his brother, he has to attend to the nuts and bolts of travel, getting his money sorted, so 'I repaired me to my friend in Bow Lane', one 'Mr. Parvish'. He sets out from his lodgings heading south, turning into Fore Street then ducking under a stone arch through Cripplegate into the walled city. The gate got its name in pre-Reformation times from cripples congregating at the church of their patron, St Giles. If anyone could intercede to make lame men walk, it was he. But now the 'age of miracles' is past, and the new regime has little tolerance for such superstitious nonsense – or its political expression. Heads of ten conspirators executed three years ago in the Babington plot to assassinate Elizabeth and restore Catholicism to England are grinning on poles overlooking London Bridge. Their quartered bodies are distributed around the city, spiked on gate tops, and tarred to preserve the gruesome message they convey. If he looks up, Harry will see bits of rotting Anthony Babington or perhaps Chidiock Tichborne, youths not much older than himself when they were hanged, cut down alive then disembowelled and cleavered like butcher's meat. (A copy of Tichborne's poem written the night before his execution will turn up in Harry's papers.) In a new playhouse on the other side of the Thames – the first to be built on the South Bank – Edward Alleyn as Tamburlaine is currently performing to packed audiences stomach-turning atrocities as 'sights of power'. They're nothing compared with the 'sights of power' the English queen stages daily as street theatre.

Harry follows Little Wood Street past the Sun tavern, crossing Silver Street (a row of 'divers fair houses') where it intersects with Addle Street. Here, Plasterers' Hall sits on one corner facing St Albans opposite, the commercial city and the worshipful city directly in each other's eye line. The situation is suggestive. This church – like every church in the city, and there are more churches in London than in any city in continental Europe – is a monument to the trades whose wealth built and beautified it. Deceased mercers and haberdashers, vintners and grocers, once lords mayor of London, now pack St Albans in silent congregation, witnesses to the glory of God made real in their earthly wealth. Past St Albans stands a different witness in stone, this one to the misery of the city's commercial failures. 'The Compter' is a debtor's prison, 'compter', the old spelling of 'counter'. Its inmates constitute an anti-city within the city: over-reaching speculators, scammers and fraudsters, or simply business fools. The prison is wedged between Lad Lane and Love Lane, so called for its 'wantons', that is, prostitutes, an irony probably not lost on Harry Wotton.

At the bottom of Wood Street he comes out onto Cheapside, the wide east–west thoroughfare that, with its crowds, trade and noise, runs like a belt across the bulging waist of the city between Old Jewry and St Paul's churchyard. It sucks up the cargo unloaded on the docks: every street running north from the Thames empties onto Cheapside. Buildings three, four, even five storeys tall line both sides of this commercial highway. Stall-holders offer Kent apples, Colchester oysters, clay pipes stuffed with tobacco, songbirds in cages.

Open-front shops sell everything from harnesses, saddles and shoes to fish, feathers, fabric – and luxury goods imported from around the world. Stepping into a dusty river of ceaseless human traffic where pedestrians have to compete with drays, carts and coaches, for these days 'the world runs on wheels', Harry is momentarily stopped by the din. The wind is blowing, as usual, from the west. The stench it carries from the slaughterhouses further along Cheapside at St Nicholas Shambles hits his nostrils. Once a religious precinct, the church now houses butchers' shops facing the aptly named Stinking Alley, where beef, pig and sheep carcasses hang by their necks, bellies ripped as if imitating some mass public execution on the common gallows at Tyburn.

He puts his back to the wind, walking east, along Goldsmith's Row, reckoned the most beautiful set of dwellings and shops in London, then crosses Bread Street, taking a slightly jiggling route that shunts Cheapside traffic down to Queenhithe, one of the city's oldest wharfs. He pauses in front of St Mary le Bow, fascinated by her architecture, the first London church to be built on stone arches. Hence the name: St Mary de Arcubus, corrupted to 'Bow', or on some maps 'Boo'. Her great bell, the fifth and heaviest in the peal, has rung the nine o'clock summer curfew for the past fifty years – earlier, as the year wanes. When the Great Bell of Bow tolls, taverns turn out their quaffers; apprentices stop work; Cripplegate – and every other gate – is locked and bolted. Thereafter, 'night walkers' are liable to arrest.

He turns right towards the Thames. Most of the trades that gave these streets names have moved elsewhere: the curriers from Cordwainer Street to Moorgate, the poulterers from the Poultry to the Shambles. Some trades have disappeared, 'almost worn out', like the fletchers of Bowyers' Row whose premises are now bowling alleys, or 'clean worn out'. There's no call in Reformation England for the 'paternoster makers … of Paternoster Row'. (They, at least, have reinvented themselves. They're now stationers, their bookstalls in St Paul's churchyard.) These redundant street names: for locals, they map a city changing with the times but they make it a mirage for a stranger trying to get his bearings. Reliably, a red cross marks Redcross Street. But where's the milk on Milk Street? Still, feeling lost in a city has to be excellent prep for the journey Harry is going on.

He finds the house of Henry Parvish, merchant and banker, or, better said, moneybroker. Parvish's trade in the Mediterranean, specifically with Venice, is extensive – and fabulously lucrative. Edward has written to make the introduction, and Harry is mightily impressed. A year hence when Parvish dies unexpectedly, he'll leave over £6,000-worth of goods in just one Venetian warehouse, quite probably a cargo of *uve passe*, currants, from Zante. England hasn't been able to get enough of them since dried currants became essential to cookery, both savoury *and* sweet. Indeed, the Venetians can't imagine what use the English make of them all – unless 'for dyeing, or to feed hogs'. Astonishingly, the import tax on currants earns the Crown as much in a year as it collects from tax on all the alehouses in the realm.

Harry is relying on 'Mr Parvish' to broker his finances, to ensure he can access funds abroad. Moving money around Europe in currencies that do not align is complicated, uncertain and expensive, and Harry is getting his first experience of a client role he'll perform time and again where he'll be at the mercy of the man sitting on the merchant's side of the table. The instrument that merchants have devised for money transfer is the 'bill of exchange', bought (for a price) in one place, and redeemed (for a further price) in another. Parvish sells him two bills worth £20 to cash when he lands in Stade, northern Germany, receiving from Parvish's factor there 'the like sum in the current money of that country'. As a gesture of 'mere courtesy' (Harry tells his brother) Parvish is not requiring 'any manner of "provision" as the merchants call it'. He's not charging commission. Even so, Harry can't resist a bit of wit. '"Provision"', he writes, is merely 'a pacified word' for taking a cut. On the rest of the transaction the merchant isn't so generous. Putting his 'silver ... into French Crowns of the Sun, which are generally received as far as the sun goes' (more wit), Harry notes that he's lost in the exchange 'one French crown in thirty'. Later, at the mercy of foreign moneylenders, he'll look back on this as a very good deal indeed.

Once the merchant has 'ballasted' the young traveller with credit and money and has agreed to be his 'conveyance' – that is, his London agent and address while abroad – Parvish helps Harry settle his passage. They saunter to Queenhithe, or maybe further down river, to the wharf at Three Cranes, to get news of what's sailing from Deptford Docks. Out of twenty ships offered, Harry settles on *Vineyard* because, he tells Edward, it reminds him of home. Already, he sounds a trifle homesick, imagining himself in Kent 'in the place that I love'.

Vineyard will make one of a mini-flotilla sailing out of Thames-mouth heading east, sticking together for mutual protection. The Spanish war in the Netherlands grinds on and English ships are targets. They're ready to sail, 'the wind large and fair', 'the ships in their full load', the passengers, 'determined to go gallantly down the river', but then the wind swings round from the east and they're becalmed. No sailor chooses to sail into a headwind, so they spend four days luffing, waiting for a southwester finally to fill their sails. We take note: in an age of sail, travellers are at the mercy of winds and tides. After that, though, it's smooth sailing, no sea sickness for Harry except 'two or three odd qualms', and swift passage, only four days at sea. (When Fynes Moryson makes the same crossing in May two years later, storms, pirates and weather beating them to shelter will make it a nine-day nightmare.)

Harry ends the letter he began from Redcross Street. He has 'delivered up' to Edward all the 'adventures' that have taken him from Graisen to Bow Street. Walking London, looking like a stranger, he has stored up impressions to set against sights just over the horizon. It only remains to bid Edward farewell, to commit his brother 'to Him to whom I commit my whole life', 'desiring Him, if it stand with His high pleasure, to bring me safe back again to … your loves'. A legal settlement at Gray's Inn. A prayer for a safe return. Book-ending Harry's letter, they intimate a deeply uncertain future. Harry is travelling alone. He's travelling without guarantees. It's 20 October. He's twenty-one years old.

Setting out, writing home

The next five years, the 'wandering time of my life', will take Harry from the North Sea to Naples, Heidelberg to Rome, Vienna to Venice, Florence, Milan and Geneva. The aim of his travel is 'knowledge', and 'to live in the seeking of that' is his 'only pleasure'. If he sounds to us like an earnest freshman, he did to himself as well, indeed 'less than a freshman' in the 'university' of 'travel'. Hitherto he'd 'been a fool' but now he's determined 'to begin my world at one and twenty'. If his friends have 'conceived' in him 'a loose humour', that's an 'error' they will need to 'correct', for his 'child's years' that 'were wont so regardlessly to look upon themselves' are now 'fully out'. My future course, he assures the family he's left behind, will 'teach my soul to run against the delights of fond youth'. So: a manifesto for a grown-up. Still, we'll want to keep an eye on the 'loose humour' his past admits even as his future self discharges it. He'll give us ample reason to doubt him.

A file of only six letters survives from his first year abroad. What's there bids us remember what's lost – all the letters Harry received from home for starters; others that he fears have gone missing. We need to handle the materials of memory diplomatically, for no matter how much we think we know, there's so much more that we don't. Philip Sidney's biographer wryly gestures at this gap when, giving the details of his 1572 licence to travel with three servants ('Lodowick Bryskett, Harry White, Griffin Maddox'), four horses and 'bags, baggages and necessaries', she remarks, 'we do not know the names of the horses'. In the five years Harry is abroad, we never know the names of the horses.

That said, these six letters, bursting with life, stand as eager first-person documents of a young man's self-fashioning, a 'freshman' traveller turning advice into action, precept into practice. He seems to be setting his course by Essex ('Look about you') and writing as if Erasmus stands at his elbow reminding him that 'letters sent and received suppose an unheard conversation between the correspondents'.

His plan to travel south via Bremen has to be scrapped. 'Malcontents', footloose renegades from Parma's Spanish garrisons stationed in the Low Countries, are targeting travellers, taking them hostage, and 'a younger brother's ransom is 20 thousand crowns', that is, a whopping £3,000. Instead, he travels via Frankfurt to Heidelberg, to take up residence in that city's ancient university, arriving there mid-December. Since 1558 it has grown into one of Europe's leading centres of activist, not to say militant, Protestantism, with a faculty that holds positions across the full range of reformist commitment.

'Apparelled and booked' – that is, enrolled and suited in the proper academic dress – and among men broadly of his own religious 'confession', Harry embarks on a course more demanding than anything he encountered at Oxford. A near-contemporary woodcut of the Heidelberg school shows students and scholars of all ages seated on two rows of forms lining the stone-built room. Some wear scholars' gowns – robes, stoles, hoods – others are in doublets; all wear hats of either academic or secular fashion; several hold books open on their laps. Plenty of cross-chat appears to be distracting some in the audience (or perhaps they're disputing some point raised). At the far end, a fierce-looking lecturer sits at an elevated dais, glaring over the top of his lectern. These Heidelberg doctors, Harry writes to his brother, 'teach so as we may weigh every syllable'. He sounds daunted. Lectures are delivered 'twelve times every week', in Latin (it must be, for Harry is 'the only Englishman in this town' and his 'High Dutch' is 'yet very low'). He has 'a chamber and a table' in the house of one of his professors, a Scot, who has made Harry 'his first sport in Germany with laughing at his dialect'. For himself, he's determined to 'bestow one hour in the day upon the German tongue' to be sure that by the time he reaches Italy 'there is no German that shall not take me for a German'. And no Italian either. Fluency is camouflage. It's a typical ruse for Englishmen to pass themselves off as German-speaking Dutchmen.

In his letters to Edward we read not just his news but the self he is scripting, a rhetorically adept public self, but also an emotional private self, both person and personality. He positions himself in a culture of deference, but deference anchored on love. Edward is his 'dear brother' whose 'love' has made him 'so necessary a person' in his little brother's life that 'I cannot reckon without you'. That word 'reckon' is doubly significant. While Parvish is his broker, Edward is Harry's banker. He controls his annuity. So Harry keeps him up to date with his expenditure, entering his 'particular expenses' in 'a book', which allows him to 'observe the sliding nature of money' and sometimes how much his 'dear ignorance' has cost him. (He's cracking a lame joke. 'Dear' means 'expensive' as well as 'loved'.) In Stade he's stunned to be charged '2^d sterling' for a 'poor pint of English beer' (but why is he drinking *English* beer?); in Heidelberg, a measure of wine costs seven times what it did a couple of years back. Despite such 'purse-crosses', Harry insists he's able to keep up appearances, to 'carry the state of a gentleman with sufficiency'. That's in December. At the beginning of January, things are slipping. He can still 'carry my self with [the] proportion [that] there is between my state & the country's charges', but he's run out of money, which means he's exhausted the two bills of exchange and the 'rest of my silver' brought from England. At this rate, he'll be in the red by Easter. For now, he asks that funds be conveyed to Frankfurt Mart in March.

This mart, held twice a year for a fortnight, has made the city famous over all Europe. Happening upon it in September 1608, Thomas Coryat will report, stunned beyond superlatives, of the 'most infinite' riches displayed there. It's not just a magnet for merchants. Scholars from across Europe trawl the 'infinite abundance of books' for sale on 'the booksellers' street', which not only 'far excels Paul's Churchyard in London' but 'seems to be a very epitome of all the principal libraries of Europe'. Beyond 'wares', though, the Frankfurt Mart sells money. It operates an international bank, an Exchange, but 'nothing like to ours in London' being 'nothing but a part of the street, under the open air'. Nevertheless, a 'concourse of wealthy merchants from all the most famous regions of Christendom' meet there to do business. And travellers like Harry go there to get cash.

Of course, for the exchange to work, letters need to be sent, delivered and acted upon in a two-way traffic that is hardly infallible and that takes, Heidelberg to London, a fortnight in each direction. Even this is unpredictable. We remember that back in October Harry's ship was holed up for days while the pilot waited for the wind to come about. Any letters on board were as delayed as the ship. Once he's in Heidelberg, Harry works out an 'easy' 'conveyance' for his letters, and with 'great security'. They can be sent from London 'by the Dutch milliner in Abchurch Lane' who 'serves the Prince's Court with gloves' in Heidelberg. This milliner 'conveys his letters to Middleburg & Antwerp, & from thence to Collen' – Cologne – '& so to Nuremberg where Mr Parvish hath a factor lying' with whom Harry will 'take order' that his own letters 'shall be conveyed unto me in the university'. Piece of cake, really. Such arrangements are his only option. In England, the postal network is organised solely to deliver royal correspondence. Private letters are sent by personal servants or entrusted to merchants and chance travellers, carriers and foot-posts. (Once, years back, the earl of Leicester sent a letter to Harry's father 'by a ryppier', a fish-peddler.) On the continent, while the postal system is well established and affordable, letters addressed in English – 'an unknown tongue' – might never reach their destination. Or, suspected for their contents, they might be unsealed, retained as evidence or simply trashed.

Across these letters, Harry's habits of address to his brother show his acute appreciation of how deference works in a system of human exchange where networks are built on patronage and where the exchange value of letters depends on making good the promises implied in them. Harry writes about this figuratively but understands it literally as the 'recompense of courtesy'. For Edward isn't just his banker. He's Harry's fixer. Where Edward's name precedes him, doors open for Harry. The 'style of an elder brother', he's discovered, is 'the only style of proof'. (He's punning again. 'Style' means 'stylus', the pen Edward uses to sign his name, but it's also Edward's actual signature, his title and family name. Being 'proof', Edward's name is like a soldier's corselet, bullet-proof. As a pun, it's hardly worth the labour of unpacking, but it tells us something about Harry's sense of humour.)

From Heidelberg Harry asks Edward to 'procure me the letters of some of the English nobility'. He wants introductions that will 'advantage me with all the great learned men of this country & the nobility besides'. In December, hoping that that superstar of the Civil Law, François Hotman, will 'be preceptor unto me', he renews his request for 'the letter of some noblemen'. Or *even better*, could Edward get some noblemen to address 'some twenty lines' *directly* to Hotman 'commending me' and (here's the spin) 'promising recompense of courtesy in England' ('recompense', tacitly, that Edward will supply)? As Gentleman of Her Majesty's Privy Chamber, Edward has the ear of aristocrats. Surely it will not be difficult along some corridor in Whitehall to bump into 'some of the English nobility' and beg those twenty lines?

Harry knows how it feels to be snubbed. We can hear the yelp of pain when he suddenly interjects 'Brother' mid-way through his account of how he's written to 'one Mercer', now secretary to an ambassador, for a letter of introduction to Hotman. He's sure his request will fall on open ears because he knew Mercer at university where he 'bound him to me' with 'the furthest courtesies I could show him'. Now, just 'as my letter was going', Mercer himself 'came to this court'. So instead of posting it, Harry 'made my self my letter', only, shockingly, to be rebuffed: 'I found him cold & after the worldly humour scarce remembering that ever he had been at Oxford', which 'blanked me'. This isn't just humiliating. It registers the sound of Harry's ambition hitting a brick wall. But then he discovers he's made a dreadful diplomatic mistake. 'Mercer' is 'the scholar of Hotman's sworn enemy'. Still, by Edward's 'loving means' Harry has 'hope … to recover', for 'In my conference with this Mercer I learn that Hotman hath a son about the court in England, some time secretary to the Earl of Leicester. My brother, thou named him once unto me.' So could Edward possibly 'procure' letters from son to father?

Harry's information is correct. Jean Hotman *is* in England. Thus we see the threads of connection spooling out: tying college acquaintance to secretary to ambassador; father to son to aristocratic patron to suitor. Again, we hear the spin: Harry has further learned that 'This son stands upon the aspiring point in the court'. Leicester is fifteen months dead. Young Jean needs new patronage. A request from Edward Wotton for a letter to Jean's father? The son 'will soon be brought to it'.

For his part, Harry immediately starts repaying the debt he owes his brother in the new currency he's pocketing as a traveller: the 'occurrenza giornale', the daily news. In Stade he sounds every inch the callow English youth, haughty in finding 'many things' to 'laugh at & especially the women which (believe me) are the most pitifully attired of any creatures since the fall of Adam'. Beyond the extortionate cost of a pint of beer he seems little aware of how the wars in the Low Countries and the collapse of Hanseatic trade have impoverished the city. He pours scorn on the 'clowns here', calling them 'scarce *Animalia*', 'the best of them' not able to 'make a leg', that is, salute a superior properly with a bow. (In Heidelberg, the boot will be on the other foot. Sitting among minds like his professors', he'll realise that he's the clown.)

Along with domestic news he's picking up political information. The rumour that 'the Turks' are 'coming into Poland' 'with an army of an hundred & twenty thousand' 'holds certain here' though he thinks it's only a ploy 'to draw' the Provinces 'to a peace & so make them tributary', blackmailing them into paying annual protection money. However that might be, the Turkish threat is a topic in letter after letter across the next five years, as Christendom wastes itself in civil wars while the Ottoman Empire advances from the east, capturing the eastern

Mediterranean with the fall of Cyprus in 1570, conquering from Budapest to Constantinople, overrunning Hungary, leaving one contemporary to envision a nightmare, 'that Satanical crew of Turkish lurdens even at our doors and ready to come into our houses'. Such alarm isn't hysterical. North African Barbary pirates are raiding the coasts of Cornwall and Devon, Waterford and Cork, snatching fair-haired children off English and Irish beaches. They fetch a premium in Turkish slave markets.

Watching Harry not just gathering news but scooping intelligence (admittedly low grade, for now) out of loud mouths over meals in ordinaries, we see him taking his first steps down the pot-holed path that leads from observation to what murky minds call espionage. He's cocky, up for the game, but to play it, to deal in the marketplace of rumour-as-communication, he needs information from London, an 'Entelligentiary out of England', to supply him with what he can trade as 'news'. 'Every letter', he tells his brother, 'shall work my credit' with 'the great men here' – where 'credit' means 'credibility' but also cash.

Often, though, Harry betrays himself in melancholic mood, plain homesick. In November he confesses he has nothing much to write about, there being 'no matters of note in this town', yet he'd 'fain … fill … up' a letter 'with trifles' because he's 'glad to be as long as I may' 'in the lively imagination of your person' – that's Edward – 'while I thus speak with you'. He writes 'From my stove in Heidelberg' as though feeling heart-pangs along with the chill the place puts in his bones, wanting to assure Edward that, by his example, 'I will spend the wandering part of my life as well as ever any but himself did before me'. He's remembering brother Ned's travels with Philip Sidney. As he writes, he's conjuring his brother's absence into presence. His pen is the magic wand of comforting ventriloquism. So, to 'hear my pen when it speaks of that brother from whom I receive the comfortablest hope of my life' makes Harry 'glad above the common measure'. Weeks ago, in his encounter with Mercer, Harry 'made my self my letter'. Here he makes his letter his self.

Regularly larding his letters to Edward with Latin tags – 'crescat saeclis innumerabilibus' (may it grow for countless centuries) – that show his education hasn't been wasted, he always ends commending his brother in plain English 'to the God of all love and mercy'. Harry's faith sounds conventional, but it's also observational. Daily prayer is as habitual as tying the points on his doublet. But in a Europe where the confessional is the political, Harry's faith is more than merely observational. It is constitutional. He begins one letter 'Ne inducas me Domine …' (Lord, lead me not [into temptation]), follows that with a bit of Italian – 'lunga vita et bel morire' (long life and a good death) – and Cicero, then proceeds to invoke the 'God of all wisdom and knowledge' to 'lead me on in His fear'. His only surviving letter to his mother assures her that his 'child's years are over' and ends leaving her in the 'protection' of the 'all-merciful Lord'. (She'll die before he returns home.) But before he signs off, he tells her he's left Heidelberg. François Hotman is dead, so he's 'determine[d] to Vienna' to study Civil Law among the 'great learned men there in the profession I follow'. He's heard they're 'all marvellous devout Papists' but he's quietly unperturbed. It 'troubles me not, because the point I study daily is to converse with all sorts, and yet in mine own manner and conscience'. It sounds like the callow youth who laughed at women in Stade has grown up some in the twelve months since he set out a traveller.

More than 'Intelligentiary Letters'

Harry's letter to his mother in September 1590, his last surviving family letter, turns up after a gap in the correspondence of nine months. In the meantime, he arrives in the small university city of Altdorf, fifteen miles east of Nuremberg, and meets Johann Richter, the renowned mathematician and astronomer who is using Copernicus's *De revolutionibus orbium coelestium* (1543) to teach the theory of the heliocentric universe. Copernicus is radical. Revising the physical model of the universe, telling man that the earth is not the centre of creation but rather an insignificant piece of cosmological property spinning around the sun, Copernicus challenges both Catholic and Reformation dogma. For now, his theories unproven, he's ignored in Rome and mocked in Geneva, Luther's collaborator, Philip Melanchthon, describing the ideas of 'that Polish astronomer who makes the earth move and the sun stand still' as 'so crazy a thing' that 'wise governments' ought to 'repress' it. In Richter Harry encounters an authority who can accelerate scientific learning first tasted at school and Oxford. In Venice years hence, Copernican theory will swing back into his ken like a blazing comet when the 'mathematical professor at Padua', one Galileo Galilei, presents to the Republic a new-fangled instrument called a 'cannocchiale' that he's using to test theory against the evidence of his eyes, training it on the heavens. That instrument in England will be called the 'telescope'.

At Altdorf Harry encounters teaching that changes the direction of his scientific thinking. And he makes an acquaintance that changes the direction of his personal life. He meets Edward de la Zouche, the thirty-four-year-old renegade baron Zouche, who's been travelling Europe in self-imposed exile for the past eight years. Except that he's a peer of the realm, and therefore qualifies as one of those noblemen who dazzle Harry, he makes a dubious companion. Zouche lost his case in the ecclesiastical court back in 1582 for putting away his estranged wife without maintenance; then refused to pay up; was excommunicated; fled abroad; returned home in 1586 to sit at the trial of Mary queen of Scots; withheld his vote for execution (the only peer to do so); and now is 'away' again. When Zouche looks back on his 'slippery' years he'll comment that 'the greatest evil' of his life was 'the fond spending of my time in my youth'. This tainted baron trailing misspent years: taking up with Harry is he about to become a misleader of youth? Or is he seeing in Harry a means of repairing the waste of his patrimony? The twenty-eight letters Harry writes to Zouche between October 1590 and August 1593 certainly show a new epistolary 'Harry' emerging. They document a relationship of patronage and service – and discover an increasingly complicated, not to say implicated, set of performances that test his inexperience. Where Harry was once 'Your loving brother', he's now 'Your Honour's servant'.

This service involves becoming Zouche's 'intelligencer' from Vienna. Clearly, Zouche has seen in the now-twenty-two-year-old Harry a youth 'enabled' by travel and furnished with 'serviceable' knowledge. No doubt Harry sees in Zouche the material object of his travel: employment. Or at least an apprenticeship in the kind of service that will gain him employment when he returns home.

Launching his 'duty unto Your Honour' from Vienna, where he arrives as a student in November 1590, he engages to send Zouche news of the 'estate of the present' in the Austrian Empire: who's up, who's down, who's in, who's out. The latest assassination attempt on the Emperor Rudolf (by a Flemish priest caught with 'an instrument' like a 'cross-bow' concealed 'in a wide sleeve'). Marriages rumoured and solemnised. The king of Poland, 'lately marvellous malcontent', grown 'a great reader of magic books'. Turkish incursions into Hungary. Poisonings. Strange apparitions. The misery of the siege of Paris.

But he has no intention of being a scavenger, raking truth from reports 'inclined' to the 'humours' of those who 'first told them'. Or culling 'tales' from the 'ordinary' 'Intelligentiary Letters' published as news sheets out of Antwerp, Lyon, Venice and Rome. Those sources are compromised, for 'as they love or hate, so they speak'. Harry is an ambitious advertiser. His news won't be second-hand. He'll report nothing 'which I have not in part, or wholly seen my self'. Already 'indifferently acquainted' in Vienna, he aims to search out the private 'letters which the German travellers in Italy send to their fathers'. He goes further. He has 'good means to learn' the 'secretest debates about the Empire' from 'the Gentleman with whom I live', secrets he can traffick *quid pro quo*, for this gentleman 'hath given me promise of meeting half way, for exchange of the like out of England'. The fresh-faced 'freshman' who left England in 1589 looks to be getting his hands dirty, or at least his fingers grubby. Within months, Harry sends Zouche ciphers so they can write some of their business in code. For now, he's ferreting out 'that which no money or charges' can purchase.

In all of this, Harry anticipates the instructions Essex gives his agent in Venice in 1595, to 'observe', 'advertize', 'gather', make 'accompt by every post', 'enter into … traffick'. To some degree, he's only following advice – like Palmer's – given to every English student going abroad, advice that makes them informants but not spies (exactly). Objectively speaking, early modern intelligence-gathering isn't espionage, nor is most secret intelligence actually secret. Subjectively, however, that's not how Harry experiences it. His duty to Zouche, he insists, is never less than 'honest' – though honest is a concept permissive of hair-raisingly wide interpretation. His duty *is*, however, less than candid, or, better said, it's candid in its practices of dissimulation, because intelligence sent from a city where he's a Protestant among a crew of 'marvellous devout Papists' involves concealment even as it aims at revelation. Such intelligence leaves a long paper trail (an 'accompt by every post'). But Harry litters that trail with misinformation. Or dead-ends it in silence. There are things he won't put on paper, but only into Zouche's ear.

In Vienna, leading a double life as scholar/intelligencer, Harry is developing habits of communication that teach him the art and craft of the politick. Does he worry about dissimulation? Certainly, dissimulation worries Fynes Moryson when he comes to consider it in his *Itineraries*, where he confesses himself 'in a dark labyrinth', having, in effect, to defend lying. Though he squirms, Moryson finally comes down on the side of necessity: 'a traveller must sometimes hide his money, change his habit, dissemble his country, and fairly conceal his religion'. Harry participates in all of these, demonstrating Moryson's oxymoronic precept that 'simulation in fit place and time is a virtue' because 'He that cannot dissemble cannot live'. Still, it has to be asked. How is the sheep who puts on wolf's clothing to be recognised as a sheep by other sheep? And what is the danger of settling so comfortably into the wolf's skin that the sheep metamorphoses into a wolf indeed?

These questions are pertinent to Harry's future. In December 1590 they're hardly thought of. In Vienna Harry is happily once more the student, surrounded by books, wrapped against the cold in academic gown and hood over padded doublet and thick English-made woollen hose, his 'feet in the stove'.

He's a bed-and-board-paying guest in the house of the Dutch scholar Hugo Blotius, master of the Imperial Library. Elatedly, he recounts his luck: 'My study joins upon the Library' and 'I have that to my free use'.

This library contains '9000 Volumes (whereof the most part are manuscript)'. It's mind-boggling. A world of learning lies at his fingertips, only a single door between it and his chamber. And Harry – so much knowledge; so little time – *does* make free use of it. In his other life, along with news, he promised Zouche books: books on 'state-life', on mathematics, books Harry can pick up 'good cheap' in Vienna because it's a town 'rather of traffick' – that is, commerce – 'than learning'. Now, in the Imperial Library, he sets up the early modern version of the photocopier: 'I live here daily at the charges of two servants, which I maintain only to write out such manuscript books as I have found of this state, and other matters of weight'.

Harry's service to Zouche doubles. He observes the news, the 'alterations of each week with us'. He sends word of mouth. But he also sends copies out of the emperor's library. Some are rare. (Including 'all such Relations as the Ambassadors of Italy have made since many years', *Relazioni*, if he reads them, that will fast-track his future in Venice.) Some are specialised ('notable discourses of military matters … written in Italian'). Some set bells ringing ('a manuscript book with certain … matters of State … wherein is more to be learned in three weeks study, than in the observation of many years otherwise'). Some are hot. Johannes Trithemius's sixty-year-old 'Book of Steganography', of secret codes and ciphers, is one. Harry writes of it warily: the manuscript he's handling is 'a notable piece of work for a statesman', but 'an Instrument of great ill, if the hand be not good that holds it'.

Alarmingly, the student has slipped back into the ways of the intelligencer – or perhaps, once 'in', it's never an option to be 'out'. He has 'caused' the Preface of Trithemius's book to be copied and smuggled secretly from the library, and hopes to send the rest. But 'I promise nothing', in case, failing, 'My Lord' should 'find me false'. He advises, 'If I chance to send it, you are wise (My Lord) to keep it secret: otherwise the bare having of the book' will cause 'many eyes about us, to observe our actions'. We cannot miss it: Harry is writing as a conspirator fearing surveillance, eyes looking into 'our actions'.

This book causes him a deal of grief. And not because of its dangerous contents. Rather, the mundane problematics of its transmission. Promised (but not *promised*) in January; mentioned in February when Zouche is clearly keen to have it and Harry is hedging, 'remember[ing] myself to have put your Honour in no further certainty than that I would go near the getting of it'; mentioned a week later when he's making 'all possible haste' to secure it, it's still not delivered in mid-April. And now Zouche thinks his servant may be playing fast and loose. Harry writes anxiously that 'your Honour suspects such a matter in me'. Far from it. To get his hands on a copy he's been moving heaven and earth – and hell too. 'The man' he first 'sounded' to 'perform it perfect' – that is, make the complete copy – 'deceived' him. (So much for honour among book thieves.) The hundred crowns Zouche sent 'persuade far in these times', but the person he needs to 'close with' – a euphemism for 'bribe' – 'is of so great a living and authority, as I dare hardly close with him that way'. Still, this 'great' person 'hath children' who may offer a softer target. 'Amongst them,' writes Harry, is

> a son of some 23 years, whom I intend to undermine with that golden instrument [the hundred crowns] and through him the father, but this very secretly, because if the son may by chance be drawn to help me to it, without his father's knowledge, I am not likely to refuse it, or if he signify the offer to his father, and he be content to let his son receive the money (for parents do now and then things by their children which they are ashamed to do by themselves), I can likewise suffer it; or lastly, if the son may move the father not to be curious in the receipt, using such arguments as youths are wont to do, it will be all one to me, so I get it.

'*So I get it*': I add the emphasis, not knowing whether that voice is calculating or cynical, or living frantically on its wits, though I do know it's not the voice of the freshman who stepped off the boat in Stade. He ends: 'I stand not much upon the means, if it be honest'. That 'honest' comes well in, like an ironic catcall. Harry's devious scheme involves secrecy, bribery, corruption, collusion: a project to 'undermine' a father using as his instrument a son just Harry's age.

Proposing it to reassure Zouche of his *bona fides* shows Harry rattled by Zouche's suggestion of double-dealing. He's then shaken to the core by Zouche's further imputation, that, sending him the Preface to *Steganographia*, he's sent him a fake. Harry scurries back to the Imperial Library. He digs out 'certain letters' written by Trithemius. He compares 'the hands' and can 'observe no difference' in the writing. He draws further 'confirmation to maintain either mine own error or judgement' 'from the style', which he dares 'pronounce to be no man's but Trithemius's', for to 'judge whether a book be the right or no', style is 'the means that cannot fail'. (On such dubious positivism hangs the whole future history of attribution studies.)

His rhetorical balancing act – poising 'error' (that he's wrong) against 'judgement' (that he's right) – is not insignificant. If his attribution is correct, Zouche's 'doubts' – which Harry diplomatically frames as 'points' he 'rashly' failed to consider – are wrong. But he can hardly say so outright to a nobleman, his master. Besides, he's sensitive to the 'displeasure' he's picked up as he reads between Zouche's lines and he's stung by what Zouche has evidently concluded, that the Preface (now smuggled back into the Imperial Library) isn't 'worth' the 'seven florins' he shelled out 'for the post's hire'. Harry's tail is firmly between his legs when he adds, concluding this sorry business, that 'repentance must teach me to correct' my 'hastiness in discovering mine own want of discretion upon others' cost'. (Now there's a motto worth copying into his commonplace book for future reference.) At the end of April, when he's leaving Vienna for Italy, the *Steganographia* is still not delivered.

Bruised and chastened by an episode that he doesn't know he'll replay more than once in future, he's delighted to be heading south. Talking about it since February, 'waiting daily upon letters out of England to resolve my self in some points concerning mine own private estate', he's always been fixed on Italy. Now, those letters arrive. Harry promises Zouche further 'advertisements' but in 'another language'. He's travelling 'in secret' because 'to have any know the time of my going ... might much endanger me'. In Italy, he'll 'change his habit' and habits, both his clothes and behaviours. He figures this 'convenient' shape-shifting epigrammatically: 'He travels with mean consideration ... that is ever one country-man'. Or, as Moryson puts it, 'He that cannot dissemble cannot live'. Not in Italy, anyway.

After Vienna, Harry must consider himself at least a BA in the university of travel. His study in Blotius's house has opened a door not just onto marvellous learning like 'Picus Mirandula's Book against Astrology' but onto a marketplace for learning: a place of 'exchange', 'gain', 'procure'-ment. He's been Zouche's 'factor' purchasing textual knowledge. But he's also been buying up 'commodities' for his own future, copying writers not published in England and certainly not in English. Among these, according to 'my profession', he says, are 'some that might make a great man beholding to me'. What, exactly, does he mean by 'my profession'? Is that simply a way of saying, 'what I profess', that is, 'think', 'believe'? Or by 'profession' does he mean his job, his employment as intelligencer? Is the student seeing himself as a 'professional'? And what does he mean by 'beholding'?

Besides books, Harry's 'study' in Vienna has been 'men and actions'. He's learned secrecy by handling news that 'I wish to come secretly unto your hands, because it contains some points of dangerous advertisement', and manuscripts purloined secretly from the library, one that he begs returned by the next post, 'no man privy to my sending it but my self'. He's gained experience: of the gap between promise and performance, of the biter bitten, of the good servant employed on less than good service, of the 'honest dissembler'. Later, as English ambassador to Venice, he'll say that he was 'plucked from the study' by his king and pitched headlong into the public life of diplomacy. Here, we see another backstory, the youth who's meant to have his head down in books raising his gaze beyond their pages, finding in 'the useful library of travel' material and practice in the 'science of policy' to fit him for 'negotiation'. He isn't just reading in this science. He's writing in it, too. Among the other discourses he advertises from Vienna, he sends Zouche 'a simple discourse of mine own', and yet perhaps not *that* 'simple', for he asks Zouche to keep 'it secret', since 'though the theme be general', its detail 'concerns some gentlemen of estate'.

A student studying contemporary politics and writing topical history, a green-horn, 'hitherto' 'a fool', but one who means 'to begin my world at one and twenty': this youth might sign his last letter from Vienna 'Your Honour's servant', but heading for Italy, he says no truer thing about himself than 'I am to travel far'.

5
A man well tumbled in the world

'A very Paradise'

Autumn, 1591. Harry crosses the Alps into Italy from Augsburg through the Brenner Pass, a journey no one forgets. 'The Alps', says Fynes Moryson, make travellers 'speak strange things ... such as will hardly be believed by those that have not seen them'. Hardly imaginable is the thrill of awe and terror that stiffens Harry's sinews as he begins trekking up mountains that loom like armies of stone Titans, rank upon rank in the distance beyond counting. He doesn't leave an account of his crossing, not one that's survived. But others do. When Thomas Coryat reaches the Alps in late spring 1608 he hands over his 'horse to another to ride for me, because I thought it was more dangerous to ride then to go a foot'. Moryson hires 'a foot-man to run by my horse and guide me', and 'sometimes (not without horror) ascended very steep passages of mountains, lying with my face on my horse's neck, whose bridle I left free to him, holding myself with one hand on his mane, and the other on the saddle'. Those so foolhardy (or so pressed with business) as to make the journey in early winter before snowfall along the routes is packed solid are 'carried upon sledges, sometimes with gloves and shoes full of nails' so they can 'creep ... on hands and feet' along paths 'enclosed ... on every side like two walls' of stone.

Harry descends into Italy along the ancient Roman road onto the fertile plains of the Veneto region, arriving in a 'very Paradise' in the final weeks of the *vendemmia*, the grape harvest that's putting every hand to work bringing in the crops. The Veneto's cities sit like stone jewels in a necklace, with small outlying towns like sparks setting them off and narrow roads threading them together like beads on a rosary. Rich in history, custom and traffic they make up the dominion that constitutes Venice's Terraferma empire: Verona, Vicenza, Bassano del Grappa, Treviso, Padua. The plains are hugged by 'fruitful hills ... abounding with vines' that Harry's English eyes find curious, tangling high into walnut trees. This odd agriculture yields rich wines. In Friuli, one the locals have been making for centuries is called 'prosecho'.

Harry rides for Venice via Verona, following the winding Adige River to enter the city across the stupendous Ponte del Castelvecchio. It's built in red brick, nearly 400 feet long, the widest bridge arch in the world, a miracle of engineering. Like all strangers entering the gates of Italian towns and cities, Harry is subject to the searches of the Sanità, the health authority. The Italians are 'so curious and scrupulous' about public health that they 'admit no stranger within the walls of their city, except he brings a bill from the last city he came from to testify that he was free from all manner of contagious sickness'. Without it, the traveller is subject to 'far la Quarantena', forty days' isolation: quarantine. Venice invented the measure to guard their port from infection sailing in from the east. No one is 'received into Venice without a bill of health' even if 'he would give a thousand ducats' in bribes. And no wonder. The devastating plague of 1576 is recent memory. The Redentore, the church of the Redeemer, built to thank God for the city's deliverance, has only just been consecrated.

Harry crosses the Veneto on horseback. In autumn he doesn't need the apparatus local horsemen fasten to their thighs in summer to 'minister shadow ... against the scorching heat of the sun'. Coryat, pop-eyed, describes these strange 'things' 'of leather', made like 'a little canopy & hooped in the inside with divers little wooden hoops', 'ombrellas', from Italian 'ombra', shadow. The river Harry follows splays fingers across this plain, its branches bridged by dozens of ferries that transport both him and his horse. But at Padua, with Venice pratically in sight, he stables his beast. It's been years since the fashion for cavallerizza died out in a city paved in water. He boards a horse-drawn barge in Padua, moving at a stately clip-clop down the twenty miles of the Brenta canal past the 'many goodly fair houses and palaces of pleasure' to which the elite of Venice escape in the summer. (Ten years hence he'll hold the lease on one of these summer retreats.) At Fusina he reaches 'the uttermost point and edge of the land', where he stares out over water.

North five miles distant is Venice. For the final leg of his journey he'll be rowed, to his eyes dubiously, by single oarsmen at helm and stern in a boat quaintly (to Moryson's eyes) 'covered with arched hatches'. He shares it with a gaggle of regional types such as Adriano Banchieri stows on board in his comic madrigal 'Barca di Venetia per Padova' (1605): a Florentine bookseller, a music master from Lucca, a student, a pair of Paduan Jews, plus three cosmetically enhanced 'donne'. As the local proverb has it, 'the boat shall be drowned, when it carries neither monk, nor student, nor courtesans'.

Since entering Italy he's been in a constant flux of adjustment. Distance, for instance: two 'Switzers miles' in the alpine region he's just left converts to fifteen Italian miles. Then coins in his purse: the Venetian 'zechine' is worth ten lire, and eight lire make six English shillings. (The ducat that merchants use for reckoning is, like the English pound, a 'money of account', not a coin in people's pockets.) These currencies, however, aren't necessarily uniform from city to city even across the Veneto. 'Little brass moneys' are paid 'by weight' not number, but twenty little brass soldi make a lira. (How uncomplicated now seem his transactions with Parvish in London.) By the time Harry reaches Padua he needs sprucing up. He's threadbare. (In the cartouche illustrating his travels, Coryat shows his travel-worn garments hung up on a gibbet, like a felon's corpse dropping disintegrating body parts.) Harry will do (and pay) as Moryson does: find a tailor to make a 'cloak, four lires' and 'doublet and hose, eight lires', and a laundress to stitch 'a shirt, a lire, that is twenty sols'. He'll pay extra to have his doublet 'lined in taffetie', having learned the traveller's trick, well worth the investment: 'lice cannot breed' in taffeta.

New landscapes. New fashions. He's adjusting also to cultural difference. He goes shopping, not something he'd do at home, where it would be considered 'unmanly'. But as Moryson reports (and we're relying on his account of local practices), here 'it is the fashion of Italy, that only men, and the masters of the family' – even patrician families – 'go into the market and buy victuals, for servants are never sent to that purpose, much less women'. The abundance is amazing: meat of all kinds and a 'very white bread, light & pleasant in taste' called 'pan-buffetto', special to the region. 'Scallops which they call holy cockles' are sold 'twelve for a lire'; 'parmesan the pound ten or twelve sols'; 'apples the pound two sols'; 'wax candles the ounce two sols'; and perhaps most attractively for a traveller writing up his daily tally along the way, 'a quire of writing paper five sols'. That means four quires of writing paper cost as much as a dozen scallops.

At inns, hostesses are ready to cook what Harry buys in the market and to serve it at the board, complete with tablecloths and napkins. But sleeping, he'll have to 'be content with a hard flock bed' since, 'by reason of the heat of the country', the Italians 'use no feather beds'. If he's 'curious to demand them', he has clean sheets. But because the beds are 'suspected for filthiness of the Venerian disease' – syphilis – he'll do what others do, 'wear linen breeches of their own'. At night, Harry will follow advice to 'bolt or lock the door of his chamber', to 'have his sword by his side' and to 'lay his purse under his pillow but always folded with his garters, or some thing he first uses in the morning, lest he forget to put it up before he goes out of his chamber'. Above all, he takes seriously the warning to avoid quarrels, for the 'Italians in our age', writes Moryson, when they're outraged, 'presently arm all their bodies ... with mails of iron, and then, compassed with their friends, servants, and hired fencers (called *bravi*) will not stick to fall upon their enemy ... though he be an unwary stranger'. Better to keep his mouth shut while he marvels at the novelties of Italy, oddities like the 'elegant and pretty' paper fans carried by both men and women that, captioned with 'witty verses', are 'curiously adorned with excellent pictures' of 'amorous things tending to dalliance' (apparently fanning their owners both hot *and* cold). Or the strange metal eating implement Coryat thinks isn't used by 'any other nation of Christendom', the 'forchetta', which the English will translate 'fork'.

God's cabinet of curiosities

Later, as ambassador in Venice, Wotton tells the doge he fell in love with Italy the moment he crossed the Alps. Now, however, he leaves no ecstatic record of first impressions such as Coryat's dazzled witness, standing at Fusina in June 1608, gazing across the lagoon at a floating city that he says is 'the most glorious and heavenly shew upon the water that ever any mortal beheld'. Harry arrives, after all, in November. Venice, floating or not, may not be visible in the distance through fog that twists down the Canal Grande into the bacino to wrap the autumn lagoon in a ghostly winding-sheet. In any case, Harry does not stop in Venice long, only four days, 'obliged' (as he writes in Latin to a friend in Vienna) to 'bring forward my departure, both because the position of the city is not conducive to good health', but also – a rare private confession – 'because I do not entirely trust my powers of restraint among Venetian women. For I am not made of stone.'

For any traveller, disembarking in Venice is like stepping into God's personal cabinet of curiosities. Everywhere he looks he sees new-age wonders. How different from Rome, a spoil-heap of antiquity's debris. This city is made modern by the architecture of Jacopo Sansovino. The Zecca, the public mint that faces the Palazzo Ducale, the fantastically decorated Loggetta adjoining the Campanile, the Biblioteca Marciana, which required the brothel that used to open its doors on that corner of the piazzetta to be demolished to make way for it: all of these are barely thirty years old. The council chambers on the second floor of the Palazzo are newly refurbished since the fire of 1577. Palazzi are rising out of the mud along the Canal Grande, built by the Corners, Dolfin Manins, Balbis. Churches – San Zulian, San Francesco della Vigna – are getting make-overs. Titian, Tintoretto, Battista Bellini, Veronese are all currently at work covering the city in modern art. Even music has a contemporary beat: Giovanni Croce is maestro di cappella in San Marco; like Croce, Giovanni Gabrieli and his uncle Andrea are masters of the new music, sacred and secular, from Mass to madrigal.

Four days are not enough for Harry to begin to know La Serenissima. It's November. Days are short. He needs a tolomazo, a guide-cum-tout such as magically appears at Coryat's elbow when he's just arrived and gazing helplessly around San Marco. ('Tolomazo': the Venetian is a corruption of German for 'translator'.) After about 3 o'clock in the afternoon Harry also needs a torchbearer to light his way along what Coryat calls 'land streets', *calle terra*, the maze of narrow bricked paths that connect the seventy-two islands linked by some 450 footbridges that make up the city. Or maybe Harry moves as the locals do 'with far more expedition' in a gondola. The Canal Grande is the city's highway. The 'channels' that 'disgorge' into it 'run even as the veins do through the body of a man'. Coryat is told that ten thousand gondolas carry the city's traffic, six thousand 'private, serving for the gentlemen', the rest 'for mercenary men' who 'get their living by the trade of rowing' – not unlike the watermen of London who ply the Thames. But here, these 'that row' 'never sit as ours do in London, but always stand, and that at the farther end of the gondola'. Astonishing! These 'little boats' aren't open, but 'fairly covered, first with some fifteen or sixteen little round pieces of timber that reach from one end to the other and make a pretty kind of arch … then with fair black cloth which is turned up at both ends of the boat, to the end that if the passenger means to be private, he may draw down the same, and after row so secretly that no man can see him'. Suggestive. The gondola is potentially a locus of assignation, of secret lives, like the closed coach in London.

Of course, it's pointed out to him that '3 o'clock in the afternoon' in November makes no sense to any Venetian. In Venice, time is reckoned by a twenty-four-hour clock that sets midnight (0 hour) at sunset, a clock, therefore, seasonally adjusted. In November, Harry will look for his torchbearer at '22 hours', a couple of hours before dark, and will want his services until '3 hours' at the latest, when the city-wide curfew sounds. In June, on a return visit, he'll again want his torchbearer's services at '22 hours', but in June '22 hours' comes several hours later than in November. If Harry goes to a festa that lasts until

'9 hours' in July, he'll see morning dawn. If he visits the Jewish Ghetto, he'll realise what the law stipulating that its gates be locked 'at midnight' actually means.

Further, although clerks and notaries and historians might record 'diary' times, Venetians in their daily lives regulate their business by the bells whose distinct voices ring out across the day. In the bell tower of San Marco the deep-toned 'Marangona' – from 'marangone', 'carpenter' – which originally ordered the work day in the Arsenale, rings across the city the start of work, the break at midday (when everyone falls to their knees to recite 'Ave Maria'), resumption an hour later and the evening end of labour. It calls elites to business too, summoning the two thousand-odd who constitute the Maggior Consiglio to assemble at the Palazzo Ducale, its peal followed by the higher-pitched insistence of 'Trottiera' telling them to 'get a trot on'. 'Mezza Terza', a sister bell in the tower, announces Senato meetings, while 'Renghiera' – 'evil deed' – tells the city of an execution. At Rialto, the 'Realtina' in the tower of San Giovanni Elemosinario rings the third hour of night, signalling (seasonally adjusted) the city-wide order to extinguish unauthorised fires, the 'coprifuoco' or 'curfew'. Its twin, 'Mattutina', tells the end of curfew, an hour before the first 'Marangona'. This soundscape fascinates Harry's Protestant ears. In England, while Bow bell still sounds the curfew, bells that rang the Catholic canonical hours have been silent since the Reformation. Young Harry is attentive to sound. He plays the viol da gamba. He sings madrigals. He listens to choirs. In Venice he's alert to a city summoned by bells.

By law, he should lodge in one of the three osterie licensed for forestieri, strangers. But that's not enforced. The influx of strangers has exploded. It started a couple of centuries back when pilgrims to the Holy Land began collecting in Venice to begin the journey east and when merchants trading west along the silk road from China made the Rialto the commercial hub of Europe. Now, there's freewheeling, not to say cutthroat, competition for guests among hundreds of private alberghi (from 'albergare', 'to shelter'). The best lodgings are between San Marco and Rialto along the Merceria that connects them. This wide calle (five men can walk abreast along it) is lined with mercers' and stationers' shops displaying incredible riches – light-catching silks, plush velvets, fine cotton, the best-quality ink to be had in Europe – and hustling for business. In either direction it's only a few minutes' walk to the most stunning sights in Venice.

In San Marco, Harry takes in the wide, red expanse that stretches the length and breadth of the brick-paved Piazza and marvels at the 'great concourse of all nations' he sees and hears. 'All manner of fashions of attire' and 'all the languages of Christendom' gather there in hordes. They come to Venice 'as well for the pleasure the City yields, as for the free conversation, and especially for the commodity of traffick'. Everywhere he looks, he gawps. He watches a mountebank, a *ciarlatano*, at the far end of the Piazza set up his stage, open his trunk to display 'a world of new-fangled trumperies' – 'oils, sovereign waters, amorous songs printed, apothecary drugs' – and launch his patter, 'hyperbolically' crying up his wares – and down his prices. Turning around Harry gazes dumbstruck at the fabulous Byzantine Basilica. Built to serve the doge as his 'chapel', with its Turkish domes, it looks like some Orientalist fantasy magically transported to Venice down the silk road. It shines with polished surfaces of inlaid marble, some set to look like flowing water, others intricately joined in curious geometrical patterns. Inside, there's splendour, mosaics composed of millions of gold-leaf tesserae: angels, evangelists, miracles, the life of Christ, the Last Judgement. It's as if the unspeakable glory of God has been captured in this dazzling interior. Outside, the medieval marble arch that spans the central door captures an altogether humbler scene, one scaled to human dimensions, a calendar of labour in sculpture: men in smocks caulking boats, pressing grapes, shearing sheep, sweating across the months of the year. Both the dazzling and down-to-earth are overlooked by four massive bronze horses, booty from Constantinople, and so life-like that it seems they might 'leap into the market place'.

From a distance, Harry observes the *broglio*. It's a strip of pavement running the length of the Palazzo Ducale. But it's also an activity. Black-robed patricians – men who have absolute sway and government in the Signoria – meet at the *broglio* to *far broglio*, saunter, share news, talk politics. Every Sunday three hundred of them assemble in an upper floor of the Palazzo to formalise the state's business, voting on agenda items by dropping *bale da balotar* – Venetian for the coloured balls that indicate 'yes', 'no', 'neutral' – into urns passed down the benches where they sit. (These *bale* give England its system of 'balloting'.) In practice, however, voting starts earlier, in the *broglio*, when votes are canvassed and nobbled. The 'vulgar sort', the *popolani*, stand well back. Any who 'use mechanical and manuary trades' are entirely 'excluded from all manner of authority in the commonweal'. A republic is no democracy. Ten years hence, Harry will follow these patricians, to enter the Palazzo as English ambassador. For now, he walks the Palazzo's portico, circling each of its colonnades and reading the stories carved into marble faces on their capitals. Turning, craning his head, he gazes at the two columns that tower over the Molo to greet every ship anchoring at this broad marble pier, the sea entrance to the Piazza; one column topped by the winged lion of San Marco, the other, Teodoro, his rather despondent dragon sulking at his feet.

Exiting San Marco into the Merceria, Harry pauses below the Torre dell'Orologio, to gaze at the clock that 'shews the course of the sun and the moon daily, and above that the gilded image of our Lady'; and above that, another winged lion; and at 'the very top two brazen images', more than life-sized, their near-naked bodies bulging with muscles, 'called the Moors, which by turns striking with a hammer upon a great bell, sound the hours'. He shoulders his way through herds milling around open shop fronts like cattle at feeding troughs to make his way to Rialto. The shimmering white bridge of Istrian marble that spans the canal in a single arch was completed just this year. Harry's feet are among the first to polish the stones of what's already 'reputed the eighth miracle of the world'.

Venetian miracles attach themselves to merchandising. To this end, the bridge is itself spanned by little shuttered goldsmiths' and jewellers' shops, no opportunity missed to turn a ducat. At one end it's anchored by the imposing Fondaco dei Tedeschi. Half residence, half warehouse it establishes German presence in the city and locates German mercantile power in the heart of the commercial district (while confining German merchants to an address the authorities can keep an eye on). At the other end is the Rialto, the banking district, the 'Exchange of Venice', and the sprawling market Harry smells before he sees it, the fragrance of fresh fish as thick on the air as a shoal of branzino. The campo that lies in front of the oldest church in Venice, San Giacomo di Rialto, is 'compassed with public houses', among them, the Banco Giro. ('Girare' means to spin, pointing to the volume of transactions the 'spinning bank' turns around.) Here, money is traded, bills of exchange passed, travellers' empty purses replenished. Here, Harry will find Henry Parvish's factor. Here, merchants and patricians gather before noon, more walking and talking – but at opposite ends of the campo whose 'middle part' lies 'open'. Here, 'news upon the Rialto' is cried up and down. Here, the cash value of news is made spatially visible.

Fleeing Venice

Harry cuts short his first visit to Venice after only four days, citing concerns about his health – not without good reason. He's already been ill for a whole month this year. But Venetians would cry 'slander' to his dismal assessment of their city's position. Not healthy? She's a *haven* of health. Rising out of the Adriatic she benefits from tides that carry 'away the filth of the city' twice a day. Moryson reports the Venetians bragging that 'by a secret virtue' (undisclosed), her air 'agrees with all strangers' complexions' and 'preserves them in health'. He's unconvinced but nevertheless admits that he's never 'observed more old men' than here in Venice. When other European princes lie mouldering in their graves, Venetian patricians are just ripening to doge-dom. The current doge, Pasquale Cicogna, elected in 1584, is eighty-three years old. He'll be succeeded in 1595 by a mere stripling, Marino Grimani, sixty-three.

In fact, of course, things are otherwise. Venice is built on salt-water swamps that breed malaria. Plague is endemic. Syphilis, a recent import from the New World, is too. The 'Necrologia', the central register of deaths in the city's seventy-six parishes, thirty monasteries, twenty-eight nunneries and Jewish Ghetto, lists page after page of names and dates followed by cause of death: 'da febre', 'da febre maligna', 'da spasimo e febre': fever, deadly fever, fever with 'pangs'. 'Fever': the English call it 'ague'. Harry knows it well. Remedies are for sale. Apothecary shops, like the Testa d'Oro situated at the foot of the Rialto bridge, unmissable under its sign, a golden head staring into the weather, make up powders and purges that cure almost anything, and one, *triaca*, that cures everything, a compound so secret that it's licensed only to selected pharmacies. These pharmacies sell more than medicines. They're gossip shops, centres of news exchange. When he returns to Venice, Harry will know them well.

His other reason for fleeing Venice – 'I do not entirely trust my powers of restraint among Venetian women. For I am not made of stone' – appears to be attending to a different category of health. This might give us pause. Except for this passing remark, Harry leaves almost no trace of his erotic life. 'In his Youth', perhaps while still at Oxford, he writes a muscular little poem that shuffles conventional tropes in interesting ways across syncopated metrics to exclaim on the perfidiousness of some lass who's thrown him over:

> O faithless world, and thy more faithless part,
>   a woman's heart!
> The true shop of variety where sits
>   nothing but fits
> And fevers of desire and pangs of love,
>   Which toys remove ...
> Untrue she was: yet, I believ'd her eyes
>   (instructed spies)
> Till I was taught, that love was but a school
>   to breed a fool.

What has this 'fool' learned from love's 'instructed' espionage? 'To know, that love lodg'd in a woman's breast / Is but a guest'. Years hence, table talk will attribute to him cynical, not to say misogynistic, wit on the subject of heterosexual relations: 'Women are not such tender fruits, but that they bear as well upon beds as plashed against the walls'; and, perhaps most revealingly, 'The best bedfellow for all times in the year is a bed without a fellow'. Harry is a young man who moves among men: at school, at university, on his travels. His future embassy in Venice will be a male domain, his *famiglia*, a band of youths brought with him from England. He'll live and die unmarried, childless. Yet here, he's clearly tempted by female flesh. And, 'not made of stone', his own flesh appears to be acting very much like any twenty-two-year-old's.

But we might wonder exactly which Venetian women he encounters on his four-day dash around the city – and where. Moryson tells travellers they will not find Venetian women of reputation in 'the market' buying 'victuals'. Chaste women 'are locked up at home'. Some *donna nobile* might be observed walking escorted across a campo to church, but Harry won't see her face. It's hidden behind a long veil. It's more likely that his 'powers of restraint' are being tested by Venice's public women, women of the street, 'courtesans' ('they love them too well to call them whores', says Moryson) 'famoused all over Christendom'. 'At least twenty thousand' of them, says Coryat, are granted 'large dispensation and indulgence' to trade in Venice (estimated civic population: 200,000), first because the patricians think that without them 'the chastity of their wives would be the sooner assaulted'. And secondly (the chink and fall of zecchini into the zecca is always music to the Signory's ears), because 'the revenues which they pay unto the Senate for their toleration do maintain a dozen of their galleys'. A tax on sex bankrolls the 'virgin' city's military defence.

Some of 'the principalest' of these courtesans are (oxymoronically) 'cortigiane oneste', like Veronica Franco, who entertained Henri III on his stopover in Venice enroute to claiming the French crown. Highly educated and culturally refined, they live in 'magnificent' palazzi 'fit for the entertainment of a great Prince'. The 'cortigiana di lume' serves other clientele. Her face 'varnished' with 'apothecary drugs', her bleached hair crimped and stacked into fashionable pyramids that look bizarrely like horns, her ruffiano (pimp) lurking, she stands formidably elevated on chopines under smoking torches, on thoroughfares that will get the name 'calle tetta' – 'tit street'. 'Tetta' is neither sluttish nor coy. It's descriptive. Gowns in the current Venetian fashion of all classes bare women's breasts while titillatingly (a *double entendre* not lost on commentators) covering their naked flesh in web-fine lawn. To make certain whom they're addressing, punters can spot a courtesan when she tweaks the hem of her gown: courtesans are required by law to wear yellow stockings. Coryat's travel log devotes page after fascinated page to these sisters of Veronica Franco in a Venice he makes 'Orbis forum', 'a marketplace of this world'. La Serenissima's flesh market, however, is evidently one market Harry has to flee. Or perhaps to retreat from? A second meaning lurking in 'non admodum confidam meis viribus' is, 'I am not entirely confident in the sufficiency of my male sexual prowess among Venetian women'.

He takes to his heels, retreats to Padua, meets up with Zouche, and spends the next four months in this university town, the *studium* of Venice where so many Englishmen across the hundred years before him – future scholars and statesmen, physicians, churchmen on both sides of Reformation controversy, mathematicians, musicians, ambassadors – have enrolled to study civil law, mathematics, physick but also, writes Moryson, 'the arts' of music, dancing, riding, fencing. The reputation of this *studium* doesn't rest on its laurels. The first 'anatomical theatre' in the world will be established in Padua a couple of years hence. This year, perhaps during the very months Harry is in residence, Galileo Galilei will return to his *alma mater*. Professor of mathematics, lecturer in mechanics, experimental astrologer, Galileo will begin in Padua the work that will eventually shatter orthodox dogma on world systems. Does Harry cross his path? If not now, he will two decades later. The same can be said of the famous fencing school attached to the university. If Harry does not practice the 'passado' and 'punto reverso' this time round, he'll be there in the future – not handling the rapiers and stilettos but mopping up a young English aristocrat's blood.

Riding for Rome

In March, Harry travels south alone. He sends news briefs in his wake, seventeen letters to Zouche across the next eighteen months. The Grand Duke Ferdinando de' Medici, grown '(as weapons do) rusty with peace', has invaded 'the State of Genova'. Ferdinando's kinswoman has married 'one of the worst faces that a man shall ordinarily see'. 'Six or eight' have been 'lately burned' in Rome 'for the fault for which Sodom was burned'. On a visit to Rome Archduke Maximilian has been given a gift by the pope, 'a hollow jewel having in it a piece of the cross on which Christ was crucified (as he made him believe) and annexed unto it an Indulgence of 8000 years'. Harry snorts parenthetically, 'notable religion'. We hear him writing with a poniard-sharp pen – and a tongue wedged firmly in his cheek.

He reports grain-hoarding. Troop movements. Plague in the 'island provinces, which we fear in our peninsula'. A 'Gentleman of Rome murdered', his corpse dumped 'in the Amphitheater of Titus' and 'for farther revenge upon the dead body, a dog (being kept hungry before) tied in such manner unto it, that he might eat human flesh'. He writes of the perfidy of the Protestant French king Henri IV, once hero of the Huguenot cause, Protestantism's strong-fisted champion in the civil wars against the Guise and Catholic League and heir to his cousin assassinated in 1589. Now, having held Paris off-and-on under siege for two years, he finally concludes what his advisers have been telling him, that Paris will never bow knee to a 'heretic' king. So he's capitulated, 'changed himself', 'forsaken the God whose mercies he had seen', renounced Protestantism, declared himself a Catholic – and 'Paris worth a mass'. While he's chopping and changing his mind, fifty thousand Parisians have died, most of starvation.

Harry sends news of 'stirs'. 'False news ... very current'. 'Public matters ... wild and raw'. Words for the fire as soon as read. These letters show him studying Italy, experiencing its specifically inflected local politics, building up thick layers of knowledge whose value for his future diplomacy he has no way of knowing now. In May 1592, he embarks on his most hair-raising journey to date – 'or rather adventure' (as he styles it). He rides for Rome.

Moryson warns English travellers off Rome: 'The Papists persecute the Reformed Church with fire and sword', and the 'crafty spies of Rome' are constantly on the look-out for English 'heretics' who can be 'known ... by some gesture or fashion', like 'muffling' their face with their cloak. Jesuit intelligencers are sure to 'advertise' them. Nine months back an Englishman was 'burned alive' in Rome, his hand cut off and his body 'scorched with lighted torches on his way to the scaffold'. His crime? Suicidally attempting to 'snatch the Host' out of the priest's hands during a Mass in St Peter's.

Since then, a Florentine has ascended St Peter's chair as Clement VIII (following three popes whose combined occupancy of the holy seat was 389 days). The papacy isn't in good health, and Clement is setting about recuperating its authority. He has dredged up old laws and imposed them with breathtaking severity. (Harry notes that no state in Christendom can ignore the Vatican. The spiritual is 'intrinsical' to the temporal. And both are political. This pope's actions will have effects far beyond Rome.) The 'taglia concerning the banditi' has been reinstated, a 'taglia' being a cut for informers. It prohibits any from carrying 'weapons by day or night', 'even ... a knife'. 'A box of the ear given in the suburbs' is 'made capital'. (We can imagine Harry's incredulity: '*suburbs?*'). 'All dishonest donne' are 'banish'd out of the city centre'. Given that a 'cense' has put their number at '40000 and certain hundreds', this evacuation will depopulate Rome's streets. Further, these 'donne' are 'prohibited to wear any sort of silk or gold, either in suits or lace' or 'to turn up or curl their hair after the manner of Rome'. Evidently this 'bando' aims to reinstate distinction in a city that can't tell its gentle from its working women. Next, Rome's three thousand Jews are targeted. They're fined either to finance '400 horse in campagnia' 'against the banditi' or 'to maintain the bread at one baiocho the pound' – this, in a year of drought, poor grain harvest and dearth. If they don't like those options they can 'imbagagliare', that is, pack their bags. Foreigners, too, are hit. To the glee of local merchants, 'all Strangers' are 'forbidden to carry out of the City above the value of five crowns of gold', less than £2 sterling. Travellers will have to leave any surplus cash behind.

It's not just the streets Clement is cleaning up. He's settling old scores. In April, 'four of the principal gentlemen of Rome' are 'secretly hang'd in the Castle' on trumped up charges of collusion with the banditi, but really in consequence of 'the natural hatred between the families of Florence and Rome'. 'Roman gentlemen' are losing 'their heads by eight, six, and four at a time'; 'principality of family makes no stop'. These, Harry comments, are 'the manifest beginnings of a dangerous time, wherein Revenge is taken for Justice'.

Next it's the turn of the priests. Clement has called 'the whole clergy of Rome to examination'. He has 'deposed certain unfit, preferred the able, sent home non-residents'. Among them are 'four Canonists' 'deposed' for 'very ridiculous matter': 'the one, for having Plutarch's *Lives* found on his table'; the rest for bad Latin, 'failing in declining of nouns and verbs'.

One clash that Harry reports between the powers spiritual and temporal gives him stark matter to ponder now and to recall fourteen years hence. It concerns the arrest and extradition back to Venice of a 'bandito'. The pope disputes the arrest, and Leonardo Donà, the Venetian ambassador to Rome, has twice been called to the Vatican to answer. There,

> he very roundly told the Pope, that the Signory wondered to understand him offended at the taking away of Marco di Sbarra, considering, that they had privilege from the seat of Rome to take any bandito whatsoever out of the ecclesiastical state, and employ him in their wars, which said, he drew forth the authentic of the privilege. The Pope answered, that their privilege extended it self no further than to banditi, but Marco di Sbarra was moreover attainted of heresy in nine articles. To which Donato replied very warily that, of that the Signory had not

understood, because as yet he was not declared an heretic, and so the disputation received an end.

Donà's 'round' assertion of the Republic's judicial privilege to punish those who offend its civil code, his eyebrow-raised tone (he 'wondered to understand'), his insubordination backed with documentary evidence ('the authentic of the privilege'): this scenario will replay in 1606, when Donà, now doge, defies Clement's successor over exactly this matter of secular v. ecclesiastical jurisdictional precedence. Here, Donà pulls in his horns and 'warily' backs down. 'Heresy' stops him in his tracks. 'Heresy' trumps every offence in the civil code, making the accused indisputably subject to the ecclesiastical courts. In 1606, there will be no backing down, and whereas now Harry drily reports that 'The Venetians are esteemed generally not [to] have done discreetly in that action', making a diplomatic error owing to a failure of information, fourteen years hence, he'll observe how expertly Venice informs its case against the pope – and he'll be one of the Republic's most enthusiastic informants. To 'study men and actions' is, he's understanding, to collect a thick portfolio of observation, a history to serve future current relations with backstory that will make sense of them. Perhaps his old tutor Alberico Gentili comes to Harry's mind, reminding him that from 'the past' are drawn 'knowledge of the present and prescience of the future'.

Clement's Rome in May 1592 is a shark tank. But Harry doesn't propose to dive in naked. He's developed one or two traits in common with that monstrously sensationalised after-birth of Machiavelli's political labour who's just then appearing on the London stage in Christopher Marlowe's *The Jew of Malta*, Mach-evil. Chief among those traits: hypocrisy. Harry travels to Rome incognito as a 'poor Dutchman', willing to 'feign my self' with 'looseness of behaviour', not so much a sheep in wolf's clothing as a loon. He makes a theatrically outrageous entrance, riding into Rome beneath

> a mighty blue feather in a black hat; which, though in it self it were a slight matter, yet surely did it work in the imaginations of men three great effects. First I was by it taken for no English, upon which depended the ground of all. Secondly, I was reputed as light in my mind as in my apparel (they are not dangerous men that are so). And thirdly, no man could think that I desired to be unknown, who, by wearing of that feather, took a course to make my self famous through Rome in few days.

What a deal of work that 'slight' but 'mighty blue feather' performs, hiding the impostor in plain sight. Sartorially, it makes Harry an audacious role-player;

someone who delights in costume, stagey gestures; who fools with signs in a place where miscalling them is fatal. But the performance costs him something. To pull it off, he has to appear 'light in my mind', that is, mad, and 'to suffer' the derisive 'judgements and discourses of the people passing', 'pointing at me'. The popular gaze is loathsome. He consoles himself. In this charade, 'safety and a conscience clear before my God were the things I sought'. 'Credit' – that is, truth, the credible – is 'to be looked unto in England'. In Italy, he'll stage a dis-'credit'-able self. He'll play the hypocrite.

Still, he doesn't push his luck. He avoids Easter in Rome. It's standard practice (says Moryson) 'some few days before Easter' for 'a Priest' to come to a traveller's lodging and take the 'names in writing' of any guests so that they 'might receive the Sacrament with [their] host's family'. Not attending Easter Mass would have blown Harry's cover, so, travelling as a Dutchman, he heads for Naples, only returning to Rome after Holy Week.

He stays another three weeks, and intends longer. He fancies himself 'grown somewhat cunning in the practick of Rome' and thinks further 'profitable points' are 'to be learned of the Pope's Court'. But he changes his mind when someone he recognises from Padua turns up. Everything about this man is 'dangerous' (from his 'suspected' acquaintance to his 'travelling to Rome without language'), and he would expose the fake Dutchman in an instant. So when a Scot 'by chance' invites this gentleman to 'supper in the place' where the Dutchman has his 'table', Harry is in serious trouble. He recounts how 'The table was covered; the salad (our first dish)' was 'served in'. 'All the Gentlemen' were 'in the chamber' except the Scot who 'in that instant' entered the house but took his guest 'first into his chamber' – giving Harry seconds to make excuses and duck out. He leaves Rome 'secretly', retreating to Florence, where the Inquisition's hitmen don't have the power to drag suspects off the streets.

Shrugging out of his disguise, Harry gives public notice that should 'any English Gentleman ... have occasion to repair to Florence', 'Henrico' is 'now very desirous of the English company'. Perhaps he needs the antidote of English company to cure the effects of three weeks' skulking under the slender shadow of a blue feather, candid company to off-set all the lies he'd told to get inside the 'misterium'. And he *has* been inside. 'No English man', he avers, 'containing himself within his allegiance to her Majesty' has 'seen more concerning the points of Rome than I have done'.

Such 'curiosity' – like handling dangerous books in Vienna – is a form of research. Moryson, for one, doesn't recommend it, but if an English traveller cannot 'restrain his curiosity to hear & see' a Mass, he should attend as if 'going to see a stage-play'. Not as a spectator. As an actor. For he must put on a performance of devotion, must imitate devotion's gestures, and 'Of two evils … choose the least, namely, rather to sign himself with the cross, or negligently to make offer, as if he dipped his hand (or his glove upon it, as their manner is) into the holy water-box.' By 'omitting these common ceremonies' he'll 'fall into suspicion'. And 'called into question', he'll be 'either driven to deny his Religion' by signing a statement of adherence to Catholicism, or 'burned with fire'.

Harry has already demonstrated his gift for stage-playing, strutting beneath his 'mighty blue feather'. The 'Points of Rome' he witnesses show him going further. He must have 'dipped his hand' in the 'holy water-box' more than once. But while he plays the part of an authentic Catholic, his Protestant eyes are never confused by the show. He has no doubts about what he's seeing. He recognises 'The Whore of Babylon'. While he's looking, however, he's also of course acting, and the problem with putting on an authentic performance is that it's persuasive. 'Excellent dissembling' is a kind of 'juggling' that 'lies like truth' (as Shakespeare's Macbeth will learn to his appalling cost). Moreover, the problem with the 'theatre' of the Catholic church, in common with the public theatres of London, is that it 'seduces' (Moryson's word) spectators with persuasive fictions; seduces them into believing false things true. For Harry, then, playing the part of 'outward reverence' too authentically puts him in double jeopardy. On the one hand, performing ritual actions, he might be seduced into believing them, turning recusant. So what started as a lie becomes the truth, and the 'cover' (as when a spy turns double agent) is pressed into performing a double deception. On the other hand, persuading spectators in Rome of the authenticity of his fake performance, Harry risks denunciation in England as one genuinely ensnared by the Whore and actually turned to Babylon, a betrayal not just of religious confession but of allegiance to his queen. And that's treason.

Shortly, Harry fears exactly such a denunciation. His double bluff has performed its work so persuasively that 'a voice' in Venice is spreading rumours that he's being investigated by 'the Inquisition', a matter that will 'very much prejudice my credit'. And not only his credit, his life. A week later, 'certain other suspicions' are circulating that are digging him deeper into danger, accusing him a secret Catholic convert. What can he do? These are now so serious that he's forced to come clean, to reveal what he'd hoped to conceal, that 'during my abode in Rome', yes, indeed, he'd had 'Conference … with Robert Bellarmine'. Yes, indeed, he'd met him regularly, the mightily learned Jesuit who had recently been appointed rector to the Roman College. For years,

Bellarmine had been walking the short distance between it and Via Monserrato to teach in the Venerable English College, founded as a seminary to re-plant England with the true seeds of Catholicism. The English know the seminary well. Protestants like Harry looking for a hide-out and willing to play the hypocrite find it a convenient cover. The English know Roberto Bellarmino very well, too. And it's precisely because of his great scholarship that sharp minds like Harry's want to dispute theology with him.

Harry succeeds too well in the part he plays as acolyte among the Jesuits. He convinces his college 'tutors' he's apt for conversion. He'll say later that one of them considered him 'uno delli suoi agnelli', 'one of his lambs'. Writing to Zouche in November 1592, Harry insists that his 'conference' with the Jesuit 'proceeded no further ... than to ordinary talk in matter of learning' and that, 'besides', he went disguised. 'To confess all' to Zouche is to pre-empt any who might use his secret life against him. Harry is discovering how dangerous a line he's treading across a gulf of religious controversy where the slightest puff of accusation might hurtle him to his doom. We pause over Harry's word 'confess': doesn't it resonate ironically? Opening his heart to Zouche, isn't he like a penitent in a confession box seeking absolution from his confessor? Whether or not their ordinary talk taints him, in Roberto Bellarmino Harry encounters another character who, like Leonardo Donà, will figure significantly in his Venetian future.

'Nail'd in Tuscany'

In July, he's hoping 'to pass ... out of Italy'. He's been living in Florence with 'little to signify' since 'private men, once settled, receive small alteration'. But the longer he's lived in the city of the Medici the more he sees it as 'a paradise inhabited with devils'. Here are 'practiced' 'those vices' which 'Venice hath scarce heard of'. For compensation, the Tuscan 'vulgar' spoken in Florence is 'very pure and correct', so his Italian is improving, and he has for 'commodity' the 'conversation of certain gentlemen' which, he remarks with characteristic wryness, gives them 'good means to speak well and to do ill'. Echoing the worry that's dogged him since he landed in Stade three years back, he's finding it hard to live within budget. 'Times' are 'dear in extremity'. He's 'not the richest man ... this present': a vast understatement. His 'Roman voyage' stood him '146 Crowns' even 'with the best frugality I could use', so while there was 'pleasure in it' and 'some profit', 'yet did it pinch the shoulder of a younger brother'. Clearly, Harry is skint.

In September, he's still in Florence. He has received 'instruction' from England 'to remain in Tuscany, not far from the Great Duke's Court'. Nothing elaborates this instruction, who issues it or to what end beyond shadowing Ferdinando de' Medici. We can speculate. Harry learns, bemused, that his brother has just been knighted, 'either against his will (as some say) or with it (as I say)'. Does Edward's business at Court bring conversation of absent Harry to the attention of someone interested in making use of eye-witness from Italy, someone who, just now, is aiming to expand his diplomatic value to the Crown? Is that man Robert Devereux, earl of Essex? Perhaps. From 1591, urged on by Francis Bacon and the veteran intelligencer Thomas Phelippes, the earl has been filling the place of chief intelligence officer to the Crown left vacant by the death of Devereux's father-in-law, Francis Walsingham. In 1593 the earl recruits the elder Bacon brother, Anthony, just returned from twelve years on the continent, as agent to organise an information network. Now, wanting intelligence 'from whence the greatest news can come, as from Rome', is Essex aiming to expand that network via Harry Wotton in Tuscany? An affiliation of affection links Essex to Edward Wotton through Philip Sidney: Devereux married Sidney's widow. There's a further affiliation of blood through the Bacons: Edward's daughter has married into the tribe, making the Wottons and Bacons 'cousins'. Then, too, Essex's self-styled 'bookishness' would find common cause with young Harry, only three years his junior, who's spent so much of the past four years in libraries, a scholar studying also the practick of policy. Such speculations gain substance from an unsigned letter to Edward in Anthony Bacon's papers, endorsed 'Dec. 20, 1594':

> Sir, having found by my Lord [that is, Essex] that you had not as yet motioned unto his lordship that which it pleased you to mention unto me yesternight of my cousin your brother [Harry], I was so bold in kindness to take the opportunity to let my Lord understand your desire and purpose, which my Lord took very kindly, and with most honourable acknowledgement of the merit of your devoted love toward him, asserted without any solicitation; and assured me with great affection that he would receive him, place him and employ him in the best sort, and do him what good he could hereafter.

'Receive him, place him and employ him': whatever has or hasn't passed as instruction to Harry in Florence in September 1592, in the new year 1595 Essex and Harry Wotton will begin a future together informed by Harry's Italian intelligence.

In October Harry finally moves to Siena via Livorno. From there he thinks his 'next stirring' will 'certainly be toward Venice'. But in December, he's still 'nail'd in Tuscany', waiting 'upon letters out of England'. They come, for by August he has worked his way north to Geneva. There he's placed 'in the house of Mr. Isaac Casaubon', Europe's greatest classicist, committed Calvinist, 'person of sober condition' – and father to a herd of children, impecunious. For the town itself, it's 'undone with war, even in manners': the women of the city, who before 'digested certain humours with walking', have taken to squatting on 'the banks in the street' shelling 'hemp till an hour or two in the night' – and offering themselves at the same time for sale. Harry mourns this great city, capital of the Protestant revolution, brought to 'intemperance and ebriety, and such other evils as follow them'. He's itching to leave Geneva in the spring, to end this 'wandering up and down in a strange land'. He's thwarted. Money troubles are piling up. He needs funds from England to pave his return. They don't arrive. Finally, he persuades his scholar-host to stand surety on local debts to the phenomenal tune of 263 crowns, nearly £80. Plus the cost of a horse. (Whose name we do not know.) He promises repayment sent to the Frankfurt Mart in September. He leaves Geneva in August. And behind him: those massive debts to Casaubon.

What are his thoughts, seeing England after five years? Impossible to know. What we can believe is that, only twenty-six years old and technically still in the 'slippery' years of youth, he has read far beyond the core syllabus he found in the 'library of travel'. He's had experiences those classmates he left 'sluggardis'd at home' could not imagine: man-eating dogs in Rome; man-eating women in Venice. And they're not over yet. Still to face: the awfulness of learning that no funds made it to Frankfurt; that he's being denounced in Casaubon's circles as 'trico ille tuus', a 'mountebank' shuffler and trickster.

When he hauls into view, climbing the steep hill to Bocton Malherbe, does his family recognise him? (When that other wanderer, Fynes Moryson, finally returns home, his family doesn't.) After five years, Harry's English clothes are worn to rags. Is he metamorphosed, a fantastical 'Italianate gentleman', a black hat on his head sprouting 'a mighty blue feather'? His last letter, written in England at the end of his travels around Christmas 1594, addressee unknown, recounts the 'occurrences out of the parts where I have been' and 'advertises' the 'ablest' of the 'acquaintances' he's made. It reads like a CV. Another letter some time later recommends for employment an Italian who, 'besides his learning and sound affection to this state', is 'well tumbled and practiced in the world'. Harry might be describing himself. That second letter is addressed to Devereux. In the gap of time between these two undated letters, young Harry's life has taken a momentous turn. He has landed service with the man they call the 'star of England', taken into the household, the employment, the confidence of 'My Most Honourable Lord' as Devereux's personal secretary. For the next five years, Harry will be a feather in the wing of this 'English Icarus', as Essex soars to the heights of courtly power and prestige, then spectacularly plummets.

Part II

A world of business

6
Mr Secretary Wotton

In a house on the Strand

January 1595. The man whose service Harry Wotton enters as personal secretary in the new year is a man in motion. When his servants draw back his bed curtains in the morning Robert Devereux's chamber is already 'stived with friends or suitors of one kind or other'. That word 'stived' is the one seamen use for stowing cargo tight in a ship's hold. It gives a sense not just of the crowd the earl of Essex deals with on a daily basis from first waking but also of the purposiveness of his dealings. The human cargo 'stived' in his chamber is going somewhere, and Essex is directing it. Harry learns the earl's daily routine. Being 'up', Devereux gives 'his legs, arms and breast to his ordinary servants to button and dress him, with little heed; his head and face to his barber, his eyes to his letters, and ears to petitions, and many times all at once'. Then, 'the gentleman of his robes throwing a cloak over his shoulders', he makes 'a step into his closet' – his private chamber – 'and after a short prayer', he's 'gone'. What he leaves behind is a world of business for his secretariat to manage.

After five years abroad travelling, sitting in libraries, listening at tables, reading, studying, collecting sources, gathering information and writing it up for onward transmission, five years observing public affairs from the fringes, Harry is now cast into the turbid centre of Elizabethan politics – and into a service whose practices and disciplines he'll have to learn. No longer a free agent but tied to a master, he's resident at an address just outside London's western limits on the Strand that is coming to be recognised by friends and foes alike as a magnet to men of influence and intrigue: Essex House.

In significant respects the England Harry returns to looks much like the England he left. On the wide stage of international politics where the queen performs, some of the scenery has shifted. But not the plot lines. War with

4 Robert Devereux, earl of Essex. In this painting by an unknown artist following Marcus Gheeraerts the Younger, the earl wears his Greater George on a riband and holds his Marshal's baton. The beard spilling over his ruff, grown on campaign in 1596, shows this as 'the face of Cadiz'.

Spain still ties up armies on several fronts: the Netherlands and the Americas, Spanish-held Portugal and the high seas where English privateers stalk the gold convoys whose treasure Spain so desperately needs to replenish her empty coffers. Meanwhile, Felipe II is putting himself deeper in hock to the Genoese cartel of moneylenders who own his colossal debt. Geriatric, gloomy, near-isolated in El Escorial where his cancer-riddled body has to be strapped into a specially designed chair to keep it upright, he's living off his obsession to build, victual and launch a new Armada in reprisal for 1588. His threat was pre-empted in 1589 when 'El Draco', Francis Drake, launched a 'counter-Armada'. Though forbidden by the queen, Essex secretly galloped to Falmouth to join the fleet. Thus, in the weeks when 21-year-old Harry Wotton was plotting his student travels in Europe, 24-year-old Robert Devereux was sailing with Drake, leading the vanguard ashore through shoulder-high surf at Peniche in Portugal and (in the kind of thrilling gesture of defiance that will characterise all his martial audacity to come) driving his lance shuddering into the city's gates. Now in 1595, as the historian William Camden records, 'Rumours' are 'abroad, and those not slight or uncertain' that 'the Spaniards were ready to set sail with a stronger and better appointed Armado than before'. 'All men' have 'buckled themselves to war'.

In France, the civil wars of religion are still thirstily gulping down the men and money Queen Elizabeth's government continues to pour into them. In August 1589, just two months before Harry Wotton sailed for Stade, and fol-lowing the double assassinations of the (rabidly Catholic) duke of Guise and the (limply tolerant) Henri III, the dead king's Protestant cousin had come to the throne as Henri IV. He failed to starve Catholic Paris into submission to his Protestant rule the following year – and backed off when Spain sent in relief. Ironically, had he held the siege 'only 3 or 4 days longer', as John Stow observes from London in his *Annales* (and Harry Wotton from Vienna in a letter), the city would have 'been glad to open their gates ... by reason they had long since not only eaten up all their oxen, sheep, horses, mules, dogs, bears, mice and rats, with all kind of carrion whatsoever' but even 'greasy leather' and bones boiled into soup. At least thirteen thousand were left 'dead in the streets ... of famine'. 'Proper knowledge' held that 'there were eaten in the town, two and twenty children'.

A year later, the English queen's care, according to Camden, was 'how she might assist and relieve the French king, now sinking'. Pressured by her chief adviser, Lord Burghley, and by the importunate young man himself (whom she'd kept ashore duing the crisis of 1588), she gave Robert Devereux leave to command a four thousand-strong expeditionary force into Normandy to aid the beleaguered king. Essex sailed in August. By December the seige of Rouen was as dismal a failure as the seige of Paris. Essex returned home reputation battered – and heart-struck. His brother Walter was a casualty of Henri's adventure. Given England's investment in France's wars, the queen was outraged when, only months later, Henri capitulated. He reconciled himself to Rome, declared himself a Catholic and walked through the gates that Paris finally opened to him, to be crowned His Most Christian King in March 1594. Elizabeth, writes Camden, 'snatched up her pen' and dashed off a series of biting rhetoricals: 'Is the world come to this pass?' Now, in 1595, this king is redirecting his attention. He declares war on Spain. And appeals to England for aid. The queen acerbically wishes him 'happy and good success' but recalls her troops from Brittany. She has troubles elsewhere, across the Irish sea.

Camden's annals for 1588 end with a tight-lipped marginal gloss: 'The beginning of a great rebellion in Ireland'. The earl of Tir-Oen – Tyrone, as the English make him – was accused of 'secret conference with certain Spaniards' who'd been 'shipwrecked upon the coast of Ireland' and left behind as their battered Armada staggered home. Summoned into England, Tyrone protested submission to the Crown, was pardoned by Elizabeth and 'made a shew and seeming' for some while of being a 'most obedient subject'. England grudgingly respects this man. He's a military expert, industrious, equipped with a 'body, able to endure labour, watching and hunger' and a 'soul large and fit for the weightiest businesses'. But he carries in his breast 'a profound dissembling heart'. Within months, then, this traitor – or freedom fighter? – was conspiring rebellion in Ulster. Or was it independence for Ireland? He signalled how dramatically he was raising the stakes of his ambitions when, contrary to his sworn vow, he took the treasonous step in 1593 of titling himself 'O'Neal', 'in comparison whereof,' writes Camden, 'the very title of Caesar is contemptible in Ireland'. Thereafter, with breathtaking impartiality, he dissembled his purposes to rival clan-chiefs and to Elizabeth's governors in Dublin alike, betraying each to each indifferently. He'll keep this up for the next twenty years, Ireland's most poisonous thorn in England's flesh. (Twelve years hence, that thorn, like a shot fired point blank from an arquebus, will threaten to split Harry Wotton's heart.)

In 1595 Tyrone assaults the English garrison at Blackwater and forces its surrender. Then this 'subtle fox', hearing the queen's hounds on his tail, switches back to 'feign submission', 'begging pardon upon his knees'. The 'wiser sort', though, see the truce he wins as merely a ploy, and 'very prejudicial … to the queen', for 'the rebels in the interim get clear time to form and ripen their secret plots and designs ... with fresh recruits'. The Nine Years War has just begun.

These grand narratives apart, the England Harry returns to, and the London he remembers, must look almost unrecognisable. The city feels like a gigantic builder's yard. North, as Stow in his *Survey* records, outside Moorgate, beyond Finsbury fields, development is pushing up Shoreditch Street along the old coaching road, crowding it with 'habitations of beggars and people without trade, stables, inns, alehouses, taverns, garden-houses converted to dwellings, ordinaries, dicing houses, bowling alleys, and brothel houses'. To the east beyond the church along Whitechapel Street, the 'common field ... which ought to be open and free for all men ... is so encroached upon by building of filthy cottages ... that in some places it scarce remaineth a sufficent highway for the meeting of carriages and droves of cattle. Much less is there any fair, pleasant, or wholesome way for people to walk on foot.' Along the Thames, now that the sailors' gallows at Wapping has gone (no seaman, it seems, wanting to live in the shadow of the admiralty hangman), a 'filthy strait passage with alleys of small tenements' housing sailors' victuallers has oozed its way a mile beyond the Tower. On the opposite bank, 'divers lanes and alleys up to St. George's Church' make a warren of crowded buildings along both sides of Long Southwark. Even Westminster has seen changes. Leicester House, new-built by the earl some twenty-five years earlier just outside Temple Bar on the Strand, is now owned by Leicester's stepson who, two years back, converted some of its forty-two apartments into accommodation for the entourage he's gathering around him. The pile is now called Essex House.

Widespread building has brought some comforts to London. The mining engineer Bevis Bulmer 'set up an engine at Broken Wharf ... to convey Thames water up into the city, sufficient to serve the whole west part thereof'. But the sprawl must also strike Harry as astonishing, given that between August 1592 and spring 1594 London lost something like ten per cent of her population. They died – eleven thousand of them – of the worst outbreak of plague since 1563. This human devastation registers in letters sent by the playhouse entrepreneur Philip Henslowe to his son-in-law, the actor Edward Alleyn, then on tour in the provinces, the London playhouses being shut by order of the Privy Council. Henslowe's household in Southwark had already endured a full year of the epidemic when he wrote in August 1593 of being 'flyted with fear of the sickness', plague 'almost in every house' around them. News of another player's family was dismal: 'Robert Brown's wife in Shoreditch & all her children & household be dead & her doors shut up'. Later that month he could 'send you no just note' of the sickness 'because there is commandment to the contrary'. (Why? What was 'commandment' worried about? Civil unrest?) He thought 'the dead number seventeen or eighteen hundreth in one week'. While 'commandment' shuffled, Londoners commended themselves to God, hung bunches of rue – herb of grace – in their windows, and carried on, not least with building projects: Henslowe moved straight from death counts to news that Alleyn's joiner had delivered the court cupboard he'd ordered for his new house.

Walking the city in January 1595, Harry must be struck by accidents that have made a lottery of ordinary London lives in his absence. Perhaps he heard in family letters news in Florence that Camden reported in 1592: 'This summer, as also the last, there was so great a drought all over England that not only the fields were parched, but fountains also were dried up, and a great many beasts died everywhere for want of water'. Unimaginably, 'The Thames ... failed so of water ... that a man might ride over it near London Bridge'. Eighteen months later, while Harry was in Geneva, the weather reversed, and for five months London was inundated: from May 'it commonly rained every day or night until Saint James day', 25 July. Drought followed by flood yields dearth: 'the price of grain grew to be such as a strike or bushel of rye was sold for 5 shillings, a bushel of wheat for five, seven or eight shillings'. Even now the price of grain is ruinously high 'to the grief of the poor'. Shortly, the queen will issue a proclamation against transporting grain into foreign lands – even as record quantities are imported from Europe through the Hanseatic towns.

For Harry, though, the most significant changes in England are happening not on London's streets but in Westminster's offices of administration, at the top of the queen's government. The old guard is dying out. The Privy Council is emptying of stalwarts who for decades have loomed over the Council table like Stonehenge over Salisbury plain: Ambrose Dudley, duke of Warwick, dead in 1589, a year behind his brother, Robert, earl of Leicester. Francis Walsingham, former ambassador to France and head of the queen's intelligence service, dead in 1590, a bankrupt, having funded the queen's service out of his own pocket, 'buried without solemnities' at night to avoid, it seems, his creditors. Two further privy counsellors depart that same year, James Croft and George Talbot, earl of Shrewsbury; and the next, Christopher Hatton, keeper of the Great Seal; followed in quick succession in 1593 and 1594 by two Stanleys, the fourth and fifth earls of Derby. A year later, William Cecil, lord Burghley, is hanging on. He's the greatest of the elders. Former secretary of state and master of the Court of Wards, latterly lord treasurer, he has served on Elizabeth's Privy

Council since her accession: the rock on which her throne is founded; the human bureaucracy machine through whose hands passes all the administration of the realm. Now, though, age and gout are at war with those hands. Just this year, seeing a shaky signature on his latest letter, the queen sends Burghley a message that he himself records, saying 'she will have a battle with my fingers'. It's a battle she'll wage for another three years, but finally lose.

Meanwhile, as the greybeards die, the smooth-faced youths are thrusting forward, young nobles like Henry Wriothesley, earl of Southampton, and Roger Manners, earl of Rutland. Chief among these smooth-faced youths is Robert Devereux – who won't grow a beard until the summer of 1596.

'Advertisers of occurrences'

Omitting to date or address it (beyond signing it 'Your Lordship's most humble servant'), Harry dictates a long memorandum of his 'occurrences' for the past five years. He profiles 'the ablest of my acquaintance' to a scribe whose writing we see punctiliously underscoring every name not to be missed. Harry is identifying a network of influence, information and intelligence. But also laying out a brief of his own serviceability.

He begins with Scipioni Alberti, a Protestant-leaning 'gentleman of Siena, well experienced in the matters of Rome', having been 'major-domo to the Count Paliano ... whose whole actions ... passed through his hands' – including Paliano's murder of his wife and subsequent execution. Such lurid histories will be turning up shortly on London stages with titles like *The White Devil* and *Women Beware Women*.

Lodging with Alberti for five months, Harry was introduced to Girolamo Emo, a Venetian, self-exiled supposedly in consequence of a spoiled love affair. But 'by long practice' – that word 'practice' reveals the intelligencer at work – Harry discovers the real reason. Emo is a secret Protestant who wants to recruit Harry's 'knowledge of the Truth' to the business of converting Venice from Catholicism. Just now, their plan stands about as much of a chance of curing Venetian Catholicism as a Venetian mountebank's of curing gout. But a decade hence, Emo's pipedream will return as part of the English ambassador's most serious diplomatic project in the Republic.

Moving on to Florence, Harry lodged with the glitteringly disreputable but entertaining geriatric Baccio Buoni, an old Satan who sent Harry 'many letters written at large and freely of the State', and more than anyone left the Englishman knowing Florence as 'a paradise inhabited with devils'.

Thus proceeds the discursive march through the gallery of useful acquaintance: in Florence, 'one Dethick' – Humphry Dethick, factor to the Cheapside merchant and moneylender, Baptist Hickes, whose brother is secretary to Lord Burghley. This younger Dethick is 'a very good scholar who, no doubt, to your Lordship, will be a most sufficient instrument in this kind'. What he means by 'in this kind' is unclear, but he's just been mentioning Buoni's indiscreet letters. Some such might be expected of Dethick. So calling him an 'instrument' is more than a little suggestive. (As it happens, Harry is wrong. Dethick won't be any use at all. He's been turned by Catholic agents in Rome.)

Beyond Italy, in Geneva there's one Rigotier; in the Grisons, the Neapolitan-turned-Protestant Scipione Lentulo; still others in High Germany, in Basel, in Vienna. Having sniffed them out on the ground, Harry fingers the 'sufficientist', scholars, secretaries, schoolmasters, merchants, doctors of law, all 'of the Religion' – that is, Protestants – as potential instruments or 'referendaries' of 'Your Lordship'.

That Lordship is surely Robert Devereux, and Harry's 'advertisers of occurrences' are just as surely his application for employment, sent on the back of Anthony Bacon's letter of 20 December 1594 to Edward Wotton, the one that assured Edward that Essex would 'receive' Harry and 'place him and employ him in the best sort'. Bacon was in a position to know. Having lived abroad for twelve years, he'd returned to England in 1592. In August 1595 he moved from slummy lodgings in Bishopsgate to an apartment in Essex House, some nine months after Secretary Wotton took up his post. There, Bacon has daily access to the earl as an intimate (and unpaid) adviser recruited as a kind of information technologist to engineer and map an intelligence grid across Europe linking reports back to Essex. The earl's father-in-law, the queen's master of intelligence, Walsingham, had died in 1590. Early in 1591 Bacon's younger brother Francis and Thomas Phelippes, the gifted code-breaker, introduced Essex to intelligence-gathering, urging him to fill the gap Walsingham had left. So far, the earl's reputation has been as a soldier. Now he's moving into covert diplomacy.

A summary of his career to date leaves a reader breathless. (No doubt Harry Wotton has studied Devereux's life as attentively as he's studied the Roman lives in Tacitus.) Born in 1565, left a royal ward when his father, sent lord lieutenant of Ireland, died there of chronic dysentery in 1576; raised in Burghley's household; sent to Trinity College, Cambridge, where he graduated MA four years later in 1581, pulling no strings of privilege but undergoing every college exhibition (thus proving himself England's best-educated nobleman); dubbed knight for conspicuous – even foolhardy – bravery under his step-father Leicester's command at Zutphen in 1585 where he refused to give up the assault even after Philip Sidney was mortally wounded; returned a war hero; adopted the queen's 'constant companion' and Master of the Horse in 1587, then Knight of the Garter the following year; sailed with Drake in the counter-Armada, 1589; secretly married Frances Walsingham Sidney, Philip's widow, in 1590; assumed independent command (with the queen's grudging approval, brokered by Burghley) of the English expeditionary force to Normandy the following spring; returned to court in the new year, the campaign a failure, a pile of debts stacked high against an already mortgaged estate (the legacy of his father whom the Crown required to fund his own lieutenancy in Ireland) and perhaps what was worse, his belief in soldiering as the highest form of service to the Crown severely knocked – not least by finding that, in his absence, Burghley's distinctly un-military son, the just-knighted twenty-eight-year-old hunchback Robert, whom the queen called her 'pygmy' and whom his ageing father was grooming to inherit his offices, had been elevated to the Privy Council.

It was in the context of this visible, personalised rivalry between the *militia* and the *togati*, a rivalry between soldiers and statesmen which increasingly would polarise around the Cecils on the one hand and Essex on the other, that the earl had to face the fact that in terms of influencing the queen and setting foreign and domestic policy, currently the statesmen were out-gunning the generals. So, as a contemporary wrote, Essex 'resolved to give this satisfaction to the queen', to 'desist for a time from his course of the wars and to intend matters of state'. He was still only twenty-six. Like twenty-three-year-old Harry, then, still in his 'slippery' years.

Thereafter, he began to show himself 'a new man'. He was sworn to the Privy Council in February 1593. Within a week, a university friend wrote in some wonderment that, 'clean forsaking all his former youthful tricks', he was 'carrying himself with honourable gravity, and singularly liked of both in Parliament and at Council table, for his speeches and judgment'. Was he cured of his 'youthful tricks'? Only as thoroughly as Harry Wotton was ever corrected of his 'loose humour'. But it's perhaps something these two young men recognise in each other's temperament that brings their minds into alignment in January 1595.

Essex is now effectively the queen's foreign secretary, 'all matters of intelligence ... wholly in his hands'. Taking on this role he sees himself as much more than a snapper up of gossip or drudge sifting stale reports purporting to be news. (We hear echoes of Harry in Vienna.) He's an actor on an international European stage, no less than an advocate for the whole of Christendom, a word that surfaces over and over in his writings. He has a sure sense of the part he's to play in a divine drama cast and directed by God whose ends include not just the defence of Christendom but its reformation. God, in Essex's book, might tolerate Catholics; might tolerate them even in Essex's own remarkably 'catholic' household, especially when Christendom needs to mobilise a united front against Turks and infidels. But Essex's God is a good Protestant.

Such ideas, such purposes chime with Harry Wotton. He, too, is dedicated to the international Protestant cause. He, too, is militant against Catholic reaction and thinks beyond England, of Christendom. He, too, is bookish. But he has attained what lies beyond Essex. The earl has campaigned as a soldier abroad but has never had time to play the scholar, to study in the 'useful library of travel'. He'll later lament: 'mon malheur a esté tel que Dieu n'aye jamais voulu permettre d'avoir veu l'Italie, le jardin de la Chrestienté'. (My misfortune has been such that God never permitted me to see Italy, the garden of Christianity.) Admitting Harry Wotton to his service Essex gains vicarious entry into that garden. Harry's 'advertisers of occurrences' landing on his desk just when Essex is expanding his covert diplomacy give him what he needs to populate his network with names and addresses across Christendom.

But for what they tell us about the young man who's entering Devereux's service, his 'advertisers' are most remarkable not for any information they give. Rather, for how they're signed. According to Harry's contemporary biographer, Essex 'first invited' him 'into a friendship', then, 'after a knowledge of his great abilities, to be one of his secretaries'. Can we seriously credit that word 'friendship'? Friendship between the aristocrat and the 'half-blood'? On the evidence of these 'advertisers', we can. Among all his papers, his family letters, his future ambassadorial dispatches, this is only one of two surviving pieces of correspondence signed familiarly 'Harry'. Here, on the earlier of the two, the signature is deferentially lowercase, 'harry wotton' crouching in the bottom corner of the page. In May 1596, after only four months' residence in the earl's household, the feathers in the secretary's cap will appear to be sitting cockier. When he signs himself to none other than Secretary of State Robert Cecil, he signs boldly, a broad flourish across the page, 'Harry Wotton'.

No 'base pen clerks'

Entering the earl's service, Harry is entering an established secretariat. Edward Reynolds has handled the earl's ordinary correspondence for the past six years, reading and annotating letters for his attention, answering petitions, blocking or admitting suitors, copying Devereux's autograph letters into letter-books and making further copies for wider distribution, writing drafts of his 'projects' and reports, communicating with the steward, Gelly Merrick, who manages Devereux's estates in Hereford and Wales. Harry Wotton's appointment after Christmas 1594 begins the process of transforming the secretariat. Essex will take on two more secretaries in 1595: William Temple in October; Henry Cuffe before the end of the year.

This flurry of activity: is it prompted by Harry's introduction to Devereux? Has the man who signs himself 'harry' to the earl given him insights that open up a world of practical possibility, Essex seeing in him the human resource, the human *instrument* he needs to make good the ambition he has nursed since the Bacons nudged him in the direction of intelligence-gathering? It's solid speculation, because from this date, Devereux's ambitions look clear. With these appointments that so greatly expand his ability to write himself into Europe, Essex declares himself not just Her Majesty's most active military commander but a statesman who, as foreign secretary, intends to take the lead role in her foreign affairs by establishing the network that will gather the intelligence that will inform England's European diplomacy. Tacitly, he's positioning himself the obvious successor to the ageing William Cecil as the queen's leading counsellor. The fact that he's putting himself on a collision course with Burghley and his son is lost on no one.

Devereux's four make an interesting group. And more than interesting, they demonstrate the intellectual fire power Essex has at his command. All are men from the shires: Dorset (Reynolds), Somerset (Cuffe), Warwickshire (Temple), Kent (Wotton). They're all one-time grammar school boys (Temple, Eton; Wotton, Winchester; Cuffe and Reynolds, local free schools). Like Essex, they're university men, educated (like Essex) according to the humanist curriculum that prepared them to serve prince and state by equipping them members of an international Latinate literary culture. Only Harry was a fee-payer at university; the others won scholarships. Only Harry is 'connected', to land-owning gentry (though as the youngest son of a second marriage, he's very far down the patriarchal pecking order). The others come from trade and local government.

Temple, born 1554, is the eldest by a decade and least visible of the lot. A fellow of King's College, Cambridge from 1576, he occupied himself with academic in-fighting before taking up an appointment as secretary to Philip Sidney in 1585. It was he who cradled Sidney in his arms as he died, horribly, of gangrene a month after being wounded at the battle of Zutphen. No doubt Temple's backstory matters to Essex. As Temple was left £30 in Sidney's will, so Essex was bequeathed Sidney's sword – and all that it symbolised.

Cuffe, born 1562, is three years older than Essex. Elected a scholar of Trinity College, Oxford in 1578, then a fellow five years later, he was a brilliant student of Greek texts, named regius professor of Greek as a mere twenty-eight-year-old in 1590. But this academic supernova also revealed rubs in his disposition, a tendency to truculence, a bantam cock of a man. By the time he was forced to resign his fellowship and migrate to Merton, he'd probably crossed paths with Harry Wotton and Jean Hotman (son of the renowned civil lawyer with whom Harry would aspire to study). As Hotman left Oxford to serve the earl of Leicester as secretary, so Cuffe left to take an appointment with Leicester's stepson, Devereux.

Reynolds, birthdate unrecorded, is probably the same age as Cuffe, judging from the dates he took his BA (1580) and MA (1584) from All Souls, Oxford. Although he held a college fellowship briefly, he – like Harry later – promptly left academia to get down to work in the world, learning the ropes of civil service before taking up employment with Devereux in 1588. He may have galloped to Falmouth with him on that mad caper to join the Portugal expedition in 1589; he certainly served Essex at the siege of Rouen in 1591. 'Good Reynolds', as Essex terms him, is the earl's secretarial anchorman. Later, he stays behind in London while Essex is campaigning, trusted to represent his master at Court – and monitor the mischief his rivals brew in his absence.

Harry Wotton is the infant of the group. Reynolds calls him 'a great languaged traveller', and whether his tone is sarcastic, bitter, awed or wary, he's taken the correct measure of the youth. What Harry brings to the table is eye-witness. Unlike any of the others, he has Europe on the tip of his tongue – and the soles of his boots. He knows the trade Essex is ambitious to invest in. As his letters to Zouche from Vienna, Venice and Florence have shown, he knows how to jolly information out of strangers. How to set snares with gold. How to plant red herrings. Of course, he's useful too in carrying in his wallet a notebook full of names and addresses.

This is the secretariat that serves Essex for the next six years, no 'base pen clerks' among them but the civil service equivalent of the well-bred aristocratic pups who are snapping at the old dogs' heels in Whitehall. In a household where perhaps fifty sit down at table, his secretaries are the 'family' at its centre, Devereux's intellectual equals, able to participate in the programme of research and learning that goes on at bookish Essex House. They read Tacitus with Essex and his aristocratic circle; discuss poetry; hear experts on magnetism, mathematics and navigation; and apply habits learned at university to politics, writing briefing papers to analyse writing and extract 'state points'. They are not like-minded. Temperamentally, they're chalk and cheese, stolid Reynolds, sober Temple, waspish Cuffe, wit-cracking Wotton, men whose personalities as much as their abilities will come into play as rivalries serving Essex. Their influence will prove ambiguous, and when Essex finally comes to grief, he'll bitterly accuse one of them of his fall.

To these four must be added a fifth man, the impressively connected Anthony Bacon, William Cecil's nephew and Robert Cecil's cousin. Seven years older than Devereux, neither secretary nor agent, he's been close to the earl for the past three years and resident in Essex House since August. His influence on the secretariat is going to be constant, felt initially by bringing his 'cousin', young Harry, to the earl's attention, later by co-ordinating the whole intelligence-gathering operation across Europe. But if we imagine Devereux's household as testosterone-fuelled and bursting with virility, Bacon is a misfit. Harry will later describe him as 'a gentleman of impotent feet but a nimble head'. By the time he knows him, Bacon's brilliant mind is trapped in an invalid's body, feet, ankles and hands crippled by gout. He douses himself with opiate-based 'physic'. He's probably addicted. Still, that nimble head stores the experience of his twelve-year absence from England, spent mainly in France functioning as the queen's unofficial contact with Henri of Navarre and feeding Burghley intelligence. There, he permitted his lodgings to be used as a 'receptacle of all rebellious Huguenots' (according to his accusers); committed sodomy, a capital offence, with one of his servants (according to his accusers); and received increasingly shrill letters from his mother calling him home, accusing him of abandoning his faith and wasting his patrimony. It's an understatement to say that the thread of Anthony Bacon's career is of a mingled yarn. That's probably why he's so valuable to Robert Devereux.

'The first thing that I must require of you'

In February 1595 the earl of Essex is in bed with ague. Edward Reynolds writes to Anthony Bacon: 'I have been a prisoner these four or five days, because my Lord hath been so himself, by reason of his indisposition. The business that hath arrested me here hath been very small, but attendance is as much necessary in sickness as in health, and somewhat more, for that the times of employment are so uncertain, and the offence of absence great.' These two sentences tell us much about the life in service of a secretary, the life Harry Wotton enters in 1595.

By his own admission Essex is a man who puts himself 'in continual labour'. We recall the morning routine Harry reports, buttoned into his doublet by one pair of hands, barbered by another, eyes reading letters, ears hearing petitions, 'and many times all at once'. We imagine the later scene when 'Even now putting my foot into the stirrup' Essex first dashes off a dozen lines to the Privy Council. Reynolds notes his master's 'watchfulness', his 'indefatigable endeavours', never sparing 'the faculties of his body or mind'. He complains of Devereux's over-work and wishes 'it were less, for it maketh him the more hard to please in his service, as all business are accompanied with a kind of chagrin'. Harry also witnesses the earl's tetchiness. When his 'humours' grow 'tart' he'll 'break forth into certain sudden recesses', exiting 'to his own chamber; doors shut, visits forbidden'.

When another secretary (Michael Hickes) to another work-horse master (Lord Burghley) apologises for his inadequacies in office, he tells us more of what should equip a secretary by what he says he lacks: 'Help of nature I have none, and, to my great shame may I speak it, [I am] in many matters of course and ordinary experience very raw and ignorant. My hand is ... not very swift and my French neither good nor ready.' But perhaps 'dutiful affection', 'careful endeavour' and 'diligence' will compensate, love and application going far, it appears, in secretarial service. Another equally deferential letter sent to recommend an inexperienced youth to his first job lists the 'ordinary' credentials a secretary should hold: 'He hath the Latin tongue perfectly both to write and speak, understandeth the Italian and speaketh somewhat, writeth a convenient speedy hand meet for dispatch of such arrants and ordinary lettres as shall pass from your Honour'. But further, 'being of a staid and secret nature he will 'be as well able to serve your Honour's turn as any unexperienced man you can choose'.

When Thomas Wilson, a future secretary to Robert Cecil, mocks the 'mechanical dunce that cannot conceive his master's drifts and policies' and those 'base pen clerks' who 'do nothing but write as they are bidden', he's proposing a secretary's free scope to anticipate and represent his master's mind. Secretary of State Robert Cecil says the opposite. A secretary's pen is tied to his master's tongue. Cecil responds briskly to a complaint about how he, acting as the queen of England's 'mere' secretary, addressed a letter to Anna, queen of Scotland. He had no agency in the matter, he writes, for 'In my dealing with foreign Princes, my part is to stand dumb, till I be directed by my sovereign what to say or write': 'my writing' is 'only by her warrant'; and, as secretary, 'my heart is fixed upon one only object, beyond which it is blind to all other prospect'.

These comments tell us that the office Harry Wotton enters is not so much employment as a way of life, and like life, ambiguous, even contradictory in its expectations and performances. A secretary is a household servant; appointed and maintained by a master whose livery he wears. He's badged with his master's coat of arms, or sartorially inscribed, like the 'Servant of King Henry VIII' whose coat lapels are ornately embroidered 'HR' (Henricus Rex), painted by Hans Holbein the Elder. Serving Essex, Harry is a marked man, his master's property in the sense that that word is used in the theatre. Playhouse properties belong to performance, enable the action as necessary drudges that sometimes achieve spectacular prominence. So, too, the secretary. He has privileges but also duties far beyond the earl's ordinary servants, the lackeys who button and barber him. At all times (and this is saying something in a household whose master admits little leisure) attendance is necessary, absence is offence. The secretary must wait at a sickbed to take dictation or, booted and spurred, ride after his master to gather up the paper he's trailing behind him. The secretary needs to be a scrupulous reader of his master, to 'conceive his master's drifts and policies'. Sometimes mute. Sometimes vocal. Always ready. He must have Latin, should have French or Italian, and the ability to write a 'convenient speedy hand'. Beyond all else – and where certain skills are lacking this will compensate – he must be 'sincere and dutiful', must fix his 'heart … upon one only object', see himself as 'dumb' until 'directed', and his writing as the extension of his master's will, a kind of surrogacy. He must be secret.

Indeed, secrecy is written into his job title. For that is the first definition of a secretary, the 'keeper or conserver of the secrets unto him committed'. That's how Angel Day puts it in *The English Secretorie*, a 'how to' manual on 'the partes, place and office of a Secretorie', published in 1599, behind times for Harry entering Devereux's service. Latterly, however, it serves as a digest of the lived experience of men like Hickes, Cecil and Reynolds, echoing their language but also articulating thoughts that their secretarial discretion would never utter while at the same time publishing in black and white the uncompromising terms of office a secretary subscribes to when he enters Devereux's household. Reynolds would recognise Day's definition: a secretary is 'a servant' who 'belongs' to a 'superior' by whose 'absolute direction his actions of service are to be ordered and commanded'; one whose office 'requires' him 'to be always near and as ready as may be' for 'sudden' employment. But Day says more than Reynolds. After he notes that the secretary needs to balance forthrightness against presumption, 'to know and discern, how, where, when, what, and to whom he ought to speak, and when, and wherein, to be likewise silent', he goes further. The secretary must never fail to advise his master of evil coming his way. Equally, and we should pause over these phrases because we'll face them again, he must never fall into that 'vain presumption' of mastering his master, to 'lead' his 'thoughts in a string'.

Harry already fits Day's job description. He's 'well studied', 'especially in the Latin tongue'; has both 'a ripe and quick conceit, aptly to receive what on a sudden shall be to him delivered' and 'a sound and good memory' to 'retain' his daily charge. We might wonder how far he yet understands how entirely 'his office is an extension of his master's will' and that 'his pen' is 'not his own'. How successfully will he discipline himself to Devereux's service, to be, on the one hand, his master's ghostwriter, a 'zealous imitator' of the 'form and manner of writing' that Devereux 'is specially addicted' to; on the other, his mind reader, 'studious' of his master's 'intents' and 'effects'? Most challenging of all, how will this young man who's been making his own way across Europe for the past five years, presenting himself to the world with such lively self-conceit, school himself to the self-effacement required of the man who would be secretary? 'In the discharge' of his office, writes Day, the secretary is 'utterly to relinquish any affectation to his own doings' or 'private judgement', 'utterly sequestered from all private regard or affection of any thing sounding to his own appetite'. He's to be self-less, literally and metaphorically a 'cifer' to his master's 'great accompt'. (It's perhaps telling that among these secretaries only Temple is married, though Reynolds writes placatingly to a woman he's had no leisure to wed.) Simultaneously, however, the secretary must be utterly self-conscious, his master's physical and mental intimate, privy to his naked thoughts, even his naked body. In this relationship, the master, it turns out, is mightily dependent.

For the next five years Secretary Wotton will stand at Robert Devereux's elbow. But not alone. Cuffe will cover his left flank, his sinister side. Reynolds will watch his back. There will be jostling for position. Some sharp digs of elbows into ribs. Their rivalries will matter. Even more than the circle of aristocrats Essex gathers around him – Southampton, Rutland, Blount, Neville, the Percies, Danvers, Henry Howard – his secretaries are his familiars. In the archives that survive them all, their hands show up in Devereux's writing, putting his words onto paper but likewise reminding us how close these men are to the earl's daily affairs. Their familiarity will grow dangerous. Right now, though, Felipe II of Spain is up to his old tricks. Statesman Essex tugs off his toga and leaps into his armour. He and his secretaries have a world of business to manage.

7
Campaigning with Essex

Cadiz, 1596

1596. A year of lists. Lists of the queen's warships, commanders and crews. Lists of costs to furnish these ships 'in warlike manner' for five months at sea: '3500 saylors and gunners ... out of divers shires at 11 pence per man'; '500 soldiers at 5 pence per man'; 'rigging wages of 800 men for vj weeks'; 'sea store' (flags, sheet lead, compasses, running glasses, spikes and nails, bolts of Ipswich sail canvas). Lists of provisions 'out of every county' (wheat, porks, malt, bacon, peas, butter, cheese, salt, beer, cider, casks, cooperage). Lists of attendant costs reckoned in the thousands down to the last four pence ('baking of biscuit'; 'transportation of victuals to the ships'). Lists of expenditure for 'pasture for the feeding of certain oxen at Barton-upon-Humber in their drift towards London'; to '8 workmen' paid '15 days for salting the beef'; to 'sundry women for bearing ... the salt beef ... to the ships'. Lists of musters out of every county (soldiers, 2 pence/day, 'forborne to be paid until their return'). Lists of instructions for maintaining good order on ship ('Imprimis ... to serve God by using of Common Prayers every day twice except urgent cause enforce the contrary'). Lists of men knighted for service. Lists of hostages. Of plunder (turkey carpets; chains of gold; cork; lead; silk tapestries; printed books; church bells 'great and small'). Lists of interrogatories put to suspects accused of embezzling booty the queen expected landed in her treasury.

These lists: they're the staggering administrative witness to a mobilisation of England from the Humber to Plymouth that sees Robert Devereux preparing, leading then mopping up the dregs of an audacious campaign Charles Howard, the lord admiral, has been pushing for months: to defend the realm by attacking Spain in her home ports. In his own mind, Essex can't act fast enough. Rumours in January of a new Armada have bred 'incredible fears in most men' but haven't shaken the queen from her palsied caution. That shock comes in March (just when, on his twenty-eighth birthday, Harry Wotton reaches manhood, a coming-of-age we'll mark by dropping 'Harry' for 'Wotton'). Certain news that Spanish troops in a sneak attack have laid siege to Calais reaches Greenwich on the air: the queen's stupefied Privy Council hear the artillery battery across the channel. They scramble for levies. (Men coming out of church on Good Friday in London are press-ganged by the lord mayor – only to be dismissed the following day: the queen has changed her mind.) Elizabeth orders Essex to Dover to command the relief of Calais. Too late. The garrison falls in the second week of April, leaving Spain squatting on England's doorstep in possession of the most strategic port in the narrow seas and 'the chiefest hold in Christendom to annoy … her Majesty's kingdom'.

Across April Essex sends message after message from Dover to the Privy Council, to the lord admiral, to Robert Cecil: 'at 9 in the morning', 'at noon', 'at 2 after noon', 'at 3 in the afternoon', 'at 10 at night', 'at midnight'. 'I am', he writes, 'toiling and breaking both my body and mind to do her Majesty service'. He urges action: 'it is time for her Majesty to draw her sword, for her doing nothing and the enemy's being so undertaking' – that is, enterprising – 'strikes a terror into the people of these parts and I fear me as much in other quarters of the realm'. He scrawls across the backs of his letters instruction to the post riders, 'haste post haste for life', and sketches a little gallows, a sign to any illiterate rider to dig his spurs in. Almost without exception, Essex writes his own dispatches, but he regularly hands them to his secretary to fold, address, seal and add the gallows, thereafter signing 'Essex' below. So it's Secretary Wotton who addresses the letter of 13 April 'about 10 of the clock in the morning' telling Cecil 'We have heard this morning shooting about Calais'. It's Wotton who twelve hours later addresses to Lord Burghley the frantic appeal for 'small munitions … spades, pickaxes, shovels' from London, for without such humble 'necessaries', 'our hands' are 'bound behind us'. The following afternoon, 14 April, 'about .6. of the clock', Wotton's hand is on the passionate dispatch that tells Cecil Essex's bitterness. His honour – and honour, for Essex, defines his essential self – has been betrayed in England's failure to relieve Calais: 'I am so full as I know not what I write'; 'I protest before God I would redeem the infamy of it with many ounces of my blood if the bargain could be made'. Next morning, Wotton is privy to the message Essex sends Cecil assuring him that any man not licensed to the queen's service – like the stripling earl of Southampton – will be returned to Court: 'Thus you see', he concludes,

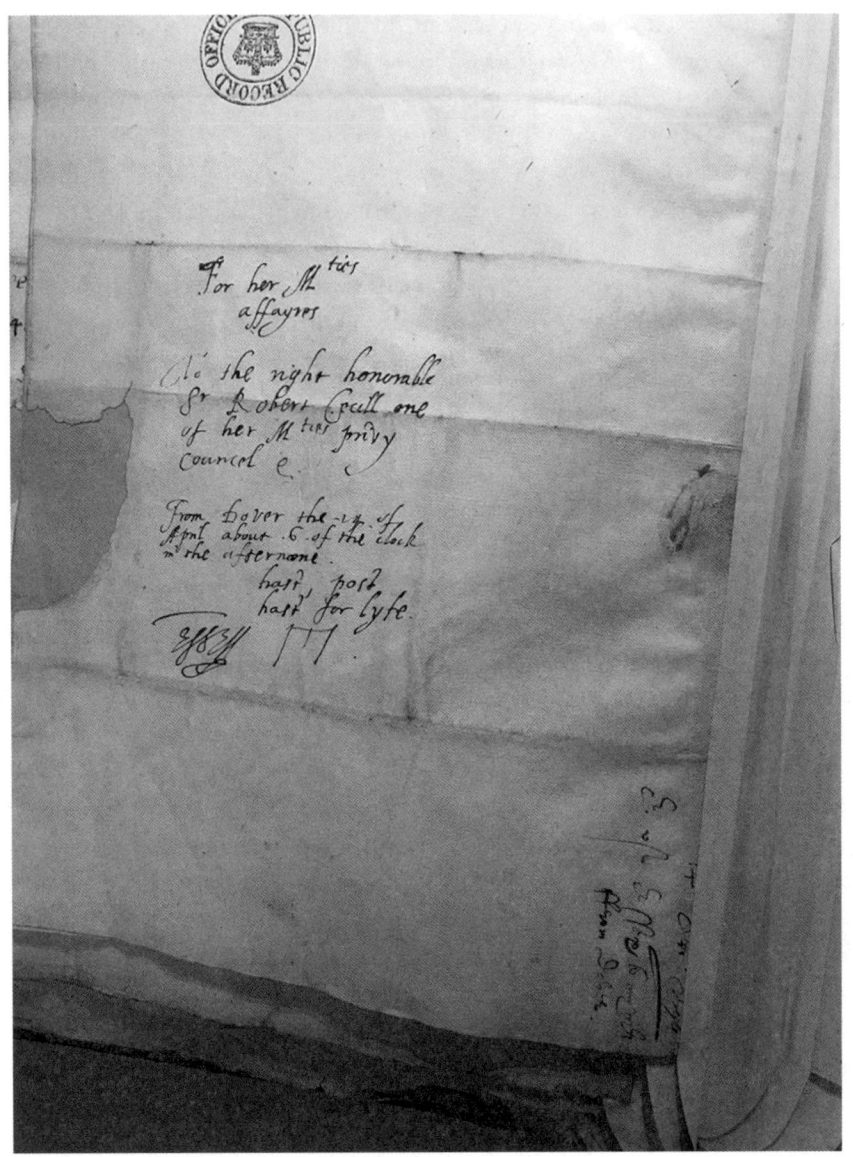

5   Addressing Essex's letter from Dover to Robert Cecil on 14 April 1596, Henry Wotton writes 'hast, post hast for lyfe' and draws a gallows to show the postmen its urgency.

with a comment that Wotton will have reason to turn over in his mind, 'I am resolved that obedience is better than sacrifice'.

Wotton's handwriting puts him alongside Essex at Dover. He attends at all hours, party to his master's moods and minds. (We remember Reynolds's remark: a secretary's attendance is necessary, his absence, offence.) Already he's observing the soul-corroding tension between obedience and sacrifice for a man like his master who's serving a mistress whose mind spins like a weathercock in a gale. A week ago, they'd obeyed orders to leave Dover and were past Canterbury when the message came that her mind was changed yet again – and they should return. The earl knows the queen's habits, knows a deep irony, that he can 'never do her service but against her will'. But his secretary, new to this relationship, might wonder how long before a man's resolved obedience simply wears itself out chomping at the bit – or would suicidally 'wish' itself 'in another world' where, Essex groans, it would 'not hear the complaints that through all Christendom will come upon us for losing such a place and in such a manner as this is like to be'.

Wotton's back-of-letter traces map his service, but they're scant, and apart from three important exceptions that we'll notice later – a letter, a witness statement, a scribal copy – they're all that survives of him this year. Still, they place him at the fraught centre of operations – where plenty of material from other sources fills out the sudden turn his pen-and-inkhorn life has taken. Young Harry of former days never stood on a war footing; never sailed aboard a fighting galleon. Certainly, he saw what a city looks like when war is finished with it: Geneva, four years earlier. He read accounts of the siege of Paris, and in Vienna, 'discorsi' on the art of war. That was theory. At Dover, 'The enemy's battery' that 'hath played all this forenoon with great fury' is real – and only thirty-one miles distant, across the water. Real, too, the 'terror' struck 'into the people of these parts'. Real the three thousand soldiers who march into the town ready to embark – just when news comes that Calais has fallen. Essex instantly regroups, redirecting the whole mobilisation to Plymouth, there to mass a fleet to sail on Spain. Across these hectic days, Secretary Wotton is learning soldiering. He's also observing the politics that frustrates it.

On 27 April, 'At Andover', Essex writes to Cecil 'at 4 in the morning'. At 8pm the same day he's at Honiton, a hundred miles on. The following day, he reaches Plymouth. His pace is punishing – no less for his secretary than his horse (whose name we do not know). He needs 'a day or two' to 'rest my brains and my bones' before 'writing anything of the state of our army', but within the week is 'busied in bringing all this chaos' around him 'to order'. The main body of the fleet sails into port with the lord admiral on 2 May. Two days later Thomas Howard, the vice-admiral, joins with further sails, but Walter Raleigh, in charge of the rear-guard victuallers and transports, is stuck in the Thames, trying to force press-ganged skippers to sail and 'dragging the mire from ale-house to ale-house' from Gravesend to London after 'runaway mariners'.

Set against all this industry is the possibility that it's wasted effort. From London, news comes from Edward Reynolds, the earl's watch-dog at Court, that 'the Queen is daily in change of humour' and using 'hard terms of my Lord's wilfulness' – as though the mobilisation were some vanity project (which is exactly how his enemies are framing it). The earl reaches the end of his tether. He writes to Cecil on 12 May:

> If I seem unpatient, think how many things concur to move my patience. Sir Walter Ralegh [sic], with the rest of our fleet, is not come ... Mr. Ashley [secretary at war] is not come with our instructions ... Mr. Dorrell [commissary general] is not [at] hand, who would help in bestowing the proportions of victual in every ship. ... I have not touched one penny of her Majesty's money, and have spent infinite sums of mine own ... I pray you, therefore, in friendship resolve me ... for except her Majesty had given out some words to shew her mislike or neglect of our going on, this slackness of all hands could not be used. I pay lendings to above 5,000 soldiers, I maintain all the poor captains and their officers. I have a little world eating upon me in my house ... yet I complain not of charge, but of want of direction and certainty in your resolutions.

While Essex chafes in a 'hellish torment', 'unpatient' that 'we are either commended unpossible things or held in irresolution', and stews over the dark suspicion that the queen's words of 'mislike' are behind 'this slackness of all hands', Wotton watches more and more ships anchor in Plymouth harbour, their masts a forest growing out of the sea. The queen's seventeen ships are joined by some seventy-six hired vessels, men-of-war of London, victuallers, coasters, flyboats. The largest, galleons like the earl's flagship, *Due Repulse*, are crewed by 340 mariners; the smallest, by under 30, in all, 6,424 sailors and gunners in 150 ships. While the fleet rides at anchor, 800 men scale their masts, rigging their sails. On land, 6,530 soldiers are training – among them, Wotton's brother. Some of these recruits, like James Wotton, are professionals; others are battle-hardened veterans of the Dutch wars. Most, though, are raw Feebles, Warts and Bullcalfs straight from the muster scene Shakespeare hasn't yet written in *Henry IV* – but so eager to 'grow perfect in all their orders and motions' that they 'march, advance, retire, file' until they're 'vying with the old soldiers' in expertise. One 'Feeble' among them is Wotton's old college friend John Donne.

Outside the city walls, the encampment sprawls across Plymouth Hoe. A population the size of Norwich, three times the size of Oxford, needs feeding, watering, billeting, clothing, arming. (A list of 'apparel' itemises 'shirts, doublets, Venetians [that is, breeches], stockings, bands, hats, shoes'.) The logistics are staggering, the pressure on Essex mind-boggling. He makes it his business to attend personally to every detail from marching in order to sanitation. (Dysentery, the bloody flux, wastes more men than combat.) 'I have my hands full', he writes in vast understatement. And: 'my helpers are a little amazed at me' – among the 'amazed', Secretary Wotton. Some of the hundreds, *thousands* of chits, dockets, orders, bills the mobilisation is producing are filling his hands, too.

When the order finally comes from London to sail, Wotton and Cuffe are both aboard *Due Repulse*. Cuffe sends a last hasty message to a friend, and Wotton writes Robert Cecil a begging letter. He apologises that 'in this buisy time of embarquinge' he is 'constreignd to be short' but promises to 'acknowledge' – whatever that means – Cecil's goodness towards him in the future. He adds parenthetically '(if I return)'. Indeed. Who knows the chances of returning? Still, the signature Harry Wotton splashes across the page swells with confidence.

Mariners, soldiers, cargo finally stived aboard, Essex goes 'from ship to ship to make our loiterers go out of the harbour'. The expedition finally sails on 3 June, but it's not until a week at sea that anyone but the commanders knows where it's heading. Cales. That is, Cadiz. A neat *quid pro quo*, Cales for Calais. But the reprisal Essex and the lord admiral intend will far out-go that recent humiliation. They aim to blockade the port, embay the Spanish gold fleet that will be resting there after its transatlantic crossing, take the citadel, and carry off unimaginable treasure, to give, says Essex, the king of Spain such 'a blow by sea' as to leave 'a thorn sticking in his foot' and deliver 'all Christendom from his fearful usurpation'.

'If I return'

For a land-lubber like Wotton, *Due Repulse* must feel safe as houses – except that she's a floating powder keg. She's a Second Rate galleon on her maiden voyage out of Deptford dockyard, designed and built by the greatest master shipwright of Tudor times, Matthew Baker. She's 105 feet long in the keel, 37 feet broad, 16 feet deep in the hold; a ship of 660 tons. She carries on her gun decks devastating fire power: three demi-cannon; two breach-loading cannon-perrier; thirteen culverin; fourteen demi-culverin; six saker; two portpiece; and two fowler: all of English manufacture. She sails with some nine hundred souls: a crew of three hundred mariners and forty gunners; 'powder boys' who, when the shooting starts, will dash between hold and gundeck to keep the gunners

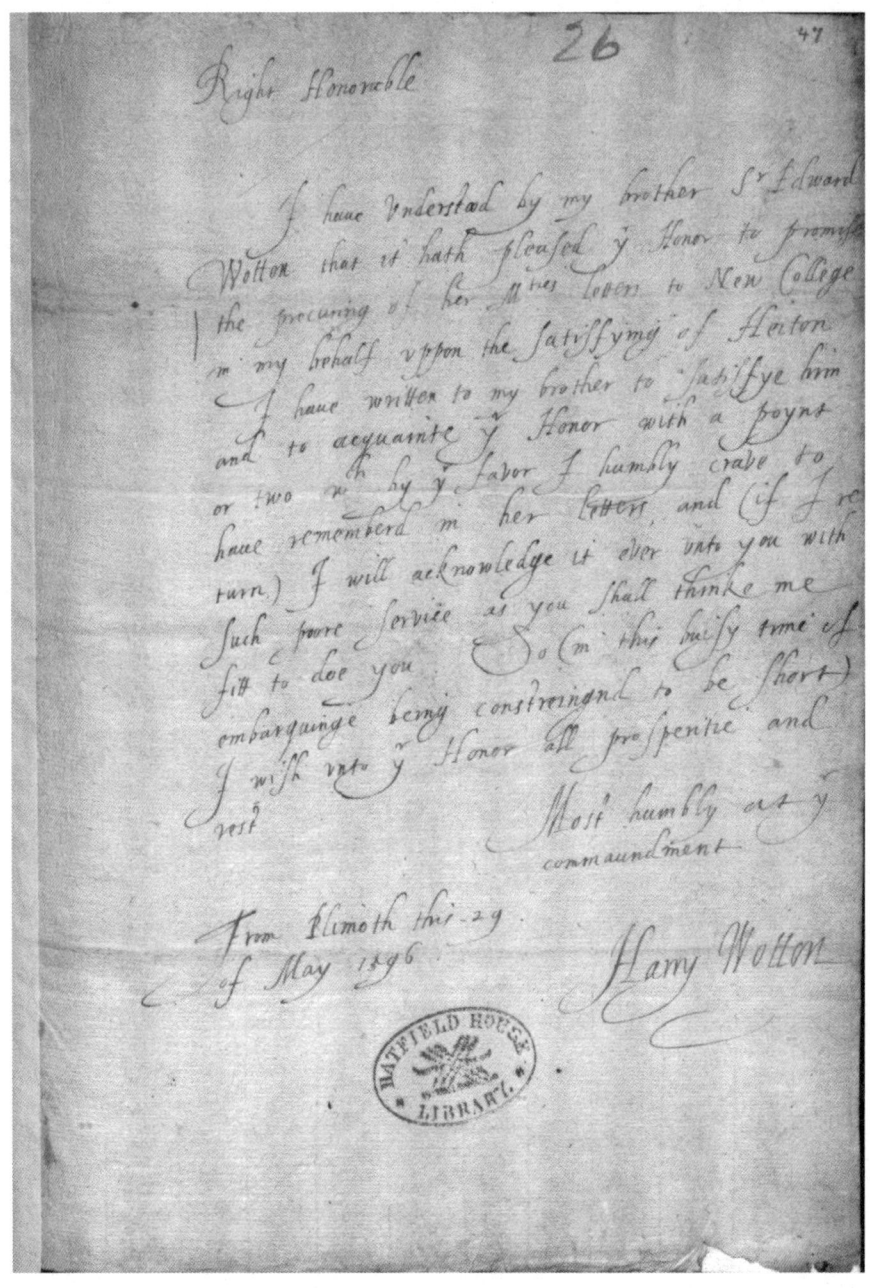

6 Writing to Robert Cecil from Plymouth 'in this buisy time of embarquinge' for Cadiz in May 1596, Wotton signs himself 'Harry'.

supplied; four hundred soldiers to fight ashore; and some thirty gentlemen volunteers attached to Essex to soak up his soldiership by example.

Veterans mock these volunteers as 'green-headed youths covered with feathers, gold and lace', mere 'ladies faces' pretending to 'fierce dragons' spleens'. But they're pouring much-needed cash into the adventure, serving without the queen's commission at their own expense and hazarding their lives to gain, as Essex puts it, 'honour and the learning of that art by whose violent arguments all the great questions of the world at this day are disputed'. What they expect in exchange is plunder – and that priceless prize, reputation. These volunteers ship their own servants.

The rest of *Due Repulse*'s human cargo is made up of Devereux's personal retinue: his bodyguard, preachers (four of them), surgeon; his lackeys, his secretaries and *their* lackeys. (Wotton himself is attended by a servant – noticed only because he's one of only two fatalities aboard *Due Repulse* at Cadiz.) Gentlemen at least have cabins; seamen and soldiers stow themselves where they may.

Nine hundred men. No room to swing a ship's cat. No bench to lie on, no stool to repose on, men crammed aboard like pilchards in a barrel. No one bothers to leave an account of conditions on *Due Repulse*, but if we sift out their exaggerations, satirical pamphlets by two Spaniards say something about what Wotton experiences shipboard. Conditions are Spartan. He's rationed 'water by the ounce, as in a pharmacy', there being 'nothing more desired' and 'less' in 'abundance, than water' on board. His daily bread is biscuit 'covered with a tapestry of cobwebs, black, worm eaten, rat eaten'. In fact, on *Due Repulse*, men eat democratically, 'in every mess alike', issued 'one £ of biscuit, one pottle of beer' in the morning 'and for every of their ij meales one £ of biscuit and one gallon of beer, and beef, pork, fish or butter or cheese'. To 'purge his belly', he (a gentleman) has to go to the common (yes, common) 'places of the forecastle' perched over the ship's gunwales where, 'sitting at his necessities', 'all men may so openly behold him' as if 'he sat banquetting at the table'. If Wotton dies he'll be spared the cost of a funeral: 'scarcely' shall he 'yield his spirit to God' than 'they shall hurl the body to the fishes'. (It goes without saying that human wastage is expected on the voyage; the miracle is that when the fleet anchors off Cadiz, not a single life on *Due Repulse* has been lost.)

The fleet sails under Essex's strict instructions. Embezzlement of vituals, munitions or powder is punishable 'upon pain of death by extreme torture'. Any who commit 'the sodomites sins' 'shall die for it, with extreme torture'. To avoid fire, no candles are to be carried without lanterns. The warning is apt. Fire is a real danger on any ship; catastrophic on a warship, and *Due Repulse* has only narrowly escaped it. Just three days out of Plymouth, fire is discovered in a volunteer's cabin 'by some negligence of his which might have much endangered us if God had not prevented it'. But God did: and only seamen on board who'd bartered their souls to the devil would doubt that God was sailing with them, for this fleet knows it's going about His business. Hence the order to serve God with common prayer twice daily.

What Wotton isn't prepared for is the constant din on deck, the groan of rope, the flap and whoosh of sail, the thunder of bare feet on wood, mariners cursing soldiers to get out of their way, the boatswain bellowing orders in a language as foreign as High Dutch that snaps sailors into action: 'steer to leeward, don't let her yaw'; 'hoist the topgallant; lower the fore-topsail'. Below, where he finds some privilege of place and comparative luxury, he's quartered within earshot of Essex, who occupies the ship's great cabin aft below the mizzen mast. That's where a pair of captured Spanish Franciscans will face interrogation, Essex 'lying on a couch of brocade, dressed in white satin'. (Really? Has Essex set this scene for propaganda purposes – or are the Spaniards lying?)

For the next three weeks the fleet sets a course south by east. Notes of 'occurrences' are recorded. On 5 June, the wind is 'hesitant'. The following day the *Mary Rose* breaks her main yard. A school of flying fish, to everyone's amazement, is encountered, their 'two large wings shaped of nature very cunningly ... like to our gentlewomen's Dutch fans'. The comet Tycho Brahe is tracking from his observatory in Sweden is sighted.

Then, twelve leagues off Cadiz, on 18 June an Irish ship meeting the fleet gives intelligence that, 'bruited in the army', 'every man skipped and leaped for joy' anticipating the 'sport' of certain combat. Twenty galleys and some sixty ships lie anchored in the outer bay of Cadiz, among them the flagship, one of the so-called 'apostle' ships, *San Felipe*, guarding the gold convoy. They first attempt a land attack, but when that fails the fleet commanders meet and push the lord admiral to signal attack by sea. Raleigh, rowing back to *Warspight*, shouts 'Entramos!' up to Essex as he crosses under his bow. On the deck of *Due Repulse* Essex throws his hat so high in the air that its feather carries it away on the wind. And four English galleons rush full-sail into the harbour.

Due Repulse stays back – the queen's command: she wants Essex out of shot. But as the fight grows hot, watching Francis Vere on *Rainbow* take the brunt of the Spanish battery, Essex ignores orders and 'upon a sudden & unlooked for of others' thrusts 'himself among the foremost into the main battle'. It continues for six hours. The action (witnessed from *Ark Royal*) is 'very terrible and most hideous ... by the continuall discharging of those roaring thundering great peeces, on all sides'. Onboard *Due Repulse* a witness recounts her throwing '350 great shot' at *San Felipe*, who, 'being bouged much' – her sides staved in – is forced to heel leeward. *Repulse*'s thirty-two gunners spend forty-eight barrels of gunpowder and fire something like four thousand round-shot in those hours. 'And so [it] continued doubtful till about one or two of the clocke in the afternoone: about which time the Philip began to yield and give over, her men that remained alive shifting for themselves as they were able, and swimming and running ashore with all the haste that they could'.

Somewhere in this mêlée, Wotton is living Dante's *Inferno*: stinking sulphur, blinding smoke, noise more deafening than all the howling demons in pandemonium. He sees flames roaring through *San Felipe*'s decks; Spanish soldiers 'tumbling into the sea … so thick as if coals had been poured out of a sack'; sailors clinging on to rope ends to avoid being burnt alive – until they drop off and drown. Later, boarding parties find the dead 'laid in heaps in the captains' cabins'. Miraculously, across the English fleet, not above '100 of our men' die in the assault.

Essex doesn't pause. Immediately, he takes the assault onto land, leading two thousand soldiers onto the beach along that tongue of land on whose rocky outcrop sits walled Cadiz. Half are sent east; Essex marches the rest – pikemen, arquebusiers, gentlemen volunteers, the earl's 'necessary gentlemen' – three miles west across 'dry deepe sliding sand' in scorching afternoon heat that turns their corselets into ovens. Tricked into an ambush, a contingent of Spanish horse turns tail and runs, clapping shut the city's gates behind them. Essex runs his men up close under the walls, and one of his captains finds an entry point by scaling a cleft in a rock 'where but one at once could enter, and if they had fallen, they had fallen very near 20 fathoms into the sea'. The captain starts handing men up and over, the first, one of the earl's, Essex making a stirrup with his own hands to hoist him. After that, men 'leap after them pesle mesle', swarming through the gap and the now-opened gates, up through the town, twisting along a maze of narrow passages fiercely defended by townspeople hurling down stones from their rooftops. Essex makes it to the city's centre with thirty men. Vere brings up his foot from another direction. Together, they clear the plaza and empty surrounding houses of resistance. Two hours after coming ashore, Essex and Vere win Cadiz. What the navy started at dawn the army finishes before sunset.

Whether Wotton is one of those necessary gentlemen who wade through the surf behind Essex or not, he surely witnesses the plundering of Cadiz that's the price of Spanish defeat. The English quarter in the town for two weeks.

An initial frenzy of random ransacking in the first twenty-four hours is shortly disciplined into orderly confiscation (not least by Essex appearing in doublet and hose among the looters in the night, threatening martial law). Lists are produced of the 'wealth of money, plate, gold and jewels ... furniture of household, of silk tapestry, cupboards of velvet' as, house by house, the town's wealthiest are assigned to the top brass for spoil; lists annotated with dry comments: 'every one went in and took what he found'; 'of all this, nothing was left for they brought it away all'. The humiliation of Cadiz is to be strictly mercenary. (Only the Dutch ignore this order. They want revenge also in blood, payback for Spain's wars in the Netherlands.) Upon pain of death, there's to be no slaughter, no woman 'insulted', all religious persons and houses to be respected. For the rest, whatever the English are minded to carry off in the killing heat of Cadiz is theirs. And they are mightily so minded.

Plunder, of course, is the return on investment the volunteers are counting on – and the common soldiers are risking their necks for. Over these days (which must strike some as a strange replay of the expedition's build-up in Plymouth), a constant train of goods trundles from the town to the shore onto barges rowed out to the fleet. Matthew Morgan dispatches gold chains, tapestries, lead, cork and fourteen church bells. Gelly Merrick sends away chests of sugar, casks of wine, burnt iron, brimstone, gold buttons, rings, chains and a box of books. Walter Raleigh makes off with Spanish plate; Thomas Howard, with 'divers of Spanish horses'. Only Essex, Coriolanus-like, refuses to pay his sword with a bribe.

His secretaries are likely standing by when he rebuffs a rich jewel sent by the marquis of Santa Cruz, telling the messenger that it's 'not his manner to receive gifts'; that, personally, he's 'not desirous of wars', being given 'rather to contemplation than action', 'naturally bookish'. That self representation may be artful, but the rhetoric isn't hollow. When Essex does accept a prize, on the return voyage, it's the contents of the bishop's library in Farol that he later donates to the shelves Thomas Bodley is currently filling in Oxford. ('Bookish': the word is a smokescreen that Wotton in future will slip behind whenever he has to apologise in Venice of busy-body meddling in affairs that shouldn't concern him. Surely it's lodged in his mind by his master.)

Not all Essex's household is so fastidious. His just-knighted steward, Merrick, for one. So where, we might wonder, does Wotton stand? Aloof with Essex? Pocketing trinkets? Sickened by the spoil that leaves three hundred of the city's thousand buildings trashed, its commerce a shambles, its miserable population turned out of doors to eat grass or starve? Or is he thrilled?

Other matters require Wotton's attention. On 23 June, Essex dictates to his secretary a proclamation ordering the streets cleansed and the dead buried. Four days later, the victors host a banquet, serving up the contents of the town's kitchens, pantries, storerooms, stalls and hen coops. What bliss, after weeks of navy biscuit and salt pork: fresh food, sweet water without stint – to say nothing of Spanish wine. Afterwards, Essex knights sixty-four men, among them, Wotton's brother, James. When they hear of it in London, the queen's carpet generals berate his 'extravagance', but Essex knows that honour is worth more than plunder. Treasure slips through fingers. A knighthood confers nobility for life. Those so endowed spur emulation in others, for they stand as a 'virtuous pattern of men of most note and accompt'.

Over the following days the commanders debate what to do next. Wotton stands by while Essex and Vere argue for further action. They're overruled. The fleet is ordered for home. On 1 July a general muster taken at the earl's command finds, miraculously, that not so many as three hundred Englishmen are missing. Neither has a single English ship been lost.

Three days later, though, the mood sours. Ready to sail, English patience with Spanish hostages who have promised ransom but failed to deliver runs out. Essex orders these 'faithless people' thrown onto ships for transportation into England, and in reprisal, Cadiz laid waste from custom house to pig sty, down to the slaughter of the plucky little mules the English have grown so attached to. No doubt this pitiless order to leave Cadiz 'baking and smoking' comes also as payback for Spanish perfidy in the harbour. Ignoring his superiors' command to save the Spanish fleet by ransoming it to the English, the admiral has ordered it torched. It burns three full days and nights. Three Levanters laden from Italy. Three treasure frigates. Two 'apostles' (including *San Felipe*), two grain-filled Lisbon galleons, thirty-four ships stowed with luxury goods for Spain's colonial market – and the rest, in all, 157 ships. The stupendous treasure the English might have taken home lies in ooze on the bottom of the bay. Or billows in smoke across its water. Thus, by a kind of 'noble stupidity', as a modern historian calls it, the Spanish disappoint the English – but entirely wreck their American trade.

If Harry Wotton is standing on deck when *Due Repulse* sails out of Cadiz on 6 July, he sees plumes rising from the still-smouldering hulls of what once were ships drifting into the thick clouds of smoke pouring into the sky above what was once a town. West and north-northeast, though, where England lies, the skies look clear.

'I pray that you will plead for me till my return'

Wotton's masterclass in the art and craft of war isn't over. Cadiz is England's greatest military triumph since 1588, but already, the backlash is taking aim. Essex anticipates that by 'report or misconceit' he'll be 'brought into Her Majesty's displeasure' and so sends a messenger ahead to 'plead for me till my return', with a letter to Burghley – dated a week before sails are ever raised for home on *Due Repulse*. Ink is as much a defensive weapon in war as gunpowder, and Essex has kept his secretaries busy building a barricade of words on paper, recording the voyage, writing up lists for audit, drafting dispatches like this politick letter that try to steal a march on calumny.

Essex isn't wrong. The queen is apoplectic. Where, she demands, is her profit? She appoints commissioners to investigate where all the booty has gone. Dozens off the voyage are interrogated. While she haggles like some Cheapside fishwife over merchandise, Essex, disembarking, discovers that the Privy Council has suppressed the 'True Relation' of Cadiz he sent ahead, so instead (more secretarial scribing) he writes a highminded defence of the expedition, answering point by point his detractors' accusations – forcing them to draw in their horns, not so much worms as snails.

The year ends as it begins, with lists. Lists of interrogatories put to deponents (including Wotton, required to testify in a corruption case). By a kind of terrible reverse alchemy, the golden opinion Essex chased sailing for Cadiz, his secretary in tow, is reduced to dross under the weight of detraction's iron tongue. Handy-dandy, though, opinion will shortly change – with the queen's mind.

But how long will *that* mind last? On some bookish evening before the next set of 'alarums and excursions' thrusts them into action, the earl (let's imagine) sits with his secretary, combing fingers through the full beard he's grown on campaign and hasn't shaved since. (From now on, he'll be recognised in public, private and portraits by the 'face of Cadiz'. On his secretary's chin, too, a new beard sprouts, somewhat weedy. But a tribute.) They replay the past months and rethink the letter the earl sent his sovereign back in May from Plymouth. They'd arrived there only days earlier, via the Court where queen and subject had wrangled. Essex wrote first to Cecil, but not immediately to the queen. Perhaps he was cooling down. What he eventually sent Her Majesty was anguished, bitter:

Most deere and most Excellent Soueraigne.

Of such things as doe belonge vnto owre charge my L. Admirall and I haue ioyntly written to my L. Treserer. This is only to protest vnto y' M:tie that the pvnt of y' vnkind dealing (If I may presume to vse that phrase) the verie day of my departure doth sticke very deeply in my verie hart and soule. And yeat nether it, nor the desperat estate I am in if by this iorny I doe not recover my self can make me so throwne downe but that I goe to this service with comfort and confidence. Perhaps it had been too much for me to goe with this force by w:ch I knowe we can doe y' M:tie exceeding great service, and to haue parted with words of encouragement from y' M:tie. but howsoever it pleaseth you to pu nish me at my going oute I knowe y' iust and royall hart will right me at my returne and then I will bury my sorrowes in the ioy I shall receaue. More my confused and troubled thoughts can not say but that as I would strive to doe as much as any man to serve and please y' M:tie, so I knowe I wish more high contentment and perfect ioys then all the harts or imaginations in the world can comprehend. from

y' Ma:ties

humblest and most
affectionat servaunt

Plimoth this 7. of
May.

7 A copy of the earl of Essex's bitter letter to Queen Elizabeth from Plymouth, 7 May 1596, written out in Wotton's hand.

Most deere and most Excellent Soveraigne

Of such things as doe belong vnto owre charge my L. Admiral and I haue iointly written to my L. Tresorer. This is only to protest vnto y^r M^{tie} that the print of y^r vnkind dealing (If I may presume to vse that phrase) the verie day of my departure doth stick very deeply in my verie hart and soule: And yeat nether It nor the desperat estate I am in if by this iorney I doe not recover my self can make me so throwne downe but that I goe to this service with comfort and confidence.

Perhaps it had been too much for me to goe with this force by wh^{ch} I knowe we can doe y^r M^{tie} exceeding great service, and to haue parted with words of encouragement from y^r M^{tie}. But howsoever it pleaseth you to punish me at my going oute I knowe y^r iust and royall hart will ryght me at my returne and then I will bury my sorrowes in the ioy I shall receaue. More my confused and troubled thought can not say but that as I would strive to doe as much as any man to serve and please y^r M^{tie} so I knowe I wish more high contentment and perfect ioys then all the harts or imaginations in the world can comprehend from

                               Y^r Maties
                               humblest and most
                               affectionat servaunt
                               Plimoth this .7. of May

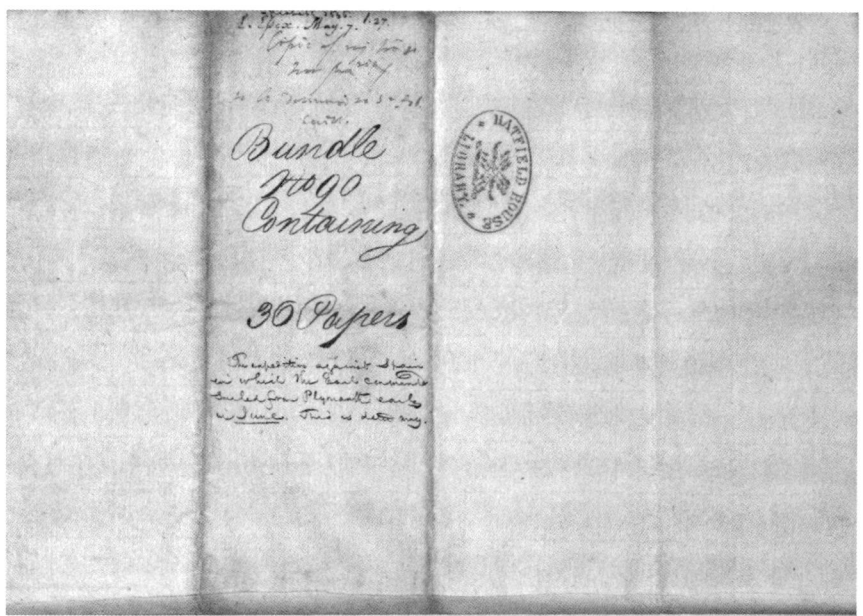

8   The endorsement in Essex's hand on the verso of the 7 May letter, 'Copie of my le*tt*re to her Ma*jes*^{tie} to be deliuered to Sr Rob. Cecill', shows that the earl intended his personal letter to the queen to be read more widely.

The original letter to the queen was undoubtedly in Devereux's hand. It's lost. But its contents survive, in a single scribal copy filed among Robert Cecil's papers, endorsed on the verso by Essex himself as a 'copie of my le*tt*re to her Majesty; to be delivered to Robt. Cecil', evidence, indisputably, that Essex wanted his 'protest' and the queen's 'unkind dealing' known to the Privy Council – and beyond. A pre-emptive defence, perhaps, against future report or misconceit? The letter's 'confused and troubled thought' must have made ominous reading for the secretary who copied it – whose handwriting we recognise. It's Henry Wotton's. Once again, he's privy to his master's 'hart and soule', to the 'desperat' 'sorrowes' of serving a queen who demands 'great service' but refuses 'words of encouragement'. A prediction of things to come? Within months he and his master are embarking on another journey, one that will cost Essex his life and Wotton his future in England.

8
This unsettled kingdom

Ireland, 1599

27 March 1599. What sounds like a premonition in that letter from Plymouth on 7 May 1596 returns as an echo three years later. Meanwhile, on this spring afternoon, Wotton and two fellow secretaries, Cuffe and Temple, are riding out with Essex from Seething Lane through the centre of London. 'Divers noblemen and many others' follow. 'For more than four miles space', the highways are 'pressed exceedingly' with people 'crying out, saying "God bless your Lordship"'. Essex himself seems 'sombre, plainly attired'. He has spent the past several months obstinately hammering out the terms of the commission appointing him lord lieutenant of Ireland, terms that give him the right of return to England at will, to appoint his own 'instruments', to confer knighthoods (for exceptional service only) and that give him instructions 'to bend his whole force against Tir-Oen, the arch-rebel'.

Since Cadiz, Wotton might reflect, his master has been thwarted at Court and stymied in action. The Azores voyage of August 1597, a gamble to recoup Spanish treasure denied them at Cadiz, was a disaster, wrecked by storms and sheer bad luck. Wotton sailed with Essex and endured four days of 'terrible tempest', 'black darkness' with the kind of 'dreadful roaring' that may be thunder or waves swallowing the topmast – or caulk splintering as a ship splits. Later, the few patched-up vessels that sailed on missed the Spanish silver fleet by three hours. Over the following months arguments in the Privy Council over proposals for peace with Spain – *togati* v. *militia* – grew furious, Burghley once shoving in Devereux's face his Psalter turned to 55:23, 'Men of blood shall not live out half their days'. Maligned as a warmonger Essex circulated an 'Apology', ostensibly a private letter, therefore deniable. It struck his standard pose of bookishness but unapologetically justifed war with Spain.

In June 1598 a 'sharp dissension' with the queen over, ironically, who should be appointed deputy to Ireland provoked Essex to an act of insupportable insolence. He turned his back on her. 'Not enduring such behaviour', she 'gave him a box on the ear', telling him to be 'gone and be hang'd' whereupon Essex, 'stung to madness clapped his hand upon his sword'. Only the lord admiral's intervention saved him from outright treason. He vanished to his country estate, replying to appeals from Lord Keeper Thomas Egerton to submit himself and return to Court with a series of rhetoricals that challenged the very basis of absolute monarchy: 'Cannot Princes err? Can they not wrong their subjects?' (Questions apparently borrowed from a dissertation Secretary Wotton wrote as a student on his travels abroad, perhaps the 'simple discourse' he secretly sent Zouche from Vienna in 1592, probing *The State of Christendom*. It had remained unpublished – for good reason.)

Since then, events have overtaken persons. Lord Burghley died in August. In September, so did Felipe II of Spain, and from Ireland came news of the total rout of Sir Henry Bagnall's forces sent to relieve the starving English garrison at Blackwater. 'Never since the time they first set foot in Ireland' had England, said one witness, 'received a greater overthrow'. Bagnall, thirteen stout captains, fifteen hundred common soldiers: all slain. Talk of peace with Spain shuts down. Directions for 'desperate' Ireland are catapulted to the top of the agenda. Clearly, Elizabeth needed her *militia*. 'Essex or none' is the cry.

They have that call in mind – Wotton, Cuffe and Temple – as they ride north that March afternoon to embark for Dublin from Chester. Sixteen thousand foot, thirteen hundred horse and 'treasure' to supply them, the largest army ever sent to Ireland, is already shipped. It's an indication of how much work he sees ahead that Essex needs all three out-rider secretaries. Reynolds, as usual, remains at Court. What else are they thinking, sober Temple, waspish Cuffe, witty Wotton? They've been intimate with every beat of Devereux's progress across the past two years. Their hands will appear all over his Irish dispatches, either taking dictation, addressing Essex's letters or making multiple copies of originals for distribution.

Now, just four days out of London, Essex writes to the Privy Council of obstacles the queen is planting in his way, obstacles that mean he's 'like to be a martyr for her'. He notes her niggardly grace and how it spoils his chances: 'if I have not inward comfort, and outward demonstration of Her Majesty's favour, I am defeated in England'. Shades of May 1596. Further, he writes before he's even left English soil that 'it is not Tyrone and the Irish rebellion that amazeth me, but to see myself sent on such an errand, at such a time, with so little comfort or ability from the Court'. How different this depressive sounds from the audacious spirit that set out for Cadiz intent on delivering 'all Christendom' from Spain's 'fearful usurpation'. No claims here for bold victory. Rather: 'What my body and mind will suffice to, I will by God's grace discharge with industry and faith'. But neither 'a rheumatick body' – we remember Essex chronically bedridden with ague – in 'a moist, rotten country', nor 'a sad' – that is, melancholic – 'mind' promise 'vigour' in a 'discomfortable voyage'. Later, dispatches reaching him from Dublin detailing the 'misery of the army' in Ireland force him – before he's embarked – to call for more soldiers. He writes to London as if walking blindfold towards a cliff: 'I had a natural antipathy against this service, because I foresaw these necessities, and knew how unpleasing they would be, not only to me, the pro-pounder, but much more to Her Majesty, the hearer of them'. Yet Secretary Wotton feels no such misgivings – and notices no cliff edge.

Rather, he feels some of his old master revive when, impatient of the 'contrariety of winds, and extreme foggy and misty weather' stalling embarkation from Chester, Essex instructs the ships' pilots 'to ride it out alongst the coast' while he, with Wotton, takes horse to gallop overnight across the towering summit of Penman Mawr, 1,500 feet above the sea. Finally sailing out of Beaumaris, the fleet fights storms for two days across a moonless Irish sea. One ship is lost with all hands, including the earl of Kildare. Two ships stowed with 'all the Queen's treasure' narrowly miss stemming each other: if they'd hit, and the gold gone to the bottom of the sea, 'we had all sunk', writes Wotton. Another ship, with Temple aboard, is eight miles short of Dublin at midnight when it strikes a rock. Essex sets off to the rescue, but 'in hasting to reach [those] who were like to have been overwhelmed' his ship dashes 'several times upon another rock'. By a miracle, the vessel clears and Essex saves 'us who were in the other boat', and just in time, for it 'turned featly upon its side before we were free from it'.

What they encounter on shore in the chill dawn of 14 April makes a grim joke of their survival. A 'public state distracted and broken in all parts'. The rebels 'even at the gates of Dublin'. A treasury in chaos – exacerbated by the colonial treasurer's death the night of Essex's arrival. An army near mutiny, who, unpaid and marching 'barefoot and barelegged', 'fall dead ... with very poverty and want of victuals'. Corruption rife. Supplies pilfered. Munitions engrossed – then handed over to rebels by 'turn-again' Irish captains double-dealing the English army. Fraudulent muster rolls, such that the queen is paying 'shadows not men' – some four thousand of them. The army from England fresh but undisciplined, a ragtag neither battle-ready nor battle-worthy, and no

9 Writing to his fellow secretary Edward Reynolds from Dublin on 19 April 1599, Wotton observes 'All things … in a good trayne' now that 'owre Lord and Master' – Essex – has taken the 'swaye of this vnsetled Kingdome into his hand'. And he predicts an 'end' of 'thease warrs' 'by treaty'.

time for training. Leaky intelligence, nay, intelligence that reaches the enemy as though gushing down a conduit. Rebel forces seriously underestimated, both in numbers (20,000) and quality (not Ulster 'roughs' and 'cowherds' but a smart guerilla force trained unwittingly by the English themselves under Tyrone's command during various of his regular 'submissions' to the Crown).

Worst of all, a colonial Privy Council in Dublin that's dead set against the new lord lieutenant's instructions. On 15 April Wotton can't have dried out from his drenching in the Irish sea when he's writing upbeat but sober to his 'honestest frend and fellow' Reynolds of 'This noble and worthy gentleman, owre Lord and Master' taking 'the sworde and sway of this vnsetled kingdome' in Dublin Cathedral; of 'things ... in a good trayne'; of 'resolutions and counsayle'. He doesn't say the counsel is bleak. But it is. Essex reports to London on 28 April. Men on the ground have detailed the 'impossibilities' of proceeding directly against Tyrone. Essex – shades of Cadiz – listens to these fainthearts and, though 'much discontented that he may not begin in Ulster', as the queen has commanded, agrees to march south, into rebellion's soft underbelly, to secure Leinster and the English Pale for England.

Plastering a gaping wound

It must have been more than fainthearted arguments about fodder, carriage-horses and the insanity of trying to plant a garrison on Tyrone's flank at Lough Foyle before summer brought longer days and better weather that persuaded Essex to march south. That 'more' is what he has himself realised. That he's on a hiding to nothing. That he's come to Ireland to stick a 'plaster' on a gaping 'wound' that 'it doth no more than cover'. He's shaken to his boots when he has the queen's proclamation, stating that Ireland is to be reduced to obedience, read out, and not a single rebel submits. Worse, keeping his alarmed 'free censure' of the English in Ireland under wraps, he confides secretly in his own hand to London that the loyalty *of the loyalists* can't be counted on: 'The same man who will draw a draught, or be a faithful guide against one rebel, will be a spy or an intelligencer for another'.

That's astonishing. The man who directs a secretariat that stretches an intelligence network across Europe, the man who hammers 'Look about you' into his agents' heads: this man appears to know nothing of the true condition of Ireland. Hasn't he read Edmund Spenser's 'View of the Present State of Ireland' (1596)? He owns a copy, was Spenser's intimate – and paid his funeral expenses in London just two months back. Or is the 'View', a blunt diagnosis of Ireland's 'disease' written by an ex-pat poet living on a once-Irish estate seized by the English, simply unpalatable? Spenser sees Ireland sick from cross-infection. The 'new English' (planters like himself sent to colonise the island) are contaminated. They've mixed with descendants of the original Anglo-Norman planters (now a generation of cross-bred mongrels). They've been exposed to the natives, 'wild Irish' (brutish, lawless, unhoused nomads who wear 'glybbs' to cover their 'thievish countenance' and mantels, their only property, to cover their nakedness). Spenser's cure: 'Great force must be the instrument, but famine must be the mean; for, till Ireland be famished, it cannot be subdued'.

Such craven brutality hardly appeals to the chivalric hero of Cadiz, though he will soon learn that the rebels pursue the same brutal agenda against the foreign land-grabbers, burning their seized castles, scorching their stolen earth, confident the English will 'never prevail' against Ireland's 'four powerful Captains': 'Captain Travel, Captain Hunger, Captain Sickness, Captain Cold'. Yet another captain, one Thomas Reade, advises Essex as 'a mere stranger unto the country of Ireland', not to expect 'Cales' in Ulster nor 'think to find a gallant enemy, which will meet him in the field'. No, as Essex will shortly discover first-hand, Tyrone's 'manner of fight will be by skirmishes in passes, bogs, woods, fords', the rebels holding it 'no dishonour to run away'. For their 'best security is their feet'.

Essex in Ireland is doomed. And Gelly Merrick sounds as though he's whistling in the dark on 7 May when he writes to Reynolds of Essex heading for Leinster, 'We speed here highly and now go a journey which please God, will end the wars for that part'. (It won't. The rebel tides simply surge in behind the English advances, erasing their tracks.) Temple, privy to his master's dispatches, writes Reynolds more warily. Officially, the expedition south aims to 'gather intelligence the better to direct his greater and subsequent expedition' into Ulster. Privately, what it 'will effect, I know not. We hope the best, and you are like to hear the worst.' Left behind to manage communications from Dublin – Cuffe and Wotton ride with Essex – Temple gives us a glance into the paper office he's running, a 'scribbling cabin' staffed by 'poor scribes tired out with an infinity of several services'.

Every dispatch from London demands results. Every dispatch to London demands more: men, money, horses, swords, armour. (Not clothing. The English stuff is useless. Boots cobbled in Northampton dissolve in Irish bogs. The army, Essex decides, should dress Irish, in brogues and mantles. Spenser turns in his grave.) Correspondence overlaps. New 'running posts' by way of Holyhead and Bristol are set up, but Essex also employs men to carry dispatches direct. Even so, it takes letters ten days or more to reach London. Thus, London learns mid-June of Essex's terrific achievement in late May far south in Tipperary, capturing the rebel stronghold Cahir Castle – reputedly impregnable, squatting like a stone toad on a rocky island in the middle of the river Suir. Back in Dublin on 2 July after what was victualled for a two-week recce stretched into an eight-week slog through torrential rain, across bogs that force troops to march defile, easy pickings for snipers or for the sumps that suck them under if they stray off the path.

Exhausted by continual toil, his body sick and his brains, he says, 'distempered', Essex receives in early August the queen's response to Cahir, a letter dated 19 July. How does Wotton react, watching Essex read the scorn she pours on his triumph, calling Cahir merely 'an Irish hold' taken 'from a rabble of rogues', nothing more than a distraction? He's heard the queen's communiques before: arch, stiff, querulous, sarcastic. But nothing like this one, acid-penned. How is it, she wonders, that the 'base bush kern' Tyrone is 'accounted so famous a rebel, as to be a person against whom so many thousands of foot and horse, besides the force of all the nobility of that kingdom, must be thought too little to be employed?'

How different things look on the ground. 'We have victualled forts', shrills one exasperated volunteer, 'we have taken castles, we have set houses on fire, we have placed garrisons and have made many knights, and yet you in England say we have done nothing but gone a progress', as if the foot-rotting, soul-destroying Irish campaign were nothing more than the queen's annual summer jolly, traipsing around her kingdom from one great house to the next. As for Elizabeth's fixation on Tyrone, the volunteer pours scorn on it: 'In England there is no rebels spoken of but Terron, but he is like a tree that to one body hath many branches which is spread over all Ireland, for there are some that march among us that, where they find opportunity, will as soon cut our throats as the rebels that fight against us'.

The queen orders Essex to Ulster. Meanwhile, her Privy Council receives on the 28th his dispatch of 15 July reporting the impossibility of attempting Ulster before 'the end of harvest' – and requesting two thousand more men.

That letter provokes a bombshell. On 30 July Elizabeth reiterates her direct command to march north – to hell with the harvest – then adds the stinger. Because 'we know that on your continuance there doth now depend the order and conduct of this important affair, and by your return suddenly (till the northern action be tried), many and great confusions may follow', she revokes Essex's 'license' – now termed 'provisionally given' – 'whereby you have liberty to return' to England. She repeats: 'we do charge you not to come out of that kingdom, by virtue of any former license whatsoever'.

Essex's thoughts have for some time sounded suicidal – thoughts recorded in dispatches by his secretaries who, grimly, know his mind. In June, he longed 'honestly and zealously' to 'end a wearisome life'. In July, cared 'not for what will happen to myself, for if a kerne kill me not, sickness will'. In August, reporting a string of disasters, defections, desertions, revolts, betrayals, a rout at Wicklow, the ambush of Henry Clifford's army that left Clifford, twenty-two 'men of note' and five hundred foot slain or wounded, he despairs: 'if I did not bear these scorns of fortune and torture of mind more for Her Majesty's service and honour than for any pleasure I take in the world, I should quickly find a fair way to free myself'. Browbeaten, bullied, ordered to impossibilities, Essex finally takes horse for Ulster on 28 August, 'even now putting my foot into the stirrup'. With him go the eighteen colonels who sent the queen a 'protestation against the journey to the north' in July – getting back a reply to rip the hide off a rhinocerous. With him goes an army outnumbered by Tyrone's 2:1. And Henry Wotton.

'Times ... bad and humours surly'

Three weeks earlier Cuffe had written to Reynolds of being 'sometimes threatened by his Lordship to be sent into England, there to argue and apologise for his virtue and true worth against those who so maliciously and sycophant-like detract from his honourable and noble endeavours'. Cuffe has no stomach for the journey: 'the times are so bad and the humours surly with you there'. Still, his loyalty is unshaken. He'd 'rather lose with' Essex 'than gain with his opposites'. (We note, however, what's anticipated in that word 'lose'.) Now in late August, he's finally sent to London to hand-deliver Essex's account of his 'negotiations' – a nicely bland term – 'with the rebels in these parts', some two days' march short of Ulster, including a long list of McDonoghs, Kavanaghs, McRorys, who have sent in the submission to the Crown. Robert Cecil endorses the dispatch for the queen's eyes, 'This is worth your reading'.

On 4 September Essex writes to his council in Dublin from Armagh with 'no news but that yesterday Tyrone and I looked one upon another from two hills'. Over the next three days the armies play Granny's Footsteps. The rebel won't be drawn to fight. Instead, Tyrone sends messages requesting a parley. Essex meets him on 7 September at Bellaclynthe, Tyrone riding his horse belly-deep into the ford while Essex keeps the hard ground. The generals talk 'near half an hour together'. What is said? Does this elder statesman of Irish independence – no bush kerne as the sneering English will have him, but a deep-chested, full-bearded man of impressive military countenance – remind the Englishman that he was sometime raised in Essex's father's household? Does he offer blandishments or, instead, *real politique*? (Not just his foot soldiers but his cavalry spread across the hillside behind him outnumbers Essex's 2:1.) What does Wotton make of a scene he sees but can't hear, observing Tyrone taking 'off his hat', the universal sign in civilised Europe of male-to-male respect, doing 'his duty unto his Lordship with very humble ceremony'? Wotton knows what he knows of Tyrone from dispatches. He knows what he knows of Ireland by inherited prejudice. And he knows of the Irish what he makes of what he's observed, that 'there is almost nothing in this country but is either savage or wanton'.

From his English supremacist point of view, he harbours few illusions about the mission Essex assigns him the following day: he is to attend Tyrone and conclude a truce. The document Wotton presents appears written in advance, four articles so perfunctory they seem copied from a diplomatic pattern-book. Tyrone signs his name in chicken scratches. But the authority is undeniable: 'Articles agreed vppon for a cessation of Armes between the Lord Liuetenant [sic] of Ireland and the Earle of Tirone on the .8.th of September 1599 in the old stile'. That 'old stile' is a giveaway. Only someone who'd travelled on the continent would think to include it. And the handwriting at the top of this document is unmistakable. It's Wotton's.

So with the ink on this unprepossessing paper hardly dry, it's over. The northern campaign monstered in so many imaginations ends after only eleven days with the sounds of horses' hooves receding in opposite directions.

London won't know of these developments until 17 September (and then, the dispatch won't include the crucial detail that a treaty has been signed, only that a six-week cessation of military action has been agreed). Three days earlier the queen answered 'such letters as we have received' hand-delivered 'by Mr. Cuff' with a series of characteristically scathing rhetoricals. Why hadn't Essex taken Tyrone? 'If sickness of the army be the reason, why was there not action undertaken when the army was in better state? If winter's approach, why were the summer's months of July and August lost? If the spring were too soon, and the summer that followed otherwise spent ... then surely we must conclude that none of the four quarters of the year will be in season for Tyrone's prosecution.' Now, 'prosecution' is done, but she's still not satisfied. From Nonsuch on 17 September she drily notes the 'quick end' that's been made 'to a slow proceeding'. She 'marvel[s]' that Essex held 'private conference' with Tyrone and

10 The title heading these 'Articles agreed vppon for a cessation of Armes' is written in Wotton's hand. 'Hughe Tirone' signs the document.

wonders at a dispatch 'so sparing in report that we cannot tell, but by divination what to think may be the issue of these proceedings'. Her sarcasm is crushing; her instruction, unequivocal: 'Pass not your word' for Tyrone's 'pardon, nor make any absolute contract for his conditions, till you do particularly advertise us by writing, and receive our pleasure hereafter for your further warrant and authority'.

Can she have missed it? The dispatch reporting the Ulster expedition clearly states that the parley concluded a cessation of arms for six weeks. And anyway, why this sudden mystification of treaties? Elizabeth's state papers, domestic and Irish, are littered with (failed) Ulster treaties. Even now, anticipating that yet another treaty with Tyrone will be brokered, Robert Cecil is searching his files of 'memorials' for copies of previous treaties that Essex might want to use as templates. Moreover, from the outset, it was rumoured that the likely outcome of England's latest Irish adventure would be a treaty, Wotton in Dublin in April opining to Reynolds, 'Of thease warrs in general I willbe bold to say this, that if they end by treaty, the Earle of Tirone must be very humble'. Perhaps on 8 September Wotton witnessed Tyrone humble.

As for the queen's letter of 17 September, which most historians assume is the final goad in the flank that spurs Essex into the headstrong action he takes a week later, can it even have been delivered by that date? Or is the last straw for Essex the letter from her dated three days earlier, 14 September, that has just reached Dublin, couriered from London by Cuffe – together with Cuffe's verbal report of the political temperature in London that sufficiently confirms the earl's mutterings about 'the malice and practice' of enemies in England who strike 'wound upon wound' on his 'unarmed back'? Does Cuffe urge what looks like the earl's impetuous, nay, insane, or perhaps overweening decision to defy the queen and leave Ireland to deputies while he posts to London to represent himself in person to his sovereign? Even now is he putting foot into stirrup? He and the queen are both shrewd readers and writers of texts. She just a month ago cited back to Essex something he'd put in an earlier dispatch, opaquely referring to it as 'your ominous parenthesis'. Now, has bookish Essex and his equally bookish secretariat applied close-reading to a letter they've dug out of their files, the one the queen sent on 30 July revoking the earl's right to return? Have they hit upon that saving parenthesis, '(till the northern action be tried)', as warrant to reinstate his right? For certainly, as the truce signed on 8 September witnesses, the northern action *has* been tried.

Whatever the case, returning to Dublin from Ulster by mid-September, Essex in the weeks following puts in place plans to leave Ireland, installing a care-taker government of deputies who clearly expect his return. He sails on the 24th with a clutch of loyalists including secretaries Cuffe and Wotton, crosses the Irish sea with almost unimaginable speed, then rides 'haste post haste for life' to reach Nonsuch Palace on the 28th, not pausing to shift shirts or wash mire from faces. What happens next inside the palace is notorious. Queen and subject play out scenes that move from romantic comedy to political tragedy via domestic farce. Essex rushes into the queen's bedchamber. Finds her 'newly up' but un-made-up, 'the hair about her face'. He kneels, kisses her hand, exchanges 'private speech with her' and leaves happy, believing he's 'found a sweet calm at home' after 'much trouble and storms abroad'. At dinner, he entertains the table with accounts 'of his travels and journeys in Ireland, of the goodness of the country, the civilities of the nobility that are true subjects'. But the trenchers are hardly cleared when the mood turns. The queen summons Essex. Begins 'to call him in question for his return'. Suddenly hands him over to interrogation. Exiting from this scene, queen and subject will never set eyes on each other again.

But if that's what's happening inside Nonsuch, what's happening *outside*, to those others, his followers, who are 'at London, but not come hither yet'? Do Wotton, Cuffe and the rest ride to Essex House? Where is 'honestest Reynolds'? When do they learn of their master's virtual arrest on Michaelmas Eve, of his three-hour-long examination the following day, standing bare-headed (no surer register of his indignity than that absence of hat) before a full Privy Council – his peers – to answer charges ranging from contemptuously disobeying orders to 'overbold going to Her Majesty's bedchamber'? Cuffe has maintained that he'd rather lose with Essex than gain with his opposites. Given who's lining up as his opposites, does Cuffe still think so? What is Wotton thinking?

In April, when the clamours of the adoring multitudes who paved Essex's way out of London were still fresh in his ears, Wotton wrote: 'For our wars, I can only say we have a good cause, and the worthiest gentleman of the world to lead it'. But now, where exactly is Essex leading them? More immediately, when does Wotton learn what Essex deposes on 30 September? That in his negotiations with Tyrone, Essex used 'Sir Wm. Constable and H. Wotton my secretary, who both are come over with me', and that 'H. Wotton hath both the articles of cessation signed by Tyrone, and the instructions I gave to them', 'the whole business being chiefly left to Sir Warham St Leger and him'? Robert Cecil needs only inspect the handwriting on the articles to confirm Essex's statement. Wotton is implicated. Directly. Is he up next for interrogation? What will he answer?

9
An interlude: executions, exile and strange encounters

London

26 February 1601. Fifty-nine names appear on the hit list drawn up for Robert Cecil. At the top are persons 'already indicted and fit to be arraigned'. Next: 'Not yet indicted but fit to be indicted'. Then: 'to be fined'. A parenthesis bracketing 'Attainted and fit to be executed' is empty. It's awaiting names to be added to those everybody knows: Robert, earl of Essex; Henry, earl of Southampton; Roger, earl of Rutland. Eight we recognise from the Irish campaign are named, 'already indicted': from the high command, Christopher Blount, Charles Danvers, John Davies, Francis Tresham, William Constable. But also Gelly Merrick (the earl's estate manager, knighted at Cadiz, latterly among his Irish lieutenants) and two more servants we know of the earl's household, 'Henrie Cuffe', 'William Temple'. On the following page, 'To be discharged without indictment, arraignment or fine' appears 'Edward Reinolds', sent 'upon bond to his own lodging'. Cecil's net has swept up Essex's innermost military circle and three of his secretaries. One name is absent.

This list draws a line under events that began when Essex burst into the queen's bedchamber at Michaelmas 1599. Eighteen months later they're ending with a bizarre replay. Again aiming to force his way into Elizabeth's presence, Essex on 8 February marches into the city of London at the head of two hundred armed followers. The 'rebellion' collapses within hours. By 3am the following morning he's in the Tower, along with Southampton and Rutland. Danvers follows later, and after ten days, Merrick and Cuffe. Cecil's list lengthens.

The months between have played out like Greek tragedy. Over the autumn, while Essex was 'in durance' under Lord Keeper Thomas Egerton, Essex House on the Strand was open 'for the family', 'his very servants afraid to meet in any [other] place to make merry lest it might be ill taken'. (John Donne is Egerton's secretary. Did he send Wotton news of his master in custody? If so, it doesn't survive.) In March 1600 the queen ordered Essex House cleared and Essex returned there, in solitary confinement, two guards only 'having all the keys'. Merrick was dismissed, Anthony Bacon sent away. In June, the earl endured a thirteen-hour-long grilling ('without either meat or drink') by an extra-judicial tribunal of eighteen commissioners. Two hundred spectators witnessed it. He was then conveyed back to Essex House to await Her Majesty's pleasure. It came in August. He was given his liberty, but still under her 'indignation', told not to approach the Court.

His faction hoped for his complete restoration. On the streets, the popular voice, remembering Cadiz and loud against the peace with Spain that the Cecil faction was pushing, clamoured for Essex. Bills appeared libelling his enemies. On the white walls of Whitehall was daubed 'much villainy' against Robert Cecil. (A lawyer's clerk was apprehended and hanged.) Across this 'long trance', as Essex put it, he sent abject letters suing 'for grace, for access, and an end of this exile'. He believed Her Majesty intended his 'correction, not ruin'.

In October, that belief collapsed. (Predictably, as one onlooker writes. The hopes of the earl's supporters always 'outran their wits'.) The queen first deferred then denied the renewal of the earl's monopoly on the importation of sweet wines, his 'chiefest maintenance' and 'only means of compounding with the merchants' who held his debts. Those debts were massive. In Ireland, he personally maintained a house of at least four hundred persons, paid surgeons and preachers, bought sheets for wounded soldiers' beds. One among his dependants reported that '40 or 50 persons sit at my Lord's table. Our expenses betwixt £35 and £40 *per diem* in meat and drink, beside the charges of the stable, servants' wages and liveries, and money that flies daily out of my Lord's purse'. Without the monopoly, Essex faced ruin – and now, he concluded, his ruin was what the queen wanted. He gave way to a mind 'full of confusion and contrariety'.

Visiting him that autumn at Essex House where Merrick, back in residence, was holding the doors open daily to crowds pumped high on the dissenting rhetoric of a slate of Puritan preachers, John Harrington, who'd marched with Essex in Ireland, found him 'devoid of good reason as of right mind', shifting erratically from 'sorrow and repentance to rage and rebellion': 'In my last discourse he uttered strange words, bordering on such strange designs, that made me hasten forth and leave his presence', 'speeches of the Queen' that 'become no man who hath *mens sana in corpore sano*'. Harrington feared Essex 'hath ill-advisers' and that 'much evil hath sprung from this source'.

Once those 'strange designs' are enacted on 8 February, with what the earl imagines is his march to liberate his queen – and his enemies, his attempted coup d'etat – his execution is inevitable. He goes to it on Tower Hill at first light on Ash Wednesday, 25 February, the most solemn penitential date in the church calendar, as observers note. But first he summons Henry Cuffe. Essex is preparing 'for another world', he says, and, resolved to 'deal clearly with God and world', needs to 'say this' to the secretary he now recognises has led his thoughts 'in a string': 'you have been one of the chiefest instigators of me in all these my disloyal courses into which I have fallen'.

Two weeks later Cuffe himself is hanged, drawn and quartered on the common gallows at Tyburn alongside Gelly Merrick, but not before sending Cecil what Cecil wants, testimony that will drive more nails into the dead earl's coffin. Cuffe confesses that for months past Essex had been secretly communicating with King James in Scotland about the English succession. (Stunningly, it will emerge a decade later, when Cecil is fretting over revelations that a treacherous secretary might make of *him*, that Cecil, too, was secretly negotiating with James. The list of traitors in February 1601 clearly misses out one name.) Secretary Cuffe's astonishing confession: we can read as his last office of loyalty to a master who'd accused him of betrayal, for in it he manages to smear Essex's busiest enemies, Cecil, Raleigh, Cobham and Carew, to their own faces, putting into the mouth of a supposed (but conspicuously unnamed) Scottish ambassador damning allegations that Cecil and his faction were working 'to the prejudice ... evident hazard and almost inevitable ruin of the whole island'. As Cecil reads, his eyes burn. On the scaffold Cuffe denies complicity in the 'ill-advised assembly' of 8 February: he 'bore but the part of a child', 'kept within doors and shut up all day long'. To the end, the scholar-turned-secretary splits hairs and chops logic, his last subversive words demonstrating why he was so useful to Essex – and so dangerous. He's been 'adjudged to die', he maintains, 'for plotting a plot never acted' and 'for acting in an act never plotted': an epigram for the whole miserable affair.

These deaths, along with Danvers's and Blount's, satisfy Elizabeth's justice. The other 'indicted' are sent away with fines; on 2 July William Temple is discharged from the Gatehouse; Henry Reynolds is already returned to his 'own lodgings'. So where is the secretariat's fourth man?

Florence

Wotton's contemporary biographer, Izaak Walton, offers a sensational account of Henry fleeing England 'so soon as the Earl was apprehended'. But six letters in the Archivio di Stato, Florence that have been known to scholars but never fitted into the jig-saw of Wotton's whereabouts, let us discover a fuller story. He may have left England before the arrest, possibly even as Essex's supporters, gathered at Robert Drury's house, were theorising how they might safely (for themselves and the kingdom) conduct 'a kind of violence' to save the state from men of 'power and malice': how, that is, they might legitimate treason. Wotton, said Walton, was 'not of that faction'. Perhaps like Harrington he heard Essex uttering strange words that prompted him to 'hasten forth and leave his presence'. Perhaps his insider big brother Edward, lodged at Court with his ear to everything echoing along the corridors, told him to get out – and sent his own son, Pickering, to travel with him to make sure he did. In an undated letter that may belong to these weeks in early 1601 of plotting and planning, Wotton writes in subdued terms to Reynolds. Despite suffering 'some little indisposition' he's 'going abroad (which I think will be to-morrow)'. More than a year earlier, at the time of his arrest, Essex had been offered the same way out, urged by Southampton and Mountjoy to escape to France. He replied that he'd 'rather run any danger than live the life of a poor fugitive'. That's the life Wotton now chooses. He returns to Italy.

On 7 April 1601 (the date is ten days earlier in England, 29 March) he's in Florence and writes from his lodgings to 'Molto Illustre Signor mio Osservantissimo', Belisario Vinta, secretary of state to Ferdinando de' Medici, Grand Duke of Tuscany. Vinta is to Florence what Robert Cecil is to England, two of the greatest ministerial minds in Europe. Vinta shows interest in the young Englishman, who appears only recently to have arrived: 'When you know me better …', the newcomer writes. (That would mean, if Wotton travelled direct to Florence from London taking the journey time of twenty-one days expected of postal couriers, he left England in early February, which would corroborate Walton's version of events. But perhaps he crossed the Channel even earlier, unsure of his destination, travelling as slowly as he would in 1604 when it would take him six weeks to reach Venice from London.)

Wotton is repaying Vinta's interest by passing on intelligence from Venice about a 'gran levata' – general muster – of foot soldiers and horse mobilised against Spain; about Venetian feints to control the Gulf with distractions in Lombardy; about the Republic's 'desperatissimo' last resort, if other appeals for allies fail, to call in the Turks. Wotton is practised in this sort of writing: minuting details, quoting verbatim, inserting humour, making the case contra as well as pro for the Medici supporting Venice against the 'grandezza' of Spain. Only in the last lines does he reveal his real reason for writing, not to pass on intelligence (which he does not presume to be 'nuove alle orrechie', news to the Grand Duke's ears) but rather to show His Highness his 'divotissime servitu', most devoted service. Wotton is pitching himself to a new master.

When he first writes to Vinta Wotton has no certain news of Essex. Five days later he knows from someone in the English Court – his brother, perhaps – of the execution, and in his second letter to Vinta bitterly notes its date. A solemn day of penitence has been made a day of torment for a man who 'perhaps wasn't innocent' but certainly was 'dragged to his death by unimaginable malice'. Wotton apologises for his passionate words: 'Perdoni in'me … la vanita, et la passione ch' Io uso'. He has lost a master 'who loved me, and who trusted me with his nearest affairs'. That same day he's emboldened to write more, to send a report from London of the execution, and to 'speak a little of myself'.

He reminds Vinta that when the Persian ambassador – that's how Antony Shirley, Wotton's scapegrace kinsman, more pirate than politician, is now touting himself – arrived lately in Florence, Wotton was given the opportunity to present a letter of introduction from 'my unhappy master', 'or better said, unhappy country, unable to uphold such virtue' to Ferdinando, who accepted his offer of service, though Wotton was only a 'forestiero', a foreigner. But now, 'things have happened in my country that have removed from my soul all thoughts of returning'. He needs the Grand Duke to know that his past fortunes and the place he held with Essex make him ashamed to come before him as a beggar, but on the other hand, that his present fortunes make him too weak to serve as he would wish without Ferdinando's grace. He asks Vinta's intervention, to assure the Grand Duke of his faithfulness and his usefulness as a 'servant and instrument'. Perhaps His Highness will have some occasion to make use of a stranger. He begs to be sent anywhere in the world. If nothing else, he can inform on those things that 'touch upon' England, Scotland, and 'all the princes confederate with them'. He has 'practice and experience' that he can use to 'interpret the truth' of matters coming from there.

Three things leap from these letters. First, that Wotton has travelled to Italy carrying, if not a licence, a letter of recognition from Essex, so he hasn't exactly, as Izaak Walton tells it, done a runner in front of Cecil's arrest warrant. (That, however, is how Wotton must have represented it to Walton, writing it up in the 'Life' years later, which gives insight into Wotton's retrospective framing of these events.) Secondly, that he's now putting himself outside Her Majesty's command, exiling himself from England. Thirdly, that he's willing to serve a foreign prince in matters 'di molta secretezza', earning his salt by discovering deep secrets and informing on England. So: an exile, an outlaw, an intelligencer, a traitor. But a traitor whose anguish makes him sound himself betrayed – by England. The envy and malice of powerful men in England killed his master. He cannot think of returning.

A week later Wotton has news of a further execution: one of the Danvers brothers is dead, Charles, the one well known to Ferdinando. Ironically, it was Charles's brother Henry who was Essex's follower, but Henry, in Ireland in February, 'scappò' – escaped – arrest. Charles was Cecil's man, and he was only drawn into the plot 'by love of Southampton'. He died on the scaffold erected for Essex. In Florence Henry Wotton might have reflected that, like that other Henry, he too scappò. Neither appears on Cecil's list of those 'not yet indicted'.

With this letter, Wotton disappears from the Grand Duke's archives. But not from his business. That summer, Ferdinando receives intelligence of a plot to poison Scotland's king, the likeliest (Protestant) heir to the English throne. His assassination would make way for the (Catholic) Spanish infanta and thus for the complete Spanish domination of Europe. A secret mission to Scotland? Vinta knows just the man for the job.

When he's summoned, Wotton is equal parts thrilled and daunted. Here's a chance to impress de' Medici and kick back at his dead master's calumniators. But there's fourteen hundred miles between Florence and Edinburgh as the crow flies. And Wotton's no crow. He's a fugitive, so the best route through Milan and France, across the channel at Calais to Dover then straight up England along the Great North Road is closed to him. He can't risk Cecil's lines of intelligence. He'll have to take the more punishing route, the horse-killing route, east towards Venice, then north to Trento, across the Alps at the Brenner Pass to Innsbruck, through Germany to Hamburg into Denmark, to Bergen in Norway, eighteen hundred miles. There he must find a ship to carry him the final five hundred miles to Leith, Edinburgh's port, across the North Sea, a stretch of water so notorious for tempests and wrecks that King James reputed it cursed by witches. Still, Wotton has weathered the Azores and survived Ireland, and he's eager to serve.

As an outlaw, of course, he has to travel incognito – but that presents no difficulty to the man who years back rode into Rome under a 'mighty blue feather'. He passes himself off as an Italian, one Ottavio Baldi, the alias perhaps a nod at the Octavians who manage King James's finances. Also a name that spares a thought for himself: 'baldo' means bold. His commission is to carry into the king's presence letters and a box of antidotes, possibly the Venetian wonder drug *triaca*. Given the Grand Duke's premonitions, there's no time to lose. We don't know how late in that summer he sets out, but he's spotted arriving at Dunfermline in September, a stranger 'of high stature, brown-haired, sober and thought-wise'. There, he learns the king is at Stirling. Back in the saddle; more miles on horseback past miserable small-holdings and stretches of wilderness that have never seen a plough. The scenery confirms English prejudice. If the Irish are wild, the Scots are beggarly.

The king is cautious when the stranger is announced. His life to date – he was crowned when he was still a babe in his nurse's arms – has been a catalogue of murders, executions, slaughters, kidnappings and attempted assassinations, so he's 'jealous' – that is, suspicious – of messengers seeking private audience. Baldi is separated from his Italian rapier at the door. He's defenceless, then, when, ushered into the king's presence, he's suddenly surrounded by king's men ready to pounce. He makes 'a stand' but finds himself more disconcerted than threatened. The figure before him hardly carries himself like a king. He's a head shorter than Baldi and looks older than the two-year age gap between them. He's bandy-legged, his beard sparse as a stubble field picked over by gleaners, his eyes 'rowling' as though any second expecting the assassin's blade and 'his fingers ever ... fiddling about his codpiece'. He's dressed so meanly, he might be taken for one of his men, but in over-stuffed doublet and hose, evidently 'quilted for stiletto proof', making him appear more a man of bombast than flesh, and one who seems anxious to keep checking his manhood.

The Italian learns something more of him when the king bids him 'be bold and deliver his message'. The king's speech has to force its way past a tongue too large for its mouth. He sounds oafish.

But what does James make of Baldi? The fake Florentine travelled across Europe in leather and frieze to avoid notice. Now, he'll present himself sumptuously arrayed in the vibrantly coloured silk and plush velvet of the city's manufacture, his fashion-plate doublet and hose matched by large Italianate gestures. He's an advertisement of Medici magnificence – and the seriousness of his mission. He looks to James like a bird of paradise. Speaking his message in Italian, a language the king understands but doesn't himself speak, the stranger then, amazingly, steps forward 'and whispers to the king in his own language' that he's 'an English man' who beseeches 'more private conference'. The audacity of this performance is stupendous, and James is charmed. For the next three months the king will collude in Wotton's fiction, allowing him to remain at the Stuart Court 'during all his abode' in the guise of the Italian. Wotton can't possibly know what's in store for Ottavio Baldi's future, but by sheer good luck he'll have three months in the king's household to study James as he once studied Essex.

Wotton discovers a man of contradictions. James is, by all reputes, the most timorous king in Christendom, one who can't abide 'the sight of a soldier'. But in the saddle, he's fearless, chasing deer pell-mell, sometimes six hours at a stint, away from Court for days, careless of absence and the state business that bores him. But as much as hunting, he loves disputation. He spends hours poring over books, a reader who's indefatigably a writer. Several long treatises are already published: *Daemonologie*, which exposes witchcraft as a fraud and admits his early persecution of it to have been over-credulous; *Basilikon Doron*, a 'how to govern' manual for his five-year-old son; and, most politically significant, *The True Law of Free Monarchies* in which he theorises the divine right of kings and the supreme sovereignty of the monarch, subordinate only to God. Ruling might be tedious, and hounds might make better company than courtiers. But of this no one should make question: he's militant on the subject of the monarch's absolute right to rule.

Wotton finds James serious-minded, certainly no oaf. Yet he's also ready with 'witty jests' (though delivered unsmiling, in so 'grave and serious manner', say observers, that they're frequently unsure whether to laugh). 'Infinitely inclined to prayer'. But given to 'cursing and swearing … verging on blasphemy'. Wedded to a queen who's been pregnant every year of their marriage so far – but besotted by pretty-boy male favourites.

While Baldi sojourns in Scotland, King James finds the seriousness of thought-wise Wotton appealing. But he also shares jokes that tickle Wotton's loose humour, like the joke of his incognito, and he pumps Baldi over the course of three months for tales of people and places, libraries and controversies, scandals and gossip far beyond his backwater Scotland before giving him leave to depart for home 'as true an Italian as he came thither'. Ever after, in all their future correspondence, they'll preserve a coded intimacy. Wotton will sign himself to the king 'Ottavio Baldi'.

Let's hope, riding south, that, more than courtly impressions, conversation and days hunting, Baldi carries away information that will matter crucially to Wotton's future. It's common knowledge in Scotland that James fears war so hysterically that, 'in sending ambassadors', he'd 'rather spend £100000 on embassies to … procure peace with dishonour than £1000 on an army that would have forced peace with honour'. When the time comes, Wotton will have to contrive – diplomatically – to override hysteria by presenting the king a scenario James finds even more horrendous than war.

London

This improbably swashbuckling story doesn't end with Baldi's exit. In March 1603 Elizabeth is dead, James has ascended the English throne and, even before arriving in London, is reviewing his household. He retains in post Elizabeth's charismatic comptroller and finds time to ask 'if he knew one Henry Wotton, that had spent much time in foreign travel'. He's my brother, Edward Wotton responds; whereupon the king requires Edward to send for him, and 'when he shall come into England, bid him repair privately to me'. Henry, in Venice, is summoned. Before heading home, he writes to Robert Cecil that life-changing letter of 23 May 1603 that we've already examined. It reframes his relationship with his ruined master. Writing to Vinta, Henry said Essex was one 'who loved me, and who trusted me with his nearest affairs'. Writing to Cecil, Essex is someone who 'owed unto me … more regard of me than I found about him'. A new master, a new pitch.

In London, King James gathers the returned exile in his arms, welcomes him by the name of Ottavio Baldi, and calls him 'the most honest and therefore the best dissembler ever he met with'. Watching this rapturous scene of rehabilitation, does Cecil have any inkling of the shadowy business Henry was performing in Florence? Perhaps Wotton, intelligencer to the Medici, like Wotton, the Essex rebel, once again simply scappò. James is pursuing a foreign peace policy across Europe, most controversially with Spain. He wants diplomatic relations with Venice restored. In October 1604, he sends Wotton, now 'Sir Henry', his ambassador, to begin the restoration.

Exile, outlaw, intelligencer, traitor: merely Wotton's most recent roles. Before that: student, secretary, soldier, scoundrel. As human architecture, he's a man built of many rooms, spacious, cramped, crooked; some sunny, some cast in shadow, others connected by twisting corridors. Winchester and Oxford formed him a humanist, made him a palimpsest of books, his mental world a compilation of minds and rhetorical styles: Cicero, Tacitus, Aesop, Ovid, Erasmus. He's studied history and the practice of embassy under Gentili; taken on Tancredi's heroics and their cost in blood; searched the human eye for what it can tell him about the soul. He's travelled across Europe and slept in strange beds. He's played the dead-keen researcher in a library in Vienna

11 King James I. A portrait from 1605 attributed to John de Critz the Elder shows the young king as Wotton knew him in Scotland and London.

(and surreptitious copyist of forbidden manuscripts), the astonished tourist in Venice, the attention-seeking hypocrite in Rome getting an eyeful of the pope's 'pretensions', the sickened observer of war-ravaged Geneva and its dead-eyed population.

Like a grub growing wings, he's metamorphosed secretary to England's Icarus. He's served Essex with his pen, gone to war and come to grief. He's watched his own dead servant slung overboard to feed fishes at Cadiz and seen raw English recruits drown in Irish bogs. He's experienced first-hand the impetuous politics of personality (and its costs), galloping break-neck across England with Icarus, and he's studied from a distance the alternative politics (and its costs) of that stoat, Robert Cecil (canny, bold: it's the stoat's pelt that dresses the monarch's robes, an apt figure for Cecil's service to James Stuart). He's learned the self-less disciplines of the secretary that he'll need as an ambassador serving as foreign secretary to Secretary of State Cecil, but also has direct experience, beyond Cecil, of the king whom Cecil serves, experience he'll use. He knows writing. The evidence it leaves in its trail. The witness of a signature. Once loose humoured, he's now thought-wise. All this has furnished Sir Henry for his newest role, spectator and actor in what he'll call a 'beautiful theatre' where he'll be making political history. From now on, this honest dissembler will fashion himself 'un vero Venetiano'. He's thirty-six years old.

Part III

Sent to lie abroad

10

Commanded in embassy

The ambassador, the Collegio and 'a year exactly'

1 October 1604. Seated on a narrow bench waiting to be admitted to his first audience, the English ambassador has a few moments to think about doors. The one he's about to enter leads into the Sala del Collegio, where the doge and his council of twenty Savii – wise men – hear the representations ambassadors bring to Venice from the world beyond. This door, he's told, will always be open to him. But the one beyond, into the Sala del Senato? Never. The Collegio is the single point of contact between foreign emissaries and the Venetian state. As Wotton will struggle to understand, it's a bureaucratic buffer zone, a 'stomack', as he'll write, where 'all things are first digested', 'a place of distribution and not of determination of affairs'. It receives, it listens, responds with questions and observations, records, refers, reports. But it makes no decisions. Decisions are reached beyond the closed door, by the three hundred or so Pregadi (so called because the Republic 'prays' their advice) elected to the Senato. They in turn serve as the deliberative body that represents the back-wall of Venetian government, the two thousand-odd *nobili* who, by birthright, constitute the Maggior Consiglio. Doge Marino Grimani, crowned in a gold-embroidered horn-shaped *corno ducale* looks like a monarch, and like a monarch serves for life, but he has no executive power. When matters reach a ballot, he doesn't have a vote.

It might strike Henry Wotton that doors are as apt an emblem of the Venetian state as the lions of San Marco. The Palazzo Ducale – the doge's residence and the seat of the Republic's government – is a warren of sumptuously decorated rooms on three floors that take their names from the magistracies that transact their business there, interconnected by doors that channel the flow of information and deliberation passing through them. Not exactly snakes

12 Henry Wotton. Odoardo Fialetti's painting, date unknown, locates the ambassador in the Collegio delivering an esposizione to Doge Leonardo Donà while Savii listen and secretaries go about their business.

and ladders, but close enough. One room has four doors. Another, one. Most, two. The floor plan directs the traffic. Business is referred, room by room, from one magistracy to the next, debated by overlapping elected memberships that rotate continuously. That's to prevent the concentration of power in anyone's, or faction's, hands – but likewise scuppers swift (they'd call it 'premature') decision-making. The efficiency of this chancery is central to the 'myth of Venice' that Europe takes for fact. But over this first year of his embassy Wotton will grow sceptical of how the Collegio's open-door policy fits the myth. For one thing, there's a contradiction between what's open and what's closed. Officially, information is 'segreta'. But 'informatione segreta' goes rogue. It seeps down corridors through cracked doors into the public space of the Piazza, escaping senators' tight lips to reach the chattering mouths of the *popolani*, the mass of Venetians who have no role in governance but whose gossip washes the city daily in tides of 'rumore'.

Supposedly, everything Wotton utters in the Collegio is confidential. His audiences – esposizioni – are delivered 'non ... di altra maniera che con la voce' (not otherwise but spoken), in Italian, with no notes and only occasional reference to letters or memoranda. The doge responds, conversation goes back and forth, the Savii occasionally add something. Notionally an oral performance, Wotton's esposizione should remain 'segreta', its words vanishing into air. But not so: for as he speaks, he's recorded verbatim by a secretary. Wotton is flattered to discover the man assigned to him is the top-ranking civil servant he mentioned in his letter to Cecil as 'Scaravella' years back. No doubt, having just survived an unplanned year in England, Giovanni Carlo Scaramelli is the Republic's expert on the place and most primed to monitor the unpredictable who's just arrived in their midst.

In esposizioni, Wotton's spoken words are captured on paper, turned into text. Then, as the ambassador's proxy, that text is taken through the door into the Senato and turned back into words, read by Scaramelli to the Pregadi. It's debated, balloted, and whatever decision is reached (or deferred) returns through the door to the Collegio as a written deliberazione, the ambassador summoned to hear it read 'ex scripto'. Finally, the secretary who's been doing all the writing and reading and moving through doors deposits his papers on a chancery shelf, where they'll be consulted for years – making Wotton an author read on English affairs long after he's ceased being England's spokesman. Eventually, the documents are consigned to the chancery's vast archive to await some distant future afterlife.

This transaction leaves a long, deep paper trail, thousands of draft pages of secretarial manuscript, gathered first by date as filze, strung on a filza, a tough thread. (Hence the name, which means each page has a thread hole at its centre.) Then they're gathered into buste – folders – bound in hide, later fair copied into registri on high-quality, durable parchment. Crossings out, interlineations, second thoughts aren't transcribed; silent edits happen; blots disappear and sometimes the stage directions the secretary occasionally writes to record 'as near as may be' the ambassador's 'passions and pauses', his tone of voice and body language ('Qui si scaldava ... Qui si fermava': here he grew heated; here he stopped). Gone, then, is the evidence the filze bear on their surfaces of their original working lives in the Collegio: not just hurried cross-hatchings and handwriting that appears struggling to keep up with speech, but wax dripped down pages, holes burnt by stray embers from candles, marks in crayon along margins scoring 'attention' to particular passages. All along this paper trail, it's vulnerable to ambush. Archives are subject to, indeed meant for, prying eyes.

So how 'segreta' is the 'segreta', Wotton wants to know six months into his embassy. (His experience of secret debates in Vienna showed him how ridiculously easy it was to penetrate them.) Outside the Collegio Wotton buttonholes Scaramelli. Clearly he's violating room-based protocols, taking 'secret' talk

13 Giovanni Carlo Scaramelli records in his distinctive handwriting the English ambassador's first audience in the Venetian Collegio, 1 October 1604.

onto the staircase. He wheedles: 'If he wanted to discuss matters of the utmost secrecy' – 'cose secretissime' – can he 'turn to someone to whom he could reveal things freely', or is it 'always necessary to refer matters to the Collegio'? Scaramelli responds briskly. The Collegio 'is the door' – the *only* door – 'to every matter', 'of whatever importance'. Wotton's prying doesn't arouse Scaramelli's suspicions. What 'matters'? How are such 'matters' reaching the ambassador's hands? Chancery secretaries don't probe. Instead, Scaramelli assures Wotton that 'ogni suo detto resterà non solo secreto, ma sepolto' ('everything you say will remain not just secret but buried'). 'This', replies Wotton with leaden sarcasm, knowing how his words move between the Collegio and the Senato, 'is amazing': I speak in secret 'to twenty-five and two hundred know everything I've said'. Besides, he knows it's untrue. He read copies of the Senato's top-secret *Relazione degli Ambasciatori* in the Imperial Library in Vienna, and *Delle Lettere di Principi* has been in print since 1562: he brought the three-volume edition with him from England.

He's been told the official line. But he won't let that stop him. This first year in office he's an apprentice in statecraft, on a steep learning curve, learning how the state operates and what his work in Venice is going to be as he talks up England to the Collegio – and Venice to London. The apprentice will keep pushing on closed doors – as we're about to see.

'Reputation … where you live'

In London, Secretary of State Robert Cecil has few ambitions for Wotton's embassy. So few, indeed, that he doesn't appear to put on file any of Wotton's dispatches during his first three months abroad. Cecil will try to 'add reputation unto you in the place where you live', but he's not hopeful, for 'the passages of affairs between us and that state are very barren; and except it be for matter of trade … I know not what other occasions we may have to deal with them'. The recently arrived Venetian ambassador in London, Nicolò Molin, takes an equally dim view, not because there's not enough business between the two states but because the English won't act as honest brokers, specifically over the matter that's most agitating the Republic – piracy. It's rumoured, Molin reports, that the newly appointed English ambassador has instructions to shrug off complaints: they 'wish all the past to be forgotten' and 'think that the execution of six or seven men and the restitution of seven or eight thousand crowns out of the hundreds of thousands they have stolen is satisfaction'. Not even Wotton, with no history of interest in trade, appears to harbour illusions about his embassy – or much sense of purpose. From Dover at the end of July 1604 on a journey he expects to take thirty-five days, he idles along the road for two months. Before crossing the Alps, he leaves in an autograph book a wisecrack that reads like future-proofing: 'An ambassador is an honest man sent to lie abroad for the sake of his country'. Only, he writes in Latin, a nod perhaps to his schoolboy self, swatting up puns. But in Latin, the pun on 'lie' doesn't translate. In Latin, the 'legatus' is 'missus ad mentiendum'. For the record, then, Wotton makes the ambassador a liar.

Against these odds, however, once installed in Venice, Ambassador Wotton looks set on a project to expand his brief – starting with his initial audience. It should be a formality but veers off course when Wotton ignores his exit line to introduce an appeal for 'a young Scotsman who finds himself a prisoner on account of a youthful fault' – no further specifics. It's a startling moment. Wotton can't be acting on instructions from London beyond the king's general commission 'to protect his subjects' because he only learned about Seget a week ago. This means the rookie ambassador is taking the diplomatic initiative, speaking for himself, not the king, and overstepping the most fundamental diplomatic protocol laid down by his Oxford tutor in diplomacy: the ambassador must never 'think beyond his instructions'. 'Thinking beyond' is exactly what he's doing. Here, we get our first inkling of the way Wotton will not just represent diplomacy – but invent it.

More disconcertingly, asking for what amounts to a judicial review, Wotton appears to be making Seget a test case for how seriously the Republic intends to take the new English embassy. He makes a similar appeal in November, again ignorant of details, this time for an exiled Paduan. The doge deftly sidelines both appeals. But as Wotton persists, Grimani grows testy: 'we govern by laws and orders'; the Collegio has no jurisdiction over criminal cases; Wotton's representations are pointless as well as irregular. Finally, Grimani thinks to silence this diplomatic upstart by telling him exactly what he's defending. He has the charge sheets dug out of the archives and read. Seget is condemned for libelling a nobleman and, for maximum insult, circulating the defamation across the *broglio*. The Paduan Dotto has been done for a string of crimes: kidnap, assault (of a priest), mutilation (cutting off a man's nose then handing him 'a mirror to look upon himself'); rape (of one Madalena whom he 'gave as spoils' to his henchman once he'd finished with her, 'for which occurrences' 'Madalena was murdered by her husband' – her violated body then refused burial by the church).

Wotton drops Dotto. But not Seget. He brings new evidence, pressures the doge to send an order to the Consiglio di Dieci, the magistracy that presides over serious crime, to re-try Seget. (In the normal way the Venetians do their headcounts, the Dieci actually numbers eighteen, 'Ten' plus seven Savii and the doge.) They ballot five times on different verdicts, finally acquitting Seget on a split vote. Wotton bundles Seget out of Venice, promises he won't be seen there again – and never mentions him to London.

'Transported in this affair'

Watching Wotton go off message, refuse to take the Signory's 'no' for an answer, ignore the rules about whom he can talk to and where, we're seeing distinctly undiplomatic diplomacy that will characterise his entire embassy. Is he inexperienced and blundering? Or deliberately challenging the system? In an earlier life he was called the 'honest dissembler'. In Venice, how far is he 'honest', how far the strategic 'dissembler'? Surely when he disparages himself as 'a nobody' ('son niente'), someone His Majesty has 'taken out of school' ('tolto dalle scuole') and 'sent as a man little practised in the ways of the world', he's striking a rhetorical pose. But when he asks that some deliberation be read a second time because he doesn't 'speak this language securely' and 'wouldn't want my defect to prejudice negotiations', is he genuinely floundering – or stalling for time? There's no question that he's speaking frankly when he asserts that he sets 'the zeal of his own conscience before all human respects'. He, a Protestant establishing an embassy at the only formally recognised Protestant address in Venice, cannot 'live without the practice of my religion'. But what about 'I love brevity' or 'it is not in my nature to search out news'?

None of this is borne out by his esposizioni. Sometimes the Savii must find interpreting him bewildering. When, for instance, he answers with a 'shrug of shoulders'. Is that acquiescence? Insolence? Pettishness? Can he be serious when he threatens to 'come no more' to the Collegio until some business that's been limping along like a corpse on crutches is finished or when, all flouncing indignation wailing 'where is respect?', 'where is honour?', he tells the Collegio they've taken so little account of him that he's going to advise His Majesty to replace him with someone 'more experienced'? Or better yet, to recall him, 'to save the costs of an ambassador who's not valued ... as much as a statue'. (This particular tantrum gets him a verbal clip round the head: he has 'let himself be transported by his affections', snaps one Savio. That's tantamount to calling him mad. The ambassador 's'impallidì', 'went white at this answer'. And was 'alquanto sopra di sè': 'for a time beside himself'.)

Of course, another name for the 'honest dissembler' is a 'politician'. On the politics of absolutism Wotton is an expert, having studied them close-up under Essex and having heard in Scotland what James Stuart thinks about the divinity of kings. Now, he's learning the politics of oligarchical republicanism in a state that fiercely defends its secular liberties while, in matters of religion, it simultaneously subjects itself humbly to the Papal See. Only this jurisdictional tension between church and state allows, as nowhere else in Italy, an English embassy to be established in Venice, an initiative that's sensitive, even politically dangerous for Wotton, his king and Venice, for it aims to settle in the city a Protestant enclave that will benefit from diplomatic immunity, including immunity from papal Inquisition. The pope's nuncio, in audiences in the Collegio, rails against a dangerous innovation: the Republic is planting heresy in its midst, officially tolerating religious difference. It hardly matters that the rationale for resuming Anglo-Venetian relations is secular, 'the matter of trade', as Cecil put it, or that Venice is, as Wotton observed back in May 1603, before he'd had much experience of the city, 'a Signory that with long neutrality of state is ... almost slipped into a neutrality of religion'. From where he sits now, Wotton can gloss 'neutrality' with more politick nuance. Church and state are co-dependants in Venice. An ambassador, he knows, should stick to matters of state and leave religion alone. But in Venice that's impossible. He'll have to risk blurring lines – as he states in syntax so blurred as to make the risk he's running practically incomprehensible: he declares he won't be 'afraid of offending with my discourse even the narrowest confiner and circumscriber of an ambassador's duty within matters of state', for anyone who takes 'religion in these countries to be anything else than a point of state' will 'peradventure be deceived'.

We see how politically sensitive this issue is from the partly ciphered 'particular directions' King James sends Wotton in an early personal message instructing his 'better government' in a 'state where formalities do sway so much'. We can shake out of that circumlocution a warning: 'Beware protocol'. Wotton is to avoid 'any great dealing with a160e': that's code for the papal nuncio. The king intends 'only to maintain civil correspondency with b134c' – the pope – 'as a secular prince', 'not otherwise', 'for the avoiding of scandal which might grow of his Majesty's sincerity and constancy in the profession of his religion'. The politics of the king's 'profession' are fraught. He bought support for his claim to the English throne from religious reformists, radicals and recusants alike, and even perhaps from Rome. But now sitting on England's throne and seeing the impossibility of reconciling all these factions, he's reneging on promises. Shortly, Catholics will be rioting in Wales. A two-hundred-strong gang of Puritans will run the king to ground where he's hunting in Berkshire to protest the new edict on conformity. James cannot risk anyone doubting his 'profession'. To be known to be communicating with Rome, if only distantly from Venice and only through a nuncio, might cause misconstructions of his 'sincerity', and be seized upon in England both by Catholics hopeful of toleration and Puritans wanting more radical reform of the English church. The king, Cecil writes to Wotton, knows he can count on his ambassador's 'discretion and soundness in religion'.

No question. Wotton promises discretion. Through Scaramelli, he tells the Venetian state that 'the practice of his religion' will be 'restricted to himself, and his famiglia', the young men he's brought with him from England to staff his embassy, 'without ever admitting any others to his house', 'such as Flemings or Germans, nor even English not in his employment', because the English 'ordinarily in Venice are for the most part Catholics', recusants in exile he'll have nothing to do with. Further, he's 'certain never to give any scandal nor disgrace, public or private, in the city' for the dubiously patriotic reason that his exercise will always be in English, which is not understood by any not of that nation.

Only weeks later, however, he's seriously worried. 'Certain rumours' have spread 'that on days of prayer, and especially when we celebrate the cena' – Holy Communion – 'the house of the Ambassador of the King of England is frequented not only by our countrymen, but by Italians'. Wotton doesn't 'know where this rumour has come from' but suspects it 'originates from one among ourselves' – that is, rogue Englishmen and recusants. These rumour-mongers might want to wreck Wotton's reputation. Or sabotage his embassy. But such rumours 'will never be true'. He'll never permit 'Italians to be pointed at'. He'll keep his 'house according to the terms to which we are restricted'. In that, he sounds 'honest' enough. But for how long? Shortly, he'll be trafficking in 'matters of great secrecy' that tangle religion and state into a Gordian knot – and involve deep dissembling.

'A ramasse of rogues'

The English ambassador, Wotton soon enough learns, is to spend most of his time in the Collegio arguing – mind-numbingly – about ships. In London, before he departed, he listened to city merchants recount decades-old grievances – and met the newly appointed ambassador Molin, just arrived from Venice, whose ship, to the Crown's mortification, was plundered by (English?) pirates enroute. Now in Venice, Wotton hears a string of complaints amounting to a Sargasso sea of claims, counterclaims and litigation that's dragged on for years, involving factors, crews, cargoes, passengers, marine insurers and long-winded tit-for-tat accusations about merchant ships mistaken for pirates, taken by pirates or, indeed, pirating.

Venice hasn't dominated trade in the Mediterranean for decades but still maintains ports and lucrative trading posts down the Adriatic (Dalmatia, Ragusa, Durazzo), across the Mediterranean (Corfu, Candia, Zante), east into the Levant (Tripoli, Tyre, Antioch) and north to Constantinople (where there's a Venetian embassy). She jealously defends laws she regularly reiterates, for example on the monopolistic export of *uve passe*, currants worth their weight in gold in England. But *uve passe* can only arrive in England legally by a single route, so restrictive as to make sense only to Venetian customs agents: exported from Zante 'to Venice in Venetian ships belonging to subjects of our Signory, officered and manned for the most part either by Venetian subjects or by Greeks as is permitted by our laws'. One English captain caught smuggling *uve passe* on an English ship bound straight for London was banned from Venice – city, sea and land territories – for life.

Meanwhile, since the 1580s, English merchantmen have increasingly challenged the Republic's dwindling power in the Mediterranean, undercutting the Venetian cloth trade to the Levant with cheap kerseys shipped direct from London and taking control of the grain shipments the Republic depends upon to feed the city. Alongside legitimate commerce, Elizabeth's government (as long as England is at war with Spain) tolerates, subsidises and takes a cut from the 'free trade' its victims call 'piracy': the harrying of the Spanish gold convoys, the dressed-up raids by Essex on Cadiz and Drake on San Juan. When the English breach the Straits of Gibraltar, they bring Atlantic habits into the Mediterranean. As one Venetian complains, although they carry 'merchandise too', the English are 'brigands' who treat 'every ship' they meet 'as an enemy, without distinguishing whether it belonged to friend or foe'. Purporting to target Spain, their real aim is 'to reach the Levant and to harry and plunder the ships and subjects' of the Republic.

English ships in these waters are peculiarly equipped for handy-dandy shifts from legitimate trade to piracy: *bertoni* – a corruption of their national origins, 'Breton' – are three-masted, crewed by sixty or so and square-rigged with miles of sail. (Venetian galleys are rowed, and these days by slaves motivated only to keep the lash off their backs.) They can move a surprising amount of cargo, measured in 'butts', 500 or so, some 14,500 English cubic feet. As merchantmen, then, they're solid, fast and deliver on investment. And this is the crucial detail: originally designed as warships, merchant *bertoni* can at any time be re-armed with twenty or thirty cannon, transformed into fearsome fighting machines.

Of course, as the man from the admiralty blandly assured Molin in June 1604, 'now that war with Spain is over', 'no corsairs would be allowed to put to sea'. The operative word is 'allowed'. Will Thomas Shirley, William Pierce, the notorious John Ward – names reeking of gunpowder that will all come before Ambassador Wotton accused of piracy – cease what they've developed into a niche commercial industry when it's not 'allowed'? Besides, even if all piracy stopped the moment the ink on the Anglo-Spanish treaty dried, dozens of cases would remain contested on both sides. It's not just English brigands who treat every ship they encounter like an enemy. Venetian galleys do, too, at least according to the English. A case Wotton brings to the Collegio in January 1605 can be taken as typical of all the complaints covering page upon page that he deals with this year.

He presents an affidavit detailing the attack on 'the *Angel* of London ... the 30th ... of June 1603', that is, two years earlier, before peace with Spain was concluded. (Here we experience the see-saw tedium of the ambassador's quotidian business and the diplomatic dance steps he must perform.) Wotton alleges: 'Four Venetian galleys near the island of Zante fired six shots of artillery' on the *Angel* before asking 'to whom it belonged or where it was headed'. The *Angel* dispatched five Englishmen in a longboat with *bona fides*. Ordered to board the lead galley, they refused, saying they'd need further orders from their captain, whereupon the Venetians opened fire, killing one, wounding two, taking command of the longboat, and continuing to fire upon the *Angel* herself, wounding 'many passengers, both Turks and others'.

At this point the *Angel*'s captain sent 'a Greek with letters written by some Italian merchants to give reassurance that the ship was not a pirate, but a merchant ship'. Only when the Greek returned and identified the galleys as authentically Venetian did the captain present himself to the commander, who, promising 'every courtesy and good treatment', offered 'to tow the ship ... to the port of Zante'. But at Zante, outrage was added to injury when, instead of receiving recompense the ship was impounded for twenty-five days, 'the merchants imprisoned and forced to unload all their goods' and further ordered to 'pay 2% for the inventory' of the cargo, as though the *Angel* were a shipwreck. The claimants say they've spent more than a thousand ducats arguing the case.

Wotton urges compensation, *maximum* financial compensation, since no amount of damages will bring back the dead. Further, 'it must be ensured in the future that ministers of this Most Serene Republic who go abroad with galleys distinguish better between pirates and honest men'. (Long-windedly, he's just incriminated the Venetian state for this debacle.) Grimani murmurs assurances but sidesteps: 'English vessels have done, and still do, great damage to our vessels'. 'They decline to make themselves known to our galleys' and so 'are themselves the cause of what results'. Wotton nods (diplomatically). Grimani's observation is 'prudent'. But he objects: the ship *did* follow procedure. The *Angel* lowered 'the top foresail', the *trinchetto di cheba*, 'which is a signal in our seas'. If Venice has a 'different custom', she should declare it so the king can 'command his subjects, and punish those who fail to obey'. 'In the final analysis,' Wotton remarks airily, 'only three or four pirates will hold out disobedient'. Grimani defers: 'This being a Republic', the dispute will be heard by the Senato. (Of course. Wotton imagines doors opening and closing as his esposizione meanders its way through consultation.)

Eleven days later he's summoned to the Collegio. Scaramelli reads the Senato's deliberazione. It's terse. 'As regards the *Angel*, we find that the disturbance was brought about by that vessel refusing to allow our Commander in those waters to search her'. Wotton is dumbfounded. 'Io fin'hora non so dir altro' (I don't know what else to say). Except: 'if things remain as they are it will be a significant concern'. Grimani agrees. 'Further consideration will be required'. More doors. Wotton exits on a parting shot. It shouldn't be 'at all difficult to tell well-meaning men from pirates': 'pirate ships ... don't carry cargo above the water'.

Not difficult? That's absurd. For what emerges from this case and the dozens like it is that recognition at sea is the fundamental problem of international maritime trade. The *Angel* thinks the galleys are Spanish and hostile; the Venetians that the *Angel*, resisting search, is a pirate. Compounding the 'misunderstanding' that 'led to the chaos of combat' is the confusion of languages. It's Babel on the Mediterranean. The *Angel* has an English captain, English sailors in her longboat, an international passenger manifest and latterly a Greek carrying a message of reassurance written in Italian. Sending English sailors in that first sally, the *Angel* might as well have sent baaing sheep: we remember John Florio (no one past Dover speaks English) and Wotton (only the English understand English). When another such case blows up, the hapless Master will depose that he 'challenged' the 'pirate' that 'bore down on us'. But didn't understand the answer. It 'came in English'.

There's also the problem of partial reporting. Or plainly self-interested reporting, like the case of the *Moresini*, attacked off Zante with the retiring governor aboard. As Michiel reports it, he shipped himself, his family and his worldly goods homeward to Venice aboard a bertone because she was a 'good, sound' and, most significantly, 'well-armed ship'. So: not unambiguously a merchantman. Even so, she was 'plundered by pirates'. He calls them 'assassins', 'robbers', most of them 'English', who, while they 'left other merchandise of value alone', 'fell upon my goods like mad dogs', giving the 'greatest proof of their cruelty' by killing 'some doves that my womenfolk were sending home for their particular delight'. Their reason? Nothing to do with piracy. Rather, vengeance on him for having pronounced justice upon 'a captain and three English sailors' in Zante. He had them hanged.

That's the version of the story Wotton hears in February, a 'complaint' 'upon a ramasse of rogues' in a 'small bark', its master, 'English'. Curiously, he observes, 'They took very little' out of the *Moresini*, 'forbearing the rest upon entreaty of some English passengers, with more temperance than I thought had been in those kind of men'. He's right to be curious. He does some digging. He informs the Collegio in language much more diplomatically couched than he uses when he writes to London on the matter, that he's 'succeeded in hearing the whole story clearly from a young merchant who was on the plundered ship'. A different account emerges. The ship 'that committed the offence' had 'a crew of 99 men aboard, all of them', Wotton allows, 'wicked men', but not all English. Now, we can hear Wotton musing thoughtfully, he has 'greatly marvelled' that 'when they had drawn alongside the Venetian ship, they damaged it only a very little'. Odd behaviour for pirates and assassins.

Oddity that's explained as more facts emerge. Both ships were captained by Englishmen. There was no attack. They 'pulled alongside' each other 'as friends', the so-called 'pirate' sailing 'to the leeward', 'which no enemy would do'. What started as friendly eating and drinking fell to drunken plundering after barrels of wine crossed between ships. Except even as Wotton tells it, it isn't that straightforward. The whole encounter lasted more than two days. Skiffs passed back and forth. The 'pirate' cruised the *Moresini* overnight. Her Master was taken hostage and clapped below decks. *Then* the plunder ensued. But not randomly. Governor Michiel's stuff was its target, for as the *Moresini*'s Master deposed, 'The chief officer' of the 'pirate' 'made us understand' 'that … anything belonging to [us] … would be restored'. Reading between the lines of events never fully recounted, it seems someone at some point in the convivialities got wind of who was aboard the *Moresini*. The hanging governor of Zante. Which triggered a rampage of mad dogs. Result: a cage of dead doves. This 'pirate', then, was no 'pirate'. It was 'The Revenge'.

From this sorry mess Wotton hopes to salvage something. It's an ambassador's job to make the best of things, so he flashes the Collegio a smile and says he's glad the *Moresini* gives him the opportunity 'to speak again' of 'how vehement his Majesty will be to punish these enormities'. Writing to London, though, his smile is more of a smirk. Setting the *Moresini* against the *Angel* he's sure 'Our complaints' trump 'the Venetians''. 'Ours' are 'far different' 'because they are laid not upon outlawed vagabonds', but 'upon the very officers of this State'. It's 'the ministers' of the Signoria, after all, not some 'ramasse of rogues', who fired upon the *Angel*. In terms of diplomacy, then, Wotton sets himself on the higher moral ground. The Venetians may bluster about 'outrages', burdening the case with 'much contumacy'. But the 'partiality' of their report makes it appear 'a mere shift'. Certainly, the 'rogues' must be condemned – but also sneakily admired. They're 'not very innocent', but that just shows them to be bully-boy Englishmen, for it's the 'timorousness of the Venetian generals' that eggs them on to a scrap.

Arguments about recognition at sea flounder along like galleys dragging their anchors. The Senato issues a 'final decision'. Wotton persists 'as if he had not heard' it. Finally, His Majesty sends a definitive proclamation. Henceforth, 'all the Captains and Masters of Ships under his Crowns – whenever they shall meet Venetian Galleys, be it in windy, or calm conditions' – et cetera, et cetera – will 'vail their topsail', 'send a boat' – et cetera, et cetera. Any who 'recuse' will 'be considered' – and persecuted – 'as corsairs'. So that settles it. But maybe not. Secretary Cecil glosses the proclamation: yes, topsails will be struck, but not 'outside the Adriatic'. For that would 'compromise the dignity of the King'. It looks, then, like ships will sail on unrecognised; that 'misunderstanding' will continue – and, consequently, the 'chaos of combat'. The king's 'dignity', it appears, counts for more than English sailors mistaken for pirates shot to pieces in longboats.

'Narrow and inglorious'

5 October 1605. On the anniversary of his first year in office, Wotton appears in the Collegio quoting Tacitus, who calls the work of ambassadors 'narrow and inglorious'. He's thinking about the long string of 'quarrels, complaints' he's brought to the Collegio across the year; about himself, moaner-in-chief; and about today's agenda item. Despite his efforts, he still hasn't managed to 'fix' the so-called 'anchorage tax'. After recognition at sea, it's the greatest stumbling block to Anglo-Venetian free trade.

In Venice, the English complain that they, alone among nations trading to the Republic, must pay 'four ducats and a half for every hundred ducats of merchandise' landed anywhere in Venetian territories, while in His Majesty's ports, Venetians pay 'no more than a ductone' (tuppence, a snip). Balderdash, say the Venetians. In London, the *only* English port licensed to their entry, they face customs so 'insupportable' that their ships have been driven out of the English trade: ten ducats a tonne on *uve passe*, six on a hogshead of wine. And more than taxes, 'insupportable' restrictions. They must sell only to London merchants; pay a ducat a head a month to the parish; and invest all their capital in England. In consequence, the number of Venetian ships docking in London has dropped to zero. It's true, more Venetian merchandise is arriving in London than a decade ago, but only on English ships. Tax, like topsails, will be disputed for years.

But not all his efforts are 'narrow and inglorious'. Certainly not the case he has pursued for months against a Venetian nobleman accused of murdering an English merchant. Wotton knows something's in the wind in late March when he stops Scaramelli outside the Collegio wanting to talk about 'Balbi'. The secretary won't. Still, Scaramelli must know that Nicolò Balbi, a 'most distinguished' scion of an illustrious family recently installed in a magnificent new palazzo on the Canal Grande, isn't at home. The Dieci arrested him a fortnight ago by unanimous ballot.

Two months later, Balbi's advocate, one Giovanni Finetti, arrives 'very freshly' at Wotton's door. No pettifogger, he's one of the Republic's most prestigious advocates, in his seventies, an orator who gathers crowds. Venetians, it's said, forget what business they're about when this Orpheus of the law captures their hearing with his 'ingenious arguments'. Wotton no doubt has Finetti ushered into his 'camera d'audientia', his formal receiving room, and offered a green velvet upholstered chair, which the avvocato no doubt declines, being used to holding forth on his feet.

Finetti begins 'running over the matter ... very rhetorically', apparently angling for the complaints against Balbi to be dropped. Wotton gives 'him good breath'. Then watches Finetti mouth air like a fish out of water when the ambassador interrupts, sarcastically opining that Finetti's client 'very well knew how to take away the life of another man, yet it seemed he was mistaken in the saving of his own', which 'was not to be done by the choice of a wise advocate' but 'by plain dealing'. Wotton tells Finetti he has 'such information of the matter' that he will 'now accuse' Balbi 'to have been not only the author but the instrument of the death' of the English merchant, Nicholas Pert. This sends Finetti flapping.

He flees the embassy, returning two days later, clutching in his fist 'certain testimonies' he's drummed out of witnesses to allege Pert died 'naturally'. Wotton is unmoved. The case will be judged in the Dieci, not here in the embassy's parlour. But he advises Finetti: it would be politick to persuade Balbi in prison to return to Pert's heirs his property, including his money and private papers. Finetti is properly shaken. He's 'ready to depart' when he 'suddenly breaks forth in a wonder' that Wotton 'should speak so constantly', that is, self-confidently.

Wotton 'should' because he's sure he's going to prove murder on Balbi. Still, he tempers certainty. He knows slips happen between cup and lip. He writes as much to Cecil: 'public ministers in relations of this kind should provide a little for their own credit, and not affirm too much of the event, but leave a certain latitude for the variety of will and opinion in a strange state'. That's diplomatic language for 'judgement is unpredictable in Venice'. 'Latitude' aside, though, he's so 'warm in this case' that 'I dare conclude' Balbi 'can not possibly escape me without some most unimaginable accident'.

Clearly, Wotton's blood is up. But what exactly is the case? Bizarrely, it's not put on record in the Collegio until the end of June, when Wotton lays out 'the circumstances that preceded, that accompanied, and that followed the death of the Englishman'. Even then, the facts have to be excavated from a mass of pertinence, impertinence, narrative leaps and random asides that Wotton crossweaves into the tangled fabric of his esposizione. Untangled, it goes something like this: Pert was sailing to the Levant via Zante on Balbi's ship. It put in to Ragusa. There Balbi took a loan from the merchant equivalent to 150 English crowns. Back at sea, 'in the morning', 'Nicolò Pert was found' in his quarters 'with his mouth, nostrils and ears all full of blood, and his strongbox [fallen] on his head'. His servant 'boy was immediately sent from the cabin so he would not see the body of his master'. Pert's 'papers and everything else, was gone'. So was 'money' in a 'little case'.

> Then followed ... Balbi's dealing with the ... boy, petting him and making much of him, telling him, 'Listen dear Gioannc. Say your master left nothing, or very little.' 'But', answered the boy, 'I have already said everything. The sailors all know.' Balbi replied, 'You are young, and you do not know the ways of the world. I want you to give ten [ducats] to one person and another ten ducats to another person, and they shall never accuse us, and I shall take you with me to Venice, where I shall give you a place in my house, and I shall love you like a son, and I shall give you a wife.'

This, for Wotton, is enough to condemn Balbi. He has pictured the scene: the body, the strongbox, the blood. He has reported the insinuating speech: the corrupting of the child. He doesn't need to 'waste time' discounting Finetti's 'witnesses' (who suggest death by natural causes, alleging 'Pert's ill-health before he took ship', 'some abscess'). Nor does he waste time on Finetti himself, who's clearly trying to throw the case. Wotton ends his statement with a flourish. In 'the name of the King of Great Britain' he requires 'civil and criminal justice against Lord Nicolò Balbi' and restitution of Pert's papers, clothes, silver and more than 6,000 ducats.

His big 'ba-boom!' moment is met with silence. Three weeks pass. On 19 July, the Dieci doesn't issue a verdict but begins an investigation, recording their 'doubt about what happened on board the ship'. They propose a ballot. The alternatives are stark: 'call on Balbi to plead' or 'proceed to torture'. Venetian justice suffers no softies. Three of the Dieci vote for torture; eight, to summon him to put in his defence; four abstain. In September they submit a 'motion to proceed'. Their deliberations aren't recorded, but it's clear by the way the investigation drags on and by voting patterns along the way that it's by no means an open-and-shut case. The first ballot in September is locked: ayes/4; noes/6; neutrals/5. So they re-jig the question and re-ballot: 4/9/2. With these numbers, Balbi is 'absolved'.

Wotton doesn't hear this verdict for another fortnight. He may be astonished. Even incredulous. What he declares in the Collegio is that he's 'contento molto bene' – delighted – with the verdict. First, because he can 'surely declare' to His Majesty 'that Nicolò Pert, his subject, did not die a violent, but a natural death'. And secondly, because the verdict runs along the bias of his own nature, 'by inclination delighting myself much more with balls, parties, comedies than tragic and baleful spectacles'. 'Balli, feste, comedie': he paints himself a gormless Andrew Aguecheek 'delight[ing] in masques and revels sometimes altogether'.

Is he serious? Or is this the 'honest dissembler' working overtime? The dispatch he writes to London doesn't survive but it's clearly less than 'contento', for Secretary Cecil is surely working from that dispatch when he addresses Molin on 'the sentence recently passed in favour of a gentleman named Balbi'. Facing Molin, Cecil is a cat walking barbed wire. Of the verdict, he says, 'One cannot say that it is unjust but one may affirm that it came as a surprise to everyone, including Signore Balbi himself; for if he knew himself innocent and able to prove it why should he have sent his relations more than once to our ambassador to beg him not to make representations to the Doge?' Molin tells Cecil he can 'take it for certain' that the verdict was 'just'. Cecil retorts: 'I do not say ... the sentence was unjust but I do say it was unexpected'. Molin's reply aims a slingshot at a cat: 'That often happens ... to those who judge by the canon of interests, not of duty, and who let their passions persuade them that anything contrary to their desire must be unjust and unreasonable'. 'Well', says Cecil, 'let us pass to another point'. The cat climbs down. Out of shot.

Putting 'interests', by which he means self-interests, against 'duty', Molin neatly sidesteps how often, in Venice, they are one and the same thing. Ambassador to a Republic that is an oligarchy, ruled by a patrician class of *nobili* whose family names echo across centuries as sonorously as the Marangona tolls daily across San Marco, what Wotton forgets to consider in the case of Pert v. Balbì is the 'unimaginable accident' of Nicolò Balbì's birth.

Standing 'generally very well with them'

If Wotton audits what he's achieved in this first year of his embassy, he can be modestly satisfied. He's confounded Secretary Cecil's predictions of 'barren' business. He's put in seventeen audiences in the Collegio, captured in some twenty-four thousand words of esposizione: that's several hours-worth of talk talked thereafter into the cocked ears of the Senato. His first audience was delivered in such a 'low voice' that Secretary Scaramelli had to strain to hear him. A year later, he's found his voice (and teeth). He's shaken Avvocato Finetti by the scruff of his neck. He's been an English bulldog in the case of Seget-the-Scot. He's long-since dumped preconceptions he arrived with about how in his esposizioni he should employ rhetoric in the florid 'Italian style'. That said, he's been keen to demonstrate his humanist credentials, dredging up Cicero, Plutarch, Tacitus – frequently misquoted in Latin his memory mangles. But that's of little consequence. He'll hardly be pulled up on his Latin by any of the Savii. They left Rome's language to the clerics long ago. He's begun to 'stand generally very well with them since I began to be somewhat plain'.

He's been the bearer of important news: the birth of an English princess; the 'Proclamation' that 'his majesty' has 'caused … his title to be changed', 'to be called henceforth King of Great Britanny', signalling the union of 'the two kingdoms of England and Scotland' – a union that won't actually be settled for another hundred years. (Sending this message, Cecil's tongue slipped. He first wrote of the union, 'England and Irela'. Wishful thinking?) Promoting Anglo-Venetian trade, Wotton has proposed major innovations, including the establishment of an English 'fondaco' along the lines of the impressive Fondaco dei Tedeschi at the Rialto, which serves German merchants as hostel, warehouse and commercial hub.

But he admits to frustrations this year, too. The 'fondaco' has been blocked. Too high a presence in the city for Protestants, perhaps. So has Wotton's attempt to buck protocol by having a private conference with the next ambassador-elect, Zorzi Giustinian, before he sets off for London. Proposing such exceptionalism, he said he was sure no 'shadow or jealousy of state' – that is, suspicion – could be 'attached to a secret channel of communication between ambassadors'. But his reasoning is as murky as candle smoke on glass: 'public figures who live with great obligations should always find an exit strategy so that certain things they say to many people are not – shall I say – thrown in their faces'. Secret channel? Exit strategy? Honest dissembling?

Men with beards as grey as Grimani's aren't likely to be taken in by such casuistry. Grimani has, this year, been educating the English ambassador on the craft of diplomacy-by-deferral. Venice knows 'about all the Princes of the world who, holding supreme authority, by their single will alone decide matters'. But: 'Things are not so here'. Here, we have 'many advisors'; 'the greater this number, the more time is required' to 'hear the opinion of each of them before resolutions are decided by a vote in the Senato'. No wonder the case of the *Angel* has dragged on for two years already and won't be resolved any time soon.

Meanwhile, even as he's been settling into his new embassy, Wotton has received schooling on diplomacy from a different direction, from Cecil, who sent him a copy of the Anglo-Spanish peace treaty concluded just as Wotton was riding for Venice. The ink on the document can hardly have dried. (Nor the paint on the group portrait commemorating the Somerset House Conference, eleven ruffed men seated across a turkey-carpeted table, Cecil down front, inkwell to hand, secretary to the proceedings.) The treaty, however, isn't politically transparent. It needs 'interpretation'. And Cecil enclosed 'interpretation'. Because, he wrote, 'it may be many glosses … will be fastened (especially of some particular articles) by some such that only regard the literal words and not the sense and coherency of the matter'. So: 'howsoever the words may seem restrictive', 'yet there can not be anything justly inferred from them'. That's breathtaking. And worth a re-read. 'The words may seem restrictive'. But 'there can not be anything … inferred from them'. So, what's this treaty worth? If its 'literal words' don't express its 'sense'? If it juggles the 'restrictive' and the 'inferred'? Cecil is scripting what later internationalists will call 'constructive ambiguity', 'plausible deniability'. He's teaching Ambassador Wotton how to 'lie abroad'.

Now, on this October afternoon when he returns to the embassy from the audience that marked his first year in office, Wotton settles into his favourite chair. He pulls it to the far end of his 'chamber of entertainment', just outside the frame of the floor-to-ceiling leaded-glass doors that open onto his shallow stone balcony. From this vantage he can hear the 'rumore' below, trafficking up and down the busy rio San Girolamo and along the fondamenta – while he stays out of sight. The October sun is mellow. September has finally coaxed August into pulling its brutal punch, gloved now in morning mists lying on the lagoon. Wotton is pensive. The lulling dip and lift of his gondolier's oars cutting the waters between San Marco and San Girolamo gave him time for a rethink. All those twenty-four thousand words. To what end? Have his dispatches *really* confounded Cecil's sour predictions of 'barren' business? Is his diplomatic future simply to be a dreary round of indecisive wrangles over *Marita*s, *Husband*s, *Angel*s? Of demands wafted aside with rhetorical gestures honed over centuries that show Venetians performing diplomacy as an art of paralysis? The man who sailed to Cadiz, who trudged across Ireland with Essex, who spurred to Scotland as Ottavio Baldi wants action.

On this October afternoon he can't imagine what's hurtling towards him, a perfect storm brewed from events in London in November and Rome in December, a storm that's about to break over the ambassador's head.

11
Household stuff

'Vicina la Chiesa à San Girolamo'

March 1605. Halfway through his first year in office, 'Arrigo VVottoni' (as he's known locally) is exchanging messages back and forth across Venice with the Jesuit Antonio Possevino. They have things in common. Both diplomats. Both well travelled. Both bookish. (The Jesuit is compiling a vast bibliography of eight thousand books on sacred Scripture.) Both students of law and fascinated by scientific questions. Both past masters in rhetorical tit-for-tatting. Both experienced in exile. (Possevino is currently banned from Rome to the Venetian territories as 'too political'.) After that, they're chalk and cheese. Besides their thirty years' age difference, they face this world and the world to come across a confessional gulf, militant Catholic v. militant Protestant. The Jesuit is the spiritual leader of the *vecchi*, the hard-line, pro-papal old-timers in the Venetian Senato. The Englishman is in sympathy with the *giovani*, the young progressives (most of them over sixty). There's always the stink of sulphur in their exchanges. As a student travelling disguised as a Dutchman in Rome a decade back, Wotton sat so rapturously at Possevino's feet soaking up doctrine that the Jesuit 'si credeva ch'io fussi uno delli suoi agnelli' ('believed that I was one of his lambs').

Now the Jesuit and the ambassador are sparring over some insults allegedly made by a drunken English sailor on shore leave. Possevino hopes that 'by the actions of some English sailors' his king's reputation won't be blemished. Wotton smells Jesuit sanctimony. He is 'stupisco' – amazed – that his king should be in any way prejudiced by such footling business, 'as if the sacred person of the Prince were charged with every particular deed and every vain word from every one of his subjects'. He suggests the Jesuits should attend to their own 'opera' and clean up 'their abuses of gold and silver', a dig that

14 2967 Cannaregio. This palazzo, shown in a modern photograph and given its modern address, housed Wotton's English embassy.

gets no rise out of Possevino. He's vowed to poverty, no doubt living in the Casa Professa attached to the Jesuit college at Santa Maria dell'Umiltà on the Zattere. He sends Wotton a book – maybe a title from among the eight thousand he's cataloguing. But Wotton excuses himself from further compliment. He's not been sent here to debate ('mandato qui per disputare'), especially 'things outside our brief'. Besides, he's busy moving house.

So far, the English ambassador has been billeted in temporary quarters while accommodation that suits both the Signoria and the delegation is found. Now, he and his *famiglia*, the seven young gentlemen who have travelled across Europe to take up residence with him in Venice as servants and apprentices in statecraft, move the embassy to its permanent address at Cannaregio. Today, *more veneto*, it is 2967 Cannaregio – though of course that means nothing in Wotton's Venice. House numbers will arrive only in 1797, on the bureaucratic coat tails of Napoleon. Before that, directions go by landmark: 'al ponte delli mori', 'nella corte del forno', 'appresso l'ospedale' (at the moors' bridge, in the baker's court, near the hospital). Anyone looking for the 'casa dell'Ambasciator d'inghilterra' from March 1605 will be told 'che sta à San Gieronimo', 'vicina la chiesa', 'where the Jewish Ghetto is': at San Girolamo, near the church, adjacent to the tiny island where, since 1516, the city's Jewish population has been contained.

The address is significant, for the English embassy is to be located as far away as possible from the Signoria's centre of government in San Marco. Venice may have invented the role of the resident ambassador, but she continues to view such residents doubtfully. They're 'honest spies', their business, to inform on their hosts, so they need to be kept under surveillance, remote from government but planted among snoopers, surrounded by working-class bustle in some of the city's most crowded corners. Spain occupies an impressive palazzo along 'calle larga', down from Santa Lucia; France, a stately but less ostentatious pile on the fondamenta della Sensa, close to Madonna dell' Orto. Now the English are installed, one fondamenta over from the French, in a modest palazzo along Rio San Girolamo – scaled perhaps to what's expected of their mission.

We can imagine Wotton looking around his new residence with satisfaction. Home. But also the ambassador's workplace. Domestic and personal; public and professional. It's self-contained, with an ample garden, enclosed by a high brick wall. The tradesmen's entrance faces the fondamenta. There's no back gate, so no separate access. Neither is there a porta d'acqua, a watergate. He understands what this means: his movements in his gondola are to be in plain sight of his neighbours, and anyone visiting the embassy will be equally visible, needing to tie up along the rio. On foot, they'll be seen walking to the embassy's front door, opening as it does onto the pavement. It's obvious that the English embassy is located deliberately for scrutiny.

The palazzo itself is one of Jacopo Sansovino's minor projects, built some forty or fifty years back while the architect was engaged in transforming Venice into a modern Renaissance city. He used rejects and off-cuts in the new-build, like the fountainhead cut from a single piece of Istrian stone that, as much for its ingenuity as its cool beauty, strikes Wotton the moment he enters. It's fixed to face onto the ground-floor *piano terra*, hiding a well in a back room that feeds it water. The simplicity of the palazzo's layout, its intimacy is appealing. Only fifteen rooms. On the *piano terra*, the entrance hall is wide, stone-paved, with storage magazines, a pantry, the servants' staircase and a 'little chamber' concealed behind wood-panelled doors. The main staircase leading off is functional, nothing grand about it. Above, galleries interconnect rooms on three floors. Servants will occupy the low-ceilinged *primo piano* one floor above: that's customary. A porthole window facing the front door lets residents eyeball anyone who comes knocking. On the top floor there's an 'upper sala' and bedchambers eventually furnished with thirteen beds. But the glory of the place is on the second floor, the *piano nobile*, the diplomatic reception area with its 'sala', 'dining chamber', 'lord's study' and 'chamber of entertainment'. This last runs the full depth of the building. It can receive thirty, maybe more at a push. The aspect facing the fondamenta is set with three pairs of floor-to-ceiling glazed doors that look northwest, to catch the evening sun.

This wall of glass strikes the English as marvellous. There's nothing like it domestically in England, where narrow lattice windows shed miserly light onto gloomy interiors. In Venice, light is a spendthrift, and glaziers' shops are everywhere, trying to keep pace with its squandering. Light reflects off the lagoon, off the canals. Let inside through glass doors, it dazzles interiors. It even bounces off the palazzo's speckled, marble-chip terrazzo floors, another wonder. There's a shallow stone balcony jutting out from the glass doors. When they're open Wotton can sit unseen and hear the 'rumore' passing with the traffic below. The English embassy, it seems, is located accidentally for eavesdropping.

Wotton knows his house will be watched. Practically the moment the Protestants arrive in Venice, the papal nuncio is crying out against heresy planted in their midst. Now, the embassy has been established at an official address as well known to the *popolani* – Wotton's immediate neighbours: bakers, bricklayers, boatmen, painters, *artefici* of all stripes – as to the *nobili* and the nuns, monks and priests whose churches and convents overlook it. He'll have to walk in felt slippers in this city. Noiselessly. He can't let the embassy be pointed at as a locus of seduction, luring the faithful to conversion. Yes, Anglican worship will be conducted there. Wotton has made it clear that he's 'not able to live without the practice of his religion'. The eucharist will be celebrated. Sermons will be heard. Prayers morning and evening will follow the English Book of Common Prayer. But only in English. All of this will be 'occasional'. And portable. So, in objective terms, deniable.

There's no room in the embassy designated as a chapel, no *place* of worship that might be denounced as the magnet of heresy the nuncio so feverishly imagines drawing gullible Venetians to damnation. It could hardly be otherwise. A chapel would need consecrating by an Anglican bishop, an intervention the Signoria, tolerant as it is, could hardly allow. Besides, English Protestants, armed with their prayer book, need none of the 'superstitious' trappings of Catholic veneration, the relics, the statues, the votives, the altars, the confession boxes that are built into the very fabric of Venice. They can worship anywhere, as Wotton has done, twice daily on ship with Essex to Cadiz in '96 and campaigning in Ireland in '99. A poop deck, a burnt-out brug, a chamber of entertainment deafened by the Catholic bells that clamour from the chiesa San Girolamo vicina: one is as 'conveniente' as the other for Protestant worship.

To make this place home, Wotton furnishes it with stuff brought by sea from England. His viol da gamba. Assorted 'holberds', 'bucklers' and 'armes' to impress visitors with material signatures of English puissance. Also among the cargo is a portrait Wotton treasures of Henry, prince of Wales, perhaps a thank-you to Wotton for delaying his journey by a couple of days to give the boy time to write his greetings to the Republic. It's bound to be a copy of the Marcus Gheeraerts original of 1603, the one that shows the pinched face of the boy-prince swamped in his Garter robes. How do Venetians view it? In Venice, signs of sovereignty aren't put onto children's shoulders.

For household stuff Wotton repairs to the Ghetto. Dealing in second-hand furniture is one of the businesses allowed the Jews. From Isaac 'Ebreo' Luzzati he leases furnishings that allow us to glimpse the material world he'll occupy, where it's austere, where it's a little plush: tables, chairs, bedsteads; hangings of 'silk', 'arras', 'damask & gilded leather'; carpets (both 'ground' and 'table'); mattresses ('flockbeds', 'straw'), sheets, bolsters, cushions (damask, embroidered). The embassy's 'chamber of entertainment' is furnished with 'green velvet chairs'; the ambassador's 'study' with 'mattress', 'stools' and 'table'; his 'chamber' with 'velvet chairs', 'hangings of arras', a 'bedstead of iron', and, perhaps the only mark of personal ostentation, a crimson 'canopy with a pavilion'. There are fires in the public rooms, but not the upper chambers or Wotton's study; the 'dining chamber' is the best-heated room, indicated by the 'pair' of 'great andirons' in the chimney. At the end of Luzzati's inventory Wotton tacks on the hire of a gondola, two iron chests – and a billiard table.

This stuff doesn't come cheap. Twenty-two ducats per month for the furnishings; 160 ducats per annum for the add-ons. There's also the lease on the palazzo itself, 50 ducats per quarter. That's extortionate. Admittedly, property values in Cannaregio have risen since the last 'Decime', the city-wide audit made for tax purposes. Still, the priciest properties in 1582 – like the artist's house and workshop at San Marcuola or the house and small garden at San Felice – fetched under 120 ducats per annum. Charging Wotton 200 ducats, the Venetian 'padrone' might be operating a stranger's surcharge such as applies in the Ghetto where the Jews must pay their Christian landlords 30 percent over the odds. Or maybe Wotton must go where the Signoria sends him – and pay what the 'padrone' demands.

It's hard to see how he can ever balance his books. Nothing unusual there. His purse has always rattled more with dead moths than ducats. He's been collecting 'diets' granted by the king's Exchequer at £3 6s. 8d. per diem since the first day of his appointment in December 1603, ten months before his arrival in Venice, 'the sum of £423 6s 8d' with another £306 13s 4d 'by way of advance' upon his next three months' 'diets'. That's £730, simply stunning for a man whose only secure income to date is the £67 annuity he collects according to his father's will. But he's never been able to live within his means, even narrowly as a student. It's anyone's guess how he supported himself in exile. Maybe he scraped a living selling information to the Medici. Maybe big brother Edward subsidised him. If he stumbled home in May 1603 down a mountain of debt, how many of his ambassadorial 'diets' will be eaten up paying creditors? Or, with that issue from the Exchequer have his fortunes turned a corner? Perhaps Sir Henry arrives in Venice feeling flush.

That can't last, with costs mounting up, 624 ducats for rents alone and prices rising relentlessly. A year hence Wotton will protest that he pays '46 ducats now for so much wine as cost me but 18 when I first came hither'. The ducat exchange rate is 2:1. That means a quarter of Wotton's annual 'diets' are allocated before he puts food on the embassy's table or makes any show of ceremony. Or indeed, figures the costs of supporting his *famiglia*.

He has seven dependants, young men barely (or not yet) out of their 'slippery' years: his chaplain, Nathaniel Fletcher (28); his secretary, William Parkhurst (23); his twenty-year-old nephew, Albertus Morton, serving under his uncle his apprenticeship in travel; and assorted others: George Rooke, a Kentishman, John Fenton, Rowland Woodward, Nicholas Ford. Henry Cogan stays behind in London, agent and listening-post to the ambassador. The whole set-up looks much like the 'family' Robert Devereux collected around himself at Essex House, men of intelligence, education, service. Woodward, thirty-one, the oldest of the *famiglia*, shares with Wotton close acquaintance with John Donne, and is the man Wotton assigns the embassy's trickiest operations. Finally, there's Wotton's Italian secretary, a Venetian, non-resident, Gregorio de Monti.

Wotton's seven will be sleeping in some of the embassy's thirteen beds. But they'll also be needing to earn their keep. The question is, how?

Bound to double-business

As ambassador, always addressing two audiences in two venues, Wotton is bound to double-business. The first he performs in that talking-shop, the Collegio, where he represents England to Venice. There, he's an orator, a mouth. The second he performs on paper, reporting Venice to England. Acting on what he sees and hears and picks up from scattered sources, he provides intelligence and information to shape England's foreign policy not just in the Republic but across Europe. In this business he's a scribbler, performing what's been called the 'craft of the hand'. He writes page after page of dispatch to King James via Secretary of State Cecil and sends briefing papers to fellow ambassadors in Paris, Madrid, Brussels. The centre of this work is the embassy, which itself is bound to double-business. It's the ambassador's private residence, nesting himself, his *famiglia* and their private entertainments. But it's also his office, a tiny patch of England's 'sceptr'd isle' set down in the Republic, privileged by the internationally agreed legal fiction of extra-territoriality that grants it sovereignty. The significance of the move to the new address Wotton tells Possevino about in March cannot be underestimated. The English, the move signals, are here to stay, and in an embassy that effectively plants a foreign enclave inside the host state, creating a mini-state and giving it diplomatic immunity which, the law of nations agrees (and Gentili drummed into Wotton's head), throws around it an unbreachable wall. Diplomatic immunity shields not just the residence but also the ambassador, his official business and his household stuff – so the chests the papal nuncio complains Wotton is using to smuggle 'heretical books' into Venice are exempt from the Inquisitor's search. Immunity, too, for his *famiglia* and any servants. They're just so much more household stuff.

So apart from giving audience to the doge every fortnight, Wotton must also manage his household and the diplomatic work that goes on there, his dispatches to London leaving a paper trail we can follow, watching him keep to the straight and narrow – or taking detours. He writes his dispatches himself. Only rarely does Secretary Parkhurst's hand show up among them (when it does, it's instantly recognisable by its even letter formation against the slouch and sprawl of Wotton's handwriting). Wotton once sends a long report dictated 'unto my secretary, my hand being, with the extremity of the hot weather faint'; once, when he's 'much tormented' with 'toothache'. From the moment he arrives in Venice, he dates his letters '*more Veneto*', 'style of the place' according to the Gregorian calendar, thus adopting himself Venetian. (Not so the next ambassador. Never truly on site, his successor will stick stubbornly to the English calendar, mentally in London, and ten days out of sync with the locals.) To the Venetians, Wotton's scribal habits are eccentric. Their ambassadors dictate all their dispatches, only signing the last page. For Wotton, though, a dispatch is a personal communication that never hides the hand that's pushing the pen.

Thanks to Cecil's negligence, few of these dispatches survive from his first year. Those that do, set down Wotton's distinctive voice in ink. (We remember

Mulcaster instructing the schoolboy: writing captures his essential 'self'; it knits the 'articulate voice' to the page; it serves 'as interpreter to the mind'.) So, for the adult Wotton, Jesuits are 'spiders that catch flies'. A notorious recusant 'enchant[s] popes and princes … with the names … of barbers and laundresses'. 'Insolencie on the one side and obstinacie on the other' make for stalemate in trade negotiations. Complaints against him 'from the Spanish side' are of no consequence to him, having 'already' been 'battered by the French'.

These earliest dispatches find Wotton worrying about the post; about interception; about miscarriage; about ambush in Milan. He worries about delay: he writes for instructions but knows he won't have an answer for at best six weeks. He worries about his own diplomatic 'immaturities', his 'boldness in a plain and confused manner to discharge … my conscience'. He begs indulgence for delivering 'things that peradventure transcend my charge', occasionally leaving a dispatch 'unsealed' so that, before it reaches the king, it 'may first pass the file' of Cecil's 'excellent judgement' – and correction. Cecil assures him, three months in, that his dispatches have all arrived. It's not like Cecil to have binned them. But they aren't filed.

Still, we know what's on the ambassador's mind. It's recorded in the matters he puts before the Collegio: the anchorage tax, recognition at sea, the Seget, Dotto and Balbi affairs, the complaints of merchants, shipowners and captains. Behind each audience lie days of preparation: research, interviews, site visits, collecting affidavits, interrogating witnesses, sifting, sifting, sifting and always writing. Wotton regularly presents himself in the Collegio as a bit of a bluffer, speaking 'off the cuff', but we know that's something of a ruse. His audiences are meticulously scripted – and can rely on a memory prodigiously trained at school. He once forwards Cecil a copy of what he's prepared for that day's appearance. The thousand-word-long esposizione he later, without notes, delivers (and Scaramelli records) is a near word-perfect oration of the prepared text. That said, such self-discipline is always, in Wotton, subject to ambush, and we regularly see him wobble just where Gentili in *De legationibus* told him he'd have to maintain a balance between affability and dignity. He can only script so much. After his opening statement, the doge will interrogate his esposizione with questions Wotton cannot fully prepare for. Under interrogation, or when the Senato delivers a decision he can't accept, discretion regularly abandons him, fails to 'confine' him within the dignified limits of his charge. In short, as we'll see, he can be rash. Prickly. Over-large in promises.

He can also be diplomatically less than candid. We know for certain, no matter what he says about how the English will restrict their activities in the

Republic, that he's hardly settled into his embassy on Cannaregio in the spring of 1605 when he's ignoring all that, looking beyond Venice, scanning Italy, broaching business far removed from topics debated in the Collegio and putting his ear to channels of communication not issuing from London. The 'craft of the hand' revealed in dispatches turns out to be crafty. He has 'confidential' sources and 'secret means' feeding him 'sufficient knowledge even from those that could wish it otherwise'. So: he admits to spying.

No wonder, given events on the ground. That March, the hard-line reformist pope Clement VIII dies. Wotton writes of feeding frenzy among Aldobrandini and Sixtine, family competitors in the papal election. Will Clement be succeeded by the Spanish-backed candidate or the man the French promote, who provokes 'distraction for the Spaniards'? The French faction carries it, but Leo XI occupies St Peter's chair for less than a month, coming 'strangely' to it and going 'doubtfully out of it'. (Wotton remains dry-eyed on the passing of popes.) Leo is succeeded by Paolo V, cut from Clement's cloth, but stiffer. He'll take watching. Only 'study' will show 'what this pope will prove'. Worryingly, some 'affirm the pope's daily inclination more and more to the Jesuits'.

Over this unbearably hot summer, when fig trees wilt and hands 'faint', Wotton takes the measure of this new pope, sending London 'troublesome dispatches of the matters of Rome'. King James's liberalisation policy has produced unintended consequences. His 'opening of his ports to all nations' means that what was possible 'under the late queen' – tracking Jesuit movements – is compromised. Wotton briefs his king on 'the restraint' of 'his subjects abroad'. He should 'lay an absolute prohibition' on travellers from 'all conference and conversation' with 'any Jesuits, priests, seminary schoolers or friars of their own language': that is, contact with English recusants like the ex-pat and increasingly radical Jesuit intriguer Robert Parsons, who's back in Rome, yapping in the pope's ear his mission to infiltrate and reconvert England to Catholicism. Wotton suggests that from his embassy he can have English travellers tailed and 'an account' given His Majesty 'of his subjects' courses' 'by our secret intelligences'.

He figures what he's doing as watching 'spiders' 'busy ... about their own objects'. The metaphor is tacitly self-referential. Spiders 'catch flies' while 'bees ... make honey', differing 'rather in their ends then in their pains'. (It's writing like this, 'notable not just for attention to ... this state' but 'enterlaced with variety of conversation' that delights King James, who says he reads 'not any foreign dispatches from any of our ministers with better contentation'.) Wotton, too, is 'busy'. He's the 'bee' in this scenario, and the 'honey' he intends is the ransacking of the spiders' webs. 'I shall much satisfy my soul', he writes, 'and reward myself with the very comfort that I take in my own labour if I can any way in these countries intercept the knowledge of their workings and counsels'.

No 'if' about it. He has already embarked on precisely such interception. Just months ago he was a man, he told the Collegio, whose 'nature' was 'not … to search out news'. Clearly, that sluggish worm has turned. In May, he writes Cecil a frank account of planting spies in Milan.

'Instructions … unto two of mine own family'

He begins by sending Cecil a draft of two instructions, one of which 'hath succeeded ill by a sudden accident', the other 'yet in contingency'. With these instructions, which we'll return to, we begin to see how Wotton employs his dependent *famiglia*. Two of the family have official duties as chaplain (Nathaniel Fletcher) and secretary (William Parkhurst). Before family business forces Fletcher to return to England in September 1606, he conducts daily prayer in Wotton's house, occasionally celebrates the 'cena', Holy Communion, and offers a programme of sermons that open up the Gospel to reformed interpretation, study, discussion and spiritual orientation. Sermons keep Protestant eyes fixed on true things while their ears are assailed by bells clanging out Catholic 'heresy' across Cannaregio day and night. This little band of Protestants in their spiritual redoubt perceive they have as much to fear from Catholics as vice versa, and Fletcher is responsible for their spiritual safety. (A case close to home: Wotton's Protestant nephew, Pickering, who travelled with him into exile in 1601, winds up in Spain four years later making a deathbed conversion, captured for Catholicism.)

The second official in the household is responsible for all the embassy's paperwork. Although Wotton writes his own dispatches to London, he dictates to Parkhurst the 'convenient correspondence' he sends his fellow ambassadors in Paris, Madrid and Brussels 'weekly' (or more often, 'from time to time'). Parkhurst copies all the embassy's correspondence into letter-books, documenting what's been sent, then later chasing what he suspects hasn't been delivered, what might have been purloined from the diplomatic courier or intercepted from the regular post. He keeps the embassy's ciphers secure in one of those iron chests leased from Luzzati, and where any of Wotton's dispatches requires it, he does the ciphering. He records the business brought to the embassy's door, drawn-out negotiations about Seget-the-Scot, tense interviews with

Avvocato Finetti, miserable complaints from English seamen. Working with Wotton's Italian secretary, Parkhurst preps the ambassador for appearances in the Collegio. He manages the embassy's finances.

That leaves five of the *famiglia* unaccounted for. How do young men like Rooke and Woodward, who have no official duties in Venice, serve the ambassador? We can make a shrewd guess if we see the embassy as the engine room for politick excursions that sends them on missions walking the city. Walking, these embassy men extend the ambassador's eyes and ears across calli, campi, Piazza. Walking, they're gathering. *News*-gathering. 'It is the disease of the place,' Wotton observes, 'to discourse much and freely'. But if 'discourse' is a disease in Venice, it's also an elixir. Every throat is dry for it. Every mouth gapes for it. Ears reach around corners to catch it on the wind. Officially, Venetian patricians are forbidden contact with foreign diplomats outside the Collegio. In practice, their paths often cross, on the Rialto, on street-corners, in churches like San Girolamo, where Wotton goes during Lent to hear the nuns sing, in printers' and booksellers' shops, in the (upmarket) pharmacies across the city that double as places of business and centres of news (but not the downmarket barber shops disdained by elites, where beards are shaved and teeth pulled). News is chewed over while apothecaries pound medicines in *farmacie* Wotton frequents like the Testa d'Oro, signposted by a golden head staring into the weather at the foot of the Rialto bridge, or the Ercole d'Oro at Cannaregio. It's beneath his dignity to enter Borsetto's barber shop in San Maurizio. But not beneath George Rooke's.

Rooke and his fellows can idle away hours in Piazza San Marco while the ambassador's loitering there would look suspicious. Wotton knows the Senators' gathering times 'al broglio', when they walk, talk, gossip, electioneer. If he thinks they'll be discussing votes that will affect English relations, political or commercial, he'll detail someone to the *broglio* to report on who's talking to whom. A watcher would be well positioned to pick up on suggestive human traffic even if he can't hear words. The *broglio* is noisy. Words get lost. Still, he can watch bodies – as do the state-sponsored *confidenti* who tail the Spanish ambassador in 1610. ('*Confidenti*': that's the grand-ish name you give spies working for *your* side.)

Reading these informants' snatched reports, scribbled on scraps of paper in a jumble of Italian and Venetian dialect, we can see how they work. One morning, they spot 'al broglio' one who hangs around the Spanish ambassador, 'Signor Antonio Calbo'. (He's a patrician already denounced for reading prohibited books, and he'll later be imprisoned for treason.) The *confidenti* watch

Calbo converse with some gentlemen until 'fora del broglio' (outside the *broglio*) 'un forestiero ben vestito' (a well-dressed foreigner) turns up. Calbo goes to speak with him, returns, and starts talking with Lorenzo Giustinian, a high-ranking nobleman, currently one of the powerful Savii sitting in the Collegio who are privy to ambassadors' audiences. 'E poi' (and then) Calbo goes back to the foreigner ('torno al foresto'), and, speaking with him, leaves, taking him home to his house nearby 'in cale di paveri' (Venetian for 'poppies'). So who is this well-dressed foreigner? What business does he have with Giustinian? And what is Calbo doing, acting as go-between? The *confidenti* can't say, but from this vignette we get the gist of the kind of surveillance watchers might bring as grist to the English ambassador's diplomatic mill.

Wotton's young men are multi-lingual. Presenting as Englishmen, though, they conceal that fact among strangers, at least in this first year, before they're known. In an apothecary's (among the better-heeled, where daily gazettes or avvisi are available to clients lingering for hours) or a barber's (over dice and local gossip) they ear-wig the chat, the chiacchiera. In crowds along the Merceria between San Marco and the Rialto or in the shadow of the Basilica at the edge of the *broglio*, they pocket up not just what's current on people's lips – and news is currency – but 'matters of secrecy'. They have an edge as English-speakers, for, as everyone knows, no one speaks English but the English. Talking with English merchants where they gather twice daily below the Rialto or with English sailors fresh in port, they gather political news and shipping updates that affect markets, and thereby international relations, communicating in what amounts to linguistic code – a code able also to hack into what's being noised in the ex-pat, English recusant community. Of course, any Venetian who wants information carried to the embassy will use these young men as human drop-boxes.

In this scenario, Wotton's *famiglia* emerges as intelligencers to the embassy. That's speculative. What's certain is that they are couriers of the ambassador's most confidential dispatches. When the message is urgent or conveys 'matters of secrecy', Wotton doesn't trust it to the ordinary post, to merchants, or even the diplomatic courier. He hands it to a 'sure messenger' from his household, messages like the eight lines he dashes off in November 1605 to report the serious illness of Doge Grimani. In all, Wotton sends six special couriers to London this first year. That's a significant investment of time and money. The journey over the Alps and across Europe takes couriers a good three weeks in each direction. Meanwhile, it leaves a sore gap in the embassy's personnel. 'Honest men', Wotton tells Cecil, are 'very precious here'. It's a measure of what's at stake that Wotton has 'resolved to send one of them home to your Lordship'.

On that occasion, the 'precious' courier is Rowland Woodward, carrying 'lines' (partly ciphered) of 'great importance and secrecy'. Woodward and his party get as far as France when they're set upon by footpads waving pistols. One Englishman is killed. Woodward is left for dead. Wotton doesn't know his fate for weeks: that he's been found alive, 'carried to a gentleman's house not far off' and then to Paris, to the residence of the English ambassador, before being returned to his brother's care in England, where the king himself pays £60 towards his 'medicines and diets'. Still, within six months, Woodward is back in Venice. (Meanwhile, Cecil is much more concerned about the whereabouts of the postbag that's been handed in to Henri IV. No wonder. It contains Wotton's explosive assessment of the French king's likely intervention in current 'differences' between Rome and Venice, with the prediction that he'll 'foment' 'war between … Britain and Spain' while keeping 'himself free'.)

Woodward is a tough bird, and he has form. This hasn't been his most dangerous assignment. Let's return to those 'instructions' of May 1605. One of them concerned Woodward, the 'one' that 'by a sudden accident' 'succeeded ill'. The story is hair-raising. 'Upon his own conceit' – that is, without instructions from London – Wotton says he's been 'drawn by diverse considerations' to focus diplomatic attention on Milan, a Spanish dependency and 'the place where all the Spanish aids for the Low Countries' are 'either originally levied or through which they must pass'. Milan, then, is strategically important for England, still fighting in the Netherlands. Seeing himself as the 'bee', Wotton knows that if he can sting the Spanish 'spider', he'll have achieved both a personal and political coup, never mind that acting upon his own conceit he is once again going rogue, inventing (in this case, very shady) diplomacy.

He resolves 'to bestow an instrument of mine own in Milan', where he hopes 'to derive some reasonable judgement upon what would follow as well within Italy as abroad'. His intelligencer is Woodward, a man 'of a very capable spirit'. It's his proficiency in Spanish that equips him for this mission. His cover story is that, coming 'into these countries' with the English ambassador, he's now 'desirous to obtain more perfection in the Spanish language'. As further cover Wotton provides Woodward a 'letter … dormant in his hand' full of 'complimenti' addressed to the Spanish governor of Milan, Count Fuentes, a stone-faced general whose beard looks like it's starched every morning into wings of mocking smiles that never reach his lips. Fuentes's determination to prosecute the northern wars shows no sign of running out of steam, despite his eighty years.

Almost immediately Woodward comes to grief – in the most sensationally alarming way. Wotton relates: 'Being ... settled there according to my directions at board where there was company of great quality, on Good Friday last at dinner he was taken rudely from the table by some 40 sbirri' – that's a small army of armed police – 'and thence carried into the prison of the inquisition, all his papers surprised'. 'Inquisition' is a word to strike terror in Protestant hearts. It operates a law unto itself, placing detainees in solitary confinement with no prospect of process or appeal. Four days later, though, Woodward is miraculously 'set at liberty'. He's brought before Fuentes 'who excuses ... not having sent for him sooner with those solemn days of devotion', the Easter weekend just passed. Fuentes 'very handsomely bestowed the whole matter upon the Inquisitors saying, 'Questi religiosi sono sospettosi'. That is, he blames the unfortunate arrest on those suspicious meddlers, the religionists. Woodward's 'papers and all things else' are 'rendered again unto him', but while nothing from either Fuentes or the Inquisitors betrays as much, Wotton realises those papers 'had doubtlessly been perused' and Woodward's 'ends discovered in them'. So Wotton aborted the mission and 'drew him hither again'.

What does Woodward make of this escapade? Arrest by the Inquisition and during Holy Week is no footling matter. We don't know. Wotton, however, is gaily unabashed. Such events, he tells Cecil, are 'as ordinary in the course which I now am in as blows are to soldiers and gusts to mariners'. That analogy bears scrutiny: spying, he's saying, is as much the ambassador's business as trimming sheets is the mariner's. Wotton fore-arms Cecil with an answer should London receive any complaint from Spain about his antics. 'There hath been here from that side the like practices upon me, for having but one servant in my family of a contrary religion' – that's Gregorio de Monti, his Italian secretary – 'the King of Spain thought him a fit subject to work upon', to spy inside the embassy. But de Monti 'detected' the plot to Wotton. So: tit-for-tat. Wotton is allowing the 'practise' to 'run on' in the embassy, no doubt to feed the Spanish false intelligence. 'These', he concludes with a mock worthy of the diplomat whose stated mission is to lie abroad, 'are the effects of this mining and countermining profession'.

And the Signoria? What will it make of covert operations managed from the embassy on Cannaregio? Wotton imagines the bee's buzzing will 'breed a little amusement in this State' and 'indeed ... give me here the more opinion'.

'Moved to entertain'

Bound to double-business in a residence also double-bound, Wotton and his *famiglia* lead double lives. The ambassador declares as much every time he asserts his double allegiance, 'primo ... Anglese', 'ma dopo Venetiano' (first an Englishman, but then, Venetian). Certainly, if this household is modelled on Essex's, it also in some senses resembles that 'little academe' the king of Navarre sets up in Shakespeare's *Love's Labour's Lost* as an idealised place of monastic male seclusion and study. In Wotton's case, his 'domestic college' is underpinned by his oft-repeated fiction that he's really only a humble scholar, 'tolto dalle scuole' – taken from school – and little versed in the ways of the world. That he's an innocent abroad, that he'll cause 'no scandal' in the city but 'always keep my house according to the terms to which we are restricted', allows the doge to treat him as if this were so, but perhaps to use him also as a willing, even amusing, pawn in the cat-and-mouse power game the Republic plays with Rome. From some angles, the 'buzzing bee' acts much like a 'busy spider'. But when the papal nuncio again complains of the ambassador importing heretical books, it's the nuncio who gets swatted. To 'rummage' in Wotton's shipments, the doge warns, would 'violate the *ius gentium*'. The ambassador 'lives with great reservedness', 'great continence, and abstinence, and goes about with great modesty'. But the doge has known for months of Wotton's covert operations.

So maybe Wotton's embassy resembles Navarre's 'little academe', too, in the way it immediately falls from 'continence' to deceptive 'practice'. Within six months of the failed Milan escapade, Wotton is planting 'instruments' (as he writes in cipher) in '205.55.11.48.22.3.47.16.45. 26.49.3.59.7.55.17.49.12.3.3 7.55.26.49.43.37.8.56.59.41.22.55.24.', that is, 'Rome, Milan, Turin, Frankfort and here' (note: 'here', *in Venice*) and dunning the Exchequer for funds to pay them. He's granted £200 the half year for 'intelligences'. It's not enough. His expenses 'grow more and more' for, he jokes ironically, while 'there be great store of knaves' ready to work for him, 'honest men are cheaper'. The king, Cecil replies, is 'pleased' with his 'dexterity', 'particularly ... in intercepting such letters as come sometimes from Rome'. So, if 'the service' requires 'some extraordinary charge more', 'you shall not need to be discouraged therein' – for 'reasonable sums'. It's significant that as a 'politique' trained by Essex to think across Christendom, Wotton sees his diplomacy locked into a political economy mapped across Europe. The eight-page brief he wrote this summer, urging 'the restraint of his Majesty's subjects abroad' from the 'foul contagion' of Jesuitical indoctrination was provoked by a 'report come hither ... of a late tumultuous insolency committed by the papists about the edge of Wales'. The borders of England, the borders of Venetian Terraferma: for Wotton, they're continuous frontiers in the global war on Jesuit-sponsored terrorism.

Wotton regularly frames his dispatches as 'entertainments', an apt word for a life lived double, for it has a double meaning. To 'entertain' is 'to engage', to 'hold the attention', but also to give 'delight'. Wotton's dispatches do both. He sends Cecil as 'a poor new year's gift' 'matter' to 'entertain your Lordship'; the king is 'entertained' with a 'bold discourse' and 'pleasant pasquinades received ... from Rome' 'entertain' the Court.

Dispatches aren't the household's only 'entertainments'. There's the billiard table. A pet monkey (that we know about because it bites a neighbour's child). And books. Wotton reads deep in Tacitus, a core text from his youth at Essex House. Books are read aloud, discussed, studied, among them, perhaps, the 'opera' Possevino has so thoughtfully sent. Wotton even applies himself fitfully to his own book, on architecture, using what he sees in Venice for examples. The embassy is interested in 'practical philosophy', science, mathematics, the latest experiments in optics coming out of Padua. Wotton sends Prince Henry 'intelligence' of an 'invention' 'to save gunpowder from all mischance of fire in their magazines' having made upon it 'mine own trial and observation'. (We can only imagine his 'trial', controlled explosions, perhaps, in the embassy garden.)

Then there's music. In-house, the embassy's 'young musicians' make up a consort, Wotton on his viol da gamba. They attempt a book of 'Spanish airs' but find it heavy going because the pieces are 'set in no measure', just notes littering a stave. Beyond the embassy, they hear the nuns of San Girolamo sing, where not just the sacred repertoire and the close harmonies astonish. It's the fact of a choir of women, unheard of in England since the dissolution of the monasteries. That first winter, Wotton climbs into the organ loft of San Marco to watch unroll below him the sonorous spectacle of the Christmas Mass. Further afield there are choirs like the one at San Rocco, sixteen instrumentalists on 'sackbutts', 'cornets', 'treble viols', 'viol da gambas of an extraordinary size' and vocalists to 'ravish and stupefy ... strangers that never heard the like'. One treble has a 'supernatural voice' of such 'sweetness' that he's supposed 'an eunuch', but isn't.

The city itself is a vast entertainment. For young men in a 'college' modelled on Essex's (but no more likely to be monastic than his *or* Navarre's), there are the pleasures of the flesh. Sex is unblushingly on sale in Venice. And young unmarried men who read Cogan on *Health* at Oxford would know, unblushingly, 'how

Venus should be used' and 'what commodities … come by moderate evacuation'. In Venice, they'd know where to find sex. In 1565 a published 'catalogo di tutte le principali et più honorate cortigianae di Venezia' offered clients the names, addresses and prices of two hundred and twelve 'donne honeste'. The highest concentration: Cannaregio. At least four of these working women operated from premises within five minutes of the future English embassy's front door. In the forty-five years since the catalogue was published, the trade hasn't diminished. Only the names of the donne have changed.

For spiritual entertainment, Wotton's gondola swings out of the rio San Girolamo northeast along the fondamenta nova to one of his favourite churches, of the double-barrelled saints, Giovanni e Paolo (Zanipolo to the locals). It's known as the noblemen's church because so many doges and generals, most in effigy mounted on life-sized horses pawing the sarcophagus, are entombed there. The church's monumental brick architecture fascinates Wotton. But he also studies Bellini and Cima paintings on the walls and stands silent below the gruesomely graphic memorial Marc Antonio Bragadin's brother recently raised to contain his remains. It shows the Turks flaying Marc Antonio, hero of Famagusta, alive, the outrage that prompted Christendom to sail to Lepanto.

Wotton's extra-curricular entertainments fit the rhythm of the calendar. Beyond Zanipolo, on the winter lagoon, he hunts ducks, a scene captured decades earlier by Carpaccio. This sport delights him not just because he can eat the birds he kills but because the Italian version introduces 'una bella cosa' unknown in England: shooting on the wing. In spring, he avoids Easter week in Venice, retreating to a villa outside Padua. In August, when the heat drapes Venice in a steaming layer of soggy felt, he and his *famiglia* take a summer house up the Brenta canal, or travel into the mountains. Throughout the year, he entertains guests at the embassy, young English travellers (like himself, a decade back) wanting to see the treasures of San Marco or inside the Collegio (some standing dumb before the doge, having no Italian).

There's also, always, the entertainment of familiar correspondence. None of Wotton's personal letters survives. Except one. From John Donne. It's a verse epistle premised on the conceit that 'More than kisses, letters mingle souls'. Wotton carried one of Donne's earlier soul-mingling efforts into Ireland in 1599, though it's anyone's guess how, as a soldier headed into a guerrilla war, he read the fantastically tortured images Donne wrapped around ideas of astonishing crassness. (The 'letter' figured Wotton's soul 'thorough crooked limbecs [di]stilled' and pronounced 'young death is best'.) Wotton has the latest of these epistles lying open on his desk. It's rather muted. It places Donne at the tail end of a paper trail. Once the new ambassador has discharged the business contained in the king's 'reverend papers', and exhausted his study of 'learned papers', and has sent 'loving papers' to his familiars, Donne meekly hopes he'll find time to receive an 'honest paper' from a friend who wants to 'swear much love' to a man who, trained up in 'schools and courts and wars', is now crowning a career 'in activity'. The poet himself sounds crushed under the weight of counter-factual hypotheticals:

> For me – if there be such a thing as I –
> Fortune – if there be such a thing as she –
> Spies that I bear so well her tyranny,
> That she thinks nothing else so fit for me.

Wotton may well sympathise. He escaped Fortune's tyranny, his Essex-shaped nemesis. But Donne can't escape the one he calls 'Anne'. He married her. As for the 'ease' the poet wishes upon his friend, Wotton perhaps hears Donne's wish more as a curse than a blessing. Right now, the ambassador's diplomatic future promises only a dreary round of indecisive wrangles over *Marita*s and *Angel*s. The man who sailed to Cadiz, who trudged across Ireland with Essex, who spurred to Scotland as Ottavio Baldi wants *action*.

He can't imagine how events hurtling towards him from London in November and San Marco in December are going to catapult him, his embassy and his *famiglia* into the centre of a perfect storm, bring Christendom to the brink of war and see him, once again, squaring up to Antonio Possevino.

12

Service in a turbulent time

'Great uncertainty'

November 1605. The English ambassador worries over the doge's health. When Grimani is absent from the Collegio, as increasingly since May, he's deputised by the 'Consiglier di maggior età', literally the body's eldest statesman, who invariably cuts Wotton less slack than the indulgent doge. And if Grimani should die? The death of a doge, like the death of a pope, is of more than local significance. It triggers a 'multi-form act' whose '9 several ballotations' (as Wotton puts it) look about as penetrable to outsiders as a moneylender's heart. It's partly lottery, partly ordered voting by the Maggior Consiglio, where ballot balls drop like Tuscan chestnuts in an autumn wind. (It took them seventy rounds to elect Grimani ten years back.)

Over the past three years, Grimani has led an increasingly bullish government that has passed laws limiting papal authority in the Republic. Will a successor continue to wag the banner of San Marco in the pope's face? Or slip it into the papal pocket like a limp handkerchief? These are disquieting questions, for in Rome, Paolo V, a Borghese who ascended St Peter's chair barely six months ago and still seems surprised to be there (his predecessor having lasted only twenty-six days), is taking his election as divine mandate personally to embody the counter-Reformation, to impose papal supremacy on spiritual sliders and slackers. He's fifty-six years old, a trained lawyer, the beard on his chin cut to a point like a surgical probe. He's tunnel-visioned. And he has Venice in his sights.

In other news, that autumn Venetian diplomacy in London is unsettled. At his own request, the ambassador is recalled. His replacement, Zorzi Giustinian, sets out from Venice in late October but, delayed by storms in Dieppe, won't arrive until 6 January. Meanwhile, in a dispatch dated 16 November, Nicoló

Molin, aghast, reports the events of the previous day, which Robert Cecil, writing to England's ambassadors abroad, makes the fifth of November. The gunpowder plot. 'Monstrous wickedness', a 'horrible conspiracy intended to bring down the state': hatched by disaffected Catholics who accuse James of reneging on promises of religious toleration made when he was angling for the English throne and needed their support. They've spent months filling 'barrels, hogsheads, and firkins' with gunpowder stowed in cellars beneath the Palace of Westminster where Parliament sits (and they've been given pre-emptive absolution for their crime by an outlawed Jesuit priest, later exposed as Father Garnet). The plot aims to waste not just the house full of MPs but the royal family attending the 'state opening'. The explosion is timed to the king's speech.

The kingdom goes into lockdown. All ports are 'stopt' 'as well for ambassadors' as others. Cecil gets this message out before chains are dragged across harbour mouths. In those same hours, Molin sends a rush of dispatches: 'The king is in terror', cowering in Whitehall's 'innermost rooms'. The 'city is in great uncertainty. Catholics fear heretics' – that is, every Protestant Englishman – 'and vice versa'. 'Both are armed'. Two days later, copies of a riddling message delivered secretly to Lord Monteagle warning him to stay away from Parliament are ricochetting around St Paul's churchyard among the booksellers and gentlemen who congregate there daily to trade news. It's the king's 'miraculous' deciphering of this anonymous letter which Cecil handed him that led to the plot's detection. Very likely, the 'discovery' is a Cecil set-up.

But Wotton in Venice knows nothing of this until the end of December, nor of the king's order enacting an Oath of Allegiance, which rattles Molin (who, mistaking 'allegiance' for 'supremacy', as so many others do, sees it clearly targeting Catholics, for how can they swear the 'supremacy' of a temporal prince?). While accidents of the post mean that Wotton's packets from Cecil are going a goose chase through France, Molin's dispatches have galloped straight to the Senato from Antwerp. So Venice has more news of London than the English ambassador does.

Then, what Wotton fears happens. Two days before Christmas, Doge Grimani dies. The electoral machine trundles into action. The Signoria shelves two briefs delivered by the papal nuncio on Christmas day, using as pretext that the dogal chair is empty. The envoy sent to Rome to report on Grimani's illness is recalled. On 10 January it is this man, Leonardo Donà, who is elected doge. Wotton is certain to remember him as the determined Republican who locked horns with Pope Clement over ecclesiastical jurisdiction a decade ago.

15 Doge Leonardo Donà. Elected doge in 1606, Donà steered the Republic through the Interdict Crisis and periodically rescued the English ambassador from diplomatic gaffes. The portrait by an unknown artist is misdated.

He's seventy, prime age for a doge, and fully equipped for a face-off with a pope. He has the better beard. White and thick as a lion's mane.

In Venice on the last day of the year the dead doge is buried 'in the foul weather' that is scouring Europe. From London Molin writes of the gunpowder conspirators hunted to Warwickshire. Of arrests made. Confessions urged under torture. Executions by hanging, drawing and quartering. The king rails against information from Rome that he's to be excommunicated, which will free English Catholics 'to dethrone me and to take my life' – and will oblige him 'to stain my hands with their blood'. Orders to 'extirpate' and 'stamp out every spark of Catholic faith in this kingdom' are drafted, among them, 'to take' Catholic children from their parents to be educated by Protestant relatives. Giustinian finally arrives – and walks into a storm of Court clamour. He reports on 10 February: 'Here they freely discuss the quarrel between the Pope and the Republic ... The Queen herself asked eagerly for information. ... We answered that we had no information on the subject. ... As to yielding to Papal pretensions, as we did not know what these pretensions were, it was impossible for us to say anything.'

What 'quarrel'? What 'pretensions'? And where is Wotton in all this? As much at sea as Giustinian, because while the Venetian in London doesn't know what the Englishman in Venice knows, neither does the Englishman in Venice know what the Venetian in London knows. Mismatched calendars, discrepant travel times, a meandering postal service mean that trying to reconcile the calendar of diplomatic correspondence criss-crossing Europe, to pin down who knows what, when, and how they're instructed to act while they await instructions would take a calculating machine not yet invented by the cunning mathematical professor of Padua. (Just now, Galileo is working on his geometrical compass.) Wotton dates all his dispatches according to the Gregorian calendar, ten days ahead of the 'old style' Julian calendar Cecil uses, ten days Cecil's secretary never accounts for in dating his receipt of Wotton's papers. Molin and Giustinian in London date *more Veneto*, thus putting the gunpowder treason on 15 November. In Venice, the Senato and the Collegio do the same. Thereafter, all these correspondents factor in a minimum twenty-one days between despatch and delivery: a six-week turn-around or, as Wotton constantly chafes, a 'loss of six weeks of time which in politick councils may breed much alteration' – an understatement.

It seems hardly possible that London knows 'freely' on 1/10 February what's only disclosed (officially) in Venice after 1/10 January when, Donà having been elected doge, the unopened briefs delivered from Rome at Christmas are finally unsealed and disclose Rome's 'papal pretensions'. Hardly possible, but Wotton knows the contents of the briefs more or less accurately within three days. For on 13 January he sends London 'A discourse of the schism betwixt the pope and the Venetians'. It's docketed by Cecil's secretary. It doesn't survive, but that discourse must be what's fuelling the eager Court chatter that hits Giustinian's ears in early February.

'Warm in the cause'

When London's news of 5 November reaches Cannaregio, Wotton shakes off the sluggish thoughts he was nursing in October. Finally, action. On 30 December, he's in the Collegio condoling the death of Grimani, a public grief that he makes particular for 'the memory of his kind manner toward me'.

Wotton defers 'business'. He's still processing the account he's just received of the gunpowder plot, 'one of the most ... prodigious conspiracies that has ever been heard of', and he can hardly bear to speak of Englishmen so perfidious. Two weeks later he's congratulating the state on the election of Leonardo Donà; the following week, he's telling London of 'times turbulent', a state 'fallen into terms of great contumacy with the Pope'.

What's the 'quarrel'? Two matters of jurisdiction. First, the pope objects to laws restricting Venetians from bequeathing property to the church: these laws have been extended to cover not just the city – dry land being a precious commodity in a city built on water – but the whole of the Veneto. Secondly, he refuses to recognise the Republic's right to try criminal clergy in secular courts, specifically two priests who've been charged with parricide, slander and rape. (Of this last, Wotton jokes sarcastically that 'Dishonouring a virgin is, in this corrupted country, esteemed the most heinous and prejudicial to papal authority of all imaginable crimes'.)

In his 'monotorial brief', as Wotton terms it, mockingly, the pope orders the Signory to heel by menacing 'the excommunicatory sentence'. He means, that is, to pressure the state into compliance by targeting the *popolani*, threatening to excommunicate the entire population not just of the city but of the Terraferma territories, to 'interdict' all clergy offices and sacraments: no Mass, no confession or absolution; no baptism, marriage, burial; children born made bastards; the dying refused extreme unction; souls lost eternally. The prospect is appalling. The pope would cut the body of the faithful, which in Venice is also the civic body, from its spiritual head to provoke mass resistance, rebellion. Wotton sees a showdown looming, what will come to be known to history as 'The Interdict Crisis' as it escalates into nothing short of pan-European war. Digging her heels in, the Republic won't hand over the accused to Rome, for while, as in 1592, the pope can insist on the prerogative of ecclesiastical courts, these priests' crimes, says the state, are civil and will be tried by civil magistrates. Neither will the laws on legacies be retracted. In Leonardo Donà the Republic has elected a match for Pope Paolo, not just 'a wise and beaten' – that is, savvy – 'man in the world', but a 'patriot' already 'warm in the cause'.

Wotton is feeding London news that is frankly astonishing. Because, officially, he shouldn't know any of it. The state aims to keep its controversy with the pope *secretissimo*, 'sepolto'. It isn't briefing its ambassadors, despite Giustinian's yelp from London in February and Wotton's complaint in April that 'la Republica ... non parla con niuno di noi' (isn't talking to any of us).

She certainly isn't informing those 'outsiders', the city's *popolani*, unrecognised as a political public, their views irrelevant to policymaking. (Over the coming months this will shift radically.) So where is Wotton's intelligence coming from? Informants across Italy? Venetian spies on the embassy's payroll? Cracks leaking from the Senato? Across the coming year he'll regularly say he's been 'secretly informed' or learned something 'by secret means'. Rooke, Fenton, Woodward: their politick excursions will make them newshounds, scavenging.

We shouldn't underestimate the crisis that's shaping up. It's going to shake regimes across Christendom, and over the coming weeks, as the English ambassador grows warm in the cause, we'll see Wotton enlisted in a year-long 'war of words' targeting the Collegio, the Papal See and Whitehall. This war will marshal mighty combatants: Catholic Spain backing the pope, Catholic France chopping and changing (her king, we remember, was once upon a time a Protestant) and Protestant England lining up behind the Republic, spurred on relentlessly by the Protestant English ambassador in Venice. From the outset, there will be a sharp point to Wotton's London briefings, for he will constantly tie papal pretensions in Venice to Catholic ambitions in England. In his mind, the Interdict Crisis is the monstrous conjoined twin to the gunpowder conspiracy. As he gets more information about the great 'equivocator', the Jesuit Father Garnet, on trial in London, and a pope in Rome 'ignorant of statecraft now being advised by the Jesuits', he'll see these twins sharing toxic blood infected by Jesuit transfusions.

Wotton's politics, then, are inflected like no other ambassador's. He's a dual national, as he'll shortly declare: 'primo ... Anglese', 'ma dopo Venetiano'. So an attack on the Signoria is an attack on Parliament. It follows that his defence of Venetian sovereignty will work to mobilise the English Crown, now hotly defending its own threatened sovereignty, and rouse King James to militancy on the one topic Wotton knows (remembering the king's thoughts on *The True Law of Free Monarchies* from Scotland) can transform the Rex Pacificus into a warrior: the temporal supremacy of princes. It follows, too, that he'll frame his 'war of words' as a war tying state politics to religious politics, Catholic v. Protestant. If the effect of the gunpowder plot is to 'extirpate' and 'stamp out every spark of Catholic faith' in England, the effect of the Interdict Crisis, he hopes, will be to ignite the Protestant revolution in Venice – where the touchpaper is just waiting to be lit. As a student traveller in Rome he saw doled out enough pieces of the 'true cross' to make a forest. In Venice, he found a Republic that 'with long neutrality of state' was 'almost slipped into a neutrality of religion'. He has seen Jesuit 'spiders' making 'conspiracy an article of their faith'. He realises that in

Italy, he's stationed 'where the root of that evil doth lie'. All this prepares him for what's coming, a crisis that will make history – and his diplomatic career. His blood races.

The Interdict Crisis that we're about to find emerging from Ambassador Wotton's papers is rather different from the one treated from hindsight in standard histories. Following Wotton, watching it through his English eyes, we'll see this year of crisis building day by day, week by week, its immediacy, its to-ings-and-fro-ings by turns riveting and stultifying, its action conveyed in the ambassador's 'working words'. This is a story of high personal stakes, frustrating switchbacks, secret intelligence, dangerous offers; a story of 'near-lies' and 'might have beens' and a Europe set to unleash the dogs of war that will turn the continent into a bear pit. It's a story of an ambassador inventing diplomacy – and a maverick hung out to dry.

Inventing diplomacy

In January 1606, writing to London, Wotton uses explosive language to position the current 'business': schism, contumacy, monitory. If he's anticipating an explosion, it doesn't happen. Instead, there's silence. He's neither summoned to the Collegio nor asks audience throughout all of February and March. Does that wrong-foot him? Not at all, for if the state is stonewalling its resident ambassadors while it negotiates behind closed doors, the English ambassador is actively digging around in other sources. He writes to Cecil on 7 April that 'the business between the Pope and these Signori propendeth to a scisme'; that he 'dare not yet say' 'what will be the event' but that, given what he knows of Donà he can predict that Venice will 'teach all the superstitious' – that is, Catholic – 'part of Christendom how to deal with an easy Pope'. Wotton can't resist sarcasm.

Three days later, 10 April, he's on to Scaramelli, requesting one of those extra-mural meetings that run athwart protocol. They meet in the church next door to the embassy. Wotton insists he's not there on his own business, but the Republic's, to tell them staggering news, that his 'instruments' have penetrated the very heart of the papacy, its 'più intimi penetralia'. He has information to convey under profound silence, because if even a whiff of it reached the Court of Rome, 'noi saressimo disconzati': we'd be ruined. (The 'we' he's thinking about is underscored by his use of Venetian dialect, 'desconzar'.) Further, he'll confide what he has to say to one person only. Diplomatic insurance, so if he's ever betrayed (which he nowise expects) he can deny having said it.

He shows Scaramelli a ciphered letter intercepted from Rome, addressed to his old sparring partner, Antonio Possevino. It's chock full of sensation. It says that the pope has turned for advice to the Jesuits, those arch-meddlers in 'the management of princes'. That Cardinal Bellarmino has written a treatise, *De Militia Ecclesiastica*, legitimating papal war on secular princes, views so provocative that it's circulating in only four manuscript copies. That the Holy See is putting on trial 'secretissimamente' (and *in absentia*) 'Brother Paolo' Sarpi, the tough-minded Servite friar the Republic has recruited as its legal and theological adviser, for writing that 'diminishes Pontifical authority' and 'defends the Signory from excommunication'. (Two months hence Wotton will learn that he, too, is being tried as a heretic in the Inquisition's courts.) Wotton repeats to Scaramelli: if 'one single iota' of what he's said 'about the king having instruments in Rome' were revealed to the Jesuits, 'they'd throw us to the fire'. Scaramelli reaches for the letter. Wotton hesitates. Then hands it over. The Senato will hear that it introduces that terrible word, 'scisma'.

A week later, Scaramelli is back at Cannaregio, delivering the Senato's thanks. Wotton is grateful, but muses (fishing) that he and his fellow ambassadors (yes, they do talk to each other) 'have concluded that Venice will bow to the pope', that 'a settlement is in hand', otherwise, the Senato would be 'opening its thoughts through us ministers', and 'most of all to us English who are waiting for them with open arms'. If only Wotton could be among the low-flying angels in the Basilica the following week when the nuncio ambushes the doge, trying to pick him off from the Collegio with wheedling words during Mass. Donà returns a broadside, muffled only by the organ's swells: 'You need to know, we couldn't be hotter or more resolved. Not just "we" the government. All our nobility and all our people. We take your excommunication per nulla', that is, for nothing. If he heard them, these fighting words that 'shake' the nuncio would sound more sweetly in Wotton's ears than the chapel choir. Wotton reports to London the 'secret office' he's performed the Signory and warns, 'For the controversies with the pope: the next Tuesday will be the critical day'.

By now, he has seen (and forwarded to London) two intercepted letters written to Rome by King Felipe III of Spain. The first laments 'how backwardly the affairs do go between your Holiness & the Venetians'; intreats a 'peace whereby the dignity of your church may be preserved'; but promises 'our arms and treasure' will 'be employed' against 'the enemies' of 'our holy faith'. The second is stiffer. Spain resolves 'to repair unto your Holiness ... both in my own person, as also with forces'. Whatever happens, the pope 'shall have me at your elbow'.

Wotton scoffs. Spain is rattling empty scabbards. Felipe III isn't his father – and at twenty-eight, he's still green. The kingdom is bankrupt. It's having trouble mustering troops for Flanders. Still, madness in the family, combined with brain-damaging piety, makes Felipe unpredictable, potentially a suicidal crusader for Catholicism. So amping up the Spanish threat is diplomatically precautious. Besides, arms are now on the table. These affairs look like they're threatening war across Christendom.

On 21 April Wotton is finally summoned to the Collegio. He hasn't crossed its threshold since the end of January. Now, the Senato officially informs him of what he already knows. Wotton was right. The pope's *Monitorio* was 'fulminato' (thundered) on that 'critical day' – and Venice simply blanked it. The Senato refused its publication. When it comes into effect after the twenty-four days the pope offered for 'penitence' expire, the clergy, under threat from the full weight of the Signoria, are told to continue in their offices. Some do, saying (Wotton reports) that while they 'had their habits from the pope, their flesh put them in mind of an other duty'. Others shed popish habits for secular clothes and flee.

Wotton puts on a sober face. He's 'no canonist', but he 'can't believe that God wants Justice ruined by Theology'. But he also can't resist a quip. 'Io vengo da un paese che intende quanto vale una scomunica' (I come from a country that knows the worth of an excommunication). Wasn't Queen Elizabeth under papal 'Interdict' for three decades? 'Scomunica'? 'Vale ... fino un quattrino' (Not worth a farthing). His exit line is resounding: 'I shall always glory to have found myself here in these times so that I might be a witness'. But he has no intention of merely witnessing anything.

For both Wotton and the Collegio, today's audience marks a turning point. The Senato must see the usefulness of a man who can intercept Possevino's letters and place 'instruments' in the 'più intimi penetrali del Papa'. They've been briefing their Catholic residents for some days but now decide to confide in him, the Protestant ambassador in Venice. They've no doubt weighed up the dangers of releasing this English maverick into the wilderness of the uncharted politics they're entering. But maybe they see him like Fra Paolo Sarpi. More of a blunt instrument, but nevertheless, a useful tool.

For his part, when he returns to the Collegio on 6 May he's playing the statesman. A week earlier he'd been in bed, 'tormented' with 'toothache' when he wrote to Cecil that he's not so much 'troubled with the pains thereof' as that they've 'fallen upon' him 'in a time which yieldeth such entertainment to his Majesty and the rest of the world': 'If I should never arise' – clearly, this toothache is a killer – 'yet it would be a great comfort to my soul to have lived to see a Pope notoriously despised by a neighbour state'. He sends a 'little taste of our spirits here'. 'Within this hour hath been published in the chief places of this town by sound of trumpet a proclamation' that anyone who has 'received from Rome any copy of a Papal Interdict' 'published against the Law of God' and 'honor of this Commonwealth' must instantly hand it over to the Consiglio di Dieci 'on pain of death'. Thus, 'not only the pope's temporal usurpations but his spiritual' will be 'defeated' in this public remonstration. Toothache or not, he's throwing off his blankets.

The first item of business he presents on 6 May is an indignant exposé of the 'artificial', that is, faked-up, account the Jesuits are circulating in Italy of the trial in London of one 'Padre Darcio'. That's the cover name of Father Garnet, implicated in the gunpowder conspiracy. In the Jesuits' version, Garnet parries three interrogatories: whether the pope has power to excommunicate King James, whether 'the English who follow the Anglican confession are heretics' and whether he's the author of a 'certain book written against the State'. But he vehemently denies the fourth: whether 'the last treason' was 'executed by his authority, council or design'. When Wotton reads Garnet's denial, he's stopped in his tracks: 'I remained dumbfounded for a good moment'. He can understand the fantastic accounts that might be produced by Jesuit missions to Moscovy ('a cold, and faraway country, not many people go there, and not many come back') or Africa ('full of strange names'), accounts that some in Europe might credit of, say, 'the conversion of a couple of crocodiles'. But this fantastic report of Garnet's innocence? It's on record in London: he *confessed* to hatching the plot and absolving the accomplices. The barefaced lie the Jesuits are pedalling? Wotton is 'truly shocked'. 'How dare' they 'treat Italy like a fool'?

The relevance of this first item of business to the second doesn't need spelling out. Wotton brings his narrative home to Venice. The 'masked fathers' have spread more than one 'false impression'. He cites the 'inveterate error' they echoed throughout Elizabeth's reign, that the diplomatic breach between the states was caused by the Republic's fear of stepping out of line with Rome, fear that will certainly make Venice toe the line now. Lies. Lies. And more lies. But implicitly (as Wotton sees it), the Jesuits' lies shade into a systematic programme to defame two sovereign states, to target with poisoned pens – and explosives – what the Jesuits find abhorrent, the confessional positions of these two states that map onto their politics. 'Your freedom', Wotton tells Donà, 'is under assault'. Like England's. In this audience, then, we hear the ambassador placing in the Collegio's imagination the image of the toxic twins. Gunpower conjoined to Interdict.

For the rest, he talks profusely in anecdotes that any fool would hear as offers of international aid. The aloofness of a month ago is shifting. He and his secretaries have clearly been busy drafting, redrafting and elaborating this high-testosterone speech that he delivers, barely pausing for breath, for twenty uninterrupted minutes to a Collegio where 'ears are cocked, spirits alert, and doors shut fast'. He cites Plato, Plutarch, Pirrone. (Scaramelli, recording this audience, notes 'lunga serie di parole': so many words!) But finally Wotton pulls off a big finish, his resounding pledge of allegiance: 'io non sono ne'Ghelfo, ne Gebellino. Ma prima son'Anglese, et poi, per Dio che io son Venetiano.' 'Neither Guelph nor Ghibelline', Wotton shunts aside dead history: those were the factions that warred pro and contra the pope for supremacy in medieval Italy. He declares for the present: First I am an Englishman, then, by God, I'm Venetian.

It comes right on time. That very morning, hours before the pope's 'repent or suffer' ultimatum expires, the state publishes its *Protesto*, drafted by Paolo Sarpi, signed by Doge Donà, addressed to the Republic's clergy but speaking beyond them to 'nostri soggetti', our people. It asserts 'the authority of princes who recognise in temporal matters no superior under God'. The pope, issuing his brief, is violating divine Scripture and canon law to 'prejudice the secular authority given us by God' and 'the quiet governance of our faithful subjects'. The *Protesto* says it has done everything – letters, ambassadors, express messengers – to inform His Holiness of our 'most valid and insoluble arguments' but has found 'chiuse le orecchie dalla santità sua' (the pope's ears closed). So it makes public its response. It declares the pope's brief not just 'unjust', but, piling up the indignation, 'per nullo, et di nissun valore, et così invalido' (null, worthless and therefore invalid). It directs the clergy to get on with their pastoral offices even as it declares the state's firm will to continue in the Holy Catholic and Apostolic faith under the holy church of Rome. (Confessionally, then, no schism.) Finally, it orders the *Protesto* to be posted everywhere in the city – printed both on wall posters and fliers – so that it 'will reach the ears of all who know about the pope's brief', and 'even come to … the pope himself'.

As a 'sign of our continuing confidence in your king', the Collegio summons Wotton ten days later, 16 May, to hear news of another escalation: the pope has recalled his nuncio to Rome and sent the Venetian ambassador packing. Answering confidence with confidence, the English ambassador decides 'to reveal a secret of my soul'. He knows he's only 'una formica', an ant, compared with the big beasts that are weighing in to Venetian 'business' with 'strepiti', clamour. But an ant just might 'bring a weighty grain to the heap' – and tip the balance of power. Wotton's 'grain'? He's been reading Venetian history and seeing that 'in turbulent times like these now, leagues have been formed among princes, some public and open, others secret'. It's come to his mind – 'venuto in pensiero' – that 'a league might be formed' for the defence of Venice, allying England, France and parts of Germany. And here's the clincher: he says Spain and the pope have already formed one.

'League'. Leaving Wotton's mouth, the word sounds so diplomatically, well, *diplomatic*. The ambassador appears to place a gift on the negotiating table. Or is it a package as explosive as anything stowed in barrels under Parliament? Donà perhaps senses both. What the ambassador 'habbia gettato qui fra questi Signori' (has thrown, mark, *thrown*, among these lords) will be considered and put safely 'in deposito', on deposit, banked for future use. Still, any doge who has served as ambassador to Rome as often as Donà will be hearing alarm bells. This offer is not made upon instructions from London. Wotton is proposing a policy of his own. That means he's violating, *again*, that basic directive: he's thinking 'beyond his instructions'. Is the maverick going dangerously rogue? Or is he simply impatient with the postal service?

Talk 'between set teeth'

With this exchange, all the balls that are going to be juggled in the Interdict Crisis are in the air. Papal obduracy matched with executive cluelessness. Republican defiance coupled to confessional obedience. Jesuit evangelism masking international terrorism. The *popolani* menaced by Rome, massaged by the Senato. The Spanish strutting. The French flip-flopping. And what about the English ambassador, is he ant, bee or fox? Proposing his league of nations without waiting for instructions, he's looking new-fangled, like a new-model diplomat, inventing diplomacy that's *immediate*. At the same time, though, he's deeply old-fangled, relying on time-worn practices, running covert operations to undermine the Holy See with networks of spies. As always, news criss-crossing Europe lags weeks behind the beat.

This growing crisis: it's certainly grave, but isn't it also slightly absurd? Are a couple of scabby priests and some vacant properties *really* going to bring Christendom to internecine war? In its details, too, the 'business' is more than a little comic. In May no one quite knows whether the pope has actually pronounced the excommunication. Contradictory messages bumble along, colliding with each other. In the Collegio, when the *Protesto* is read to the nuncio, he snatches off his 'priest's cap' and beats it against his thigh in rage. It turns out that the Jesuits promised him the Senato vote would kill the bill. In fact, not a single senator voted 'no'. Days later the Senato orders the Jesuits banished from Venice and her territories and (echoing English policy) the children in their custody returned to approved tutorial care. They struggle out, Possevino among them, permitted to leave with only 'their quotidian habits' and 'breviaries'. Their exit prompts sarcasm from above, that the Jesuit college will be turned into 'botteghe', common shops, and its confiscated wealth used to fund the war against Rome. And from below bubble up scabrous jokes, that now in Venice there's 'buon mercato di vitello. Et di puti': cheap trade in calf skin (since nobody will be needing vellum anymore). And catamites. The *Protesto* itself is not without its comic value, located in self-contradiction. Since the state didn't permit the publication of the *Monitorio*, the *Protesto* can only object to 'a brief against us' that doesn't exist.

Meanwhile, in London on 18 May, Zorzi Giustinian opens a dispatch that gives him his first solid news of the excommunication that, around him, 'the great and small' are discussing 'tra denti' (between set teeth) while merchants' letters talk of 'apparati da guerra', preparations for war. Giustinian is instructed to inform King James. He knows that will be tricky. This is a monarch who, as Scaramelli reported back in 1603, prefers hunting to reigning and appears to conduct his audiences in public corridors, on the hoof, tossing over his shoulder 'see Salisbury on this matter' as he exits to horse. (How different the diplomatic protocols in the 'sealed' chamber of the Collegio.) Cecil, now earl of Salisbury, is, Giustinian knows, 'the master of the king's counsellors'. 'The king himself' is 'completely his' and no one can 'count upon anything for certain in the conduct of affairs here' except through Cecil.

If Giustinian feels frustrated by the absent landlord king, so do the king's subjects. They've taken to pinning graffiti to the privy chamber door complaining that they've been left victims of his rapacious ministers. (When this dispatch is read in Venice, this alarming comment is scored for attention in red crayon down the margin.) Given Wotton's offer of a defensive league, Venice needs to know if it can depend on King James. His talk is ample – and like his stiletto-proof doublets, well-padded. Catching him between doors, Giustinian listens as James launches into 'an exceedingly long discourse' on the pope's 'usurpation' of 'temporal sovereignty', the bone of contention that sticks in the king's craw. Nothing is as monstrous as this: the pope would overthrow kings. (Has Wotton copied to his king the line from the *Protesto* about 'the authority of princes' recognising 'in temporal matters no superior under God'? Smart move.) Giustinian reports him arguing with 'such a force of reasoning, such riches of citation from the holy scriptures' that, if he heard it, the pope himself would be convinced. But are his words merely air? Will he *act*? Everyone knows his reputation as the most timorous king in Christendom. Worryingly, while the king remarks that the Republic's 'business' is 'the sole topic of conversation at Court' and opines that 'there will be war in Italy and all the powers of Europe drawn into it', he's apparently giving no thought to the 'effetti che potessero nascer', what effects on Christendom might (no, *will*) ensue.

Another question: how will Cecil manipulate the 'conduct of affairs'? Cecil makes a habit of reversing the king's large promises, for example on grain shipments to Venice, which the Republic urgently needs to fill its storehouses 'in anticipo'. Any dearth in the city will be exploited by Rome as divine punishment for disobedience and used to foment popular rebellion. Giustinian petitions an export licence. The king agrees. Exits. Enter Cecil, who cannot 'imagine how the king can issue orders' to 'take bread out of the mouths of his own people'. But, the counsellor shrugs, the king 'is sovereign and one must obey'. Only, a week later the licence is refused, leaving the ambassador to wail against (Cecil's?) 'artifices', 'Would to God I had to deal with no other here than with this excellent king, a model of frankness and sincerity'. *Is* this king 'frank'? Or stupendously inept? Cecil in these documents certainly emerges as a manipulator. But he's also a plumber, constantly plugging holes the king's bluster punches through diplomatic dykes.

For King James, as for Wotton, the Interdict Crisis and the gunpowder conspiracy are toxic twins, the 'usurpation of temporal sovereignty' their connecting tissue. Discoursing, the king moves between the crisis and the conspiracy in one breath, approving the Republic's determination to exhaust 'their goods, their children and their lives' in 'defense of their civil liberty and jurisdiction'. In England, he has the same iron bit between his teeth. His 'Oath of Allegiance' will be sworn by all subjects serving foreign princes abroad to guarantee loyalty to the English Crown, and he's putting his own pen to a 'discourse' on sovereignty.

For his part, however, Cecil is unconvinced: the master of the king's counsellors thinks the Republic will back down, that an 'accommodation' will be 'compassed before ever any blow be given', leaving England as an ally high and dry. Cecil is not above misreporting the king to the Venetian ambassador. It's obvious that he's putting his own words into the king's mouth when he informs Giustinian that 'his Majesty's own judgement' persuades him 'there will be some means wrought' – accommodation – to 'reduce that divided member again, rather than it shall bring the whole body into danger'. (In Venice, any mention of accommodation hits Wotton like boiling water scalding a cat.)

Throughout late spring and early summer Wotton observes Venice mobilising: appointing generals by land and sea; securing her frontier with Milan; setting the arsenal to work around the clock; choosing *cittadini* as watchmen 'against sudden casualties that happen in the night'. The state is 'proceeding ... with exemplary wisdom and magnanimity'. The 'minds of the vulgar' are being 'settled by discourses and translations in print'. Issuing publication 'daily' (so Wotton says, exaggerating for effect), the Senato is reversing its early policy of ignoring the *popolani*. Civic unity is displayed in public shows, like the Feast of Corpus Christi on 25 May, 'celebrated by express commandment of the state' with 'the most sumptuous procession that ever had been seen here': parades of incalculable riches and 'curious pageants' designed (says Protestant Wotton) to 'contain the people in good order with superstition' but also 'to let the pope know' via his 'intelligencers' planted in Venice 'that notwithstanding his interdict they had friars enough ... to furnish out the day'. He writes to Cecil that 'matters here ... go forward with great appearance of war' and to the king, signed 'Ottavio Baldi', a long discourse, intricately argued, setting out, *pro* and *contra*, possible ways matters in Venice might pan out. His discourse wears Wotton's university training on its sleeve. It reads like a rhetorical 'persuasion' – or like the large print on a recruiting poster sent to get the king on side. Nowhere does he mention that word 'league'.

It should be noted that, reporting Venice to London, the English ambassador is, strictly speaking, conscientious. He soberly relays the official line: the Republic's defiance of Rome extends no further than the assertion of her inalienable sovereignty in temporal matters; confessionally, she remains as she has been for a thousand years, a devout daughter of Holy Mother Church. So, as the long view of history will put it, Venice is in no way verging on schism. On the ground, though, Wotton sees plenty to contradict this – and it fills him with glee. The 'variance' is calling 'into examination and discourse' the 'great mystery' of the Roman church, the very foundation on which its 'authority' is 'built' and 'conserved by ignorance'. He feels sure that once 'human reason' exposes its doctrines as superstition, this church will 'lose much of that foolish reverence which maintained it'. He's 'transported with the secret comfort' he takes in 'these things'. The breach with Rome and the expulsion of the Jesuits show the state coming 'nearer unto his Majesty not only in civil friendship but even in religion' and Venice on the brink of Protestant reformation. 'By such a beginning' he hopes 'God hath appointed the re-entrance of his truth ... unto this goodly country' where 'error' 'hath so long slept'. And where his 'poor family' – his covey of Protestants at Cannaregio – has given Venice 'the first example ... of God's incorrupted service on this side of the mountains since the Goths and Vandals did pass them'. The *nobili* are ripe for conversion. Donà shows 'a very great degree' of 'illumination of God's truth', and, 'likewise', 'upon my secret knowledge', 'many of the rest'. Wotton tells London that, in the Collegio, he'll remain po-faced: he'll echo the official line and 'labour' in his 'discourses nothing but the mere point of sovereignty'. But, ever the honest dissembler, he'll be two-faced. He'll use the cover of sovereigny to make sure that 'religion will slide along'.

He's not the only one thinking such thoughts. In France, Henri IV fears 'a new religion' is 'being introduced' in Italy. In England, King James hopes 'to see God's church reformed of Rome's abuses' and claims to have 'in hand' that which allows him 'to promise himself that the Serene Republic would presently shake off the yoke of the Roman church'. 'In hand': is he referring to Wotton's dispatches or to other intelligence? Evidently, reformation in Venice has been discussed in Parliament – though on that topic, Cecil isn't the only cynic. 'Whatsoever tales were told in the end of the last parliament', scoffs one observer, 'Those pantaloons will sooner turn Turks than Protestants'.

In late July Wotton is summoned to hear what the Senato has sent as instructions to their ambassador in London. The pope's 'naught'-y censures, his 'insidious snares' to trap our subjects' allegiances, his call to arms all make war inevitable. Giustinian is to 'dig out' of the king a declaration of his mind. And to report Cecil's mind, too. Wotton listens, satisfied. He's 'full of zeal and great intention' and happens to hold in his hand his king's latest dispatch, which calls on God, 'protector of justice', to defend the Republic's 'most just cause'. Wotton renews his thoughts on a league. Before, his offer was put 'in deposito'. Now, says the doge, 'the time is somewhat close' to take it out of storage. That afternoon, Wotton writes up his audience for Cecil, endorsing the Senato's petition for the king's declaration, and reporting that Venice is making 'provisions' for the defence of 'their civil liberty and jurisdiction'. Any rumour of accommodation is just that. He still says nothing about a league.

Giustinian in London receives his 'digging' instructions on 8 August when the king is out of the city, hunting. He takes coach, chasing him to Hatfield House, Cecil's country estate, ordering his sweating servant on horseback ahead. The king is at table, entertaining. The Italians are sent away unheard. Two days later, Giustinian is finally granted audience, and pours out the whole dispatch. The traps. The threats. The rumours. The warlike preparations. With 'forcible and lively language' he aims to 'draw out the king's true opinion'. And it seems he succeeds. The king assures the ambassador that he is 'justified in promising' to the Republic 'every help as far as His Majesty is concerned'. England is not stirring up trouble, and (despite what he's said elsewhere) the king knows, he tells Giustinian, Venice 'would never abandon her religion'. But the Republic's cause is just and right, the people are constant, the Senato is united. Thus, James has 'written to my ambassador to make this promise in my name': 'I will assist her with all my heart in all that depends on me'.

Exit king. Enter Cecil. He confirms 'lo istesso' (the same). The 'dechiaratione' looks solid. No loopholes. But then Giustinian adds a diplomatically hair-raising postscript. Their audience was conducted 'tra noi nella lingua Francese et Italiana' (between us in French and Italian), the king not speaking Italian, and Giustinian judging that it wouldn't be a good idea to use a paid interpreter for such sensitive negotiations, for the king would speak more freely thus. So Giustinian may have mistaken the king's exact words ('vi potrebbe esser qualche improprietà') but not, he thinks, his sense, because to make sure, he repeated himself several times. (He'd be less optimistic if he'd seen Cecil juggling 'words' against 'sense' lately in his instructions to Wotton on interpreting the recently negotiated Spanish treaty.) There's no way we can miss it: the staggering abyss of potential misunderstanding that's just opened up in London.

In Venice, the summer of 1606 gives way to autumn, and Wotton, waiting to be admitted to his latest audience on 5 September, sits on his usual wooden bench in the Collegio's anteroom. He's gazing out of its tall windows, reflecting on how he's watched the seasons turn in the nine months since this 'business' with the pope began. The weather has been more decided than the politicians. Still, his own mind is settled. He, Arrigo VVottoni, is to be God's agent for 'the re-entrance of his truth' into this 'goodly country' where 'error' 'hath so long slept'. Defeating the pope's political supremacism in Venice will, collaterally, defeat his confessional supremacism. Wotton knows he must use every audience to trumpet the case for resistance to papal violations of Republican sovereignty. The liberty and honour of Venice are at stake. There can be no accommodation. But he also knows that for Venice to arm without allies would be suicide, so to stiffen her spine against Roman aggression backed by Spain, Wotton must convince her that England will mobilise in her defence – and bring the rest of right-thinking Europe on board. The war that ensues will be holy. (Is he experiencing flashbacks to university and Tancredi liberating Jerusalem?) At the same time, he must persuade the king – and Cecil – of the Venetians' tenacity, that they won't back down, that they aren't using England as a stalking horse, and that not just the honour of King James participates in this cause, but his sovereignty, threatened by Catholic gunpowder plotters ten months back.

Words are the ambassador's weapons, and, as usual, Wotton knows he's aiming them at a double audience. Today, seated on the dais on Doge Donà's right hand, he triumphantly ventriloquises his king to the Collegio. King James agrees the league. The English ambassador underscores parenthetically that 'these are the very words of his Majesty': he has the king's 'authority to oblige his word to unite with this Republic all of his friends, his council, and his forces, both terrestrial and naval, as far as in him' rests. The king is handing Venice the 'dechiaratione' Giustinian was instructed to 'cavar', and he's also saying, significantly, that he's making his declaration 'senza prender consiglio da alcuno', without taking anyone's advice. Not even Cecil's?

This dispatch does not survive. So we have no way of knowing whether these really are 'the very words of his Majesty' or whether Wotton is elaborating, garnishing for his own political ends. Shortly, we'll be able to make some shrewd guesses. What we do know is that instead of grabbing the 'dechiaratione' with both hands, Venice hedges. The pontiff, says Donà, 'having realised that he ran too inconsiderately in those resolutions of his, shows his desire to subside somewhat'. Negotiations with Rome are proceeding. No sense rocking the boat. The ambassador should keep the king's declaration 'in his heart', a secret. If 'the differences are mended', it won't be needed. If they aren't, well …. Wotton appears dumbfounded, lamely repeating, 'Your serenity commands me to keep secret what I have here exposed of the offers of my king?'

He's hardly out the door when he's called back. Those negotiations with that 'inconsiderate' pope were either a time-serving alibi or hit a brick wall. The pope has created eight new cardinals – red hats purchased with cash to fill a war chest – and has announced his intention to 'proceed against Venice', raising horse and foot. 'In view of this', the Senato now leaves 'it to the pleasure of His Majesty to publish his offer of support'. Has he heard right? Wotton asks to hear the resolution read twice. He replies: he won't just publish his king's declaration; he'll make it 'manifest to the world'. Then he adds (ominously or triumphantly?): 'Transivimus Rubiconem'.

13

Crossing the Rubicon

Promises

Over the coming days Wotton bombards Cecil and the king with fevered dispatches – a wonder the paper doesn't burst into flame. They contain 'matter' so 'very secret and tender' (and awash with pope-bashing comments) that they aren't just ciphered, but couriered, one by his chaplain, another by his 'confident messenger'. It's on this journey that Rowland Woodward is ambushed and left for dead outside Paris and his postbags sent on to the French king. If they're deciphered and read, Wotton's dispatches will constitute a catastrophic security breach. Henri will know what the English ambassador in Venice is telling London to expect of France: that she'll watch from the riverbank but never dip a toe in the Rubicon, happily fomenting war between Spain and England – but keeping herself dry from any action. He's not wrong.

Wotton repeats to Cecil what he's told the Collegio of King James's promise, quoting the 'parts' His Majesty expressly declared, that his 'concurrence … should be with all his counsels, friends, and forces both terrestrial and maritime, sincerely and seriously'. In the Collegio the secretary records Wotton's 'long and ornate speeches', the ambassador as diplomatic hurdy-gurdy, droning on about lessons from history, his king's honour, the pope's usurpations, pressing constantly for war. Periodically Wotton pulls something new from his sleeve, like his appeal to be adopted a 'gentleman and citizen Venetian with the same privileges of voting' in the Maggior Consiglio 'as other men attained at 25-years'. He can hardly push his devotion harder. (Imagine, then, how irked this bustling ambassador will be to read the brief Cecil is currently drafting in London saying that he'd almost 'deferred … to write', there being 'so small occasion … ministered from the place where you live'.)

Meanwhile in Whitehall, Giustinian snags the king's attention long enough to relay the Senato's gratitude for his declaration. His Majesty replies that he's 'come to his resolve' to 'defend the Republic' with 'that readiness and courage', 'loyalty and intrepidity' 'which you observe' 'without the aid of my Council'. (Note: the same words Wotton quoted to the Collegio.) 'Nothing', he assures Venice, 'shall move me or make me draw back', for this is 'not a question of the church but the common cause of all Princes for the preservation of their rights and liberties'. Moreover, he will rally his friends Denmark and Germany, 'con tutto il spirito'. The Senato 'will find me disposed to do even more than I promise'. Exit king. His voice drifts in his wake, 'I am leaving tomorrow'; 'see the Earl of Salisbury on this subject'. Enter Cecil. Giustinian repeats the king's asseverations. Cecil confirms them. But then the audience is interrupted. Cecil is summoned to the king. Is there thunder in his face as he leaves?

For in the morning, Cecil has his secretary draft to Wotton a dispatch that does to him with words what the Turks' knives did to Bragadin on Cyprus: flays him alive. The surviving draft shows Cecil vigorously editing, crossing out, interlining, scratching up the margins, turning phrases like thumbscrews. He recaps Giustinian's audience then scathingly accuses the English ambassador of overstepping the 'limits' that should 'contain' both him and the 'speeches' he's making. Cecil hisses his understanding (and he's right about this) that the 'motion of dealing with his Majesty's confederates for a joint association against the Pope and the particularising of his aid, by sea and by land' 'proceedeth from your own speech' in the Collegio. He offers as a slight excuse for the 'motion' that it may 'happily have fallen from you by way of dilating', but then hammers the ambassador with an about-face that dismisses excuses: 'yet I thought fit particularly to note it unto you, that you may be the more wary hereafter, how to carry yourself'.

The Venetians, in Cecil's view, are both machiavels and opportunists, 'apt to make applications of any thing to their advantage'. 'It is considerable, that by this motion of soliciting Princes, which they would fain impose upon his Majesty, their principal drift is, either to draw in his Majesty to be the head of that quarrel, or at least, by this rumour of association to serve their turn, to terrify the Pope, and so to make their own conditions the better; which latter, I think to be the very motive and ground of all, and am of opinion, that it will be compassed before ever any blow be given either on the one side or other'. As for the king's 'more particular engaging himself or dealing with his confederates in Denmark and Germany', His Majesty, says Cecil, 'held that' to be 'somewhat an untimely motion, and not so fit [Cecil strikes this out to add more toughly] very improper to be undertaken by him, seeing that neither the pope had as yet proceeded to open action of hostility, nor the Venetians resolved if he did to stand upon other but a defensive' position.

Reading this on 3 November, the English ambassador's bowels turn to water. He, of course, sees the letter's fair copy, which doesn't show any of Cecil's ragged edits, cancellations and insertions churning up the lines on the draft page like bullocks charging. The 'joint association', the league, *was* his idea, first bruited six months ago. Uninstructed. In his 'own speech'. And constantly reiterated in audiences since. But the king's support: that was being offered by the king himself only two months later, that is, practically as soon as the diplomatic postbags could go their round-trip journeys over the Alps. Self-doubt floods Wotton's mind. Weren't those words 'particularising … aid, by sea and by land', the 'very words of his majesty', Wotton merely quoting him? Or *has* he been guilty of dilating?

An ugly thought that probably doesn't occur to Wotton certainly does to us, having seen how Cecil manipulated negotiations over corn exports to Venice: Cecil looks to be making Wotton the fall guy for the king's over-large promises, hanging the English ambassador out to dry by rewriting the king's speech for his own purposes. Most definitely, the king did *not* tell Giustinian that 'dealing with his [Danish and German] confederates' was 'untimely' and 'improper'. Rather, James unstintingly undertook 'offices with those princes' and promised 'fruitful results'. So that's a bald-faced lie – though Wotton can't know it. Or is it possible that the Venetian ambassador mistook the king's words in the slippage between one man's Italian and the other's French?

Cecil's anti-Italian prejudices are certainly poisoning his pen, making the Venetians craven, saying they're using the king's declaration to 'terrify the Pope' into submission or making England their stooge in a proxy war that will end without a shot fired. (But really, what would be wrong with that? If Wotton's league acts as a deterrent to stop a war, doesn't that constitute effective diplomacy?) Cecil's prejudices must appal the 'vero Venetiano', who perhaps hears in this dispatch echoes of Elizabeth's excoriating letters to Essex in Ireland – or, more likely, echoes of the secretary who drafted them. But maybe the bottom of Cecil's rebuke lies elsewhere, in the sentence instructing Wotton 'not to engage himself further' than 'the condition of his Majesty's own affairs may well permit'. Cecil knows just how parlous the king's 'own affairs' are. While the royal huntsman chases sparrows, his latest infatuation, and heaps mind-boggling riches on young male favourites, the civil servant counts farthings. There's no money in the Exchequer to fund Venetian adventures.

'Be the more wary how you carry yourself': caution or threat? In the Collegio, Wotton tries. He rows back on the king's declaration; casts himself the injured party; accuses the ambassador in London of misrepresenting him; then rows back on his grievances, admitting he 'went overboard' 'overstepping suitable terms', his speech an 'outburst of his soul'. He maunders on about how he's merely a scholar, unapt for diplomatic service; how he's begged the king's leave 'to come home, to serve him with orations and with my life and blood, but never again with my pen'. It's perhaps Wotton's bleating that provokes the normally imperturbable Donà to explode with his own 'unsuitable terms'. He tells the English ambassador exactly what he thinks of Rome's machinations. The pope puts on a 'show of calm' but acts 'opposite', 'sending every day more and more writing, thinking that in multiplying his writing he can justify his – yes', says Donà, 'we will use the word – *errors*'. 'And if all the writing he has circulated were stacked up', including what's been written by 'that generation of friars, priests and busy-body parasites of Rome', it 'would make a pile higher than the chair I'm sitting on'. We can imagine Wotton's astonished ears pinned back even as he hears the diatribe's subtext: that the doge and the ambassador think alike on Rome. And that far from having to cringe, making a volte-face, Wotton is Donà's diplomatic golden lad. His influence, he reports Donà telling him, somewhat 'dilating', is such that Wotton can 'do more with them than any public minister he had ever known in this state'. With this, a rocky moment in diplomatic relations steadies. No thanks to Cecil, who, reading Wotton's 'recovery', quite possibly spits nails.

His wounded self-confidence may feel salved, but Wotton sees no end to the 'business' with Rome. In London that November, celebrations with bells and bonfires mark the first anniversary of the kingdom's miraculous escape from the gunpowder plot. In Venice, late in December, it's observed that the pope's first threatening briefs arrived a year ago. Rumours of an accommodation are (again) rife. Cecil tells Giustinian what he's heard. (And what he's heard sounds suspiciously like Cecil ventriloquising Cecil, even down to the oily parenthetical disclaimer.) 'People are saying' ('but I do not believe it') 'the Republic will withdraw from the position she now assumes and will be obliged to make public demonstration of obedience and subservience to the Pope, even on the points which she now maintains to be temporal'. Wotton is confused. Should he congratulate the Signory? 'People' are saying the Interdict is 'fixed', though for the *popolani*, it's the *pope* who's conceding. The chat on the Piazza is amplified by the arrival of Don Francisco de Castro with terms from Spain. He's one of those arrogant Captain Spurios, all pose and puff, currently being caricatured on the English stage, and at twenty-six, a whippersnapper far too callow for weighty diplomacy. Wotton instantly loathes him. Indeed, when they meet, he provokes a rage that avoids fisticuffs only when another ambassador 'throws himself between them'.

In any case, the terms are unacceptable. Castro's 'importunities' only resolve the Senato to 'confirm their former decrees' with tougher measures. Preparations for war proceed. From a brief vacation duck-hunting on the winter lagoon, Wotton returns beaming, taking 'from his sleeve' a 'little printed book', to report to the Collegio that it names him on Rome's charge sheet as 'the first "capo d'accusa" to show why Venice has been excommunicated'. How delicious! To be so cited: Arrigo VVottoni, chief heretic. The book's author? Supposedly 'Don Paolo'. But reading it, Wotton recognises its author as one of those Jesuit 'masked fathers': 'this is Possevino's work'. It was he who, years back in Rome, mistook Wotton for 'one of his lambs'.

At Christmas, Wotton is straining for action. He reports to the Collegio news just in from London: English ships are 'tied up, ready, on the banks of the Thames'. England's 'roused blood' wants 'the occasion to do something in service' of the Republic's 'great cause'. But the Senato again says 'pause': wait 'until the Pope moves first'. Wotton slumps.

More promises

A week later, things take an astonishing turn. The French ambassador, Philippe Canaye, arranges to meet Wotton privately, whereupon (as Wotton reports in a ciphered dispatch to London) he 'brake with me into the matter following'. The matter is sensational, once it's dug out of Canaye's diplomatic circumlocution: 'That if it shall please His Majesty to hold some understanding (so was his phrase, though meaning without doubt a direct combination with the French king) touching the means to foment and advance the present troubles here, His Majesty shall find the French king much disposed thereunto'.

Canaye is Wotton's closest professional colleague in Venice. The men share information and visit each other in their embassies. And Canaye is still perhaps at heart a Protestant, though recently converted to Catholicism. So Wotton trusts what he dispatches to Cecil, heavily ciphered, as 'a most important deliberative', itemising how the two diplomats have put their heads together, once the bombshell of the 'general proposition' lands, to come up with 'the manner' of achieving it – including what Canaye 'let fall', 'that the church of Rome was grown to such irregularity … as could not be reformed by ordinary remedies'.

(That being the case, Wotton thinks, *extraordinary* remedies must be applied, and he can suggest some.)

It's been said for months that if only Henri would declare for Venice, the controversy would end. Now, France's rather opaquely rendered 'understanding' makes the moment look critical to 'foment' a 'just war'. It's time to end the game of leapfrog the hawks and doves have been playing at across Europe. In Venice, hawks drag Wotton out of bed in the middle of the night to learn just-intercepted news that Fuentes, in Milan, has instructions to invade. In London, the Spanish ambassador, newly dovish 'ever since England declared for Venice', now 'goes about asserting his master's determination to maintain peace in Italy'.

Depressingly, though, 'worse news than ever' comes only days later: the servite friar Paolo Sarpi has been excommunicated in Rome, and Father Fulgenzio Manfredi, the popular pro-Republican preacher, on the pretext of reconciliation, has been 'cyted thither'. (He'll eventually go, but wind up burned as a heretic there.) And Henri of France suddenly withdraws his 'understanding', declaring himself neutral. Poor Canaye! A frog o'er-leaped. Watching him haplessly negotiating smoke-and-mirrors diplomacy for a wind-changing king makes Wotton 'stagger'. He knows how it feels to be left dangling, exposed.

Two weeks into January: another convulsion. The English ambassador first sends one of his household to the Collegio to seek an audience, then, when he's told to come back in the morning, the ambassador appears himself, to 'beat on the doors', even 'to break them down so as to be let in'. The letters he's just received from his intelligencer in Milan can't wait. General Fuentes is assembling 6,000 foot, 1,000 horse on Venice's borders. The pope is 'pounding the war drum everywhere'; Spain is levying '24 thousand men in his states of Italy'; the beaches of the Mediterranean 'where any vessels can disembark men' have been militarised for 'fear of English ships' landing forces. France, ever the hooked haddock, flip-flops. Henri now declares positively for Rome. (Canaye in Venice shows 'much perturbation of spirit' and takes to his bed. There will be three more 'turn and turn agains' from the French king before things finish.) Wotton sees no option but war, a holy war, 'because Christ in this case came into the world to bring a sword and not peace'. But when the Senato finally votes to adopt the league of nations that he's been touting for eight months, Wotton starts quibbling. (Is Cecil's 'be more wary' chiming in his head?) He wants to know if the Senato's resolution has been properly written to show the initiative coming from Venice, not London? Donà's reply would wither grapes on the vine. The 'Senato's intention is so well expressed that it needs no interpreting'. Does Wotton want to hear it read again? The ambassador says that won't be necessary.

Unbelievably, action *again* stalls. Wotton kicks his heels in Cannaregio, writes long dispatches to London analysing the constitution of the Venetian government as a form of diplomatic crystal ball gazing and practises Spanish airs on his viol da gamba. Although he's 'urged here by diverse selves (who differ not much from my opinion touching the pope) to appear often in College', Wotton won't put in an appearance throughout all of February. He's boycotting indecisiveness. Suspicious, he reports the arrival of the French cardinal Joyeuse, who's given an 'extraordinary reception', then conveyed to a 'secret audience', not up the Palazzo's common stairs but 'by private ways through the prince's lodging'. What's Joyeuse doing there? The same as Castro, proposing 'certain researched subtilties' (Wotton's scorn is thick) towards an accommodation.

These 'subtilties' are rejected, and 'pericoli della guerra' (danger of war) is scrawled down the margin of the meeting's transcript. The following day, 3 March, Wotton hears that Joyeuse's embassy has changed nothing: the Senato is resolved to 'maintain preparations', since the pope 'maintains his pretensions'. Wotton replies with an old saw, something he might have read in an almanac. In England, to claim your title to disputed property, you must stand on it once a year and, *viva voce*, assert your rights. By analogy, and in the face of all the Castros and Joyeuses coming to Venice with this and that offer, he's standing his ground: reiterating the promises of his king, the Republic's surest defender, and his own faith that Venice will never submit to craven conditions. Mostly, though, the English ambassador is weary. He writes to Cecil, 'My lord, I am, as God help me, tired in my very soul with the sluggishness of this business'. Yet he remains hopeful, watching Joyeuse (and his ultimata) leave for Rome empty-handed on 19 March, 'that the Divine Providence will lead on that which he hath begun for his glory through a secret and sweet disposition of these inferior causes, wherein His will be done'.

Peace without bells

Then, suddenly, it's over. On 30 March the preening Spaniard, Castro, struts down the Scala d'Oro proclaiming the repeal of the Interdict. Apparently, Wotton hears, the news is already public in Rome. He sounds stunned, that the papal city is 'full of nothing but voices of peace which have engendered the like here and in the towns by the way and perhaps farther, finding ears and minds open for it'. The news has travelled like witches riding a storm. But he's deeply sceptical. When 'we come to examine the substance of the thing', is it likely? Joyeuse carried from Venice 'no other matter' than what the Senato had roundly rejected. The ambassador confesses that his 'understanding is much troubled how to conceive any grounds of these impressions', 'among which uncertainties, fuller of imagination than substance', he's 'forced to suspend mine own conceit'.

Five days later the English ambassador walks into the Collegio to congratulate the Republic. He's had to accept it. An 'accommodation' – 'for so they will have it styled', he writes pointedly, 'and not a rebenediction or absolution' – has ended the Interdict.

Or has it? Holy Week is fast approaching, and just in time for Palm Sunday, 8 April, Joyeuse arrives again from Rome bearing the 'forms' to be used 'in the knitting up of this business'. Speaking in the Collegio, he declares 'the pope's paternal clemency', but then he begins 'a new song', listing the pope's 'conditions': 'That they should receive again the Jesuits, suspend their decrees, send an ambassador to the pope, and thereupon he would pronounce the rebenediction'.

The Collegio explodes: 'what confusion, what despight and scorn' could not 'be related unto His Majesty', writes Wotton, 'without a better pen than mine'. It takes Ambassador Canaye pouring in 'all kinds of lenitives' to restore the French cardinal's credentials who, 'slacking his spirit', 'speaketh no more of Jesuits' but 'will be contented to give them the public rebenediction'. Even that is absolutely refused, as giving 'sotto parole tacite' – that is, tacitly – 'a recognition of validity in the pope's interdict'. And that would be monstrous. What the state *will* allow is 'simply in College the revocation of the said interdict', then the cardinal, being a priest, may say 'Mass in any church of the town ... except the Cathedral' – the Basilica – without 'any of the Signory or Senate present', and without any 'public note of joy or so much as acknowledgement'. No bells. No bonfires.

Now, on Easter Monday, it's over. The pope lifts the Interdict. Donà revokes the *Protesto*. Cecil is right. It *is* 'compassed' without 'any blow' on 'either side'. But he's also wrong. The Republic does not 'withdraw' from her original 'position'; does not 'make any public demonstration of obedience and subservience to the Pope'; does not revoke 'the perpetual exclusive of the Jesuits'; does not refrain from prosecuting delinquent clergy. The Venetian 'pantaloons', 'on the points' maintained 'to be temporal', concede not one.

In his study, writing up these events for Cecil, Wotton puts down his pen. He's been on the front line of the Republic's war of words for a full sixteen months and he's exhausted. No matter what he urges so optimistically to London, that 'our troubles here are likely and almost certain to be concluded with more honour unto this State and the cause then ever hath happened in these countries since the deformation of the truth', he's depressed that his diplomacy may have been 'over run by the nimbleness of others', Joyeuse and that blasted Castro. What has he actually achieved? He imagined himself leading the charge across the Rubicon but perhaps was merely a foot soldier in other men's manoeuvres. An instrument, hardly instrumental.

Gloom, however, never settles on the English ambassador for long. In the coming days, as he gathers his strength, with Parkhurst, perhaps, impressing upon him that, diplomatically speaking, he's a war hero, Arrigo VVottoni rethinks his role as one of Divine Providence's 'inferior causes'. And changes his mind.

14

Some particular men

After words

April 1607. Leonardo Donà greets the pope's 'accommodation' with an adjectival flourish. Venetians, he tells Christendom, are what they've always been, '*ossequentissimi* figlioli della santa sede': not just children of the Holy See, but her *most obsequious* children. The pope buys a villa outside Rome, where he retires, according to Wotton, to take 'upon him the form of a wiser man than he appeared in the whole action'. Cardinal Joyeuse exits Venice down the silent back stairs of the Palazzo Ducale without crossing the path of the English ambassador, who makes his way to the Collegio, as usual, up the Scala d'Oro. Is Wotton licking his wounds? Probably not. The Protestant revolution did not take place. But neither did war in Christendom, which, a bare hundred years back, when a pope last excommunicated Venice and declared war on the Republic, ended in the humiliations of Agnadello: the rout of the Venetians and the loss of mainland territories that (as Machiavelli wrote in *The Prince*) 'it had taken them eight hundred years' exertion to conquer'.

Now it dawns on the English ambassador that he could be credited with war averted. He was only an ant in the business. Nevertheless, the ant acted on his own initiative when he put the league, his diplomatic grain, on the negotiating table, and he didn't just drop it there; he kept pushing it in Venice such that Giustianian pushed it in London, pushing the king into his declaration. Without the league and the English king's declaration, where would the Republic have stood as the long months of contumacy dragged on? Once the Senato finally ungagged him in September 1606, allowing him to broadcast the league to his fellow ambassadors, and they began passing it up the diplomatic chain, the political rhetoric shifted. Result: Spain's ambassador in Venice now went 'about asserting his master's determination to maintain peace in Italy'. The king of Spain himself a scant month later began 'to distinguish upon his offers to the pope, that he meant them [only] defensively', 'such sober interpretations of the matter' having evidently 'grown upon' the English king's 'declaration of himself'. In February 1607, the Venetian ambassador in Spain reported in a ciphered message that Spain was 'convinced that had it not been for the King of England the Republic would not have shown so bold a front to the Pope: for she could never have resisted these two powers united, and from France she knew quite well she could look for nothing but words'.

The ant heaps all credit upon His Majesty. Of course. While others have spent the year 'twiddling their thumbs' or 'in shameful connivance', his king can 'boast now and for the future that he alone declared himself in favour of the right'. His 'patronage' means that the 'honourable and memorable conclusion of this business' should 'be ascribed absolutely unto the King of Great Britain'. Doge Donà agrees. In the 'most fervent, serious and affectionate' speech Wotton has ever heard from him, Donà attributes 'the glory of this conclusion' 'unto his Majesty's so clear, so magnanimous, and so disinterested protection'. Not only would the Signory's 'eternal obligation ... be imprinted on the hearts of the living'; it would 'be delivered over to their posterity forever'. Less effusive, the Senate minutes the king as 'a principal cause of this result by his generous, heroic and spontaneous declaration in our favour'.

In post-Interdict Venice Wotton's reputation rides high. Both the French and Spanish ambassadors having been recalled, he who was once 'the youngest is now the oldest of the ministers' serving Venice, and (the doge adds) 'the most loving'. Reciprocally, to show 'what extraordinary weight you have with us', the Signory will regularly grant Wotton 'more than what is ordinary'. A short four years ago, *nobili* begrudged appointment to England. Now, they're competing for the honour, men 'of greater quality than any before sent', like Marc' Antonio Correr, who tells Wotton he has 'petitioned of this office' and will 'devour the length of the way' to London, even taking with him his only son.

More astonishingly, where two years earlier the Signory turned down flat Wotton's request to meet Zorzi Giustinian 'in public or privately without shadow' to 'discuss together the greater good' before the ambassador-elect's departure for England, now the state is sending its diplomats to the English embassy to hear Wotton's thoughts. Correr in January 1608. And after Correr, Piero Contarini. In the Collegio, before they get down to business, familiarities pass between doge and ambassador: they commiserate over dismal weather and rejoice in a beautiful spring morning; they compare aches and pains; they joke about the calendar reforms Pope Gregory introduced two decades back that have divided Europe and bamboozled farmers, who complain that they don't know when to sow their crops. Wotton reports disaster averted in the embassy after a chimney catches fire. Donà advises Wotton to 'arm himself' with heavy cloaks against the cold on the winter lagoon and suggests points of interest when the ambassador goes on holiday. There's a new confidence in Wotton's replies, even occasionally 'demanding pardon' to interrupt the doge.

Otherwise, Wotton is all modesty. To be 'a poor scholar', he says, is 'the highest of my own titles'. (We've heard that one before.) And: the 'farthest end of mine ambition' is the 'honour wherewith it hath pleased his Majesty to clothe my unworthiness', sending him to Venice where he's been a 'spectator in this beautiful theatre', privileged to watch the 'glorious action' of the Interdict Crisis play out. But claiming he's 'both born and formed in my education fitter to be an instrument of truth than art' (by which he means 'artfulness') is deferential tosh. And does he really wish, 'as Vitruvius says', that 'the chests of all the ministers that reside by the Signory could have windows'? What would Donà see if he could peer through a window into Wotton's interior, heart and mind? Truth? Or art? Is the 'candour' Wotton says would show there an anatomical mirage?

For despite what he avers in the Collegio, Wotton knows the 'glorious action' isn't finished, not least because while the matter of the Republic's sovereignty has been settled, that other matter, the one Wotton undertook to help 'slide along', hasn't. Even as the 'articles of the agreement' were being hammered out, 'two of the mainest and in all opinion most irreconcilable points were passed over in silence', both bearing down on religious differences with Rome. First, what to do about 'the books written in justification of the cause on each side'? Secondly, what to do about 'the persons of the writers' of those books? Rome makes them – both books and persons – heretics. And in Rome, heretics burn. Wotton informs Cecil: 'Those of the pope's side continue to write as maliciously as before, and there is preparation here to answer them'. So, he hopes, 'we shall keep on foot the war of the quill, as your lordship has called it'.

'Our young noblemen travellers'

The Protestant revolution goes underground. Or maybe better said in Venice, underwater, like a deep-diving cormorant on the lagoon. It will resurface, but the interim offers us some relief from statecraft's incessant broils to look at a series of domestic episodes that show what else is occupying the English ambassador in the post-Interdict years, obliged as he is by the king's commission to 'protect his subjects abroad'. That totalising clause expands Wotton's brief far beyond anything covered in Gentili's *De legationibus* to make him not just the king's toiling ant but his sheep-dog, herding the wandering flock of fresh-faced English youths and noblemen travellers who are arriving in Venice in a steady stream – most of them kin to Robert Cecil. Wotton sees himself in them, though of course when he was the student traveller two decades back he had no resident ambassador to make introductions or snatch him out of harm's way. The tricks these lads get up to aren't much different from his of yore. (We remember the brash youth riding into Rome in '92 and ducking out of dinner seconds before his cover was blown.) Only now, when young men come to grief, they're a diplomatic problem for Wotton.

Such is the case of William, lord Roos, Robert Cecil's great-nephew. Roos spells trouble even before he's within striking distance of Venice. Eighteen years old, travelling through Italy in the spring of 1608 with another youth, Baron St John, and their tutors, he's one of those epicene aristos whose slightly bulging spaniel eyes and pouting lips speak inbred entitlement. He's keen to see Rome. Most student travellers are. But in these months after the Interdict, it's 'never worse' time 'for his majesty's true subjects', that is, Protestants, to attempt the journey. On the Italian frontier at Milan, Protestants 'can very hardly be suffered to pass without searching' (baggage, boxes, books, body) 'and a hundred other intrigues'. In Rome they're 'secretly' and 'straitly looked into', the pope having 'professed that not one of our nation shall be safe there unless he will live "catholicamente"'. Roos wants to reach Rome (of all times) 'this Holy Week' and, 'underhand', he has 'moved some about the pope' for 'a safe conduct'. It's denied.

Getting wind of these lunatic plans, Wotton warns Roos off Rome as a matter of 'public consequence', never mind 'Christian wisdom'. Imagine the Inquisition getting their hands on Cecil's kin, what propaganda might be made out of claims that he's turned to Mother Church. Roos retorts haughtily. Wotton's information is a 'base lie' from an 'impertinent traitor', a shrill denial that shows the lady protesting too much. These travelling barons have already lost one tutor, St John's Master Lomax. He died in Florence. But not before spending his last breaths revealing himself a 'professed Catholic', his religion concealed so 'he might not be thought to persuade' St John 'of the same'. It's Roos's tutor, John Mole, who, clearly stunned to have been travelling with a cloaked heretic in their midst, writes Wotton troubled news of this 'dissimulation', of seeing 'the poor lord', before, '*Ovem lupo*', a lamb entrusted to a wolf, 'now left destitute of an adviser'.

Let's hope Master Mole didn't worry overmuch about that lamb, for what the prerogatived aristocrats do next costs their remaining tutor his life. They ignore instructions. They travel to Rome. Entering the Holy City their entourage is promptly stopped by the Inquisition. Mole is arrested, recognised as the author of anti-Catholic titles. The lads are given leave to continue their sightseeing. They travel to Naples, then Venice. There, Wotton deals 'very seriously' with Roos 'touching his Roman journey' and propounds 'a course' for Mole's 'delivery', 'to transport by oblique means' 'some portion of money'. (He means bribery.) It fails. Shortly, reports start reaching London that Cecil's kinsman is lapsed into 'unsavoury & obscene discourse', profligate spending, depravity (he once insults some locals by exposing 'his privy member' 'in the presence of divers men & women') and, most worryingly, his constant consorting with continental Catholics. Mole meanwhile remains in the Inquisition's prison. Thirty years later, he'll die there.

Roos's progress prompts Wotton to redouble his efforts to warn London about Catholic predations on English innocents abroad. Four years earlier he briefed Cecil on the dangers. Now he exposes new machinations (his pen dripping sarcasm): 'council ... infused into the pope by his artisans' (more sarcasm) 'the Jesuits', to 'separate by some device their guides from our young noblemen' and afterwards to show them 'much kindness and security but yet with restraint when they come to Rome of departing thence without leave'. Baldly stated, the Jesuits hold these youths captive to ply them with indoctrination, 'which form was held ... with the Lords Roos and St John'. On at least one of then, Rome's ministrations stuck.

For Wotton, Rome is Babylon. So it's a relief that for some gentlemen travellers it holds no allure. In the autumn of 1610 Cecil sends his own son, titled lord Cranborne, to Venice, ordering him to avoid all the 'dangerous' parts of Italy. Cranborne and his entourage lodge in the embassy, but he intends only a brief stay because, 'having married just before leaving England', he's anxious to get home. Besides (and Wotton doesn't tell the Venetians this), Cecil's son 'finds relish in nothing on this side the mountains, nor much in anything on this side the sea'. He certainly isn't interested in Rome. His father has ordered him abroad, evidently thinking the seventeen-year-old needs a couple more years on his back before bedding his bride. Cranborne has other ideas. What can Wotton do? In Padua, on the first leg of a journey homeward, Cranborne falls ill to a life-threatening flux: 'shivering ... ague ... looseness'. Wotton goes to his bedside. In a letter to Cecil he juggles the pros and cons of 'your son's farther travel'. 'It were pity' that, by failing to visit the 'courts of Italy', 'such a capacity' as Cranborne's 'should want objects to work upon'. On the other hand, there's 'his present weakness and attenuation'. Like other prerogatived youths, however, Cranborne makes up his own mind: 'he casts no perils in going where his desire leads him'. The ambassador resigns him to his physician.

Wotton has more clout with Cecil than any tutor or physician. Still, reporting on Cecil's loathsome great-nephew and headstrong son tests his diplomatic resources. John Harington gives him no such trouble. He arrives in Venice at the end of 1608, 'having refrained' from a 'Roman journey though he was thither enticed by the letters' of a notorious ex-pat English recusant, and takes a house in San Polo: the embassy is too small to accommodate the dozen in his suite. He intends to reside six months, 'determined to study the form of this government'. Wotton rhapsodises. Never has he seen in a youth of Harington's years 'such a desire of knowledge nor a more religious dispostion joined with so quick a temper'. Who is this wonder? The ambassador basks almost ridiculously hyperbolic, introducing him in the Collegio with a speech lasting a full five minutes (while Harington waits outside the door): little more than sixteen years old; his father ... his mother ... his sister ... learned in philosophy ... possessing Latin and Greek 'perfettamente'.

Most significantly, he's 'l'occhio dritto del Principe nostro': Prince Henry's 'right eye', installed as his 'henchman' in 1603 when the nine-year-old Stuart arrived in England and at his side ever since. (A double portrait of the prince and companion by Robert Peake dated 1603 shows a hunting scene of precocious, over-dressed 'blooding', Henry in green velvet sheathing his sword having made the kill while John, kneeling, holds the stag's antlers.) It's rumoured (says Wotton) that Cecil intends Harington for his daughter and that this gentleman will one day 'haver tutto il governo del Regno', have complete rule of the kingdom. It's taken tears and hard work to wring from the prince a licence for a year's travel. Wotton says James jokes about Harington's almost-magic sway over his son, asking, 'What art have you used?' It can't be flattery. Harington is too young to know the ways of the court flatterer. His reply gives us the measure of this youth. No, he says, not flattery, 'ma bene con la verità' (but rather, truth).

Harington disappears from Wotton's official notice after his audience with the doge. So he stays out of diplomatic trouble – but not out of view. In post-Interdict Venice, he's precisely positioned to report on the after-effects, indeed, the future likelihoods of the 'glorious action'. He's a determined Protestant who serves an equally determined Protestant, a prince who, having survived the gunpower plot, zealously opposes Catholicism. Harington writes to his prince weekly as he travels across Europe and compiles a diary to show him on his return. He notes the 'trifles and trickeries of the false religion' he sees in Italy and the 'superstitions, false miracles and relics' he encounters in Venice 'in this time of Lent'. His own habitual devotions include prayers and psalms before meals, an hour's daily study of Scripture and unfailing observance of the Sabbath, so in Venice, he's under the ambassador's watchful eye as he attends services, sermons and lectures in the English embassy, now staffed with a new chaplain, William Bedell. But Harington also listens to local preaching.

Having picked up Italian 'indifferently well ... by the way' (according to his tutor), he attends at least some of the Lenten sermons Fra Fulgenzio Micanzio is delivering daily at San Lorenzo, preaching in Italian, not Latin, his sermons thus meant for the ears of the *popolani*. A papal intelligencer calls them 'calvinistical', and in his report to Rome they certainly sound so, for Fulgenzio 'stoutly maintains justification of faith without works' and, urging 'the people to read the scripture' and pray in their own 'tongue', 'preaches against legends ... against pilgrimage, against confession as it is used' and says 'the people should not care for excommunication so [long as] they followed the scripture'. Harington reports to Prince Henry that these sermons preach 'the word of God' 'purely and without intermixture', and he relates some gossip about this preaching that he probably hears from Wotton (who has it from the Collegio and puts it in a dispatch to Cecil). When the Venetian ambassador in Rome insisted to the pope that Fulgenzio preached nothing but the Scriptures, the pope 'in a great passion' retorted, 'Et non sapete voi che il predicare la pura scrittura et il puro Evangelio è un voler ruinare et distruggere la fede Catholica?' (But don't you know that preaching the pure Scripture and the pure Gospel will ruin and destroy the Catholic faith?)

Prince Henry has followed the Interdict controversy avidly. Unlike his father, the Rex Pacificus, he's a militarist of the earl of Essex stripe, likely to stand behind Wotton's league and to urge military action in defence of Christendom. We might speculate, then, that in Venice in 1609 Harington is like Wotton in Florence all those years ago, the eyes, ears and pen informing someone higher up, feeding intelligence that will shape international relations and the future of Christendom. Possibly Harington, like Bedell (but not Wotton, forbidden by protocol) has direct access through Fulgenzio to the man Fulgenzio serves, Fra Paolo Sarpi, architect of the Republic's theological and legal position during the crisis, and to Sarpi's continuing conversations. That is, access to what's still hanging unresolved, the matter of 'the books' and 'the persons of the writers' of those books. With such access would come access to those persons' current thinking. (An unnamed informant tells Cecil in April 1609 that 'your cousin

Sir John Harington' is 'with this Fulgenzio ... very great'.) Does Wotton, who, we remember, hangs Prince Henry's portrait on an embassy wall and writes to him regularly, have, through Harington, a confidential channel of communication to the kingdom's heir? Might the Protestant revolution in Venice yet take place?

Death brings an end to that promise. Prince Henry dies in 1612, never reaching full maturity, and Harington, only fifteen months later. No record survives of Wotton's reactions to these deaths, catastrophic to his hopes, beyond a passing reference to 'a time of so public grief'. Elsewhere, however, we see how deeply he feels the deaths of young men in his diplomatic charge, and how, diplomatically, he has to deal with them.

In the middle of an August night in 1607 Wotton scribbles lines to Cecil telling him he's making 'as much haste as my grief will suffer me towards Padua'. Richard Cave lies near death. He's another of Cecil's kinsmen, only introduced in the Collegio with two companions and kissed 'alla venetiana' four months earlier when they arrived intending study at the great university of Padua – and just in time to revel with Wotton in the glorious end of the Interdict Crisis. Young men get sick in Venice. The symptoms are general: fever, ague, what today we'd diagnose as malaria or flu. They usually recover. Cave won't. His illness as Wotton describes it is not just horrific ('hardness of his belly, turgidity and inflamation of his bladder', continuous fever and headaches); it's also mysterious. It baffles all the 'ordinary physicians ... called to consult of him', for Cave, counter-symptomatically, also shows 'strength of pulse, constancy of color, and appetite'. He suffers thus a fortnight, Wotton at his bedside for the final three days. He then departs 'to a better life', 'well settled and seasoned in God's truth'.

Cave's soul is provided for, but he leaves behind the diplomatic problem of his mortal remains. First, there has to be an investigation of the body. Mysterious death always brings suspicion of poisoning. So, in the interests of forensic science, the physicians' satisfaction and 'the common benefit', Wotton 'yielded to have his body afterwards opened' so that 'the principal parts might be seen'. He orders an autopsy, calling in a surgeon from the university's renowned anatomy theatre to make the cuts. They find a kidney 'apostemated' by a tumor and a bladder 'so inflamed that even .6. hours after his death when the rest of his body was cold, the surgeon ... could hardly support the heat with his hand'. They make 'no farther search'. Later though, in the night, 'his body we brought up ... to Venice', and in the morning, 'accompanied with almost all the gentlemen of our religion and my family', Wotton heads a cortege of black-draped gondolas to row Cave's corpse across the lagoon, beyond Malamocco. There, wrapped in a winding-sheet, weighted, it's slipped overboard, 'buried in the gulf'.

Recounting these events, Wotton acknowledges that he commands enough respect in the Venetian state that young Cave might have been 'buried in any of these churches with their ordinary solemnities'. He hasn't made the request, however, unwilling that any 'popish rites' be performed on Cave's body. Worse would be the imputation, if he were 'buried with these rites', that he 'died in this faith', a Catholic. Wotton won't countenance a Roman 'triumph amongst them', which is why, consulting his chaplain and Cave's colleagues, he decides 'to commit his body to the sea which in the expected day of our Redeemer shall yield up her dead: contenting our selves out of the necessity which this place doth lay upon us only with a meeting together privately at a sermon in my house for the solemnization of his remembrance'. We hear Wotton's emotions tugging against his diplomacy in this dispatch. He'd like to do so much more for Cave than 'this place' allows them. Privately, 'Christian wisdom' reconciles him to the loss of 'this sweet gentleman'. But he's bereft of further words, unable to 'intermingle ... any other matter' with his message. Still, as ambassador, he must dress himself in official language to assure Cecil that 'on our parts, here nothing was wanting' for Cave 'which might be provided by human reason'. 'Reason': in the operation of his Protestant faith, that's Wotton's default position.

When he buries Cave secretly at sea, Wotton ducks diplomatic controversy. When he learns that Julius, the son of Sir Julius Caesar, chancellor of the Exchequer, lies dead in the street outside Padua's famous fencing school, he can't avoid it.

The only thing that's certain about the incident is the weather. Across Europe in January 1608 'the cold is intenser than any within the memory of man'. In London, the Thames is frozen, the city reportedly in a state of siege. Throughout Italy, Wotton writes, the 'asperity of the weather and depth of snows ... exceedeth all example'. The posts aren't getting through. But that hardly matters. No one is 'hearkening after news', rather, 'after meat', that is, food. Venetians are 'breaking their heads with falls in the street'; 'citizens that went a-fowling' are 'frozen to death'; 'the courier of Feltri and his horse' have been 'eaten up with a troop of wolves that were driven with famine down into the plain'. On the back of all this, Wotton has to report 'a grievous accident' that 'happened at Padua amongst the little number of our nation there'.

The story is a tangle of cross-accusations and contradictions. Admittedly, eighteen-year-old Caesar was 'a bit too full of youth', only just having hit his 'slippery' years. His 'excessive vivacity' was the reason his father sent him to

Padua, 'hoping he would absorb learning, manners and devotion' to Venice, which should have been 'native to his blood', the family having originated, only a generation back, in Treviso. He enrols in the university but exercises his vivacity in Bartolomeo Tagliaferro's fencing school. On the day in question (as Wotton tells it), challenged by one of Tagliaferro's students, Caesar bests him, then lays down his weapon and makes to leave. But he's called back by the master of school who leans out of a window saying that because the youth he bested is his student, he wants Caesar to return for another bout, with Tagliaferro himself. Caesar consents, returns, puts himself *en garde* to begin 'the game', but instead is attacked for real, 'furiously and with insulting words'. His sword hand is badly wounded. 'Reason had it', Wotton continues, that if the wounding were only an accident, the following morning Tagliaferro should have apologised. Instead, 'he armed himself with weapons and friends, and went to attack the youth', but – here's where the weather steps in – Caesar, defending himself with 'a little weapon that he had in his bed', 'slipped on the ice' and fell. Instantly, 'the other leaped upon him with a dagger and killed him'.

That's not the story the Podestà, the mayor, reports from Padua. His investigation claims that, infuriated by the wounding and leaving the school shouting 'that he wanted to kill' the student fencer, Tommaso Brochetta, it was Caesar who returned the next day with a terzaruolo, a type of short musket. He shot at Brochetta, missed, then was set upon by Brochetta who 'unsheathed his sword and wounded the Englishman with a thrust that killed him instantly'. Not so, say witnesses, changing Wotton's original account. Yes, Caesar armed himself with the firearm, an offence in Padua. But he never fired on Brochetta. (Here's the weather again.) Caesar slipped, and the weapon falling on the ground fired on its own.

Howls of protest come from the English students at Padua. They want Brochetta arrested for homicide. Wotton formally supports them in the Collegio, petitioning that 'Brochetta as the executor, and Tagliaferro as incendiary and instigator ... of the homicide' be brought to law. Given the place Caesar's father occupies in the English government, there may be trouble ahead, Wotton implies, were the crime to go unpunished. A new Podestà is installed. A new investigation produces yet another account. It still has Caesar firing on Brochetta, but also includes testimony from witnesses who produce Caesar's cloak to show from holes and burning in the fabric that the gun went off under his clothing. There's nothing for it but another trial. The case drags on through April. But at least the accused are arrested.

Meanwhile, for weeks Caesar's body lies unburied, 'the clergy refusing its admittance to holy ground' because they're 'informed that the man was a Calvinist'. Finally, they give him a public funeral, but then secretly, at night, remove the body (as 'incapable' of sacred burial) to a separate place. Who knows where the corpse winds up, but Wotton at least tries to repatriate Caesar's personal effects, having hoped to send home to his father for his 'especial comfort' a Greek New Testament that young Julius 'was wont every day to read two chapters'. This shows 'that though his end was fatal and sudden, yet he had always good thought about him, even in the midst of some imperfections, rather of his age than of his nature'. Thus, Wotton offers comfort, man to man. But he's forced to admit that as ambassador, he has failed: 'this book I can by no means recover out of the hands of the Inquisitor, whom I have urged so far both by private and public means, as that he hath been forced to deny the having of it'. We hear, under the diplomatic language, Wotton's rage. He despairs of securing a result, for he knows Venice is a place where 'a respect of State' frequently 'hath drowned the respect of Justice'.

'Extravagant persons'

We're seeing in these episodes the repertoire Wotton developed for managing the troubles English youths brought to the embassy's door, but they weren't the king's subjects who gave him the most sleepless nights. Rather, it was the footloose renegades he calls 'extravagant persons': recusants, outlaws, the disaffected, men holding grudges, men holding secrets, men posing significant danger to kingdom, Republic and Anglo-Venetian relations. Like Robert Dudley, who pitches up in Florence in spring 1607, just as Venice is reaching her accommodation with Rome. Wotton is instantly alert.

This Dudley is the bastard son of Robert, earl of Leicester, Queen Elizabeth's particular favourite, her 'Robin'. Failing in a two-year-long court case to establish his legitimacy, the bastard leaves England. He's married, but takes with him his lover and cousin, Elizabeth Southwell, disguised as a boy page, later using a papal dispensation to marry her on the grounds that his Protestant marriage was null. Dudley is a master theorist and practical engineer of ship-building, and he arrives in Florence when Ferdinando de' Medici, the Grand Duke, is intent on opening a school of naval construction, assembling a world-class fleet, and recruiting to his service 'as many mariners and seamasters as with money and words he can corrupt', including Dudley as his sharpest instrument.

Venice fears de' Medici's military build-up (which Wotton was already nervously reporting a decade ago as he travelled through Florence, though now he can also mock Ferdinando's 'strange and vast opinions', including a project to send his fleet 'to fetch the holy sepulcher' from Jerusalem and to reassemble it as a tourist attraction in a new Medici chapel in Florence). England is less fearful than angry: Florence is stealing English ships and ordnance and 'withdrawing ... our mariners from mercantile to little better than piratical employment', putting English mariners in chains as galeots or slaves if they refuse de' Medici's service.

England knows de' Medici's designs will fail if Dudley is removed, so the king orders Wotton to serve privy seals on him and Southwell, ordering them home. Dudley refuses them: they aren't properly addressed to him as 'earl of Leicester'. Hers can't be delivered. She's 'lying sick at present of a late abort', a miscarriage. The mission is stonewalled. Bizarrely, Wotton confesses he does 'much compassionate' Southwell, a 'gentlewoman whose mind as her blood' is 'assuredly noble but deceived'. More bizarrely, he thinks of her as a 'fellow traveller', both of them having 'tasted of peregrination'. Nevertheless, England declares the pair outlaws and bigamists. They'll remain exiles in de' Medici's Court. For his part, the Grand Duke (who once sent young Arrigo VVottoni on an errand to Scotland disguised as Ottavio Baldi) shows his contempt for England by tearing up the paper brought in claim of the king's ships: 'That for you king', he smirks. 'Your ships are full of traders. Mine of soldiers and arms.' But that's his last roar. Two days later, time catches up with him. The old man dies.

More threatening to Wotton's diplomacy is John Ward, who goes by a dozen other names according to local pronunciation across the Mediterranean. A Kentishman, like Wotton, and ten years older, he sailed as a privateer licensed by Queen Elizabeth to plunder Spanish ships after the Armada's defeat in 1588. When peace with Spain in 1604 ended such enterprise, Ward turned pirate in the Mediterranean, taking ships of all nations, their crews and booty indiscriminately. Impossible to capture. A legend. Not much to look at, according to a profile read in the Collegio: 'very small in stature, with not much hair ... black in complexion and beard, speaks little and almost always cursing, drunk from the morning to night ... outwardly, mangled and oafish'. Still, according to Leonardo Donà (in distinctly un-doge-like language), he's a legend every Englishman who owns even 'dui palmi di terreno sul mare' aspires to imitate. (Two palms of land on the sea-front: that's sarcasm. A 'palm' is a measurement, the width of a man's hand.)

For the Venetians, Ward's depredations cross a line in April 1607, just as they're otherwise engaged ending their business with the pope, when he captures the *Soderina*. She's stived with silks, indigo, the riches of the east, too heavily laden to manoeuvre when Ward's cruiser blasts her broadside. After three hours' firefight, he takes her, adding insult to injury when he tows her to Tunis, his pasha-protected bolthole, refitting her as his flagship, with twenty artillery in the casemates and another twenty on deck. On her first voyage out, though, she breaks up in a storm. The gundecks can't carry the added weight of cannon. Three hundred and fifty Turkish sailors drown. Back in Tunis, locals bay for Ward's blood. Rumours circulate: that he's 'in desperate plight'; that he's dead; that he's seeking pardon from King James, prepared to buy pardon with spoils. In Venice, this last causes uproar. They know from their ambassador in London the state of the king's finances, the Exchequer empty, the Commons compiling thirty-two grievances against taxation and extravagance at Court. Ward's loot would hand King James a golden ladder to climb out of his fiscal hole.

Meanwhile, Ward's piracy threatens Anglo-Venetian trade and markets around the globe. Every ship pirated is a diplomatic nightmare that produces welters of claims crossing national boundaries and engaging 'foreign' laws on confiscation and 'adventure of sea', plus the danger that merchants will transfer their business to safer ports. Wotton stands head bowed in the Collegio hearing complaint after complaint against England: the *Husband*, the *Corsaletta*, the *Seraphim*. In January 1609 King James issues a 'Proclamation Against Pirates': 'Death and confiscation for any act of piracy'; 'No subject ... to aid, abet or deal with pirates'. Fine words. How to enforce them? Ward 'turns Turk'. As 'Ysuf Reis', he remains at large.

The bald-faced, the outlaw: stymied, the ambassador must despair at what little shift diplomacy can make with 'extravagant persons'. We can imagine his horror, then, when he learns of the next one coming his way, in autumn 1607, across a mist-shrouded lagoon. It's a ghost from his past whose 'remember me?' returns Wotton to Ireland, to campaigning with Essex, to rain and mud, to ambush and failures of men and supplies, to young Harry's first real experience of diplomacy, negotiating a disastrous treaty with an 'extravagant person' whose memory has haunted him for a decade: Hugh O'Neill, earl of Tyrone.

To dodge a summons to London and likely arrest, Tyrone with ninety others, wife, family, Ulstermen, sailed from Donegal in September in what history will call the 'Flight of the Earls'. Destination: Spain. Then Italy, Rome, perhaps Venice. Purpose: conjectured. Likely: to raise rebellion in Ireland with Spain and Rome on side. Wotton reports news from Cecil to the Collegio in

November. Donà interjects that he remembers Tyrone from thirty-four years ago, when he was Venetian ambassador to Spain and 'heard of many commotions and troubles in that province' which 'the late queen had taken steps and remedied with her great prudence'. Remedied? Wotton recounts his own experience of the queen's steps, how 'at the time of our past wars', he 'frequented' Tyrone and 'got to know the nature of this Earl well'. He remembers standing far off, watching the encounter of the generals, Tyrone riding his horse into the Lagan, Essex, reined-in on the riverbank. Whatever was said in that parley, Essex 'decided to negotiate a truce of arms' and 'sent me with the necessary instructions ... to the army of this Tyrone, which was of twenty thousand Irishmen'. Wotton 'negotiated with him for an entire day', the diplomatic effort hardly showing in the resulting document, four articles scratched on a half sheet of paper. Still, it was enough, says Wotton, to be fatal to Essex.

Now Essex's nemesis is travelling in convoy across Europe. In London, King James sits in council around the clock. Ireland occupies his sole attention. Those earls on the run have the power to wreck the Spanish peace negotiated just three years earlier, a peace on which King James stakes his reputation as the Pacificus; a peace popularly spat on in London as craven. Suspicions grow daily. One source reports Tyrone's mission is 'to Rome to persuade the pope to undertake an Irish expedition' to stir 'sedition and intestine rebellion'; another, that the pope has sent 'certain Jesuits' across the Irish sea 'whose sole mission is supposed to be the setting of Ireland in a blaze'; still others, by contrast, that Spain has given the fugitive 'crew' short shrift while the pope, who welcomed Tyrone open-handed to Rome, has since reduced his 'board to twelve persons' and grown so tight-fisted that 'those few that are there already' can only 'with much difficulty get their .8. ducats monthly'. In the new year, Tyrone reportedly 'begins to find himself cheated in those hopes which led him to fly precipately [sic] from Ireland'; is looking to 'obtain pardon'; is 'selling his horses and pawning his plate'; is begging the French king to permit him residence in France.

For eighteen months, Wotton dogs Tyrone's progress. Surely the old earl feels his sixty-seven years in his bones, rattling across Europe. Wotton dispatches 'one to Milan who shall accompany Tyrone and his going over all Italy'. He promises that 'his majesty shall have accompt of every step that he treadeth'. Such an accompt carries a price tag. Wotton requests his extraordinary allowance be bumped up by this extraordinary charge. But it's worth it. He produces, via his secret instrument, alarming intelligence that the king of Spain is being solicited to Tyrone's 'pretences'. What he's broaching is 'wars ... for a kingdom', that kingdom being Ireland, which, 'being gotten, would force the king of England to yield his obedience to the See of Rome'. The council in London stays awake.

Then, across the summer of 1609, the grand pretences vanish like morning mist. In Ireland the rebels are defeated when Tyrone's nephew is slain. In Rome, the earl of Tirconnel dies of fever while Tyrone and his son look to be next. Followers no longer follow. They're destitute. Their property, like the property of all those who've taken part in the uprising, is confiscated, earmarked for building projects and repaying the king's debts. By this means Cecil finally succeeds in replenishing the Exchequer, and King James orders two new towns in Ulster. They'll be planted with English Protestants and called Coleraine and Derry.

Officially, Wotton scorns the Irish fugitives as 'zingari', gipsies, 'Aegiptian vagabonds'. His efforts in the Collegio, however, show him taking a far greater account of them. Without waiting for 'a word' from 'anyone from England' (Cecil, for instance), he offers 'an idea that came from my own heart', that if Tyrone came to Venice, the Signoria 'would have him retained', arrested. As with his league of nations, the ambassador is inventing diplomacy. But if he really believes that his king's 'honour could not be hurt with what bruit soever such a handful of traitorous vagabonds should scatter as they go', why is he so keen to see the Senato resolved that 'should Tyrone enter Venetian territories he'll be required to retire, and warned not to enter beforehand'? Could it be that the ambassador fears coming face to face with a ghost?

A most particular man

In April 1608 Wotton opens a letter from Robert Cecil. Nothing he's attended to domestically in post-Interdict Venice prepares him for its contents, confessional writing that cuts so close to the bone it feels like vivisection. The man Wotton calls 'my lord' writes to 'open my self' with 'more freedom than I would to others'. Confiding in Wotton, he's counting on both Wotton's 'discretion' and his 'observation of my disposition to be free from revenge'. (Cecil's 'disposition' 'free from revenge'? That's debatable.) His 'unpleasing subject' is 'the ingratitude of a creature of mine own', one Simon Willis, his personal secretary, 'discharged from my service' 'some two' (corrected to 'about a year') 'before the queen died': that is, 1602, to put this well after the Essex trial. The reason 'I put this man from me'? 'Partly for his pride whom provender had pricked' – he'd grown fat on Cecil's service, it appears – 'but principally because I was loath he should have come to some discovery of that correspondency which I had with the King our sovereign'. (This 'king', of course, in 1602 was neither 'our sovereign' nor Elizabeth's heir but James VI of Scotland.)

Willis must necessarily have discovered this secret 'correspondency', 'considering his daily and near attendance as my secretary, to whose eyes a pacquet or a paper might have been so visible as he might have raised some such inferences thereof as might have bred some jealousy' – that is, suspicion – 'in the queen's mind if she had known it'. Listing all those 'mights', Cecil is paltering, trying to cover his back by relying on Wotton to 'remain secure' in the knowledge that 'if her majesty had known all I did' she likewise 'should have known the innocency and constancy of my private faith'. 'Yet', he continues, and it's a mighty big 'yet', 'her age and … the jealousy of her soul might' – another 'might' – 'have moved her to think that ill meant which helped to preserve her'. Cecil makes several attempts at that last sentence. The letter survives in draft, and its edits, interlines and crossings-out show him struggling: 'jealousy of her soul might have [moved her] <~~thought that ill~~> [to think ~~ill of~~] that [ill meant] which helped …'.

We can imagine, as he reads, Wotton's blood draining from his face. 'Correspondency' with James before Elizabeth's death. That was exactly the coal of fire Cecil heaped on Essex's head, making him a traitor. How can Cecil now frame such secret communication as acting to 'preserve' the queen, except by casuistically claiming that to 'quiet the expectation of a successor' was all for her good? There's worse. Cecil reveals that he didn't act alone. 'In this correspondency I was associated' with 'those great men' who would know the reasons why Willis needed cashiering. They were all in on it, the clandestine communication. All in on it, sending Essex to the block.

It takes Wotton some time to read on. He's stuck on that word 'ingratitude'. Another word, 'treachery', might pound in his brain. For his part, Cecil could take timely instruction from Macbeth in a play that's just now hitting the London stage. Those who 'teach bloody instructions' discover that their instructions 'return to plague the inventor'. Cecil thought Willis long gone. But Willis is back. The disaffected servant is smearing Cecil's name, 'especially in foreign parts', even as he collects the pension – the hush money? – Cecil is paying him 'out of mine own purse £40 per annum during his life'. Such ingratitude! Cecil pretends only to 'despise' the calumnies Willis is spreading about him, dismissing him as a man 'bereaved' of both 'discretion and good manners', but he's clearly stung, and anxious, returning to those calumnies twice in a letter that goes on for some 1,700 words. The real trouble is that

Willis has travelled to Rome, 'revolted from his faith', and, 'practising in some kind', revealed the identities of 'divers with whom I held correspondency there'. Cecil adds 'for his Maiesties service', interlined, to leave no doubt for whom he's acting in this 'correspondency'. Several of Cecil's informants have been 'discovered and upon the sudden', 'an accident happening so rarely … as it can have but one cause and one author' (Willis), whose 'former experience with my courses in those matters of intelligence' and 'his particular acquaintance with some of the parties employed' point the finger (Willis again).

Willis (Cecil claims) is spreading rumours of Wotton, too, that the English ambassador entertains in his house 'a bravo' hired 'to do some assassination upon him'. These are 'ridiculous', 'idle favors' that 'no man … will think … worthy to be believed', but Cecil relays them anyway, putting the goad of gossip into Wotton's flank before returning to 'the matter that troubles me the most'. 'By discovering some persons employed', Willis has blocked 'the passage to all intelligence' in Italy. The upshot? 'His majesty's service is like to suffer, and also my reputation, as Secretary, which you know, consists in a great part in that business'. Wotton's assignment: salvage Cecil's reputation. Discover 'how far this canker hath spread' so that, 'in time', the 'service' can be again 'settle[d] and secure[d]'.

Of course Wotton will follow instructions. He who has instruments in Milan, Florence and the 'più intimi penetrali del Papa' will root out Willis's spoiling. Correspondency with intelligencers is part of his day's work. But, as for the other correspondency Cecil confesses, does that stagger Wotton's opinion of this man? (Shortly, Cecil will sign letters to Wotton 'your assured loving friend'.) Or is Wotton now so coolly politick that he'll forget how he once wrote passionately of Essex 'dragged to his death by unimaginable malice'? Will he take the hypocrisy that Cecil's letter reveals in his stride, even as he continues protecting His Majesty's subjects abroad?

For Wotton *does* continue. He searches in-coming ships for Englishmen enslaved in their crews. He springs a couple of English lads from arrest in Padua where they've been handled 'very villainously' by the police, their only fault, 'youth and ignorance of the world'. Happening by in his gondola he plucks Thomas Coryat to saftey when that gormless tourist, having ventured into the Jewish Ghetto where he buttonholes a rabbi and begins browbeating him on the subject of conversion, finds himself surrounded by an angry mob manhandling him towards the canal. The ambassador reports, perhaps amused that local lads, too, get up to laddish behaviour, the outrage of nine young Venetian *nobili* who've broken into a nunnery to 'convey' some 'votaries to their private chambers', later dancing them 'up and down in masquing attire at festival assemblies'. (The girls no doubt wanted conveying: too many third and fourth daughters of *nobili* are stuck in cloisters because their fathers can't raise dowries.)

But what about the Protestant revolution? If like the cormorant it's taken a deep dive, like the cormorant it reveals its whereabouts in bubbles breaking the lagoon's surface. Its oxygen is writing. Soon enough, it will come up for air.

15
So many sheets of paper

Armies of writers

2 March 1607. Wotton sends King James the Interdict's left-overs: 'all those treatises and discourses which have been here or elsewhere printed in defence or oppugnation of the present cause, which are now grown to a pretty bulk'. That's an understatement. If it were stacked up, says Leonardo Donà, the 'pretty bulk' that just the pope and his 'parasites' have produced would reach higher than his dogal chair. Pamphlets, pasquinades, prophecies, printed letters and replies, single-sheet broadsheets, learned treatises, scurrilous libels, translations, more pamphlets; in print, in manuscript; in Latin, Italian, Venetian, even English; for readers noble, middling, 'idiota' and foreign. Wotton bundles them all up for London. They've been appearing daily in Venice since the crisis began. Even 'the poets', says Wotton, 'have plentifully rained showers of their wit upon the season'.

In London, the king has been reading 'everything out of Italy, serious or satirical' for months, studying the Jesuit cardinal Roberto Bellarmino 'every day' (particularly, hot off the press, his *Risposta* denouncing Venetian anti-papalism) while churning out an 'interlinear reply' to Cardinal Baronio's aggressively pro-papalist *Paraenesis*. The king's appetite for picking over the dry bones of theological disputation is phenomenal. But he's also reading attacks on sovereignty that he takes as direct attacks on *his* sovereignty. He has seen in print Baronio's chilling instruction to the pope, telling him his duties are 'two-fold: to feed and to kill'.

The 'populace', too, have been following the controversy, and not through idle curiosity. It was only in May 1606 that Londoners saw the Jesuit Father Garnet of the gunpowder conspiracy dragged on a hurdle to St Paul's churchyard to a traitor's execution, so it's no wonder, when Leonardo Donà's pro-Republican

Protesto arrived in London that summer, printed in English, it was said to be 'in everybody's hands'. The threat of Jesuit terrorism is real. In September, Paolo Sarpi's 'defence of the Republic' made clear, if anyone needed reminding, how high the stakes were for those who opposed Rome. Wotton sent Cecil a 'copy from Venice' direct.

All this publication mattered because the 'war of the quill' was the stand-in for the war on the ground that was constantly threatened but always postponed, and it laid out as effectively as armies facing each other across battle lines drawn the ideas men were prepared to kill and die for. The Interdict was fought with words (though there was no guarantee it would end with words). Foot soldiers in this war? Writers, and the weapons they snatched out of scabbards were pens, though many did so anonymously or pseudonymously. Title pages name publishers – but not authors. Ascriptions take the form 'said to be …'. Of course, everybody knew who wrote those libellous pasquinades that regularly appeared on the city's walls. 'Pasquino', obviously. And no matter what alias Possevino used, Wotton knew him as clearly in print as if he stood facing him.

It was Paolo Sarpi who fired the first paper bullet in this war in early 1606. He aimed to hit by ricochet. His pamphlet wasn't attributed to him, purported (fictitiously) to issue from Paris, and seemed only to produce a new edition of two obscure *libretti* by a two-centuries-dead French conciliarist, Jean Gerson. Their relevance? Gerson's topic in the 1390s was the pope's (strictly limited) power to excommunicate – the same as Sarpi's in 1606. Obscure or not, publication was provocation. Over that summer, Bellarmino returned fire with his *Risposta* and Sarpi replied with an *Apologia* which, published in Venice in Italian (not Latin) and English, was clearly aimed at a readership far beyond Bellarmino's Latin-literate scholastics. Moreover, it blazoned both Sarpi's and the bookseller's names on the title page: the war would no longer be fought behind stalking horses.

By summer, everybody seemed to be signing up. Zorzi Giustinian was 'credibly informed' that Robert Cecil so admired the *Apologia* that he had taken up the pen to write 'a book about the differences', 'printed in England' (though as we'll now see, Cecil was only the proxy for the real author).

This book runs to a hundred pages, with an 'advertisement' on the title page that reads like a dispatch from a combat zone, billing it as a *Letter from Venice, setting foorth the variance between the Pope and that State: Declaring the causes, proceedings, and present issue thereof.* Inside, the book gives a blow-by-blow account of the first three months of the 'variance', up to the present, 'this June'. The author-cum-war correspondent isn't identified. But he's clearly Henry Wotton. We recognise him by his stylistic fingerprint, his habit of parenthetical remark, eight of them interrupting the fifty-six opening lines of the quarto text. He's like an actor constantly double-talking his audience with asides.

Further along, we realise this *Letter* is Wotton's pastiche, put together from extracts lifted from ten dispatches he sent to King James between the end of March and late June 1606. Words (particularly those calling out the pope's 'presumptuous' 'usurpation' of 'authority'), phrases, sentences, whole paragraphs, jokes (the one about the furious nuncio beating his thigh with his 'priest's cap') are copied, interlaced with a running narrative that makes readers eye-witnesses: 'About December last …'; 'The clergy thus startled …'; 'Hereupon Leonardo Donà …'; 'Whereupon …'; 'Thereupon …'. In this version of events, the pope is all 'raging passions'; the Republic is confident in 'the execution of Justice'. Wotton's *Letter* doesn't mince matters. It knows exactly who the local heroes are: Donà, Sarpi, the resolute Senato, the Rome-shy clergy who would 'rather be excommunicated twelve years than hang half an hour'. The villains too are obvious: not just the pope and his overweening cardinals (Baronio's terrible 'feed and kill' is quoted), but that 'swarm' of 'kites', the Jesuits. Wotton repeats himself from a May dispatch, crowing that the Jesuits have been 'thrown out' of Venice with 'only their quotidian habits and breviaries'.

In case anyone missed it, the *Letter* reprints Donà's *Protesto* (but Londoners have had their hands on that manifesto for weeks). More importantly, it contextualises Venetian grievances, puts wounded flesh on the bare bones of the Republic's formal complaints, and widens dissemination. As in all his Interdict dispatches, Wotton here twins Venice with England, making England's past – 'King H.8 … did eject [the] pope's … false and ill-gotten supremacy' – prologue to a Republican future where the pope's 'consistorial power' is 'contemptible'. Reciprocally, though, Venice is England's precedent. If, without direct experience of Jesuit treasons, the Republic can permanently discard these firebrands, aren't we English bound likewise to expel them, having seen proof of their designs in 'the vault treason' of 5 November? We hear the ambassador as political agitator and now can see this *Letter* as a brilliant exercise in smuggling, putting extracts of dispatches meant for the king into the public domain; state papers leaked to common view, diplomacy wooing public opinion. (Now there's an innovation.)

Across these weeks on Cannaregio the industry of paper, ink and pen is intense. Wotton is not just making weekly appearances in the Collegio and shooting volleys of dispatches to London. After hours, he's burning candles down to wax puddles putting together this *Letter*. (By the way, is it he or someone else in the embassy who's translating Sarpi?) Never out of his mind are Gentili's words from two decades back, that 'the only things consigned' to an ambassador 'are words and opportunities'. Now, he's mobilising both to wage war on Rome.

His *Letter* concludes by analogy: if God's eternal clock worked slowly but surely to bring truth to England, why shouldn't time be working to the same end in Venice, 'the eyes and hearts of the Venetians ... by the touch of God's finger ... opened wider' to become 'God's harbingers ... throughout that goodly country'? Why not indeed? Via such analogies, Wotton's *Letter* starts by 'Setting forth the variance' between the pope and Venice but ends justifying England. It outlines provisions for war in Italy but rouses Londoners to the defence of their freedoms. Strikingly, it bristles with emotion: the ambassador has to curb 'passions that make me to forget my ... orderly proceeding in this relation'. He has never written anything finer.

More remarkably, he reaches a point he rarely comes to in diplomatic dispatches, giving himself 'leave to tell that I think'. That's a revelation. Diplomatic opinion is normally framed obliquely: 'some think', 'the wiser discourse', 'rumour has it'. Writing what 'I think', Wotton is owning ideas that directly challenge papal supremacy – and challenge 'us' in England to be 'the exemplary instance' of resistance. Like the 'recruitment' dispatch he sent his monarch a month back, Wotton's *Letter* reaches far beyond the never-named 'Sir' it's putatively addressed to. It aims to recruit an entire reading public to the Venetian cause, fulminating the Protestant revolution with an apostrophe that calls Protestant Christendom to the barricades: 'O that the honourably minded Venetians would ... hold themselves to their freedom and shake off [the pope's] shackles!'

It's this *Letter*, leaving Venice in manuscript sometime in late June, 'printed in England' in August, that Giustinian thinks is Cecil's work. He's half right. Cecil has certainly authorised its publication and ensured that no name, certainly no English ambassador's name, appears on its title page. No one at Court is fooled. (Nor in Rome: Wotton is as easily discovered to Possevino as the Jesuit is to the ambassador.) But that's hardly the point. What matters is that, like everyone else adopting the conceit of self-concealment in this 'war of the quill', Wotton is able to extend the reach of his arguments through publication, to widen participation, to address an audience of 'us English'.

Does anonymity signal that writing is dangerous? It should. In both Rome and Venice the Interdict's left-overs are a problem. Books and writers are targets. And now Wotton, who considers himself and his *famiglia* among those inferior causes keeping Protestant hopes in Venice alive, has made himself one. The left-overs bring to an international readership a canon of anti-papal texts that challenge the fundamentals of Catholicism. But equally, they publish plenty that makes nonsense of the Republic's self-legitimating myth of civic unity during the crisis. The pope wants books he calls heretical banned and destroyed. That's futile, as the history of communication in Venice shows. Print evades control. It escapes local licensing the minute it changes hands or crosses a border. It keeps the bubbling pot of controversy stirred. It lasts, surviving censorship, confiscation, book-burning. It refuses to give 'accommodation' the final word. States (like Venice) that begin by thinking the *popolani* have no function in political discussion rapidly realise the public is a 'many-headed multitude' that will wag its tongue in yellow print ignorantly and seditiously if it isn't given intelligent publication to inform it. Both sides of the controversy rightly reckon the power of learned *discorsi* – and rightly fear the tickle of scurrilous ridicule.

Now among the published left-overs, Wotton must know he's put himself in the firing line. A word warrior. What he can't know is that it won't be his own book but a future left-over, a book just now forming in the mind of its author, that, in July 1609, will very nearly wreck his diplomatic career. And when it blows up, he'll be the one holding it.

Arresting writing

Rome's strategy in the post-Interdict years (as Wotton reports it) is to target the movement of books into and out of Italy. In June 1607 the pope lets 'fall some few words touching the fitness of recalling such books as had been printed here'. 'Recall' is a euphemism. Three months earlier, approaching the border crossing at Milan, 'the courier of Spain was assaulted ... and all his letters and other things was robbed'. In September, when, having delayed sending for 'danger of the portage', Wotton finally posts 'books ... written ... of the late variance on either side', his courier is roughed-up at Milan. He's safe, but his portmanteau with its cargo for King James is seized by the Inquisitor. In Rome, books printed by the Venetian Roberto Meietti are publicly burnt, and in Venice 'a practice of powder' is 'laid' to torch his shop, 'loose papers to the quantity of twenty pounds with pieces of wax candles set burning ... to give it fire'. Only, the pope's hitmen get the wrong address. They cremate a rival print shop instead.

Undeterred, Rome keeps up the pressure. And the violence. Two coffers of books shipped from England, some English, some Latin ('part of my collection', says Wotton) pass the regular quarantine on shipments coming into Venice but are arrested by the Inquisition. The doge orders their release – then staves off the papal nuncio who comes fuming. 'Two coffers' of books belonging 'to the Ambassador's sect'? 'What does he want to do with them' unless 'to scatter' them 'to the hands of many to the detriment of our religion'? The doge tells the nuncio to stop 'rummaging' in the ambassador's 'secret things'. They're covered by diplomatic immunity. Books? Well, the ambassador *is* 'a man of letters'. (And also a student of optics. Wotton knows a blind eye when he sees one.)

Clearly, he *is* importing books 'to scatter', and with English government sanction, books 'touching the progress of reformation', Bibles in English and Bishop Jewel's *Apology of the Church of England*, which Wotton wishes 'were reprinted in the little form' – octavo – 'and some two hundred of them sent me', for they're both 'eloquently penned and in respect of the smallness, of easy dispersion'. Note: easy dispersion. Wotton knows that Donà has received some such book from someone he summoned 'of purpose to his private lodgings'. No wonder, then, that Wotton imagines Donà ripe for conversion (and upon his 'secret knowledge', 'many of the rest').

When a 'voice ... from Rome' informs Venice that the pope now 'intendeth to proceed against the writers of this state' as heretics, Wotton reports with alarm this sinister ramping up of Inquisition. Rome, we remember, burns heretics. One of the accused is Henry Wotton. It would doubtless give the pope satisfaction to bring down the English ambassador, a man he calls 'mal huomo', a 'viper', that Venice is 'nursing ... in their breast'. Maybe it's the pope, or one of his Jesuit black hoods, Possevino even, who's behind the nuncio's accusation that Wotton runs a 'printing press in his house' (disguised as a billiard table?). Any of them could have arranged the hoax delivery to the embassy's door of a bundle of Baronio's writing, a dirty trick to smear the ambassador by making him look like the mouthpiece for the cardinal's anti-Venetian 'thunder'. Wotton is small fry, though, compared with the whale Paolo V is hunting.

A year earlier the pope had cited Paolo Sarpi to the Court of Inquisition in Rome. The Servite, just then ink-bombing the Holy See as he masterminded the theological defence of Venice, refused to appear. Post-Interdict, the pope tries dangling bait. He speaks 'not only charitably of the authors' of those 'heretical' books that he's just summoned for burning 'but also (which was little expected) very worthily and in particular of Maestro Paolo'. So Wotton reports, noticeably bemused by the pope's blatancy. The bait isn't swallowed. Honied words won't 'serve the turn' to bring Fra Paolo to Rome along a booby-trapped road. He's under state protection in Venice, receiving a generous pension.

Wotton wants London to know this man. Packed among the books in that portmanteau he sent London three months back was a painting he'd commissioned, Sarpi's 'true picture in portable form'. Wotton adds a pen portrait: 'by birth a Venetian, and well skilled in the humours of his own country'; for learning, 'the most deep and general scholar of the world'; 'a fitter instrument to overthrow the falsehood by degrees then on a sudden, which accordeth with a frequent saying of his own: that in these operations *non bisogna far salti*' (no need to leap). When the king looks on Sarpi's portrait he will 'behold a sound protestant', though 'yet' 'in the habit of a friar'.

Wotton has this from his chaplain, William Bedell, who has 'sounded' Sarpi 'in the principal points of our religion' during regular meetings: he and the Servite spend 'upon agreement together every week almost one half a day', which gives Bedell opportunity to act as Wotton's cover. 'By him', Wotton tells Cecil, he can 'deal' with Sarpi 'for less observation in diverse things of importance', a ruse that means in the Collegio Wotton can indignantly daff aside the rumour someone 'had the gall to put into print' that Sarpi frequents the English embassy; that he and the ambassador engage in 'long conversations'. In almost the same breath, Wotton can assure London that 'by the public writings and more by the private discourses of Maestro Paolo' – private discourses channelled to Wotton through Bedell – 'the light of God's truth increaseth here'.

One thing Wotton extracts from these discourses must be communicated to King James urgently: Sarpi's frank assessment 'that the pope's ends' extend far beyond the Republic. Rome aims to 'contest secular sovereignty', 'resist all natural obedience' 'and finally to dissolve the jurisdiction of princes and states'. Sarpi touches the king's rawest nerve: only this, the threatened usurpation of temporal sovereignty, will push the timorous English king to back Venice with arms. And Wotton knows it.

His Majesty never sees this portrait of Sarpi. It's confiscated in Milan with the rest of the September consignment. Just a month later, the pope gives a brutal demonstration of how far he'll go to hunt down men he calls heretics. He sends assassins to Venice. They attack Fra Sarpi as he is crossing the bridge to his monastery not far from the English embassy, thrusting a stiletto through his right cheek and jaw, leaving the weapon in the wound and him for dead. But Sarpi doesn't die. 'The most excellent ... surgeon of the world' is 'fetched from Padua' while news of the 'enormous accident' races from mouth to mouth across Venice, 'from the Senator to the gondolier'. 'Pursuit of the offenders' springs into action 'with no less provision than if the Prince himself had been assailed', everyone suspecting Rome of hiring the blades, even the papal nuncio

16　Fra Paolo Sarpi. Commissioned by Wotton for King James to show him the face of the Servite friar who masterminded the theological defence of Venice throughout the Interdict Crisis, this portrait also documents the assassination attempt on Sarpi, showing the wound on his cheek. The inscription was Wotton's addition. Date unknown.

(who, Wotton reports with grim satisfaction, is 'fallen ill at the news' and 'like to die'). Seeing Sarpi's recovery as 'a pattern of God's miraculous providence', the English ambassador is 'transported'. The pope has revealed his murderous hand – and God has thwarted him.

Shown the stiletto pulled from his wound, Sarpi quips, 'Agnosco stylum Romanae Curiae' (I recognise the style of the Roman Curia). The pun is a triple entendre. 'Style' means 'method'; but a 'stylus' is also a pen and the Latin root of 'stiletto'. We get the joke. Rome will play the war of the quill *dirty*; will send assassins with daggers to cut down the pen that writes Venetian liberty.

The King's Book

King James receives news of Sarpi on the second anniversary of the gunpowder plot. 'Cruel conspiracies', 'providential' escapes: the parallels between November 1605 and October 1607 are obvious. Wotton balefully marks them while Giustinian in London predicts that the 'iniquitous' Sarpi affair will shortly be mass-marketed, turned to the 'pulpit' and 'theatre' where, 'as is the custom in this country', preachers and players will sensationalise it in sermons and on stage – disseminating it to vast audiences of London illiterates who don't read newsletters but thrill to news played out live before their eyes.

King James rewinds history. In the immediate after-shock of 5 November, he reached for his pen. By December, he and his Privy Council had drafted a new 'Oath of Allegiance', passed into law by Parliament in June 1606. Having granted his subjects liberty to serve foreign princes abroad as part of the Spanish peace concluded two years earlier, he now needs to make sure their service isn't with princes who design to depose and murder him: the powder plotters were all discovered Catholics conspiring with Jesuit 'seminators' directed by Rome.

Originally the 'Oath' was to be administered only to subjects serving abroad, a 'means', Cecil tells Wotton, to show that 'those that go to serve Catholick princes' are 'of better affection than they have been hitherto or else they must stay behind'. Later, with dark consequences for English Catholics, it's expanded to take in all Englishmen. It opens uncontroversially, with an affirmation 'before God and the world that our Sovereign Lord King James is lawful and rightful King of this realm'. The next sentence, though, begins targeting Catholic 'usurpations'. The deponent must swear that 'The Pope' has no 'power or authority to depose the King'; to 'authorise any foreign prince to invade or annoy him'; or 'to discharge any of his Subjects of their allegiance and obedience to his Majesty'. The 'damnable doctrine' that allows 'princes which be excommunicated by the Pope' to be 'deposed or murdered by their subjects' must be abjured as 'impious and heretical'. The deponent must swear, finally, that 'the Pope has no power to absolve me from this oath'. It's a concise – and bullish – declaration of the king's 'differences' with Rome. It's also an oath English Catholics can't swear.

And it's on its way to Venice the moment Parliament passes it into law, Giustinian mistakenly calling it a 'new oath of supremacy', an error Rome echoes. When Wotton presents to the Collegio the copy he's received from Cecil (theatrically drawing 'from under his cloak a book' that he 'lays on the bench where he's sitting'), he says it's what 'all subjects of His Majesty who take service with foreign Princes will be expected to subscribe'. But he immediately connects 'this resolution' to 'questions now pending between your Serenity and the pope'. We're into July 1606, and the crisis that's been simmering throughout this summer is on the point of exploding: the pope arming his frontiers; Spain mobilising; de-frocked abbots secretly scuttling out of Venice with as much loot as they can stash under borrowed robes. The king's 'Oath' is relevant to the Republic's self-defence, 'aimed at no other end than establishing and conserving temporal dominion'. And temporal dominion is the king's pedal drone underscoring the pope's shrill chorus of excommunication.

The 'Oath' arrives in Rome. Now Rome must wage the 'war of the quill' on two fronts. The arch-priest George Blackwell, leader of the clandestine Catholic Mission in England, tells English Catholics they may swear, since the 'Oath' refers only to civil matters. Bellarmino condemns Blackwell for misleading English Catholics, and the pope issues a breve instructing those Catholics that the Oath 'cannot be taken, for it contains many things evidently contrary to faith and salvation'. *Which* 'things' aren't specified, *ex cathedra* wooliness that's mocked in *An Apology for the oath of allegiance*, published as a counter-blast to Bellarmino. 'Set forth without a name', its author is evidently King James. He's been 'pressing ahead' 'under a feigned name' with a book for months, 'living in almost absolute retirement' at Royston, not hunting but writing, and attacking the exercise of pen and paper with the sort of relish and intellectual certainty that, in Scotland a decade back, energised his treatise on *The True Law of Free Monarchies*. James will have among his piles of sources Wotton's *Letter from Venice*, lately arrived, with its constant harping on papal presumptions and usurpations and with its history from Henry I to Henry VIII of English resistance to the pope's 'false and ill-gotten supremacy'. The *Letter* is a provocation no less than the dispatch Wotton as Ottavio Baldi sent his king early in the crisis, stating the Republic's grievances, that 'Paulus .V.[us] questioneth theire whole jurisdiction: intruding at once both upon theire Civil and Criminal decrees and finaly tending to the dissolution of theire soveraignitie'. The *Apology* will borrow some of this history and recite its central themes.

In late February 1608 the *Apology*'s still-anonymous author sends the French and Venetian ambassadors in London copies of the book via Cecil with individual messages. To Giustinian the 'ignoto' writes that it is a 'defence of the freedom and sovereignty of princes in matters temporal', 'precisely the point which the Republic had sustained with so much glory and reputation' throughout the Interdict Crisis. He adds that he doesn't 'wish his name to appear for reasons which he would subsequently explain'.

Then, the royal swot having handed in his homework, he eagerly awaits feedback. The French say little, quibbling over 'a passage about the French king's fear of the pope'. The Venetians make it a 'subject of much discourse', sharing copies with their resident ambassadors 'and other instruments of state'. Paolo Sarpi will no doubt add the *Apology* to his growing library of English writing. A year back Wotton knew Sarpi was eager to get his hands on the 'Oath' so he might 'inform the Senato palpably and authentically' on the pope's challenge to secular sovereignty, for 'he holdeth this position' (which happened also to be Wotton's position), that sovereignty 'is the point ... under which other parts of God's truth must be replanted' in the Republic. (Is the English ambassador quoting – or dilating?) By now, a new portrait of Sarpi is on its way to London, a trifle late because the freezing weather in January 1608 kept the paint from drying. This one carries 'the late addition of his scars' and a provocative caption Wotton has devised to fly above Sarpi's right shoulder, 'Concilii Tridentini Eviscerator' (he who ripped the guts out of the Catholic counter-Reformation.)

When it comes nearly a year later, Rome's reply to the *Apology* takes the form of 'a certain scandalous pamphlet ... by one Tortus', actually Bellarmino. It does a hatchet job on King James, and baits him. So England tools up for a final campaign. In London in January 1609 the new Venetian ambassador, Marc' Antonio Correr, hears that a 'reply' to 'Bellarmino's work' is 'now quite ready'. (He jumps the gun. The 'King's Book', as it will be known, won't be published until June.) In cipher, Correr continues: 'in the preface the king warns all princes to note the great authority of the Pontiff. ... The French ambassador has twice urged the king not to reply in person ... the Council is of the opinion that it would be more dignified to reply by another hand.' Wotton in Venice volunteers to be that 'hand'; the king declines his offer.

Firmly seated on his high horse, James is careless of pot-shots at dignity. His new book bundles up, tit-for-tat, a dossier of his argument with the pope, most of it old hat. What's new is the 'preface' written as a 'Premonition', tagged 'Be wise now therefore, O ye kings: be instructed, ye judges of the earth' from Psalm 2. It addresses his 'brethren', 'right excellent Free Princes', and it's dynamite, a 'warning' that 'concerneth the authority and privilege of kings in general and all supereminent temporal powers'. Elsewhere, he has accused the pope not only of intruding 'himself into the sole power and authority for matters belonging to religion' but of seeking 'cunningly to wind himself, by little and little, into the civil government and so lift himself up, above all the monarchs of the earth'. Now King James urges his 'brethren', 'Awake' 'while it is time, and suffer not, by your longer sleep, the strings of your authority to be cut'.

Running on for a hundred and thirty-five pages (over the course of which the royal author hits his stride and the modern reader sinks in a slough of pedantry), this 'Premonition' is framed as self-justification: there would be no 'Oath' without the gunpowder treason; no gunpowder treason without the pope's asserting his 'power over Kings, to throne or dethrone them at his pleasure' by inciting subjects to rebel and murder them. But 'the kings of England', even 'when the world was fullest of darkened blindness and ignorance' – before, we gather, the Reformation – have 'withstood this temporal usurpation and encroachment of ambitious popes'. Scottish King James makes himself one of those English kings. He commands in this 'Premonition' the same 'force of reasoning' and 'riches of citation' that so impressed Ambassador Giustinian at the beginning of the Interdict Crisis. Only now, he's not only dogged. He's 'biting': 'free in speech', making 'frequent jokes'. So Correr reports to Venice in April, having read an advance copy.

Logic or laughter? Which is more devastating? Countering the accusation of Tortus that he's a 'heretic', King James renders a 'free confession of my faith' – which, as it disgorges more and more words, bloats into a lampoon of Catholic doctrine. Ritual practices are derided: veneration of the cross ('a piece of stick'); prayers to saints ('courtiers of God'); adoration of images ('idolatry'); 'jubilees, pardons, relics' ('juggling wares and merchandise', 'delusions'). 'Purgatory' is 'trash', but sarcastically seeming to keep his eternal options open 'in case I come there', the king hopes it has 'a brook running through it, that ... I may have my hawking upon it'. If this is 'wit' from a king known for his wit, 'wit' crosses a line into blasphemy when it belittles the Virgin Mary, mocking Marian intercession: James can't 'think that she hath no other thing to do in heaven than to hear every idle man's suit and busy her self in their errands'.

King James asserts repeatedly that he makes 'no question of faith or religion'; that his subject is 'temporal sovereignty', 'civil law', 'the liberties of free princes'. But if the secular is his sole business, why does he end his 'Premonition' urging 'the planting and spreading of the true worship of God' according to the 'truth which I profess'? Can the 'ambitious pope' be put down otherwise than through the overthrow of Catholicism? Surely, that's a declaration of war.

Confident that he's struck the *coup de grace* in the 'war of the quill', the king throws down the pen and goes hunting – chasing stags at such a gallop that horses die under him. Meanwhile the King's Book is being translated into Latin and French and presentation copies 'bound in velvet with arms and cornerpieces of solid gold' prepared for England's resident ambassadors to place in royal hands abroad in June. Someone at Court (is it Cecil?) 'is very ill-affected to this child-birth of his majesty, fearing that it may not prove acceptable to the world'. Prophetic words.

More zeal than wisdom

In Venice in the new year 1609 the English ambassador is much occupied with matters domestic and international (squiring John Harington; Tyrone's halting progress across Europe; Ward's insolence in the Mediterranean). He spends half of January and all of February in bed, knocked off his feet by 'a continual ague of forty days with the accesses of a double tertian in the night' that leaves him 'weak' in the 'head' and out of pocket, 'exhausted with the rewarding of my physicians'. He makes no appearances in the Collegio until 30 March. He manages patchy dispatches dictated to his secretary and, for the first time, writes of going home: London has evidently proposed his 'revocation' for the end of September, 'this next Michaelmas'.

By March, he's back on form. Easter is late this year, so the public preaching of the annual Lenten sermons doesn't begin until 4 March, Ash Wednesday. The pope's spy reports that, at San Lorenzo, Fulgenzio Micanzio's 'schismatical & calvinistical' preaching draws crowds. Wotton attends, sees 'never less than between 5. and 600' including 'principal senators and gentlemen' and can 'scarcely believe his own eyes and ears': Fulgenzio preaches justification of faith without works and prayer in the vernacular. He discounts legends, the veneration of saints, auricular confession, pilgrimage. No wonder Wotton hears militancy deserving 'immortal praise' in these sermons. Fulgenzio 'is the first which in a quiet time' – post-Interdict – 'hath entered the list against the pope'. The 'war of the quill' has moved to the pulpit. So between Fulgenzio's sermons, Sarpi's weekly 'discourses' with Wotton's chaplain and the importation of contraband books in crates protected from search by diplomatic immunity, the English ambassador keeps alive through God's so-called inferior causes his hopes 'touching the progress of reformation' in Venice.

Of the King's Book Wotton evidently has no notice until his presentation copy arrives that summer, the Senato, meanwhile, having stewed over its troubling contents since Correr reported them in April. Since March, Wotton has again been absent from the Collegio, 'wantonly much abroad, flattering' – that is, indulging – 'myself since my sickness': his physicians have advised him 'to drink of a mineral water … at the baths of Abano against a calcular disposition whereof I am somewhat afraid'. The English ambassador suffers in the heat.

Now, in July, Wotton asks audience to present the King's Book. He knows 'Spain have refused it' and France 'openly approved it'. (He's wrong. Handed the book, Henri IV 'threw it down on a small table', quipping, 'Writing books is no business for a king'.) He's blissfully confident that 'here' in Venice 'our good Master's excellent work' 'will be kissed'. 'At present', however, 'our famous Duke is a little confined within his chamber by a humour fallen down into one of his legs'. He decides to wait for Donà's return. Meanwhile, the Senato goes into a huddle. What to do with this unsolicited royal gift? The pope has condemned it and ordered Venice to suppress it. But the Senato has no intention of taking a bullet for Rome. Venetian-style, it will do what's 'conveniente'. It hatches a plot. The doge will be instructed to accept the book on behalf of the Senato as 'another proof of his Majesty's goodwill towards the Republic', return 'due thanks for the honour and courtesy', then 'at once hand it to the Grand Chancellor who immediately and without allowing anyone to see it, shall place it under lock and key in the Secret Chancery', very much a dead letter, 'until a further decision be taken about it'.

Wotton enters the Collegio on 25 July thinking auspicious thoughts. It's St James's Day, the anniversary of his king's coronation, and he has solemn business to perform. He takes his seat beside Donà, and without further 'complimenti' pulls from under his cloak a book. Bound in crimson and held against his chest while he speaks, it must, to the Catholic Collegio, bizarrely recall images of the Sacred Heart. His Majesty's gift, intones the ambassador, will 'tie more tightly' 'friendship ... and good understanding' between 'Great Britain and this happy Signory'. 'This work' (he's been commanded to say) no way aims 'to catechise Princes or to sow in their states a new religion'. Rather it warns 'Princes that whilst the Pope touches upon their crowns, sovereignty, and temporal jurisdiction, they should not suffer their power to be offended'.

Wotton gives a brief history of the book, starting with the gunpowder conspiracy, the Oath of Allegiance and the 'many sheets of paper' that weaponised the 'variance'. He leaves out the king's debunking of Catholic worship and comes close to joking only when he analogises the pope's 'usurpations' to 'leaving his proper bed': modern Italian equivalent, pissing outside his chamber pot. Through all of this, the Savii keep straight faces. They know what's coming. Donà accepts the gift as a pledge, not 'to imprint the seeds of a new religion but to preserve temporal jurisdiction'. The English ambassador expresses 'great pleasure that his office had been received by His Serenity in that sense', and rises to leave, only pausing to add that the 'rumour' that 'the King was about to call him home' is false. The recall expected for Michaelmas is evidently cancelled. The doge is happy to hear it: Ambassador Wotton is 'much loved and esteemed by the Republic'. Then: 'as soon as he had left', His Serenity executes 'what the Senato had deliberated'. The book is removed to the 'secreto' and put under lock and key.

Mission accomplished, elated, Wotton retires to Cannaregio to write Cecil a minute-by-minute report of his performance, promising to 'entertain him with ... the event'. When it comes at the end of August, however, the event first bemuses then enrages him. He learns that the King's Book has been banned, order 'given to all the booksellers of this town ... to consign immediately to the General Inquisitor all copies that have or shall come to their hands'. He doesn't believe it. So, 'for trial', he sends one of his *famiglia* to Ciotti's bookshop 'underhand, as out of his own curiosity to deal ... for a copy or two of the said books'. This Ciotti is 'of all our stationers the most Jesuitical', the one most likely to uphold the ban. But he's Venetian first, even more disposed to turning a ducat. He draws Wotton's man 'into a corner of his shop' and tells him 'they had been newly in a sort forbidden, but notwithstanding, (said he) if you return within a few days I hope to furnish you, for we expect some from Basil where we hear it hath been reprinted'.

Wotton shrugs off the ban: prohibition will only 'increase the desire and price of the thing prohibited'. Then, informed 'by secret intelligence' that the papal nuncio is at the bottom of this skulduggery, using Donà's absence – he's ill again – to push through the ban, he's furious. To refuse the book would be one thing. But to accept it *then* exclude it: that's insufferable. He demands audience in the Collegio; demands the ban's repeal. Twelve days pass. He returns to the Collegio, Donà still absent. He oozes irony. That nothing has been done to repair the 'real offense' 'done to the honour of his Majesty' must be his fault, not presenting his 'office ... clearly'. He'll try again. Starting with self-abnegation (the usual refrain), 'not a man of State ... plucked from school', he then demands punishment for 'the temerity and presumption' of the Inquisitor. He talks of friendships cooling, even terminating. He's promised a result.

The following day he's back. He hears the Senato's deliberation. The ban stands. He repeats his arguments – and won't accept the Senato's. Several of the Savii weigh in, in no mood to humour the English ambassador, not least because two weeks back, high in choler, he fumed over a negotiation still not finalised, 'What should I tell my king?' 'Tell him', they'd replied, acid, 'what you like'. Now, a war of words erupts. Tempers flare. We've seen Ambassador Wotton inventing diplomacy before. Now he does so again – sensationally.

He resigns his office. If he cannot, as servant and minister, defend His Majesty's reputation, he 'should not be known … as that qualified person which I have been until this present hour'. A long-winded way of saying 'I quit'. The Savii doggedly latch onto him with explanations and excuses, but even now he's shedding his robes: 'it saddens me not to have been able to do enough'; 'I shall go out to the country'; 'if anything should be ordered of me from Your Excellencies, I shall not fail, as a private person, to serve them'. He bows and exits. A private person.

The Venetian state doesn't do 'panic'. But what comes next looks very much like it. A late-night session of the Senato is convened. It votes to send an extraordinary ambassador to London to talk their way out of this diplomatic debacle: England is, after all, their staunchest European ally. Post-Interdict Venice can't afford to be cut loose. A 'staffetta' (a 'stirrup', as Venice calls its couriers) is ordered, post-post-haste to carry advance notice of the extraordinary ambassador. The journey normally takes twenty-one days. Pietro Carrara – his name should be remembered even if we do not know the names of the horses – gets there in nine. This 'stirrup' costs the state a staggering two hundred and fifty ducats.

The Venetian ambassador in London grabs Carrara's dispatch and spurs to Wanstead in pouring rain to find the king half-dressed after a day's hunting. He blurts out his message, the readiness of the Signory to receive the royal book; the intervention of the Inquisition; the 'dexterous and cautious way in which the booksellers had been told not to sell it'. (He doesn't say so, but all the instructions were oral, leaving no paper trail of what was actually said.) Then he gets onto Ambassador Wotton: 'the extent of his extraordinary resentment', his 'protestations that the friendship with this Crown was injured', his 'resolve to lay down his quality of Ambassador without considering' what the Signory 'can do or ought to do, rather than what his superabundant zeal of office blindly led him to wish [it] to do'. Wotton's 'outburst', he thinks, doesn't represent English policy but was 'due to the Ambassador alone, who by his zeal … allowed himself to be swept into such disagreeable representations'. A secretary standing by takes notes and asks the Signory 'not to feel resentment against the Ambassador for verily they knew not where to lay hands on a person more skilful or more attached' to serving Venice.

The king must be itching to get out of his muddy breeches but allows Correr to run his story into the ground. Later, though, he sends Cecil, 'My littil beagle', a note. It deserves quoting in the original: it allows us to hear the king's style, Scottish voice and distinctly royal condescension:

My littil beagle I haue bene this nighte surprysed by the venetian ambassadoure quho for all my hunting hathe not spaired to hunte me out heir, to be shorte his cheife earande was to tell me of a greate frayne [fray] in venice betwixte my ambassadoure thaire, & that staite anent [about] a prohibition that the inquisiton of venice hathe sett foorthe against the publishing of my booke thaire, he hathe complained that my ambassadoure takis this so hoatlie as passeth, in disorder he hathe bestowid an houris vehement oration upon me for this purpose, my answre was, that I coulde neuer dreame, that ather the State of venice, wolde euer giue me any iuste cause of offence, or yett that euer my ambassadoure thaire wolde doe thaime any euill office, but as to giue him any particulaire ansoure I tolde him I muste first heare from my owin ambassadoure, for he new well anewgh that euerie prince or state muste haue a greate truste in thaire owin ministers, I only wryte this unto you now, that incace this pantalone [pantaloon] come unto you ye may giue him the lyke deferring ansoure, albeit if I shoulde tell you my conscience, if all this mannis tale be trewe, my ambassadoure hathe usid this maitter with a littel more feruent zeale, then temperate wisdome ... & so fair well

James R.

'A littel more feruent zeale, then temperate wisdome': that about sums things up.

For his part, Wotton can't have made it to the bottom of the Scala d'Oro before realising that in his latest diplomatic improvisation he has over-reached himself. Perhaps too confident of his post-Interdict reputation. Too secure in a special relationship that professes to grant him 'more than what is ordinary'. Or perhaps, experiencing the kind of blindingly headstrong 'Essex moment' that doomed the earl, he literally lost his mind. He's been rash before. He's recovered before. Can he fix this indiscretion?

Three days later he uses the excuse of rumours on the Piazza to deem his master's (and, by proxy, his own) honour restored: he's heard that an extraordinary ambassador is to be sent to King James. So, 'notwithstanding the manner of my last departure' (there's a phrase that will raise eyebrows) he demands audience in the Collegio, happily, on 'the first day of the prince's return to the dogal seat'. Donà greets him 'kindly', but he's also severe. Ambassadors have no authority to act without instructions. They are 'mezzani': go-betweens, pimps, brokers connecting princes to other parties, exactly what Gentili told him two decades ago. Resigning, Wotton was insubordinate, acting wide of his brief. He 'could have taken another road'. But Donà offers the delinquent a sop: none of this would have happened if the doge had been there, for he 'would not have accepted the resignation'. Once again, Leonardo Donà extends a hand to salvage the English ambassador's diplomatic career.

Wotton writes the king, via Cecil, a robust account of this audience, stretched across four thousand words. In it, his tail feathers are up. But the one hundred and fifty words he encloses only to Cecil present a very different man. Crushed. He's always needed Cecil's 'noble patronage of my imperfections', and 'never more than at the present'. He begs Cecil's 'favourable representation unto his Majesty' of 'my part'. What next? 'I yet know not'. But 'I have already in mine own person learnt hereby the definition of a Republic: it is a kind of government where one may lose all the goodwill in a morning which he hath hardly' – that is, by hard work – 'gotten in five years'.

Wotton's depression will lift. He'll survive. For Donà really does cherish the English ambassador. Then, too, Wotton the political scientist will shortly have cause to consider that James's 'brethren' should have taken his 'Premonition' much more seriously. Nine months hence, in May 1610, Henri IV, the Protestant-turned-Catholic king of France, will be assassinated by a fanatical Catholic zealot. By then, Wotton the natural philosopher will already know of discoveries afoot that will blow the 'truth' debates fought over in the theologians' 'war of the quill' sky high. He sends London news in March 1610 of a book – yet *another* book – 'come abroad this very day' from 'the Mathematical Professor at Padua' – Galileo Galilei – 'who by the help of an optical glass instrument … hath discovered four new planets rolling about the sphere of Jupiter, besides many other unknown fixed stars; likewise, the true cause of the Via Lactea so long searched, and lastly that the Moon is not spherical but indued with many prominencies, and (which is of all the strangest) illuminated with the solar light by reflexion from the body of the earth'.

This is revolutionary stuff. Wotton realises that Galileo with his 'cannocchiale' (the English call it a telescope) has proven what Copernicus and Giordano Bruno only theorised: the heliocentric universe and, in consequence, that man is not the centre of God's creation. Galileo has 'overthrown all former astronomy' and 'next, all astrology', for 'these new planets' necessarily challenge universal truth. 'And why may there not yet be more?' With that rhetorical question Wotton sees the bare outlines of things to come. Galileo's book, his science, will make redundant all the left-over books that argued theology to such mind-numbing particulars across the Interdict. Even now, as Wotton's friend John Donne will write, the 'new philosophy calls all in doubt', starting with that mind-blowing existential doubt about mankind's place in creation. The English ambassador, though, is troubled by doubts much closer to home. For Arrigo VVottoni has begun to doubt himself.

16

Return into our sweet England

'Touching my revocation'

October 1609. The English ambassador is homesick. He's been in post now full five years while, in England, three Venetian ambassadors have come and gone. He shuffles towards a recall at the beginning of the year, obliquely proposing that 'some other suffitienter instrument' might work upon his 'small beginnings' while he 'resolve[s] ... again into those plain and simple elements' – air and water – 'whereof I am compounded'. He sounds like Prince Hamlet at his most self-loathing, wishing that his 'too too solid flesh' would 'resolve itself into a dew' and simply vanish, but where before Wotton's self-disparagement seemed merely rhetorical, now he sounds as though he means it.

He wants to go home, and, as in his student days, he asks his brother Edward's help. In March he's wonderfully 'surprised' by a letter from Edward 'wherein he hath signified unto me the late conference' which Robert Cecil 'was pleased to have with him touching my revocation this next Michaelmas', news so thrilling that, though desperately ill, he shunts himself up on his pillows to dictate thanks to Cecil for his 'love and care' of 'one of the furthest removed from your remembrance'. Meanwhile, Correr in London hears that the king is considering 'a general change of ambassadors'. Who is destined for Venice isn't known, but several candidates have offered themselves. (Against the odds, it appears from the competition to replace him that London thinks Wotton has made a serious fist of his diplomatic posting.) Wotton himself counts on the autumn revocation, hoping to be 'shortly restored' to the 'happy sight' of his king's 'sacred person'.

A month later, his hopes are dashed. The rumour of his recall is false, he tells the Collegio. While a fellow ambassador has 'leave to return into our sweet England', 'his Majesty hath been pleased to tolerate my poor endeavours here somewhat longer'. In August, he hears as much from the king, receiving 'with much cheerfulness ... and humble thankfulness' a 'change' of the 'resolution about my return before winter'. Every set-back must be couched as a privilege. Now, he barely disguises his disappointment behind hyperbole, his 'fervent desire' to 'behold again the face of so good a master'.

The problem for London is not just finding an adequate successor for Wotton but deciding 'how to dispose of him at his return'. Officially, the Crown makes 'great count' of him (so diplomatic rumour has it) and will want to assign him to a high-profile post elsewhere, but the embassy in France is occupied and 'the Spanish air is thought somewhat too hot for his crazedness'. 'Crazed': it's the word that describes porcelain when its glaze cracks, or a man when his health is about to break. Increasingly Wotton's crazedness is evident. He's had regular recurrences of ague – malaria – since his student days, and now his relapses are growing more severe. This February, too weak to write, he dictates a dispatch, asking Cecil to 'conjecture the present estate of my body after a continual ague of forty days', wracked with fever and convulsions, an 'extremity of ... sickness' that doesn't just 'strain' his 'weak head' but empties his purse. Physicians are expensive. Especially the one 'fetcht from Padua'. So is their advice. They warn against a 'calcular disposition' so he rents a villa at the baths of Abano near Padua where he can 'drink of a mineral water'.

Illness excuses some of his increasingly frequent, increasingly protracted absences from the Collegio, those between 13 January–30 March and 27 April–7 July this year. But not all. Earlier, when he hadn't put in an appearance throughout March 1608, he excused his absence as a 'sign of two things', 'a peaceful time' and 'a solid friendship'. Then, there was 'little business to do'. Now, though, he may be hiding. Since 11 September when, with such crass stupidity, he protested the banning of the King's Book by driving his ship of state onto the rocks then leaping overboard, he's been treading water. The Senato's decision to send an extraordinary ambassador to London threw him a buoy: that honour (he says) repaired the insult. He returns to the Collegio. In esposizioni on 15 and 26 September he attempts to justify his 'termine assai sgarbo' (rude words) by glossing over with vast understatement the 'poco disparer nato circa il suo libro' ('small variance' arisen from the King's Book). Then he vanishes to Cannaregio to await the event. Does he have flashbacks to May 1603, again having to 'tumble' opinion up and down wondering what Cecil is thinking of him? Or indeed, to September 1599, holed up inside Essex House, wondering what the queen at Nonsuch was making of the sudden appearance of Essex and his gang from Ireland?

He'd perhaps be heartened to know his reputation in Rome is unchanged: the pope declares he's 'in Venice ... to do all the mischief he can to the Catholic faith'. The Republic's regard, too, remains unchanged: the matter of 'the book'? Donà considers it 'dimenticato', forgotten. And when a drunken Greek commanding a galley that Wotton boards, having been tipped off that there's an Englishman among the slave crew, insults the ambassador and knocks the captive to the deck 'with a great cudgel', the Signoria instantly demonstrates how it values the English ambassador. 'The Greek' is 'drawn out of the galley to prison through the common piazza with a long chain at his heels like a slave', sentenced 'to perpetual close imprisonment' and just misses hanging. It takes some fast talking from Wotton to persuade them the public shaming (and the freeing of the Englishman) are enough reparation and that the drunk, stone-cold sober after days in a freezing prison pozzo, should be reprieved.

But what about London? In November Wotton delivers to the Collegio King James's formal letter in Latin responding to the diplomatic embarrassment his ambassador has caused. It stresses the reciprocal love between the two states, pours oil on troubled waters, and wafts aside any tit-for-tat point-scoring he might gain from complaining about the obscene book libelling him as 'Pruritanus' recently discovered smuggled into the Venetian embassy in London (to the Venetian ambassador's horror). Quality of the dirt dished in that book? The scandalmonger says the king 'manggiasse rospi', eats toads. The dispatch Cecil contributes to this damage limitation exercise doesn't survive, but we can guess its contents from a single sentence in Wotton's reply: 'I will precisely perform his Majesty's commandments ... being indeed (as your Lordship hath made me well understand) better at obedience then voluntary sacrifice'. (Eerily, 'obedience ... sacrifice' is a direct echo, Essex to Elizabeth in 1596. Does Wotton hear it? Does it, as instruction from Cecil, send ice through his veins?)

After he introduces John Harington to the Collegio on 23 November and puts in a brief appearance on 13 January 1610 to congratulate the doge on the new year, Wotton again disappears until the middle of May. He excuses himself. Lamely. He says he's been thinking as he walks up the Scala d'Oro about how 'li mercanti et li ambasciatori siano simili' (merchants and ambassadors are alike). 'Ma in effetto, sono diversi' (but in fact, they're different). If a merchant isn't seen on the Piazza they say his business is bad, a ship is sunk or taken by pirates, he's bankrupt. But if an ambassador doesn't show, it goes for certain that things are going well, there's perfect friendship and little business.

In truth, the present times *are* quiet. Practically the only stirring is in Savoy, where the duke, nicknamed 'Testa Calda', Hothead, and known to Wotton as 'the most discontented prince in the world', has some 'enterprise' in (not so) secret combination with Henri IV 'to assay the Duchy of Milan'. Wotton considers these 'purposes' 'things tacked together with such threads as are woven in men's imaginations'. Nevertheless, this 'ridiculous enterprise' might push France 'to a total rupture with Spain', thus shattering the 'present tranquillity'. (That threat will be stopped in its tracks when Henri IV is assassinated in May.) But if the times are quiet, Wotton isn't.

'No season or weather can be ill to go homewards'

He carries bruises into the new year 1610. Clearly, the King's Book debacle has battered him. His new year's eve message to London remembers 'that I have been so unfortunate this year ... as to stir some public complaint ... against me from this state'. He's still 'craving pardon ... for all my presumptions and imperfections' at the end of the month and grovelling before Cecil about that 'uncheerful subject', 'the faults of my indiscretion'.

The English ambassador is more homesick than ever. In those same January dispatches he hopes 'to beg' the king's pardon in person 'ere it be long at your royal feet', and 'to profess' his 'zeal' towards Cecil 'in your presence [so] that your Lordship may see my heart in my face'.

He is overjoyed when shortly 'ere it be long' looks like turning into 'now'. At the end of February, he has a dispatch from Cecil notifying 'the tyme' 'drawing now onwards apace which his Majesty hath prefixed for my return'. Days later, when this latest recall is withdrawn (Cecil at least having the decency to write the bad news himself, though as an after-thought, in a postscript) he's despondent. He replies in March. The king 'rejorneth my return till Allhollantide' (31 October): 'I must humbly and cheerfully obey'. 'In truth', though, he's been fantasising thoughts of home, 'devoured in mine own cogitation', and beseeching 'my brother' to back his 'humble suit', 'that a month or two of the prefixed time may be shortened for the more commodity of travel'. He writes again to Cecil. A begging letter – and a study in diplomatic rhetoric:

> My Lord, I can easily consider how unfit it is for me to importune a release from this employment wherewith his Majesty did first honour me so much above my merit, and then more, by the toleration of my poor endeavours here, but your Lordship, by whose recommendation I came unto it, and by whose patronage only I must acknowledge myself to have been kept in his Majesty's good opinion,

will I hope likewise continue the same favour in excusing my desire which at least is not unnatural: for all natural bodies do tend to their own centre. In the meantime, I shall proceed very cheerfully: for his Majesty I see hath not only pardoned my errors by his goodness but healed them with his wisdom.

'All natural bodies do tend to their own centre', a metaphor from natural philosophy. For 'centre' we read 'home', and in every repetition of 'cheerfully' we hear Wotton's gloom.

There's nothing for it but to continue, observing, gathering, informing, writing, reporting entertainments and 'rhapsodies'. He sends news flashes: the vexed question of nuns' dowries is settled; disputes about the *Corsaletta* remain unresolved; the Venetian ambassador returning home from plague-stricken London is stopped at the frontiers of the Veneto 'per far contumacia', quarantine; one of Galileo's instruments is promised Cecil by the next ship; and Fulgenzio Manfredi, who gained such popularity during the Interdict for his pro-Republican preaching and who, long since, was enticed to Rome with promises of reconciliation, is accused of practising with Wotton for a safe conduct to London. (This allegation Wotton dismisses as 'a thing merely surmised and coined in that shop of lies', the Vatican.)

The news rolls on. The footling. The shocking. But somehow it all feels routine. In May Wotton appears in the Collegio to comment on 'l'horrendo, et essecrabile' assassination of Henri IV (but confesses to Cecil that the sudden death gives him some 'private comfort', not least because the turn-about Catholic king died without last rites: he received no comfort from the church Wotton thinks 'abused' Henri by converting him to Catholicism's false doctrine). In June Wotton quashes the 'headless rumour' that King James 'era stato amazzato d' un'archibugiata in una spalla': was killed in his privy chamber by a carpenter who fired an arquebus into his shoulder. (Where do these bizarre stories come from? A carpenter smuggling a gun the size of a musket into the king's bedroom?) In early July Wotton reports himself 'cast into a little febrous disposition' that worsened into 'a painful fever which, falling into these Canicular heats' (the dog-days of summer this year having been 'very excessive and almost beyond example') 'did in the space of three weeks bring me to a greater weakness than my former long infirmity'.

Perhaps it's realising the toll such 'crazedness' is having on the English ambassador, and not just him, his *famiglia*, that prompts Cecil finally to send him assurance of his discharge, 'about Allhollantyde', only weeks away. A dispatch received 6 August 'hath brought me', says Wotton, 'new blood and new strength', being 'now in truth desirous … to lay off this garment', his robes of office, to put on instead 'outward ... plainness'. 'As for the incommodiousness of the season towards winter to journey in', he's no longer quibbling. Cecil should 'take no care of us' (note 'us': his entire household is being recalled) 'for no doubt the maxime is good, that no season or weather can be ill to go homewards and besides we are now uccelli di bosco et di riviera' – forest birds, sea birds – 'after the trial of many airs'. They'll fly home in any weather.

Even now, Dudley Carleton, Wotton's replacement, writes to arrange the handover, beginning with 'economical affairs, as to leave me your house ... household stuff ... servants'. On 3 September Wotton says he's 'in qualità di sgombrante': already clearing out. He and his *famiglia*. Going home.

But not, as it happens, before Christmas.

'A few collections'

Wotton ties up business. In terms of trade: after three years browbeating the Collegio, he finally folds. 'Dio m'aiuto' (God help me), he concedes that Mr Cordal will have to accept 'compensation' not 'restitution' for the *Corsaletta* (long since stripped to a hulk, her cargo rotted). He attends to external relations: he introduces Cecil's son, Lord Cranborne. And to internal relations: learning that poor, miserable, duped Manfredi was strangled and burnt just days ago in Rome upon the false imputation that he'd practised with Wotton for conveyance to England, Wotton has to protest that in making him the instrument of Manfredi's death, Rome lies. Leonardo Donà absolves the ambassador. He shouldn't doubt himself. Manfredi lived 'accarezzato' (cherished) in Venice. And safe. He was lured by hope to Rome. He had only himself to blame.

Thinking about his successor (and the final 'relazione' he'll make to the king in London, giving an account of his embassy), Wotton begins putting together 'a few collections' concerning 'the estate of Italy' and 'the condition wherein I leave it', a user's guide to statecraft in Venice. The new ambassador will find it a place of 'uncertain and narrow negotiation'; a government 'where businesses are carried per via di broglio and by the secret banding of families and affinities'; where the constant rotation of magistracies makes for 'mysterious ballotations', uncertain 'even in the best and clearest causes'. In this state, 'good answers ... are cheaper than good resolutions, or at least than hasty'; but conversely, 'upon some occasions' the Republic is 'as precipitous peradventure as it is generally sober'. In sum, La Serenissima's counsels 'participate much ... of the fluctuation of that element wherein they are planted': her political decisions, like the sea on which she's built, ebb and flow.

Meanwhile, Carleton, is grumbling his way across Europe, travelling, as he puts it, *'cum impedimentis'*, a 'wife and some other women-kind', in four coaches with a suite totalling twenty-four, including his elderly surrogate father, John Chamberlain (who so memorably, during the Interdict Crisis, called the Venetian senators 'pantaloons'). Neither of them thinks much of Wotton, mocking him in private letters as 'Fabritio', the 'father of lies', while they munch sour grapes. Wotton and Carleton have led parallel lives for decades, but when each in turn comes a cropper, Wotton over Essex, Carleton over the gunpowder conspiracy (he's the unwitting secretary who leased the cellars beneath Parliament to the plotters), Wotton first scappò then turned up basking under King James's sunny beams while Carleton was nailed to disgrace, sent to that particular Court limbo where suitors stand like gallows-fodder, cap-in-hand, waiting. Carleton's appointment to Venice is his last throw of the dice. He's been angling for years for diplomatic postings – and this one is at least better than the alternative he's offered, Ireland.

In Italy Carleton complains of everything from inferior accommodation to the fussy 'rinfrescamenti' offered as refreshments by hospitable locals that delay his progress, to the 'heap of holydays' that delay him further. At Cremona he's furious that the Sanità (the same Sanità Correr obeyed when it quarantined him) locks the city gates against his convoy, fearing the English have brought from London the plague that is currently devastating that city, and he rages to Wotton about answers from officials that come with 'but a shrug of the shoulder'. Later, he'll tell the Collegio he 'hopes to trouble his Serenity as little as possible' while making his secretary his messenger-of-business. How very different is this new ambassador showing himself to be from the 'vero Venetiano' currently in residence. Cremona advertises him 'troppo vivace e risentito' (too heated and indignant). In the Collegio Wotton smoothes things. Stava brontolando? 'Stanco dalla lunghezza del viaggio'. Was he bellowing? Probably tired from the journey.

Wotton does everything to accommodate his successor. He sends the noble guest, Cranborne, who is currently staying in the embassy, on a jaunt so that Carleton, now in Padua, might 'make a step hither unknown and so take a view and possession of this your own house'. (Already, we hear Wotton handing his house over.) He fits 'the lower hall with cloth of arras', as agreed with Carleton's secretary. He takes the 'pattern of your arms' from Carleton's 'sumpter cloths' to make his robes of state. He advises him to give 'some civil warning' to 'all those English gentlemen and students' in Padua 'to come hither with you' to bulk up the numbers for his 'entrata', 'which point I touch the rather because our nation is in truth ... more defective therein than the French'. He arranges 'these rooms' – *his* rooms – 'for your reception, which will be sufficient (with a little help abroad) to contain us both for those few days of mine own abode here after your coming, whereof I shall be glad, both that the friendship between us may be the more confirmed under one roof, and that my Lady' – Carleton's wife – 'be not disobeyed by any want on my part in her just commandment'. (Little does he know of the poisoned paper darts his 'friend' exchanges with Chamberlain.) He's leaving behind especially for Lady Carleton 'a new carnation [coloured] satin coverlet', 'a poor relique', he apologises, but meant to keep 'her from the cold this winter'.

Wotton gives his last *esposizione* on 30 November and leaves, as the Collegio secretary records, 'non mostrando ... di partir sodisfatto', not satisfied. He's grumpy, having asked, as is customary, a 'grace' to end his embassy, the release of one Count Lombardo from life imprisonment. The Senato is willing only to commute the sentence to four years' confinement in the fort at Palma. Wotton persists. Donà advises 'di restar di quello' (stop there). The doge knows how many votes it took to wangle even this much out of the Senato. And Palma? 'Un giardino' (a garden). After six years, Wotton might have wished a cheerier exit.

Already, though, he has in hand a bigger take-away than this 'grace'. A souvenir: the whole city. Recorded on canvas. A painter is currently living in the English embassy. Perhaps he's Odoardo Fialetti, whose anatomy-indebted manual on how to draw the human body was published in Venice in 1608. He has worked for Wotton before, painting portraits of four doges and the ambassador himself, in long view, giving audience in a busy Collegio. Now, Wotton commissions Fialetti to paint a map of Venice. It's going to be magnificent, and massive. (Fourteen years hence, when it hangs in rooms Wotton occupies as provost of Eton College, it covers an entire wall.) It won't be architecturally exact: Fialetti will paint only five arches across the façade of the Palazzo Ducale instead of seventeen. Churches will be missing, Palladio's Redentore most glaringly. In the far northwest, the Jewish Ghetto will be noticed, and San Girolamo, but nothing distinguished of the huddle of buildings beyond to mark the English embassy: Wotton wouldn't presume to have himself and his 'poor endeavors' put on the map.

This bird's eye 'View' will riff on Jacopo de' Barbari's map of 1500, but Fialetti will go beyond de' Barbari to paint the living city Wotton knows and loves. He'll people Venice: senators sauntering along the *broglio*, a mountebank crying his stuff along the piazzetta, gondolieri threading canal and rio, one cruising beneath the Rialto bridge; in the Arsenale, marangoni working on a galley, on the lagoon, marinari pulling sheets holding full-blown sails on galleons taut; in the Piazza, on a raised platform surrounded by jostling spettatori, a scena in full swing. Fialetti will paint the orologio, the clock tower built over the entrance to the Merceria, in beautiful detail, right up to the *mori* with their hammers beating the bell at the top. A child will play, a dog bark. The winged lion and Teodoro with his glum crocodile will gaze down from their columns. This map will be Wotton's cartographic archive rendered as civic theatre. When it's finished it will be sent after the ambassador. Paint (we remember of Sarpi's portrait) takes forever to dry in Venetian winters, and this huge canvas, five canvas panels stitched together, will need to travel rolled.

But more than a souvenir, Wotton's map will be his trophy. Among much impressionistic fudging, the one façade Fialetti paints for him with draughtsman-like accuracy is the face of the Jesuit church and college, Santa Maria dell'Umiltà along the Zattere. It's been empty of Jesuits since 1606 when they were expelled, permanently, from Venice at the beginning of the Interdict Crisis, among them, Antonio Possevino, who once thought 'Arrigo' one of his 'agnelli', his lambs. In fact Arrigo was a wolf pup biding his time. Ambassador Wotton takes as among his greatest triumphs during the 'war of the quill' the part he played to expose the 'mascherato', the masked man, and to ransack the 'spiders' nest'. Ever since, the French government has demanded that the Jesuits be allowed to return to Venice. Wotton crows: 'never ... in the age of the living'. Fialetti's map, then, hides in plain sight a tribute to the English ambassador's achievement, secretly coding for Wotton his Protestant victory, a boast in paint, 'ce l'ho fatto': I did it.

'My last leave from this place'

Arrigo VVottoni formally resigns his charge in a public audience on 7 December, introducing the new ambassador to Doge Leonardo Donà, the Collegio and a mass of spectators packed into the chamber. The Englishmen have by an 'express agreement at home' worked out the terms of their speeches – compliment, assurance, thanks. But when Donà, after lavishly praising the retiring ambassador and every one of his household, goes on to make it not just praiseworthy but no small wonder – 'non poca meraviglia' – 'that, despite diversity of religion, not the slightest scandal has occurred' during his tenure, words Wotton thinks 'purposely insinuated for some contentment of the pope's spies' in the audience, Wotton 'non voglio lasciar di dire ...': can't help saying …. And so the retiring ambassador launches into a defence of his king's policies. Thus, as in his first audience six years back, the English ambassador misses his exit cue and speaks more than is set down for him before, for the last time, 'si licentiò, et partí': he's dismissed and leaves.

The weather is terrible, and worsening, but in Padua on the first leg of the journey homeward he tarries some days, looking after Cecil's sick son, when a message from Venice catches up with him. He wasn't still in residence when Carleton's secretary went room by room writing up an inventory of the embassy's furnishings, and now Carleton is fussing over costs, terms and get-out clauses with 'the Jew' – Isaac Luzzati – who leases them the stuff and who's 'a little unsatisfied for not having been dealt with clearly' in the 'confusion' of Wotton's departure. Wotton replies on Christmas eve, hoping to 'put an end unto it'. But maybe not. There's an even longer letter itemising pictures, sheets, holberds, the gondola, the iron chests and the billiard table sent on St Steven's day, 27 December – but no reply, doubtless because Wotton never receives it. That day, as he writes to Robert Cecil, 'our riding suits on our backs', he and his *famiglia* are at their 'departure from Padua'.

Not many days later, though, with wonderful irony, it appears that the homesick Englishman is one homesick Venetiano, looking east as his horse (whose name we do not know) takes him west. 'From a filthy inn at the foot of the hill of Sanserre on the Loire this 4th of February' 1611 he writes that he's 'dispatched to Paris before me … my secretary to see there how I may be accommodated at the Hostel de Venice to which place I have some peculiar fancy for the very name's sake'. He'll leave arrangements there 'in bilancia, as we Italians use to speak'.

When he writes 'From my lodging in King St', Westminster, on 2 April, we know the 'uccello' 'di bosco et di riviera' is landed. That's his brother's London address. Three days earlier, he marked his birthday. He is forty-three years old.

'Touching the public affairs'

Behind in Venice Wotton leaves not just furniture and a billiard table but an innovation, a fully functioning English embassy: Gregorio de Monti in place as Venetian secretary; an intelligence network planted across Italy and beyond that sends the ambassador 'informatione' up to the moment he departs; a back-channel to Sarpi and that 'calvinistical' preacher Fulgenzio Micanzio; iron chests filled with dispatches, letter-books, memoranda, affidavits, ciphers and his 'collections' on 'the estate of Italy' as 'I leave it' that document the restoration of Anglo-Venetian relations, that show Wotton the architect of that restoration, and that detail the daily life of a jobbing ambassador.

Wotton has talked his embassy into being with no previous experience of diplomacy but his humanist education, his travels in Europe, his campaigning with Essex and his skills of observation and reporting, which underpin his embassy the way the tree trunk piles driven into the lagoon underpin Venetian palazzi. He has always recognised the fiction built into embassy, that an ambassador is a stand-in, a proxy. His particular strength has been to exploit the theatricality which constitutes his everyday life, equipping him to perform a number of 'selves' that position him to get his work in the world done. The affable. The prickly. The deeply read and bookish, a man who does his homework. The mindlessly superficial. Witty. Witless. Shrewd and analytical. Selectively deaf. Constructively imprudent. Never pompous. Never buffoonish. Able to derive from events insights of startling political implication: in the Grisons, a frenzied uprising of the 'base multitude' demonstrates that 'a Senate can rule the mass of their people no longer, nor no farther than themselves list'.

His personal style has eased him into connections that have enabled his diplomacy: with Philippe Canaye (the French ambassador, who shares intelligence with Wotton and can turn up at his door unannounced); Giovanni Carlo Scaramelli (shadow-man to Wotton in the Collegio whose secretarial hand comes in and out of the filza record until Wotton mourns his death in 1608); and most significantly, Leonardo Donà, who trains him in 'reserved' diplomacy – but whose reserve the English ambassador occasionally cracks, luring him (as Donà himself says) into frankness like Wotton's. Wotton talks to Donà as no other ambassador talks to Donà. And Donà talks to him as to no other ambassador. Wotton's familiarity with Donà is echoed, though more distant geographically, in his personal address to King James, begun in Scotland and ever since sustained by Ottavio Baldi, which makes him an influencer in Whitehall. The king reads his dispatches 'with better contentation' than any other ambassador's because they don't just stick to state matters: they're 'enterlaced with variety of conversation'. Perhaps the king even plagiarises Wotton, borrowing from his ambassador's *Letter from Venice* thoughts that turn up in his 'Premonition'.

Wotton leaves behind solid achievements for international trade: abolition of the anchorage tax, protocols on recognition at sea, a declaration on piracy (though John Ward is still running amok in the Mediterranean). He has scored personal successes: nameless Englishmen freed from galley slavery; gormless student delinquents saved from prosecution; Thomas Coryat plucked from the riot he's crassly inciting in the Ghetto; a nine-year-old orphan granted admission to the seminary school of San Marco; the Venetian ambassador, Correr, excused of the 'Pruritanus' scandal by Wotton's good words and so saved from immediate recall to face 'fire on his feet'. It must be said, though, that some of his interventions seem incomprehensible. Why, after five years, does he renew his appeal for the rapist and mutilator Antonio Dotto? Others look indefensible. Perhaps he was naive, or simply 'normally' misogynist, believing Agustin Carpan's protestation that he'd been accused by 'una puttana', a whore. But when he heard the Consiglio di Dieci's sickening file on Carpan, that he'd sexually abused 'una putta di anni otto', not just deflowering but sodomising the eight-year-old 'più et più volti' (over and over), how could he continue defending him?

He leaves behind, too, solid achievements as a cultural ambassador. He exports Venice to England. He sends books. Galileo's cannocchiale and *Sidereus Nuncius*. Paintings to whet the soon-voracious English appetite for Italian art and to launch royal collections: Fialetti's doges; the Sarpi portrait ('done truly and naturally but roughly ala Venetiana and therefore to be set at some good distance from the sight'); 'Prometheus devoured by the eagle done by Giacobo Palma in concurrence with Titiano … (bothe of no smale name)'; a finely wrought mosaic of Cecil made from the de Critz pattern (enshrined, when it arrived at Cecil's Hatfield House, in a marble surround). Glass from Murano. Finocchio from Chioggia. (Until then, fennel had been used homeopathically in England, but not eaten.) An account of Venetian architecture.

His legacy to Carleton is continuity: a change of 'instruments', not 'ends'. But also expectation. What will Carleton make of the house Wotton built?

Riding west in winter 1611 through papal territories – Milan, Turin – into France, retired ambassador Henry Wotton spends some thoughts on the state of Christendom. It's a mixed picture. In Florence, twenty-year-old Cosimo de' Medici, who inherited the title 'Grand Duke' a year earlier, is already showing signs of the tuberculosis that will kill him. In Milan, Cardinal Baronio is rumoured canonised, and that creaking geriatric Count Fuentes spends his last breaths arming Spain against Savoy, while in Turin the duke of Savoy begins lobbying London for royal marriages. In Paris, a nine-year-old sits on the throne of France. In Rome, Pope Paolo pulls in his horns so far that, when the Venetian Senato not only publicly hangs a priest for theft between the two pillars on San Marco but orders the body to twist in the wind there overnight, he makes no protest.

As for La Serenissima herself: Wotton leaves behind a Republic that has defied the pope, stopped Rome's land-grab across the Veneto, hobbled the *papalini* and the moves these pro-papal patricians in the Senato might make to limit commerce with 'infidels' and 'heretics', asserted her inviolable sovereignty – and avoided war in Christendom. While the papacy extends its authority over one Italian state after the other, Venice remains independent, defending her publishing industry and her minorities, crucial to the circulation of knowledge and commerce. That, across the harrowing year of the Interdict, Venice didn't capitulate must be credited in large measure to Henry Wotton. His obstinacy. His recklessness. His league. As ambassador his role was to represent, and never to exceed his instruction. But he overstepped that limit. No longer the actor playing the part, he made himself the dramatist scripting it. With each one of those acts, he invented diplomacy that nudged Venetian history. In terms of inventions, Henry Wotton's was no mean achievement.

Epilogue: no longer Sisyphus

Henry Wotton was sent twice more ambassador to Venice, from 1616 to 1619 and 1621 to 1623. Both embassies were largely uneventful. Gregorio de Monti continued to serve him as Venetian secretary until his death in 1621.

In other business, as extraordinary ambassador Wotton negotiated (fruitlessly) a double marriage between Prince Henry, Princess Elizabeth and the

17 Henry Wotton. Painted late in his life, this portrait shows the former ambassador as provost of Eton College, an elderly 'philosopher' leaning thoughtfully on his hand, who yet retains his youthful (though greying) 'beard of Cadiz'. Unknown artist, date unknown.

heirs of Protestant-leaning Savoy in 1612 (terminated when the heir to the English throne died that November); represented (haplessly) English interests in The Hague (1614); sat in the Addled Parliament that year and returned briefly to Parliament in 1625. He was tipped (endorsed by the great man himself) to succeed Robert Cecil as secretary of state but was passed over – luckily for England and himself, for he had neither the temperament of a stoat nor the work ethic of a little beagle. Besides, he was currently disgraced. The fuse on the explosive left in the autograph book in Austria eight years earlier was finally lit by the mischief-making German scholar Caspar Schoppe, who quoted 'Legatus est vir bonus peregre missus ad mentiendum Reipublicae causa' literally to make England's ambassador the lying tongue of the lying king he spoke for. King James was not amused – although he himself called Wotton his 'honest dissembler'. Wotton managed, eventually, to survive disgrace. Again.

In July 1613 Wotton gave history the only detailed account of what 'happened this week at the Bank's side' in London when, during a performance by the King's Players of a new play called *All is True*, wadding shot from a cannon landed in the thatch covering the theatre's upper gallery. 'Being thought at first but an idle smoke', fire 'kindled inwardly, and ran round like a train, consuming within less than an hour the whole house to the very grounds'. The only casualty – except for 'a few forsaken cloaks' and, likely, the company's entire store of costumes and playbooks that Wotton doesn't think about – was a man who 'had his breeches set on fire' and would 'have broiled' if he hadn't doused himself 'with bottle ale'. With this, he, who as secretary to Essex had missed the after-dinner row across the Thames with a gaggle of aristos to see a specially commissioned performance of Shakespeare's *Richard II* on the eve of the so-called Essex 'rebellion', now documented the burning down of Shakespeare's playhouse, the Globe. And during a performance of one of Shakespeare's plays. *All is True* is otherwise titled *Henry VIII*.

In July 1624, on the king's writ, Wotton was elected provost of Eton College. He took minor clerical orders, casting off the scholar's gown, the courtier's ruff, the ambassador's robes for a surplice. No longer 'Sisyphus' rolling 'the restless stone of state employment' through 'multitudes of men', he who so often claimed to have been 'tolto dal scuola' and thrust into tumultuous public business now found 'sweet content' in Eton's 'scuola', in a 'private study' that he made his 'theatre' – while that other theatre, Venice, hung, mapped, on his college wall. At Eton, he was 'a constant cherisher of all those youths' he found diligent in learning. There, he 'seemed to have his youth renewed'. Along the Thames in the meadow beyond the college walls at Black Potts, he spent 'his idle time which was then not idly spent' fishing, frequently in the company of Izaak Walton, who would write his 'Life' and remember him in *The Compleat Angler*. Wotton never completed his *Philosophical Survey of Education*, begun at Eton in his sixties, on the education of children or 'how I could build a man'. But then, he didn't finish his history of the Interdict Crisis either.

In 1637 he wrote his will. He bequeathed his soul to God, his body to earth and his earthly goods to King Charles (paintings of the doges of Venice), Queen Henrietta (Dioscorides 'with the plants naturally coloured'), the bishop of London ('a picture of Heraclitus bewailing and Democritus laughing at the world') and friends (more paintings, books, his 'cabinet of instruments', a lodestone and 'my viol de gamba which hath been twice with me to Italy'). He outlived Carleton (now secretary of state, Viscount Dorchester), five years his junior, by seven years. He died in College in December 1639, just as the first skirmishes broke out in England's civil wars in three kingdoms, wars partly of religion. He is buried in the chapel, his grave marked by a black marble slab. It carries a Latin inscription (in English, 'The Itch of Disputation Will Prove the Scab of the Church'). But not his name. We who stand reading are told: 'Seek His Name Elsewhere'. That's as much as to say: Henry Wotton? He's lying abroad.

Illustrations

Endpapers Odoardo Fialetti, *View of Venice* (1611). Reproduced by permission of the Provost and Fellows of Eton College, ref. FDA-P.166-2010.

1. From Henry Wotton, self-exiled in Venice, this letter to Secretary of State Robert Cecil dated May 1603 worked his pardon and rehabilitation. Reproduced by permission of The National Archives, ref. SP99/2.167-169.   26
2. Derived from a pattern taken by John de Critz the Elder, this portrait showing Cecil in his Garter robes was commissioned by Henry Wotton in 1609 to be produced in Venice in mosaic. Now at Hatfield House. Reproduced with permission of the Marquess of Salisbury, Hatfield House, ref. CP67.   29
3. Abraham Ortelius map of Europe, 1595. Public domain.   50
4. Robert Devereux, earl of Essex. In this painting by an unknown artist following Marcus Gheeraerts the Younger, the earl wears his Greater George on a riband and holds his Marshal's baton. The beard spilling over his ruff, grown on campaign in 1596, shows this as 'the face of Cadiz'. Reproduced by permission of the Provost and Fellows of Eton College, ref. FDA-P.262-2010.   100
5. Addressing Essex's letter from Dover to Robert Cecil on 14 April 1596, Henry Wotton writes 'hast, post hast for lyfe' and draws a gallows to show the postmen its urgency. Reproduced by permission of The National Archives, ref. SP12/259 f.45v, ref. TNA SP12/259 f.45v.   118
6. Writing to Robert Cecil from Plymouth 'in this buisy time of embarquinge' for Cadiz in May 1596, Wotton signs himself 'Harry'. Reproduced with permission of the Marquess of Salisbury, Hatfield House, ref. CP41_26.   122

LIST OF ILLUSTRATIONS

7   A copy of the earl of Essex's bitter letter to Queen Elizabeth from Plymouth, 7 May 1596, written out in Wotton's hand. Reproduced with permission of the Marquess of Salisbury, Hatfield House, ref. CP40_66.   129

8   The endorsement in Essex's hand on the verso of the 7 May letter, 'Copie of my le*tt*re to her Ma*jes*tie to be deliuered to Sr Rob. Cecill', shows that the earl intended his personal letter to the queen to be read more widely. Reproduced with permission of the Marquess of Salisbury, Hatfield House, ref. CP40.66.   130

9   Writing to his fellow secretary Edward Reynolds from Dublin on 19 April 1599, Wotton observes 'All things ... in a good trayne' now that 'owre Lord and Master' – Essex – has taken the 'swaye of this vnsetled Kingdome into his hand'. And he predicts an 'end' of 'thease warrs' 'by treaty'. Reproduced with permission of the Marquess of Salisbury, Hatfield House, ref. CP179.2.   135

10   The title heading these 'Articles agreed vppon for a cessation of Armes' is written in Wotton's hand. 'Hughe Tirone' signs the document. Reproduced with permission of the Marquess of Salisbury, Hatfield House, ref. CP73_90.   141

11   King James I. A portrait from 1605 attributed to John de Critz the Elder shows the young king as Wotton knew him in Scotland and London. Wikimedia Commons, public domain.   153

12   Henry Wotton. Odoardo Fialetti's painting, date unknown, locates the ambassador in the Collegio delivering an esposizione to Doge Leonardo Donà while Savii listen and secretaries go about their business. Royal Collection Trust © His Majesty King Charles III.   158

13   Giovanni Carlo Scaramelli records in his distinctive handwriting the English ambassador's first audience in the Venetian Collegio, 1 October 1604. Reproduced by courtesy of the Archivio di Stato di Venezia, Campo dei Frari, Venice.   160

14   2967 Cannaregio. This palazzo, shown in a modern photograph and given its modern address, housed Wotton's English embassy. Photo Micky White.   178

15   Doge Leonardo Donà. Elected doge in 1606, Donà steered the Republic through the Interdict Crisis and periodically rescued the English ambassador from diplomatic gaffes. The portrait by an unknown artist is misdated. Wikimedia Commons, public domain.   197

16 Fra Paolo Sarpi. Commissioned by Wotton for King James to show him the face of the Servite friar who masterminded the theological defence of Venice throughout the Interdict Crisis, this portrait also documents the assassination attempt on Sarpi, showing the wound on his cheek. The inscription was Wotton's addition. Date unknown. © National Trust Images, ref. CMS_PCF_1139719. 247

17 Henry Wotton. Painted late in his life, this portrait shows the former ambassador as provost of Eton College, an elderly 'philosopher' leaning thoughtfully on his hand, who yet retains his youthful (though greying) 'beard of Cadiz'. Unknown artist, date unknown. Wikimedia Commons, public domain. 271

Acknowledgements

This book is a collaboration, and it is a great pleasure to record my gratitude to the many who have worked on it with me. William Ingram first infected me with 'archive fever' as a graduate student researching early modern playhouse records. Fifty years on, Bill is still my mentor, wise and generous. He read chapters as they emerged and the whole thing again in final draft. My colleague at Warwick University, Peter Mack, gave me the courage to start the project. His instructions were: 'Go to Venice. Learn Italian. Find Carpaccio'. I wish he'd lived to see finished what he started. Other colleagues at Warwick and elsewhere have given me enormous support: Thomas Docherty read chapters and sharpened my political thinking; Paul Botley translated Wotton's Latin; Susan Brock checked transcriptions and deciphered Robert Cecil's execrable handwriting when it defeated me (ironic that Cecil had the gall to complain about his son's poor penmanship); Julian Richards collaborated with me on an exhibition at the Shakespeare Birthplace Trust that placed Wotton among the 'peacemakers' celebrated in the centenary marking the end of the Great War; Peter Holland hurried into print in *Shakespeare Survey* my early findings on Wotton and Shakespeare; Marion O'Connor drove me up the hill to Bocton Hall and found Thomas Wotton's letter-book; Bernhard Klein educated me on ships; Stefano Villani complicated my understanding of Protestantism in Venice; Werner Sollors walked Cannaregio with me and challenged me to prove my claims about the address of Wotton's embassy; Paul Hammer sent transcripts of documents from his personal Essex file; Giulia Boitani took on the daunting job of translating Wotton. Invitations by Diego Pirillo and Eloise Davies and Alana Mailes gave me the opportunity to present parts of this book at the CRSS 'Global Reformations' conference (University of Toronto) and the 'Stuart Serenissima' conference (University of Cambridge), and Diego brought to my grateful attention Wotton's letters archived in Florence. All of these colleagues have given more than collegiality. They've given the kind of listening, conversation, intellectual rigour and prompting that signals friendship.

Much of this book was written in Venice. From the first day, walking into the Archivio di Stato with my three words of Italian, I benefited from the expertise, generosity and infinite patience both of archivists and the Archivio's research community. It was sheer good fortune to meet Maria Fusaro on that first day and to be taken under her stern wing. I cannot thank her enough. Good fortune, too, to be handed, when I didn't know what I was looking for, Wotton's esposizioni in filza, not registro, files which meant that I was set to work on the 'foul papers' (rather than the corrected 'fair copy') that showed me the material evidence of the Collegio at work written out in Scaramelli's beautifully legible hand. It was good fortune beyond any expectation to benefit from the deep knowledge, exemplary archival research, practical help and sheer kindness of Mauro Bondioli and Isabella Cecchini who have made my every return to the Archivio a homecoming. The wider archive community gave me daily support: Jan-Christoph Rößler with invaluable information about where to look for the English embassy's address, Micky White with hundreds of document photographs, and Antonio Mazzucco and Roberto Zago with help navigating the Archivio's wall of red catalogue books. Mariangela Nicolardi 'oft invited me' and encouraged my bumbling Italian.

I want to thank my Venetian hosts over several years, Kent and Pam Cartwright, for hospitality and for reading drafts of chapters; and Shaul Bassi, Susanne Franco and PK for making me family. I am grateful to Shaul for adopting me a 'una vera Venetiana': for collaborations over many years, for inviting me to take a visiting lectureship in Ca' Foscari, University of Venice, that gave me time to write the book's final chapter, and for reading and commenting on the full draft. He made it possible for me to spend an afternoon with the Borgo family, walking through rooms at 2967 Cannaregio Wotton would have known. I gratefully acknowledge the Borgos's hospitality, opening their doors to me.

In England, I am indebted to the numerous archivists that made this book possible: at the Shakespeare Birthplace Trust, the British Library, The National Archive, Hatfield House (particularly Sarah Whale and Vannis Jones Rahi) and Eton College (particularly Sally Jennings). Thanks to Eva Rice and Phil Breen, I was able to spend a day at Eton College where Justin Nolan, whose admiration of Wotton rides as high as my own, gave me a full tour of Wotton's Eton and allowed me to linger over his map of Venice, portrait and marble slab in the College chapel. At Winchester College, Geoffrey Day shared a copy of his unpublished history of the school. Hours spent there among records in the library and in the classroom where Wotton was taught allowed me to imagine Harry the schoolboy. At St Edmund's Hall, Oxford, Filippo de Vivo welcomed me into the Early Modern Italian World Seminar and made it possible for me to finish this book by attentive and generous readings of its Venice chapters. They are everywhere informed by his scholarship, publication and always ebullient energy. I owe him a massive debt.

This book was enabled by grants from the Delmas Foundation and the Warwick Research Fund along with extensive periods of research leave. I thank my agent, Charlie Viney, for believing in it; my editor at MUP, Alun Richards, for helping to whip it into shape; Diane Wardle, for sharp-eyed copy editing; and Siân Chapman for her super-human effort to get this book across the finish line.

As I've written, I've kept in mind (thanks to James Shapiro) comments made by Wotton's cousin, Francis Bacon, that anyone who 'undertaketh the story of a time … cannot but meet with many blanks and spaces which he must be forced to fill up out of his own wit and conjecture'. But also Hermione Lee quoting Thomas Carlyle on life-writing, that '"To have an open loving heart" was the primary qualification of a biographer'. I hope readers will see both wit and love in this book.

Finally, none of this would have happened without my family, willing to go the distance with me, prepared to keep home together (thank you Cheryl Asthana) and the Warwickshire wilderness at bay while I decamped to Venice for months at a time. Mary Lowance told me I needed to write the Prologue; Pete Atkin, that I needed to write for the human voice; Roberta and David Skelton, Irene Musumeci, Ben Fowler, Matt Armstrong, Ibo Ozhan and Jenny Warren reminded me that there was 'a world elsewhere' and regularly took me there. My daughters, Bryony (who photographed documents and meticulously checked transcriptions) and Rowan (who read copy and added numbers of full stops) told me I needed to finish. During the time I've been working on Wotton, they have produced the next generation. This book is dedicated to my grandchildren.

Appendix

Right Honorable

The good opinion which it hath pleased youre honor first to conceaue in youre self of me, and then to deliuer it vnto my brother (who is in nature and in loue the neerest vnto me) doth assure me that how full of care so ever the tymes are now at home (whereof I can easily vnderstand the greatest waight next his Matie to lie vppon youre wisdome) yet that you will pardon in me this troubling of you from abroade, and honorably interpret the offer of my poore service though it come both vnseasonably and late.

    Sir, I will gayne youre fauor with plain^{n}esse: which is my best occupation and when I stepp out of it I doe nothing handsomely: Therfore it may please youre Honor to give me leaue to tell you, that of all those which sometyme were of that vnfortunat familie I only peraduenture had reason to deliberat whether after the death of owre Master (between whom and youre Honor theare was so publique vnkindnesse) it were fitt for me to apply my self vnto youre service because mine owne person hauing been remoued into thease parts (ether of porpose or by accident) from the knowledg and participation of ill, the world (which must somewhat be satisfyed) might thinke me more obliged to a tender and reuerent remembrance of my Master then they that knew him worthy of opposition: And yet as I owed him a dubble duty: the duty of fidelitie to his person while he lived and the duty of reuerense to his memorie after his death: So (I thinke I may iustly say) that he owed vnto me in some respects more regard of me then I found about him, which I would not confesse vnto youre Honor but rather couer my disestimation if from that interest first of kindred and then of affection into which it pleased youre Honor to receaue my brother theare had not (as I may speake it) reflected some little distrust vppon me: wherewith the corrupt instruments of families did worke vppon one that was not worthe the considering.

APPENDIX

Youre Honor seeth how I tumble my self vp and downe strengthening and weakoning the obligations of a servant. It is not (I protest vnto youre Honor) ~~my natural~~ ingratitude, or new ambition, or tediousenesse of my present estate how narrow so ever it be: But as I was free by birthe, so I seeke to proue my self free by reason: and being so, I must confesse vnto youre Honor that first the obligations of nature doe take hold of me: which binde me to carry towards youre Honorable person the same vnfeined zeale and deuotion with my brothers next the heigth and dignitie rather of youre wisdome and vertue then of youre place, and lastly, youre Honors good and graciouse concept of me wherewith it pleaseth you to deceaue youre self.

Right Honorable. I should haue presumed to haue written thus much vnto youre Honor albeit theare had falne out no difference between the tymes when my brother dated his letter (wherein se [sic] sent me that noble testimonie of y^r fauor) and the present: But besides those privat respects it may now please youre Honor to receaue a poore traueler for his part into the publique obligation since contrarie to malitiouse imaginations God hath made you in this greate buisinesse so apparent an instrument of the vnitie and glory of that whole Iland.

I am at this present with my nephew vppon owre departure from Venice: a Signorie that with long neutralitie of state is at length (as it seemeth) almost slipped into a neutralitie of religion: which I adde to give youre Honor a short accoumpt in what condition I leaue it.

We bend owre selvs towards Fraunce: but with some circuit about the ciuilest of Germanie. That cuntrie can yeld me little sober matter to intertayn my duties with youre Honor.

I shalbe in Franckfurt on the Mayne this next <blot> September aboute the tyme of the Mart: whether if it may please youre Honor by any of youre servants to direct vnto me youre commaundments, and with them to fashion me vnto youre self: I doe ingage my brothers word and mine owne honestie for my perpetual fidelitie, and observation toward you. And indeed it is necessarie even in the order of nature that youre Honor should with youre excellent instructions first inable my vnderstanding of your service, and then applye it.

The God of heauen preserve y^r Honor in his blessed fauor.

this .23. of May from Venice 1603. style of the place.

Youre Honors from the day aboue
written to the end of my lyfe.
henry Wotton

[Afterword:] This state hath newly chosen two principal gentlemen to be sent Embassadors to his Matie Pietro Dodi and Nicolo Molini: the first, to congratulate,

281

the other, to reside. Pietro Dodi hath performed before Embassages to the Emperor and King of Fraunce with good opinion. Nicolo Molini is at this present savio di terra ferma: an office of great reputation among them. They thinke to depart about the beginning of August accompagned with diuerse young Clarissimi: who (since the introduction of horsemanship into this citie) are more subiect then they were to noveltie and motion. Carolo Scarauella must return home for want of nothing but nobilitie: being otherwise esteemed one of theire ablest instruments.

[Addressed:]   To the right Honorable
              S^{ir} Robert Cicil Knight
              one of his Maties most
              Honorable privie Counsailers
              and Secretarie of Estate

Sources

The great bulk of the documents I cite are conserved in two archives, The National Archives, London (TNA) and the Archivio di Stato di Venezia (ASV). I quote from my own full transcriptions of both sets of files. Translations of the Italian papers are Giulia Boitani's. At TNA, Wotton's dispatches are filed as SP99.2–SP99.6; in ASV, his audiences are conserved in *Collegio, Secreta, Esposizioni Principi*, buste XIV–XIX and *Roma*, IX–XII. My transcriptions of the esposizioni are from filza files except where deterioration makes them illegible. Then I revert to registro files. I abbreviate citations to (for example): SP99.2 and *Coll. Esposizioni Principi* XIV. Other ASV *fonti* I use are: *Consiglio di Dieci, Inquisitori di Stato, Sanità*, and *Senato* (where the *Dispacci degli ambasciatori e residenti, Inghilterra* are filed).

Extracts and summaries of Wotton's state papers can be consulted in volumes IX, X and XI of the *Calendar of State Papers ... Venice* (*CSPV*) edited by Horatio F. Brown (London, 1897, 1900, 1904), available online at http://books.google.com. Further calendars of state papers I cite include *CSP Ireland* (Elizabeth) and *CSP Domestic* (Elizabeth, James), online at http://books.google.com. Additional archival sources include, in Florence, the Archivio di Stato di Firenze; at the British Library (London), *Stowe* manuscripts 168–171; at Hatfield House, the Cecil Papers, calendared by British History Online as the *Calendar of the Cecil Papers in Hatfield House* and accessible in a handsomely sophisticated online archive at https://about.proquest.com/en/products-services/cecil_papers/.

Wotton's contemporary biographer is Izaak Walton. 'The Life of Sir Henry Wotton' is published in *Reliquiæ Wottonianæ* (1685), available digitally through *Early English Books Online* (*EEBO*). Walton is quoted throughout from the 'Life'. Logan Pearsall Smith's impressive two-volume *The Life and Letters of Sir Henry*

Wotton (1907) remains the fullest cradle-to-grave biography and the starting point for any research on the English ambassador. Necessarily, however, Pearsall Smith publishes only extracts of most 'letters', doesn't distinguish between 'letters' and 'dispatches', and gives only the barest mention in footnotes of Wotton's audiences in the Collegio. Thus, he notices only half of the diplomat's life. Otherwise, Wotton biography is thin. See A.J. Loomie's compact life in the *Dictionary of National Biography* (now online) and Gerald Curzon's entertaining but uneven partial view in *Wotton and his Worlds: Spying, Science and Venetian Intrigues* (2003).

Indispensable sources on early modern diplomacy are Alberico Gentili, *De legationibus, libri tres* (1585; ed. E. Nys, tr. G.J. Laing, 1924); Jean Hotman, *The Ambassador* (1603, available through *EEBO*); Torquato Tasso, *Il Messagiero* (1582); Garrett Mattingly, *Renaissance Diplomacy* (1955); Luigi Firpo's edited volumes, *Relazioni di ambasciatori veneti al Senato* (1975–96); and Filippo de Vivo's, 'Archives of Speech: Recording Diplomatic Negotiation in Late Medieval and Early Modern Italy', *European History Quarterly* 46:3 (2016), 519–544. See also Timothy Hampton, *Fictions of Embassy: Literature and Diplomacy in Early Modern Europe* (2009); Michael Mallett, 'Ambassadors and their Audiences in Renaissance Italy', *Renaissance Studies* 8 (1994), 229–243; Monica Azzonlini and Isabella Lazzarini, *Italian Renaissance Diplomacy: A Sourcebook* (2017); and, in Robyn Adams and Rosanna Cox (eds), *Diplomacy and Early Modern Culture* (2011), Joanna Craigwood, 'Sidney, Gentili, and the Poetics of Embassy'.

On 'archive fever' and biography see Carolyn Steedman, *Dust* (2001); Peter France and William St Clair (eds), *Mapping Lives: The Uses of Biography* (2002); Allan Pritchard, *English Biography in the Seventeenth Century* (2005); Kevin Sharpe and Steven Zwicker, *Writing Lives: Biography and Textuality, Identity and Representation in Early Modern England* (2008); and Hermione Lee, *Body Parts* (2005).

Several dictionaries, accessible online, have been my constant companions: *Dictionary of National Biography* (*ODNB*); *Dizionario biografico degli Italiani*; Giuseppe Boerio, *Dizionario del Dialetto Veneziano* (1829); Fabio Mutinelli, *Lessico Veneto* (1852); and Gasparo Patriarchi, *Vocaborlario Veneziano e Padovano* (1775).

Early modern printed books can be accessed through *EEBO*.

Shakespeare is quoted from single-play editions in Arden, series two and three.

Prologue

For Wotton's 'entrata' and first audience see ASV *Ceremoniali* III and *Coll. Esposizioni Principi* XIV. For recent attempts to restore diplomatic relations see *CSPV* 2 November 1596, 14 February 1598, October 1601. The description of the Palazzo Ducale is my own. On Sansovino, see Deborah Howard, *Jacopo Sansovino: Architecture and Patronage in Renaissance Venice* (1975). For Cecil's dim view see TNA SP99.2.

Chapter 1

For Wotton's letter see TNA SP99.2. His *Elements* and *Philosophical Survey* appears in *Reliquiæ Wottonianæ* (1685). For Cecil's biography see Alan Haynes Robert, *Robert Cecil Earl of Salisbury 1563–1612* (1989) and the long-overdue (but misleadingly titled) *All His Spies: The Secret World of Robert Cecil* (2004) by Stephen Alford (which makes no mention of Harry Wotton). For Wotton at Bocton Malherbe see Izaak Walton, 'The Life of Sir Henry Wotton'; E. Eland (ed.), *Thomas Wotton's Letter Book 1574–1586* (1960); entries in *ODNB*; and Elizabeth Goldring et al. (eds), *John Nichols's The Progresses and Public Processions of Queen Elizabeth: A New Edition of the Early Modern Sources, Vol 2: 1572–1578* (2014). The queen's dress is documented in Janet Arnold's *Queen Elizabeth's Wardrobe Unlock'd* (1988). On bureaucratic administrations see Steve Hindle quoted by Norman Jones in *Governing by Virtue: Lord Burghley and the Management of Elizabethan England* (2015) and Diarmaid MacCulloch, *Thomas Cromwell: A Life* (2018). Mulcaster's *Positions* is accessible on *EEBO*. The history of Winchester College is given by Geoffrey Day in an unpublished study, 'Wykehamical Foundations' and by Sheila Himsworth in *Winchester College* (1976). For pedagogy see Desiderius Erasmus, 'On the Method of Study', 'On Education for Children', 'On Good Manners for Boys' and 'On the Writing of Letters' in vols 24 (1978) and 25 (1985) of the *Collected Works of Erasmus* (general editor, J.K. Soward). See also Thomas Elyot, *The boke named the Governor* (1537); Roger Ascham, *The Scholemaster* (1570); and John Brinsley, *Ludus Literarius* (1612) and *A Consolation for our Grammar Schools* (1622), all on *EEBO*. See, too, T.W. Baldwin, *William Shakspere's small Latine & less Greeke* (1944); Carol Chillington Rutter, 'Shakespeare in School', in Paul Edmondson and Stanley Wells (eds), *Shakespeare Beyond Doubt* (2013); M.H. Curtis, 'Education and Apprenticeship', *Shakespeare Survey* 17 (1964); and Lynn Enterline, *Shakespeare's Schoolroom: Rhetoric, Discipline, Emotion* (2012), which, failing to take account of Erasmus et al., is overly influenced by Jesuit-inspired accounts of the classroom as a 'disciplinary setting' where 'disciplinary scene[s]' of 'flogging' were played out on a daily basis. To see English pedagogy fitting into a pan-European scheme see Paul Grendler, *Schooling in Renaissance Italy: Literacy and Learning, 1300–1600* (1989). Wotton's letters to his brother appear in Logan Pearsall Smith, *The Life and Letters of Sir Henry Wotton* (1907). Scaramelli's reports are filed in ASV *Dispacci*. Extracts appear in *CSPV*. On letter-writing see Lynne Magnusson, *Shakespeare and Social Dialogue* (1999) and James Daybell, *The Material Letter in Early Modern England: Manuscript Letters and the Culture and Practices of Letter-Writing 1512–1635* (2012). Robert Cecil refers to his letter in SP99.5 Part 1.

Chapter 2

James McConica (ed.) informs Wotton's likely life at Oxford in Vol. 3, *The Collegiate University*, of *The History of Oxford* (1986) and Peter Mack (ed.) deals comprehensively with the syllabus in *Renaissance Rhetoric* (1994), where Brian Vickers contributes 'Some Reflections on the Rhetoric Textbook'. See Mack, too, in *Elizabethan Rhetoric: Theory and Practice* (2002). For Marlowe, see *ODNB*, and for the 1604 edition of Marlowe's *Dr Faustus* see *EEBO*; for Donne, see Herbert Grierson, *The Poems of John Donne: 2 Vols.* (1912); Thomas Docherty, *John Donne Undone* (1981); John Carey, *John Donne: Life, Mind and Art* (1981); and Katherine Rundell, *Super-infinite: The Transformations of John Donne* (2022). 'Mr Smith' can be found in TNA SP.12. Michael Riordan, Archivist, St. John's and The Queen's Colleges, Oxford, confirms academic dress in the 1590s (personal communication). On 'youth's dross' see Walton's 'On a Portrait of Donne taken in his eighteenth year' (1635), available from Project Gutenberg (2021). Tasso's *Liberata* is quoted from R[ichard] C[arew]'s Italian edition, 1594, accessible on *EEBO*, and Edward Fairfax's translation (1600), online at www.gutenberg.org (accessed 30 August 2021). Scipione Gentili's *Annotationi* (1586) and Alberico Gentili's *De iure belli* are available on *EEBO*. For Rainoldes v. Gentili see Rainoldes in *ODNB* and 'The overthrow of stage playes' (1629) on *EEBO*; John Binns edits and translates 'Alberico Gentili in Defense of Poetry and Acting', *Studies in the Renaissance* 19 (1972). On the 'Optique Question' see Jacques Guillemeau, *A Worthy Treatise of the eyes* (n.d.) and Helkiah Crooke, *Mikrokosmographia* Book 8 (1615) on *EEBO*. *De legationibus* (1585) is accessible on *EEBO*; a modern translation by G.J. Laing is edited by Ernest Nys (1924). See, too, Richard Langhorne, 'Alberico Gentili on Diplomacy', *The Hague Journal of Diplomacy* 4 (2009). For Essex at Cambridge see Appendix D in Vol. II of Walter

Bourchier Devereux's *Lives and Letters of the Devereux Earls of Essex* (2005 facsimile edition). Cogan's *Haven* (1589) is available on *EEBO*.

Chapter 3

Garrett Mattingly's *The Defeat of the Spanish Armada* (1959) remains the classic telling of this history. See, too, Geoffrey Parker's *The Grand Strategy of Philip II* (1998) and essays in *God's Obvious Design*, edited by P. Gallagher and D.W. Cruickshank (1988), including Francisco de Cuéllar's eye-witness account. William Camden's *Annales* (1625, accessible on *EEBO*) and John Stow's *The Annales of England* (1601) provide additional contemporary accounts. On beacons see Francesco Gradenigo's account, visiting England, November 1596, *CSPV* IX. 'Dancing and leaping' is from Stow, *Annales*. On 'slippery youth' see Roger Ascham, *The Scholemaster* (1570) on *EEBO*, and Bruce Smith, *Shakespeare and Masculinity* (2000). Essex's instructions are transcribed by Paul Hammer in 'Essex and Europe: Evidence from Confidential Instructions by the Earl of Essex, 1595–6', *English Historical Review* CXI:441 (1996). See also Essex's advice to the earl of Rutland in Devereux, *Lives and Letters*. Harry's letters to Edward (whose biography appears in *ODNB*) are published in Pearsall Smith, *Life and Letters*. On travel licences see John Ghazvinian, *'A certain tickling humour': English Travellers, 1560–1660* (unpublished D.Phil, Oxford, 2003). The travel writers I depend on most heavily are Fynes Moryson, his four volumes of *An Itinerary: containing his ten yeeres travell* ... (1617), rpt. Glasgow (1907), shortened to *Itineraries*, and Thomas Coryat, *Coryats crudities* (1611; facsimile rpt., 1978), shortened to *Crudities*. Elyot, Ascham, Hakluyt and Sidney are all accessible on *EEBO*, as are Palmer's *Essay* (1606) and Florio's *Florio his firste fruites* (1578). Daybell describes the postal service in *The Material Letter*. On the cultural exchange rate see G.K. Hunter, 'Elizabethans and Foreigners', *Shakespeare Survey* 17 (1964). See also John Stoye, *English Travellers Abroad 1604–1667* (1952); Sara Warneke, *Images of the Educational Traveller in Early Modern England* (1995); and Natalya Din Kariuki, *Gifted Travellers: Rhetorical Invention in Seventeenth Century Travel Writing* (unpublished D.Phil, Oxford, 2018). On 'return', see John Gallagher, 'The Italian London of John North: Cultural Contact and Linguistic Encounter in Early Modern England', *Renaissance Quarterly* 70 (2017).

Chapter 4

Harry's letters to Edward are published in Pearsall Smith, *Life and Letters*. For Moryson, see *Itineraries*, 'Of Travelling in General' and 'Precepts for Travellers'. Harry's moves through London can be followed on the brilliant interactive *Agas Map of London*, digitally at uvic.ca/edition/7.0/map.htm (accessed 20 July 2021) and across John Stow, *A Survey of London* (1598, 1603) online by Project Gutenberg (2013). See, too, William Harrison, *The Description of England* (1577), available on *EEBO*; Adrian Procter and Robert Taylor (eds), *The A to Z of Elizabethan London* (1979); and Peter Ackroyd, *London: The Biography* (2001). On currants see Maria Fusaro, *L'uva passa: una guerra commerciale tra Venezia e l'Inghilterra 1540–1640* (1997). Katherine Duncan-Jones writes Sidney's biography – and that of his nameless horses – in *Philip Sidney* (1991). For Erasmus see 'On the Writing of Letters', in *Collected Works*. The woodcut of Heidelberg University is Sebastian Münster's in *Cosmographia universalis* (1550). Coryat in *Crudities* describes Frankfurt Mart. On the Turkish threat in Europe see Daniel Vitkus, *Turning Turk: English Theatre and the Multicultural Mediterranean, 1570–1630* (2003) and Christopher de Bellaigue, *The Lion House* (2022). On Copernicus and Melanchthon see Patrick Ferry, 'The Guiding Lights of the University of Wittenberg and the Emergence of Copernican Astronomy', *Concordia Theological Quarterly* 57:4 (1993). For Zouche, see *ODNB* and letters published in Wotton, *Reliquiæ Wottonianæ*. On 'intelligence', 'information' and 'spying' see Hammer, 'Essex in Europe' and Paul Hammer, *The Polarisation of Elizabethan Politics: The Political Career of Robert Devereux* (1999), Stephen Alford's *The Watchers: A Secret History of the Reign of Elizabeth I* (2012) and Ioanna Iordanou's *Venice's Secret Service: Organizing Intelligence in the Renaissance* (2019). Harry's 'discourse of my own' is, I will argue elsewhere, *The State of Christendom* (1679). For another view of its authorship see Alexandra Gajda, '*The State of Christendom*: History, Political Thought and the Essex Circle', *Historical Research* 8 (2008).

Chapter 5

For Harry's travels through Europe see Coryat, *Crudities* and Moryson, 'The Situation of Italy'; 'Of my journey from Padvoa to Venice'; 'Comments upon Venice'; 'Of my journey to Vicenza …'; and 'Of the Fit Meanes to Travell', in *Itineraries*. On Venice see Vaughan Hart and Peter Hicks, *Sansovino's Venice: A Translation of Francesco Tatti da Sansovino's Guidebook to Venice of 1561* (2017); Patricia Labalme and Laura Sanguineti (eds) and Linda Carroll (tr.), *Venice: Città*

Excelentissima: Selections from the Renaissance Diaries of Marin Sanudo (2008); Robert Davis and Garry Marvin, *Venice, the Tourist Maze* (2004); and Peter Ackroyd, *Venice: Pure City* (2010). Filippo de Vivo describes the *broglio* in 'Walking in Sixteenth-Century Venice', *I Tatti Studies in the Italian Renaissance* 19:1 (2016). Paul Botley translates Wotton to Blotius (personal communication). Harry's's poem and letters to Zouche appear in *Reliquiæ Wottonianæ*; his 'table talk' in Pearsall Smith, *Life and Letters*. On the University at Padua and its students see Jonathan Woolfson, 'Padua and English Students Revisited', *Renaissance Studies* 27:4 (2013). On behaviour in Rome, see Moryson, 'Precepts for Travellers', in *Itineraries*. The earl's unrivalled biographer and interpreter is Hammer in *The Polarisation of Elizabethan Politics*. I follow his revisionist account that shifts Essex's reputation: Essex was no 'political butterfly' but a heavyweight intellectual and political thinker. Bacon's letter is conserved in Lambeth Palace Library. Paul Botley is Casaubon's editor and writes of him in *Richard 'Dutch' Thomson, c. 1569–1613* (2016).

Chapter 6

Harry writes 'The Parallel Life of Robert Devereux, Earl of Essex, and George Villiers, Duke of Buckingham' in *Reliquiæ Wottonianæ*. On contemporary accounts of these histories see Camden, *Annales*; and Stow, *A Survey* and *Annales of England*. For Henslowe see R.A. Foakes and R.T. Rickert (eds), *Henslowe's Diary* (1960) and for Burghley, Alford, *Burghley* (2008). For biographies of guards old and new see *ODNB* and also Arthur Kinney, *Titled Elizabethans: A Directory of Elizabethan State and Church Officers and Knights, with Peers of England, Scotland and Ireland 1558–1603* (1973). Harry's manuscript letter is filed in Hatfield House/Cecil Papers online and given in Pearsall Smith, *Life and Letters*. Lives of the Bacon brothers appear in *ODNB* and in Lisa Jardine and Alan Stewart, *Hostage to Fortune: The Troubled Life of Francis Bacon* (1999). For Essex, see Hammer, *Polarisation*; *ODNB*; and Devereux, *Lives and Letters*. On the household see Annaliese Connolly and Lisa Hopkins (eds), *Essex: The Cultural Impact of an Elizabethan Courtier* (2013); and on the secretariat, *ODNB* and Hammer in *Polarisation* and in 'The Uses of Scholarship: The Secretariat of Robert Devereux, Second Earl of Essex, c. 1585–1605', *English Historical Review* 109:430 (1994). Devereux, *Lives and Letters*, gives Reynolds's letter to Bacon. Alan Smith writes of Burghley's secretary in *Servant of the Cecils: The Life of Sir Michael Hickes* (1977). For the deferential letter, see William Philippes writing to William Davison in Jardine and Stewart, *Hostage*. Wilson is quoted in Smith, *Servant*. Cecil to Queen Anna is reproduced in Rayne Allison, *A Monarchy of Letters: Royal Correspondence and English Diplomacy in the Reign of Elizabeth I* (2012). Angel Day's *The English Secretorie* (1599) is accessible on *EEBO*.

Chapter 7

Lists, letters exchanged between Essex, Cecil, the Privy Council and others, and accounts of 'sundry matters' (including 'Instructions ... to be observed') that document the mobilisation for Cadiz and Wotton's hand in these affairs are conserved in SP12. See, too, Devereux, *Lives and Letters*. The satirical accounts are given by two Spaniards, Antonio de Guevara, *Arte del marear* (1539), where the pun on 'marear' meaning 'to navigate' and 'to vomit' should be noted, translated in 1578 as 'The Art of Navigation' by Edward Hellowes, accessible on *EEBO*; and Eugenio de Salazar, 'Letter' (unpublished, transcript supplied by Bernard Klein). For Wotton to Cecil and Essex to Cecil and to Burghley see Hatfield/Cecil Papers. For *Due Repulse* see Brian Lavery, *The Ship of the Line*, 2 vols (1983) and Julian Stafford Corbett, *The Successors of Drake* (1916), who recounts the battle of Cadiz. (The phrase 'noble stupidity' is Corbett's.) See also Devereux (Essex to Burghley) and SP12 (lists). 'Spoils' are documented in Hatfield/Cecil papers. For Essex to Elizabeth see Hatfield/Cecil papers.

Chapter 8

Essex's departure is recounted by Stow in *Annales*. His Irish papers are conserved in TNA SP63; in Hatfield/Cecil papers; published in Devereux, *Lives and Letters*; and calendared in *CSP Ireland*. His secretaries' letters appear in Hatfield/Cecil and TNA SP63. His departure to Ireland from London is recorded by Nichols in *Progresses*, Vol. 4. Corbett, *Successors of Drake*, recounts the Azores expedition. For arguments in the Privy Council, the earl's insolence and *An Apology of the Earl of Essex ... 1598* (1603) see *EEBO* and Devereux, *Lives and Letters*. Spenser's 'View' is accessible on *EEBO* and edited by Andrew Hadfield and Willy Maley in *A View of the State of Ireland* (1997). William Segar writes of *Honour, Military and Civil* (1602), accessible on *EEBO*. For contemporary accounts of Ireland and Tyrone, see Camden, *Annales* and Moryson, *Itineraries*. See, too, James Shapiro, *1599: A Year in the Life of William Shakespeare* (2006); and (from the vast literature on Ireland), Paul Hammer, '"Base Rogues" and "Gentlemen of Quality": The Earl of Essex's Knights and Royal Displeasure', in Brendan Kane and Valerie McGowan-Doyle (eds), *Elizabethan I and Ireland* (2014);

James O'Neill, 'Irish Savage and English Butcher', in Matthew Woodcock and Cian O'Mahony (eds), *Early Modern Military Identities, 1560–1639* (2019); Brendan Bradshaw, Andrew Hadfield and Willy Maley (eds), *Representing Ireland: Literature and the Origins of Conflict 1534–1660* (2019). For Essex's return see Devereux, *Lives and Letters*.

Chapter 9

Documents relevant to the 'rebellion', including Cecil's list, affidavits from Reynolds and Temple, the earl's confession and Cuffe's account to Cecil are calendared by British History Online in Vol. 11 of the *Calendar of the Cecil Papers in Hatfield House* and produced in the online Cecil archive, https://about.proquest.com/en/products-services/cecil_papers/, Vol. 83 (accessed 11 January 2021). On events leading up to the 'rebellion' see Devereux, *Lives and Letters*. Witless 'hopes' quotes John Chamberlain in N.E. McClure, *The Letters of John Chamberlain* (1939). Harrington on Essex and Essex to Cuffe are reported in Devereux, *Lives and Letters*. For Cuffe on the scaffold see *ODNB*. Walton's account of Wotton's involvement appears in the 'Life', *Reliquiæ*. See also Paul Hammer, 'Shakespeare's *Richard II*, the Play of 7 February 1601, and the Essex Rising', *Shakespeare Quarterly* 59:1 (2008). Wotton's Florence letters are conserved in the Archivio di Stato di Firenze, *Mediceo del Principato* 903. 'Baldi's' story is told by Walton, 'Life'. Contemporary description of King James appears in Anthony Weldon, *The Court and Character of King James I* (1651), accessible on *EEBO*, and elaborated in Lucy Hughes-Hallett, *The Scapegoat: The Brilliant Brief Life of the Duke of Buckingham* (2025).

Chapter 10

Wotton's audiences are conserved in ASV *Coll. Esposizioni Principi* XIV and XV; his London dispatches (and Cecil's to Venice) in TNA SP99.2. Both are calendared in *CSPV* X. On the government of the Republic see Gasparo Contarini, *The Commonwealth and Government of Venice*, tr. Lewis Lewkenor (1599), accessible on *EEBO*; Francesco Sansovino, *Venetia città nobilissima e singolare, descritta in XIII libri*, in Venetia appresso Steffano Curti (1663); and Marin Sanudo, *La Città di Venetia (1493–1530)*, edited by Angela Caracciolo Aricò (1980). See, too, William Bouwsma, *Venice and the Defense of Republican Liberty* (1968); Fredric Lane, *Venice: A Maritime Republic* (1973); entries in David Chambers and Brian Pullan (eds), *Venice: A Documentary History 1450–1630* (1992); and, most significantly, Filippo de Vivo's magisterial *Information & Communication in Venice: Rethinking Early Modern Politics* (2007), together with a number of important essays: 'Ordering the Archive in Early Modern Venice (1400–1650)', *Archival Science* 10 (2010); 'Heart of the State, Site of Tension', *Annales: Histoire, Sciences Sociales* (2013); and 'Archives of Speech: Recording Diplomatic Negotiation in Late Medieval and Early Modern Italy', *European History Quarterly* 46:3 (2016). For the 'myth' see David MacPherson, *Shakespeare, Jonson and the Myth of Venice* (1990). Scaramelli's dispatches from England 1603–1604 that document regime change are conserved in ASV *Senato, Dispacci, Dispacci degli ambasciatori e residenti, Inghilterra*, Filze, Pezzo 2 and in extracts in *CSPV* IX and X; his biography appears in *Dizionario biografico degli Italiani*. See, too, Wotton's letter to Cecil of May 1604, SP99.2, and Carol Chillington Rutter, '"Hear the Ambassadors!": Marking Shakespeare's Venice Connection', *Shakespeare Survey* 66 (2013). On the challenge of Protestantism see Eamon Duffy, *The Stripping of the Altars: Traditional Religion in England 1400–c.1580* (1992); Diarmaid MacCulloch, *Reformation: Europe's House Divided 1490–1700* (2003); and Diego Pirillo, *The Refugee-Diplomat: Venice, England, and the Reformation* (2018). On commercial Venice see Maria Fusaro, *Political Economies of Empire in the Early Modern Mediterranean* (2015); P.L. Cottrell and D.H. Aldcroft (eds), *Shipping, Trade and Commerce* (1981); extracts in Chambers and Pullan, *Venice*; and Alberto Teneti, *Piracy and the Decline of Venice 1580–1616* (1967).

Chapter 11

For Wotton's audiences see ASV *Coll. Esposizioni Principi* XIV and XV; for his London dispatches, TNA SP99.2 and SP99.3. For Wotton's exchange with Possevino, see SP99.2. On the address of the English embassy, correcting Pearsall Smith in *Life and Letters* (and all who quote him), see Carol Chillington Rutter, '2967 Cannaregio: The Only (Official) Protestant Address in Venice', forthcoming in Eloise Davies and Alana Mailes (eds), *Stuart Serenissima*. My description of 2967 depends on personal observation, conducted on a tour of the palazzo by the head of the Borgo family, resident there for five generations, supported by Patricia Fortini Brown, 'The Venetian Casa', in Marta Ajmar-Wollheim and Flora Dennis (eds), *At Home in Renaissance Italy* (2006). On the household see Pearsall Smith, *Life and Letters*, and derivative work that repeats him, such as Daniel McReynolds, 'Lying Abroad for the Good of his Country', in Deborah Howard and Henrietta McBurney (eds), *The Image of Venice: Fialetti's View and Sir Henry Wotton* (2014). Mark Netzloff's 'The Ambassador's Household: Sir Henry Wotton, Domesticity, and Diplomatic Writing', in

Robyn Adams and Rosanna Cox (eds), *Diplomacy and Early Modern Culture* (2011) is finally unreliable, marred by errors of fact (including ignorance of Venetian law) and interpretation (the most egregious, sensationalising the embassy into a nest of spies even as it's 'queered' into a nest of sodomites). Comments on a 'private chapel' in the embassy correct Pirillo in *The Refugee-Diplomat*. On the embassy's finances see Frederick Devon, *Issues of the Exchequer* (1836) and on rents in the Ghetto see the *Decree of the Senate* 1516. The inventory appears in TNA SP99.6. For the *famiglia* see entries in *ODNB*. On *confidenti* see ASV *Osservationi Inquisitori di Stato*, Busta 606; de Vivo, *Information and Communication* (2007), 'Walking in Sixteenth-Century Venice' and 'Pharmacies as Centres of Communication in Early Modern Venice', *Renaissance Studies* 21:4 (2007). See, too, Liz Horodowich, 'The Gossiping Tongue: Oral Networks, Public Life and Political Culture in Early Modern Venice', *Renaissance Studies* 19 (2005). For the 'catalogo' of 'donne honeste' see Hannah Johnston, 'A Sexual Tour of Venice: Mapping a Sixteenth-Century Catalogue of Courtesans' online at https://historyjournal.org.uk/2022/01/05 (accessed 17 March 2023). Donne can be accessed online.

Chapter 12

On 'The Election of the New Duke of Venice' see *Reliquiæ* and ASV *Coll. Esposizioni Principi* XV. The course of the Interdict Crisis (and Wotton's involvement) progresses daily from December 1605 to April 1607 across his audiences in *Coll. Esposizioni Principi* XV, XVI and *Coll. Esposizioni Roma* X, XI (with occasional reference to *Roma Registro XV*). For Wotton to Cecil (and King James) and Cecil (and the king) to Wotton see SP99.3 and SP99.4. Dispatches from the Venetian ambassadors in London (Molin, Giustinian) to the Republic are calendared in *CSPV* X; Giustinian's *Dispacci* appear in ASV *Senato, Dispacci*, Pezzo 5. I quote from my transcriptions and translations; Pezzo 4, Molin's, is 'non consultabile', too fragile to handle. Ambassadors reporting from other capitals are calendared in *CSPV* X. See also letters to Edmondes in *Stowe* MSS 168–169 and Pearsall Smith, *Life and Letters*. On the gunpowder treason see *CSPV* X; *CSP Dom* (James) XVI; Chamberlain in McClure, *Letters*; and Antonia Fraser, *The Gunpowder Plot: Terror and Faith in 1605* (1996). The Interdict Crisis is dealt with masterfully in de Vivo, *Information and Communication*, where an extensive bibliography points to a vast territory of further reading. On the *Protesto* and its circulation see de Vivo. The Venetians as 'pantaloons' quotes Chamberlain in McClure, *Letters*. 'Transivimus Rubiconem' appears in the verbatim filza transcript of Wotton's audience. It was not copied into the registro. It was not, that is, made part of the permanent record of that audience.

Chapter 13

On the Woodward ambush see SP99.3. Cecil's excoriation appears in SP99.3/ff. 187–190; Wotton's audiences and Donà's reaction appear in *Coll. Esposizioni Roma* X. Giustinian is calendared in *CSPV* X; for his full *Dispacci* see ASV Senato, *Dispacci*, Pezzo 5. Canaye's discussion with Wotton appears in SP99.3/ff. 244–246v. For the end of the Interdict Crisis see SP99.4 and *Coll. Esposizioni Roma* XI.

Chapter 14

Wotton sends Donà's statement to London, TNA SP99.4. His audiences and dispatches documenting the end of the Interdict (including comments on the pope) are conserved in TNA SP99.4 and in *Coll. Esposizioni Roma* XI. For Spanish interventions see *CSPV* X. For Wotton's reputation see *Coll. Esposizioni Roma* XI and *Coll. Esposizioni Principi* XVI. His comment on Vitruvius is recorded in *Coll. Esposizioni Principi* XVI; he writes to King James as Ottavio Baldi on 'points … passed over' in SP99.4. Roos's progress (and Mole's fate) can be tracked across SP99.5 and *Coll. Esposizioni Principi* XVIII. See, too, *ODNB*. For Cranborne see SP99.5 Part 2 and SP99.6 and *Coll. Esposizioni Principi* XIX. For Harington see SP99.5 Part 2 and for his introduction in the Collegio as 'Arenton', *Coll. Esposizioni Principi* XVII. See, too, Harington's entry in *The History of Parliament*, www.historyofparliamentonline.org/volume/1604-1629/member/harington-sir-john-1592-1614 (accessed 16 October 2023). The report of the papal intelligencer can be found at SP99.5 f. 234. Cave's story is reported in SP99.4; Caesar's (and the weather's) in *Coll. Esposizioni Principi* XVI, *Coll. Esposizioni Roma* XI, SP99.5 and *Stowe* MS 169. Giustinian's reports to Venice on Dudley and de' Medici's designs are calendared in *CSPV* XI; Wotton and Rooke report extensively to Cecil and King James (Wotton writing as 'Baldi') throughout in SP99.4. See also *ODNB*. For Ward see *Coll. Esposizioni Principi* XVII, SP99.4, *CSPV* XI and *ODNB*. Wotton tracks Tyrone across SP99.4 and SP99.5 and reports him in *Coll. Esposizioni Principi* XVII. For Wotton's proposal to detain him see *Coll. Esposizioni Roma* XI. See, too, reports from ambassadors in England, France and Spain on Tyrone's progress across Europe in *CSPV* XI and *ODNB*. Cecil's 'confession' appears in SP99.5. For the arrests see *Coll.*

Esposizioni Principi XVIII. Coryat reports this cultural encounter in *Crudities*. For the kidnapped nuns see Wotton to Edmondes, *Stowe* MS 170 and Mary Laven, *Virgins of Venice: Enclosed Lives and Broken Vows in the Renaissance Convent* (2002).

Chapter 15

The 'war of the pen' is recounted in de Vivo, *Information & Communication*. For Wotton's dispatches, see SP99.3 and SP99.4; for Giustinian's, *Dispacci* filza 5 and *CSPV* XI. On Sarpi see de Vivo, who navigates the Servite's extensive bibliography in *Information & Communication*. See, too, *Dizionario biografico degli Italiani* and Jaska Kainulainen, *Paolo Sarpi: A Servant of God and State* (2014). Wotton's *Letter*, otherwise titled *A Declaration of the Variance betweene the Pope, and the Segniory of Venice* (1606), accessible on *EEBO*, was first identified as his work by de Vivo in 'Francia e Inghilterra di fronte all'Interdetto di Venezia' in *Paolo Sarpi* (Paris, 2010), 163–188. On the movement of books see Wotton to Cecil, SP99.4, *Coll. Esposizioni Principi* XVII and *Roma* XI. Meietti's story is told by de Vivo, *Information & Communication*. On books to 'scatter', see SP99.5. On Sarpi's portrait and assassination attempt, see SP99.4 and *CSPV* XI. The 'Oath of Allegiance' in Italian translation is sent to Venice from Giustinian, *Dispacci* filza 5; and to Wotton from Cecil, SP99.3. Wotton complains of Bellarmino in *Coll. Esposizioni Roma* IX. The nuncio's complaint about 'schismatical' preaching is reported in SP99.5. King James's *Apology* with its 'Premonition' is accessed on *EEBO*. First Giustinian then Correr tracks the progress of the 'King's Book' through *CSPV* XI. For the king's 'beagle' letter see SP99.5 Part 2. Wotton's dispatches across this period (and Cecil's to him) are conserved in SP99.5 Part 2 and SP99.6 (including reference to the 'mathematical professor'). His audiences are preserved in *Coll. Esposizioni Roma* XII. Wotton writes to Edmondes, assured that the book will be 'kissed in Venice' in *Stowe* MS 171. Wotton records the courier's nine-day gallop in SP99.5 and Correr in *CSPV* XI. On the assassination of Henri IV see SP99.6. Donne is quoted from 'An Anatomy of the World' (1611).

Chapter 16

Wotton's London dispatches for 1609 are filed as SP99.5 Part 2; for 1610, in SP99.6. All his audiences from January 1610 onwards are filed in *Coll. Esposizioni Principi* XVIII and XIX. Correr reports on Wotton in *CSPV* XI. On the drunken Greek captain episode, see *Coll. Esposizioni Principi* XVII. For Carleton see *ODNB*. His progress across Europe and letters to Wotton are filed in SP996.

For his exchanges with Chamberlain see McClure, *Letters* and Maurice Lee, *Dudley Carleton to John Chamberlain 1603–1624* (1972). On Fialetti and Wotton's map see Howard and McBurney (eds), *The Image of Venice*, which provides an excellent documentation of the restoration of the Eton map but is unreliable on Wotton's biography and diplomacy. Not noticing Wotton's implication in Interdict politics or his relationship with Possevino, it misreads the significance of the 'Jesuit church' and so (to my mind) is forced to produce a tangled account of the map's commissioning and how it came to Eton. The 'Inventory of goods left in the Ambassador's house after his departure', SP99.6, itemises furnishings in 'The painters chamber'. Was that painter Fialetti? Or one 'Bilford', whom Wotton, returned to England, thought 'better than Isaach [Isaac Oliver], the French painter in the Blackfriers' (quoted in Chamberlain, *Letters*)? The Carpan case is documented in *Consiglio di dieci, Deliberazioni, Criminali*, Registri, Pezzo 22.

Epilogue

For Wotton's career after 1611 see Walton, 'Life' in *Reliquiæ* (including his will and instructions for his tomb); *ODNB*; and Pearsall Smith, *Life and Letters*. Wotton recounts the Globe fire in a letter to Edmund Bacon. See *Reliquiæ*.

Index

N.B., italicised page numbers denote an illustration

Adige River 78
Adriatic, the 8, 85, 166, 170
Aesop 20, 39, 152
Alberti, Scipioni 105
All Souls College Oxford 110
   see also *individual colleges*
Alleyn, Edward 61, 103–4
Alps, the 77, 80, 149, 162, 188, 215
Altdorf 70–71
ambassador
   angels as original 6, 39
   freedom of speech 40
   French in Venice *see* Canaye, Philippe
   history 39
   qualities 38–39, 40–42
   Spanish in England *see* Mendoza, Bernardino de
   Spanish in Venice *see* Cardenas, Don Inigo de
   see also diplomacy: diplomatic immunity; embassy; Wotton, Henry
Anglo-Spanish peace
   and Robert Cecil 145
   and Elizabeth I's reign 132, 133
   and James VI/I 152, 235, 248
   Somerset House Conference 175
   treaty 167, 175, 211
Anna, queen of Scotland, later queen of England 113, 151, 198

Aristotle 31, 33, 39, 52
Armada, 'The Invincible' 43, 44–47, 48, 102, 233
Ascham, Roger 51, 52
astronomy and astrology 31, 70, 75, 87, 257
   see also Copernicus, Nicolaus; Galileo, Galilei

Babington, Anthony 61
Bacon, Anthony 94, 106, 111–12, 145
Bacon, Francis 94, 106
Bagnall, Henry 133
Baker, Matthew 121
Balbi, Nicolò 171–74
Banchieri, Adriano 78
Banister, John *see* medicine and anatomy
de' Barbari, Jacopo 265
Baronio, Cesare 245, 269
   Paraenesis ad rempublicam Venetam 240, 242
   see also Interdict Crisis: books and publishing
Basel 15, 48, 51, 60, 106
beacons 44, 46–47
   see also Armada, 'The Invincible'
Bedell, William 228, 246
Bellarmino, Roberto 93
   De Militia Ecclesiastica 202
   Risposta 240, 241
   'war of the quill' 249, 250

INDEX

Bellini, Battista 81, 193
Bergen 149
Bible, Old Testament 7, 38, 39
Blackwell, George 249
Blotius, Hugo 73, 75
Blount, Charles Eighth Baron Mountjoy 147
Blount, Christopher 115, 144, 146
Boccaccio 31
Bodley, Thomas 126
Bragadin, Marc Antonio 193, 214
Brahe, Tycho 124
Bremen 65
Brenner Pass 77, 149
Brenta canal 78, 193
Bristol 44, 137
Brochetta, Tommaso 231
broglio 83, 162, 187–88, 263, 265
Brown, Robert 103
Bruno, Giordano 257
Bryskett, Lodowick 64
Budapest 69
Bulmer, Bevis 103
Buoni, Baccio 105–6

Cadiz 5, 19, 23, 100, 145
   backlash 128–30, *129*
   mobilisation 120–24, *122*
   raid 125
   sack 125–27
Caesar 3, 20, 39, 40, 54, 102
Caesar, Julius, Chancellor of the Exchequer 230–32
Caesar, Julius (son) 230–32
Calais 15, 38, 46, 49, 57, 117, 119, 121, 149
Calbo, Antonio 187–88
calendar
   Gregorian 54, 183, 198, 223–24
   Julian 54, 183, 198
Cales *see* Cadiz
Cambridge *see individual colleges*
Camden, William 31, 45, 101–2, 104
Canaye, Philippe (French ambassador in Venice) 217–18, 200, 223, 268
Cannaregio *see* embassy
cannocchiale see telescope

Canterbury 15
Cardenas, Don Inigo de (Spanish ambassador in Venice), 8, 187, 223
Carew, George 146
Carleton, Anne 264, 265
Carleton, Dudley 263–65, 267, 269, 273
Carpaccio, Vittore 193
Carpan, Agustin 269
Carrara, Pietro, 'staffetta' 255
Casaubon, Isaac 95
de Castro, Francisco Ruiz count Lemos 216–17, 219, 221
Catholic League 45, 88
Catholicism 28, 35, 45, 48, 53, 61, 70, 88, 92–93, 105, 164, 185, 186, 200, 228
   in England, Wales and Scotland 164, 191–92, 227, 248
   versus Protestant burial 53, 229–30, 232
   see also Interdict Crisis; James VI/I: gunpowder plot; *popolani*: the Venetian State; Roman Curia
Cave, Richard 229–30
Cecil, Robert
   'entertainments' 192
   and earl of Essex 23, 27, 28, 107, 109, 117–20, 128–31, *130*, 142, 144–45, 146
   gunpowder plot 196
   and Henry Wotton 4, 13, 108, 117, *118*, 121, *122*, 152, 159, 161, 165, 172, 175, 183
   correspondence 23, 24–29, *26*, *29*, 184, 186, 189, 190, 191, 196, 198, 201, 203–4, 209, 210, 213–15, 217, 219, 220–21, 224, 226–27, 228, 229–30, 234, 236–37, 241, 246, 248, 254, 257, 258, 260, 262, 280–82
   proxy author of *Letter from Venice* 241, 243
   return to England 258, 261–63
   on Italians 4, 220

intelligence network 149, 238
Interdict Crisis 207, 211, 214–16, 241
'littil beagle' 13, 24, 255–56
manipulating state affairs 208–9, 214–15
secretary of state 4, 10, 13, 24, 112–13, 139, 144–45, 146, 161, 164, 173–74, 175, 183, 189, 207, 236, 238
traitor 28, 146, 236–38
see also Willis, Simon
Cecil, William lord Burghley 15–16, 56, 102, 104–5, 106–7, 109, 111, 112, 117, 128, 132, 133
see also Elizabeth I: government and governance; Privy Council
Chamberlain, John 145, 264, 265
Charles I, king of England 273
Cicero 3, 20, 21, 31, 39, 40, 41, 55, 69, 152, 174
Cima, Giovanni Battista da Conegliano 193
Ciotti, Giovanni Battista, bookseller 254
cittadini 28, 209
Clifford, Henry 139
Clorinda (in *La Gerusalemme liberata*) 34–35, 36
clothing 75, 79, 90–91, 150
ambassador attire 5, 8, 40, 41, 225
dogal and senatorial attire 5, 6, 8, 157
intelligencer attire 90–91, 150
professional attire 60, 113
student attire 32–33, 65
Cobham, Henry Brooke eighth lord 146
Cogan, Henry 182
Cogan, Thomas, *The Haven of Health* 43, 192
Coleraine 236
Committee of Sixteen 45
confidenti see Calbo, Antonio; spies and spying
Consiglieri 8, 9
Constable, William 143, 144

Constantinople 69, 83, 166
Contarini, Piero 223
Copernicus, Nicolaus 31, 70, 257
see also astronomy and astrology
Cordal, shipowner 263
Cork 69
Cornwall 44, 69
Corpus Christi, Cambridge 31, 32
see also individual colleges
Correr, Marc' Antonio 223, 250, 251, 252, 255, 258, 264, 269
Coryat, Thomas 54, 56, 58, 66, 77, 78, 80, 81, 86, 87, 238, 268
see also travel: advice to travellers *and* travel writing
Court 16, 24, 49, 55, 56, 68, 91, 94, 110, 117, 120, 128, 132–33, 134, 145, 147, 148, 151, 192, 197, 198, 201, 208, 233, 234, 243, 251, 264
courtesans
Rome 88–89
Venice 79, 86, 87, 193
cortigiana di lume 86–87
cortigiane oneste 86, 193
see also Franco, Veronica
Cranborne, Robert Cecil lord 226–27, 263, 264
Cremona 264
Croce, Giovanni 81
Croft, James 104
Cuffe, Henry
childhood and education 109–10
secretary to earl of Essex 111, 114
arrest and execution 144, 146
on campaigns 121, 132, 133, 137, 139, 142–43
see also Essex, earl of: secretariat

Dante, *Inferno* 125
Danvers, Charles 115, 144, 146, 149
Danvers Henry 149
Davies, John 144
Day, Angel, *The English Secretorie* 113–14
Derby, Henry Stanley fourth earl of 104
Derby, Henry Stanley fifth earl of 104
Derry 236

INDEX

Dethick, Humphry 106
Devon 69
diplomacy 1, 2, 3, 7–9, 22, 35, 170, 175, 190, 229
  diplomatic immunity 38, 39–40, 164, 183, 245, 252
  history 38, 39
  theory 38
  training in 31–32, 38–39, 439–41
  'undiplomatic diplomacy' 162–63
  Wotton's style of 9–10, 162–63 174, 184, 206, 216, 224, 236, 242, 254–55, 268
  see also ambassador; embassy
Donà, Leonardo, Doge 90, *197*, 233
  election of 196–97, 198–99
    familiarity and kindness 256–57, 260, 268
    resignation as English ambassador 266–67
    Interdict Crisis 199, 201, 202, 204–6, 210, 218–19, 220, 222, 223, 240, 242
    Venetian ambassador to Rome 89–90, 235
    and Henry Wotton 3, *158*, 216, 219, 223–24, 242, 245, 253–54, 263, 265
  see also Wotton, Henry: esposizioni with doge and Collegio
Donne, John 182, 257
  Cadiz 120
  Egerton's secretary 145
  portrait 32
  Wotton's life-long friend 31, 33, 193–94
Dotto, Antonio 162, 184, 269
Dover 23, 38, 44, 46, 49, 55, 57, 117–19
Drake, Francis, 'il Draco' 46, 101, 107, 166
Dudley, Robert supposed earl of Leicester 232–33
Dunfermline 150

Edinburgh 2, 13, 149
education *see* grammar school
Edward VI, king 2, 15

Egerton, Thomas 133, 144–45
Elizabeth, princess 271
Elizabeth I, queen of England 2, 35, 38, 45, 47, 56, 117, 120, 152, 203, 215, 232, 233, 237, 260
  assassination plots 46, 61
  and Robert Cecil 28, 215
  and earl of Essex *129*, 133, 138–42, 143, 144–45
  government and governing 48, 101, 102, 104, 107, 117, 119, 120, 128, 138–39, 142, 166
  and James VI/I's succession 13, 146, 152
  and Henry Wotton's family 15, 16
  see also Armada, 'The Invincible'; Court; Essex, earl of: execution *and* rebellion; Irish campaign; Mary, queen of Scots; Mendoza, Bernardino de; Privy Council
Elyot, Thomas 51
embassy
  English in Brussels 183, 186
  English in Madrid 183, 186, 259
  English in Paris 183, 186, 189, 259
  English in Venice
    Cannaregio, English embassy 4, 40, 163, 164, 165, 171–72, 175, *178*, 179–81, 183, 185 186, 190, 193, 210, 219, 223, 224, 226, 227, 228, 232 245, 254
    interior 171, 176, 179–81, 264–65, 267
    meeting place 238, 246
    and successor Carleton 264–65, 267
    see also Luzzati, Isaac 'Ebreo'
    see also Venice, churches: San Girolamo
  entertainment 22, 192–93
  finances 181–82, 187
  protocols and immunities 39, 40, 164, 183, 191, 245
  religious observance 165, 180, 186

staff 6, 86, 165 178, 182, 186–190, 191, 194
English in Vienna 48
French in Venice 179
Spanish in Venice 179
Venetian in London 260
see also Wotton, Henry: *famiglia*; spies and spying
Emo, Girolamo 105
English Book of Common Prayer 17, 40, 180
Erasmus, Desiderius 15, 20, 21, 24–25, 27, 39, 52, 65, 152
Essex, Robert Devereux, earl of
  appointed lord lieutenant of Ireland 132
  Azores voyage 132
  beard of Cadiz 5, 33, *100*, 105, 128, 271
  brother, Walter 102
  Cadiz 5, 10, 19, 23, *100*, 116, 121–28, *122*, *129*, 130–31, 132, 134, 136, 137, 144, 145, 154, 166, 176, 180, 194
  Calais 117
  campaigning with earl of Leicester 107
  childhood 106
  employs Henry Wotton 106
  execution 23, 25, 28–29, 144, 146, 148, 238
  foreign secretary 107–8, 109
  intelligencer to the Crown 72, 94, 106, 109
  Knight of the Garter 107
  marriage 49, 107
  Master of the Horse 107
  Privy Council 105, 107, 117, 131, 143
  Portugal 101, 110
  rebellion 13, 23, 144–45
  returns to London 142–43
  secretariat 99, 109–11, 123, 126, 128, 136, 142, 146
    see also Cuffe, Henry; Reynolds, Edward; Temple, William; Wotton, Henry
  travel 52
  university 43, 106

  writes to Robert Cecil 117–20, *118*, 128, 139
  writes to Elizabeth I 128–30, *129*, 140–42
  writes to Privy Council 133–34, 138–39
  see also see also Irish campaign; Wotton, Henry: and earl of Essex
Eton College 14, 15, 109, 265, 272, 273
  see also Wotton, Henry: Provost at Eton College

Falmouth 44, 101, 110
farmacie 85, 187, 188
  Ercole d'Oro 187
  Testa d'Oro 85, 187
  triaca 85, 150
Farol 126
fashion see clothing
Felipe II, king of Spain 46, 101, 115, 121, 133
Felipe III, king of Spain 202–3, 223, 235
Fenton, John 182
Fialetti, Odoardo
  'Doge Leonardo Donato Giving Audience to Sir Henry Wotton' *158*, 265
  'View' of Venice 265–66
Finetti, Giovanni 171–72, 173, 174
Fletcher, Nathaniel 182, 186
Flight of the Earls see earl of Tyrone
Florence 225, 228
  and Robert Dudley
  Dudley, Robert 232–33
  families of 89, 269
  intelligencers 238
  Wotton in the city 64, 91, 93–94, 104, 105–6, 110, 147–49, 152
Florio, John 55, 56, 58, 168
Folkestone 44, 46
Ford, Nicholas 182
France 15, 23, 27, 45, 46, 49, 51, 56, 101
  siege of Rouen 102, 110
  see also Henri III; Interdict Crisis; Paris

Franco, Veronica *see* courtesans: Venice: cortigiane oneste
Frankfurt 54, 65, 66, 95, 281
Frankfurt Mart 95, 281
Fuentes, Pedro Enriquez de Acevedo count of 189–90, 218, 269
Fulgenzio, Manfredi 218, 262, 263
Fulgenzio, Micanzio 228–29, 252, 267
  see also Protestant revolution, hopes of; Wotton, Henry
Fusina 78

Gabrieli, Andrea 81
Gabrieli, Giovanni 81
Galileo, Galilei 37, 70, 87, 198, 257, 262, 269
  see also astronomy and astrology
Garnet, Henry (Father, Padre Darcio) 196, 200, 204, 240
  see also gunpowder plot; Jesuits
Geneva 64, 70, 95, 104, 106, 119, 154
Gentili, Alberico 35–43, 48, 55, 56, 90, 152, 183, 243, 256
  De iure belli 36
  De legationibus libri tres 38–39, 40, 42, 57, 184, 225
Gentili, Scipione 35
  Annotationi to *La Gerusalemme liberata* 35–36
  '*pious arms*' 36
Germany 35, 51, 56, 63, 65, 106, 149, 206, 214
Gheeraerts, Marcus 181
giovani 7, 177
Giustinian, Lorenzo 188
Giustinian, Zorzi 175, 195, 197–98, 199, 223, 248
  Interdict Crisis 207–8, 210, 212, 214, 215, 251
  and Robert Cecil 207, 208, 211, 212, 214, 215, 216, 241, 243
  and James VI/I 207–8, 210–11, 214, 215, 248, 249, 251
Globe playhouse, London Southwark 1, 5, 272
gondolas 81, 179, 181, 193, 229, 238, 267
grammar school 14–15, 17–22
  curriculum and pedagogy 17, 19–22
  see also Eton College; Winchester College
Gravesend 120
Grimani, Marino, Doge 5, 9, 85, 157, 162, 168, 175, 188, 195, 196–97, 198
  see also Venetian, government: doge
Guicciardini 39
Guise, Henri I de Lorraine duke of 45–46, 49, 88, 101
gunpowder plot 196–97, 198, 200, 204, 208, 212, 216, 240, 251, 253, 264

Hague 2, 272
Hakluyt, Richard 51
Hamburg 149
Harington, John [n.b., not the same as John Harrington] 227–29, 252
Harrington, John [n.b., not the same as John Harington] 145–46, 147
Hatton, Christopher 104
Hawkyns, John 44
health and illness 43, 53, 78, 85, 88, 103, 112, 138–39, 140, 192–93, 229, 233, 252, 259, 262, 264, 267
  see also medicine and anatomy
Heidelberg 64, 65–67, 68, 69, 70
Henrietta, Queen of England 273
Henri III, king of France 45–46, 49, 86, 101
  see also Paris: siege of
Henri of Navarre, Henri IV king of France
  assassination 257, 262
  England 111, 189, 213
  Interdict Crisis 210, 218
  political stage 102, 218, 261
  religion 88
  succession 49, 101, 261
  'war of the quill' 253
  see also Interdict Crisis: France
Henry VIII, king 2, 15, 113
Henry, Prince of Wales 9, 181, 192, 227, 228–29, 271

Henslowe, Philip 103–4
heresy, heretic 53, 88, 89–90, 164, 180, 186, 196, 204, 218, 225, 245, 246, 248, 270
  books 183, 191, 224, 244, 245
  and Elizabeth I 2, 45, 203
  and James VI/I 197, 251
  and Wotton, Henry 53, 202, 217
  see also Roman Curia: papal Inquisition; Rome, city of: punishment and persecution
Hickes, Baptist 106, 113
Hickes, Michael 112
Hilliard, Nicholas 16
Holbein, Hans the Elder 113
Horace 31
horses (unnamed) 64–5, 95, 119, 255
Hotman, François 67–68, 70
Hotman, Jean 68, 110
Howard, Charles, lord admiral 116, 119, 121, 133
Howard, Henry 115
Howard, Thomas, duke of Norfolk 16
Howard, Thomas, vice-admiral 119, 126
Huguenot 45, 49, 51, 88, 111
humanism and humanist education 15, 30–31, 51–52, 109, 152, 174
Hungary 69, 71

Imperial Library, Vienna 73–75, 161
intelligencers *see* spies, spying
Interdict Crisis
  argument 198–203
  books and printing 205, 224, 240
    Monitorio 203, 207
    Protesto 205, 206–7, 220, 241, 242
    'war of the quill' 224, 241–52, 257
    see also Wotton, Henry: *Letter from Venice* and Protestant revolution, hopes of
  conclusion 219–21, 222–23, 240
  England 197–98, 211, 214, 217, 218, 223
  France 217–18, 223
  proposed league 206–7, 209, 210, 212, 214–15, 218, 222, 228, 236, 270
    Cecil's rebuke 214–16

Spain 211, 216, 218, 222–23
Venice mobilising 207, 209, 217, 219
see also Cecil, Robert: manipulating state affairs; James VI/I; Roman Curia
Irish campaign
  Armagh 139
  Bellaclynthe 139–40
  Cahir Castle, Tipperary 128
  communications 133–34, *135*, 136, 137–42
  Crown's instructions 136, 138–39, 140, 142, 143
  Dublin 102, 133–36, *135*, 137–38, 139, 142
  earl of Tir-Oen (Tyrone) 102–3, 133, 136, 137, 138, 139–42, *141*, 143, 234–36
  Leinster 136, 137
  mobilisation 132–34, 136
  treaty with Tyrone *135*, 140, 142, 234
  truce 139–40, *141*, 143, 235
  Ulster 102, 136, 137, 138–39, 142, 236
  Wicklow 139
  see also Spenser, Edmund: 'View of the Present State of Ireland'

James VI/I, king
  as author 208
    An Apology for the oath of allegiance 249
    Basilikon Doron 151
    Daemonologie 151
    'The King's Book' 250–55
    'Premonition' 250–51, 257, 268
    The True Law of Free Monarchies 151, 200, 249
  and Robert Cecil, 4, 23, 28, *29*, 146, 170, 249, 251–52
    see also Cecil, Robert: manipulating state affairs
  and earl of Essex 23, 146
  gunpowder plot 196–97, 204, 208, 212, 227, 251
  Interdict Crisis

James VI/I, king (*cont.*)
   and Zorzi Giustinian 207–9, 210–11, 214
      league 206, 207, 210–12
      sovereignty 200, 207–8, 212, 223, 240
   Ireland 235–36
   liberalisation policy 185
   Oath of Allegiance 196, 208, 248–49, 250, 251, 253
   portrait *153*
   Rex Pacificus 2, 152, 200, 228
   and Fra Sarpi 248
   succeeds to the English throne 2, 13, 23, 152
   and Henry Wotton 5, 23–24, 150, 185, 191, 192, 213, 240, 242, 244, 246, 249, 260, 262, 272
      Ottavio Baldi 149–52, 176, 194, 209, 217, 233, 249, 268
      correspondence 3, 9, 18, 164–65, 209, 183, 185, 249, 257, 268
      in Scotland 149–151
      sent ambassador to Venice 2–3, 80, 152
   see also Henry, Prince of Wales; pirates and piracy: 'Proclamation Against Pirates'; Roman Curia
Jesuits 88, 92, 93, 177–78, 184, 185, 191–92, 196, 200, 202, 204, 206, 207, 210, 226
   England 235, 240–41
   Interdict crisis 206–7, 209, 220, 242, 266
   Italy 242, 266
   papal 235, 243, 245, 248
   Wotton's map of Venice 266
Jews
   Padua 78, 239
   Rome 89
   Venice 4, 58, 82, 85, 178–79, 181, 267
   see also Luzzati, Isaac 'Ebreo'
Jewel, John bishop of Salisbury
   Apology of the Church of England 245
Joyeuse, François de 219–22

Kent 15, 16, 23, 46, 59, 61, 63, 109
King's College, Cambridge 110
   see also individual colleges

law of nations 35, 38, 39, 183
Leicester, Robert Dudley earl of 45, 47, 49, 67, 68, 104, 107, 110, 232
Leith 149
Lentulo, Scipione 106
Lepanto 8, 193
Levant 166, 172
Lipsius 39
Livorno 94
Livy 39
Lomax, tutor 225
London 1, 2, 3, 5, 13, 18, 23, 24, 35, 38, 44, 45, 46, 47, 52, 54, 59, 60
   Addle Street 60, 61
   Bow Lane 60
   Bread Street 62
   Cheapside 61, 62
   Cordwainer Street 62
   Cripplegate 60–61, 62
   Deptford Docks 63, 121
   Essex House 99, 103, 106, 111, 143, 144–45, 182, 192, 259
   Finsbury fields 103
   Fore Street 60
   Golding Lane 60
   Goldsmith's Row 62
   Gray's Inn 59, 64
   King Street 267
   Lad Lane 61
   Leicester House 103
   Little Wood Street 61
   London Bridge 61
   Love Lane 61
   Milk Street 62
   Monkswell Street 60
   Moorgate 62, 103
   Old Jewry 61
   Paternoster Row 62
   Poultry 62
   Queenhithe 62, 63
   Redcross Street 60, 62, 64
   Shoreditch 103
   Silver Street 61

St Nicholas Shambles 62
Stinking Alley 62
Strand 99, 103, 145
Temple Bar 103
Thames 45, 61, 62, 63, 81, 103, 104, 119, 217, 230, 272
Three Cranes 63
Tower of London 27, 103
Tyburn 62, 146
Wapping 103
Westminster 103, 196, 267
Whitechapel Street 103
Whitehall 67, 111, 145, 196, 200, 214, 268
see also plague
London churches
  St Albans 61
  St Giles 61
  St Mary le Bow 62
  St Paul's 61, 62, 66, 196, 240
London guilds 60–61
Luther, Martin 35–36, 70
Luzzati, Isaac 'Ebreo' 181, 186, 267

Machiavelli 39, 90, 222
Madalena, raped and murdered 162
Maddox, Griffin 64
Madrid 2, 183
Margate 44, 45
Marlowe, Christopher 31
  Dr Faustus 32
  The Jew of Malta 90
  portrait 32
  Tamburlaine 31, 61
Mary, queen of England 2, 7
Mary, queen of Scots 16, 38, 45, 71
de' Medici, Cosimo, Grand Duke of Tuscany 269
de' Medici, Ferdinando, Grand Duke of Tuscany 29, 87, 94, 147–49, 150, 232–33
medicine and anatomy 17, 22, 37, 40, 42, 43, 53–54, 60, 78, 80, 85, 87, 229, 257, 265
  see also farmacie; health and illness
Mediterranean 2, 8, 62, 69, 166, 168, 172, 218, 233, 252, 268
  see also piracy

Meietti, Roberto, bookseller 244
Melanchthon, Philip 70
Mendoza, Bernardino de (Spanish ambassador in England) 38, 43, 46
merchants 39, 56, 84, 89, 174, 184, 260
  currency exchange and credit 54, 63, 66, 79, 145
  intelligencers and informers 106, 188, 207
  piracy 165–67, 169, 234
  postal service and communication 54, 67, 207
  trade 66, 82, 166–67, 171, 234
  see also Parvish, Henry; Pert, Nicholas; trade routes
Merrick, Gelly 109, 126, 137, 144, 145, 146
Merton College, Oxford 110
Milan 64, 149, 184, 186, 189, 191, 209, 218, 225, 235, 238, 244, 246, 261, 269
Mole, John 225–26
Molin, Nicolò 161, 165, 167, 173–74, 195–96, 197, 198, 282
Monteagle, William Parker lord 196
de Monti, Gregorio 182, 190, 267, 271
Morgan, Matthew 126
Morton, Albertus 182
Moryson, Fynes *see* travel: advice to travellers *and* travel writing
Mountjoy *see* Blount, Charles
Mulcaster, Richard 17, 18, 55, 184
  see also grammar school: curriculum and pedagogy

Naples 48, 49, 64, 91, 226
Netherlands *see* Spain: war in the Netherlands and Low Countries
Neville, Henry 115
New College, Oxford 19
Nine Years War *see* Irish campaign
nobili 8, 157, 174, 180, 202, 210, 223, 238–39, 282
North Sea 46, 47, 64, 149
Nuremberg 67, 70

Ortelius 31, *50*
Ottoman Empire 68–69
Ovid 20, 31, 33, 152
Oxford
   city of 18, 19, 39, 43, 44, 120, 126
   university 19, 30, 31, 32, 33, 35, 36, 37, 38, 43, 46, 48, 60, 65, 68, 70, 85, 110, 152, 162, 192
   see also individual colleges

Palma 265
Palma, Giacobo 269
Palmer, Thomas 55, 56–57, 72
Paris 2, 45–46, 183, 186, 241, 267, 269
   Bartholomew's Day massacre 51
   siege of 71, 88, 101–2, 119
   and Rowland Woodward 189, 213
   see also Committee of Sixteen
Parker, Matthew, archbishop of Canterbury 15, 31
Parkhurst, William 182, 183, 186, 187, 221
Parma, Alexander Farnese, duke of 45–46, 65
Parvish, Henry 60, 62–63, 66, 67, 79, 84
pasquinades 192, 240, 241
Peake, Robert 227
Percy, Thomas earl of Northumberland 16
Pert, Nicholas 171–74
Phelippes, Thomas 94, 106
physicians *see* medicine and anatomy
Piers, William 167
pirates and piracy
   accusations of 161, 165–67
   attempt to remedy 170, 268
   Barbary 69
   'diplomatic nightmare' 234
   England 69, 166–68
   Ireland 69
   Mediterranean 2, 166, 167–69, 233–34
   'Proclamation Against Pirates' 234
   Wotton's audience with the Collegio 167–68, 169–70
   see also Piers, William; Shirley, Thomas; Ward, John

Pirrone 205
plague 88
   London 103–4, 262, 264
   Oxford 43
   Venice 78, 85
Plato 39, 205
Plautus 20, 39
playwriting and literary entertainment 31, 33–35, 105, 192
   see also Globe playhouse; Marlowe, Christopher; Shakespeare, William
Plutarch 39, 89, 174, 205
Plymouth 44, 116, 119–21, *122*, 124, 126, 128, *129*, 132
poetry 35, 36, 38, 49, 52, 111
Ponte del Casetlvecchio 78
popes *see* Roman Curia
popolani 56, 83, 158, 180, 199, 200, 206, 209, 216
   the Church 228
   the Venetian State 244
Possevino, Antonio 177–78, 183, 192, 194, 202, 203, 207, 217, 241, 243, 245, 266
   see also Jesuits
postal service, sending and receiving letters 54, 66–67, 184, 186, 188–89, 196, 206, 215, 230, 244
prison, 'The Compter' 61
Privy Council 19, 23, 38, 48, 51, 103, 104–5, 107, 112, 117, 128, 131, 132, 133, 138, 143, 248
   in Ireland 136, 142–43
Protestantism 17, 35, 53, 65, 88, 105, 108
   hostility in Italy 53, 88, 225, 229, 231
   ritual observance 40, 154, 180, 186, 228
   see also Huguenot; Wotton, Henry: *Letters from Venice and Protestant revolution, hopes of*
Puritans 36, 145, 164–65
putta di anni otto, 269
   see also Carpan, Agustin

Queen's College, Oxford 30–33, 46, 85
  alternative curriculum 31, 33, 36, 37, 38, 43, 68
  college curriculum 31–32, 42, 43
  see also clothing: student attire; *individual colleges*

Rainoldes, John
  attacks college plays 36
Raleigh, Walter 119–20, 124, 126, 146
Ramsgate 44
Reade, Thomas 137
Reformation 17, 45, 47, 60, 62, 70, 82, 192, 195, 250, 251
Reynolds, Edward
  character 111, 143
  correspondences between the secretariat *135*, 136, 137, 139, 142, 147
  education 109, 110
  marriage 114
  secretary to earl of Essex 109, 110, 111–12, 113, 114–15, 118–19, 120, 133, 143
    Essex arrested 143, 146
Richter, Johann 70
Roman Curia
  control of books 244–45, 254–56
    see also Interdict Crisis: books and printing
  Holy See 202, 206, 222, 245
  and James VI/I 164–65, 197, 204
  papal Inquisition
    Court of Inquisition 245
    investigations and arrests 53, 91, 92, 190, 202, 225, 226, 245
    seizing possessions and books 232, 244–45, 254, 255, 256
    Wotton's diplomatic immunity 40, 164, 183, 245
  papal jurisdiction 199
  papal nuncio in Venice 164–65, 180, 183, 191, 196, 202, 205, 206–7, 242, 245, 246–47, 254
  popes
    Clement VIII 88–90, 185, 196
    Gregory 54
    Leo XI 185
    Paolo V 3, 185, 195, 199, 222, 245, 246, 249, 269
      and Robert Parsons 185
    Pio V 2
    see also Catholicism; Interdict Crisis: books and publishing: 'war of the quill'; James VI/I: 'The King's Book', *Oath of Allegiance;* Sarpi: assassination attempt
Rome
  city of 1, 4, 22, 28, 36, 55, 60, 64, 70, 71, 80, 106, 177, 189, 219, 222, 249
  English College 93
  punishment and persecution 87–89, 263
  Roman College 92–93
  travel 88, 225–26, 238
  and earl of Tyrone 234–36
  see also Roman Curia: control of books; spies and spying: Wotton's network: Rome; Wotton, Henry: travel to/in Rome
Rooke, George 182, 187
Roos, William Cecil lord 225–26
Rudolf II, Holy Roman Emperor 49, 71
Rutland, Roger Manners earl of 105, 115, 144

St John, Oliver baron Bletso 225–26
St Leger, Warham 143
Sansovino, Jacopo 7, 80, 179
Sarpi, Paolo
  Apologia 241, 243
  assassination attempt 246–48
  Court of Inquisition 245
  excommunicated 202, 218
  and James VI/I's writing 250
  libretti 241
  pamphlet 241
  portrait 246, *247*, 250
  Protesto see Interdict Crisis: books and printing
  Rome and the Church 218, 245
  and Henry Wotton 203, 242, 243, 246, *247*, 250, 252, 267
  see also Wotton, Henry: Protestant revolution, hopes of

Savoy, Charles Emmanuel duke of
    261, 269
Sbarra, Marco di 89
Scaramelli, Giovanni Carlo
    England 2, 24, 28, 207
    and Henry Wotton 8–10, 159–61,
        160, 165, 168, 171, 174, 184,
        201–2, 205, 268
Schoppe, Caspar 272
Scotland *see individual monarchs, towns and
    cities*
Seget, Scottish youth arrested in
    Venice 9, 162–63, 174
Shakespeare, John 15
Shakespeare, William 13, 15, 19
    Hamlet 20, 21, 258
    Henry IV 120
    Henry VIII or All is True 1, 272
    Love's Labour's Lost 191, 192
    Macbeth 92, 237
    Merry Wives of Windsor, The 14
    Othello 5
    Richard II 272
    Taming of the Shrew, The 31
    Two Gentlemen of Verona, The 47, 52
    Venus and Adonis 31
ships
    The Angel 167–68, 170, 175, 176
    Ark Royal 124
    bertone 166–67, 169
    Corsaletta 234, 262, 263
    Due Repulse 23, 120, 121, 123–25,
        127, 128
    Husband 176, 234
    Marita 176, 194
    Mary Rose 124
    Moresini 168–70
    Rainbow 124
    recognition at sea 168–70, 184,
        268
    San Felipe (*The Philip*) 124–25, 127
    Seraphim 234
    Soderina 234
    Victory 44
    Vineyard 63
    Warspight 124
Shirley, Antony 148
Shirley, Thomas 167

Shrewsbury, George Talbot earl of 104
Sidney, Frances 107
    see also Walsingham, Frances
Sidney, Henry 15
Sidney, Philip
    death 107, 110
    Defence of Poesy 49
    and earl of Essex 94, 107
    family 49
    Gentili dedicates *De legationibus libri
        tres* 42–43
    licence to travel 64
    reading 35
    travel advice to brother Robert 51,
        52
    and Edward Wotton 42, 48, 69, 94
    and Henry Wotton 42
Siena 94, 105
Sigismund III Vasa, king of Poland 71
silk road 82
Smith, Mr (Cambridge University
    undergraduate) 31, 32
Southampton, Henry Wriothesley earl
    of 27, 105, 117, 144, 147,
    149
Southwell, Elizabeth 232, 233
Spain
    England and the English throne 45,
        166–67
    France 101, 102, 189
    inquisition 190
    intelligence gathering 189–190
    and earl of Tyrone 235–36
    Venice 147–48, 179
    war in the Netherlands and Low
        Countries 45, 63, 65, 68,
        101, 126, 189
    see also Anglo-Spanish peace;
        Armada, 'The Invincible';
        Cadiz; Catholic League;
        Essex, earl of: Azores voyage;
        Felipe II, king of Spain;
        Interdict Crisis; Mendoza,
        Bernardino de
Spenser, Edmund 35
    The Faerie Queene 31
    'View of the Present State of Ireland'
        136–37

spies and spying 4, 37, 42, 57, 58, 85, 190
   confidenti 58, 187–88
   informants 72, 182, 229
   intelligence and intelligencers 48, 69, 71–75, 111, 136, 147–48, 149, 179, 190, 209, 228, 238
   and Wotton's network 105–6, 185–86, 191, 200, 206, 235, 238, 254
   famiglia 187–90
   Milan 186, 189, 218
   Rome 88, 201–2, 266
   see also Canaye, Philippe; Wotton, Henry: informant/intelligencer
Stade 63, 66, 68, 70, 74
Steganography, Book of 73–75
Stirling 150
Stow, John 47, 101, 103
Suetonius 31

Tacitus 3, 39, 106, 111, 152, 170, 174, 192
Tagliaferro, Bartolomeo 231
Tancredi (in *La Gerusalemme liberata*) 33–34, 36, 42, 152, 211
   see also Tasso, Torquato
Tasso, Torquato 34–36, 38–39, 52
telescope 70, 257, 269
Temple, William 109–10, 111, 114, 132, 133, 134, 137, 144, 146
   see also Essex, earl of: secretariat
Terence 20
Tichborne, Chidiock 61
Tilbury 45, 47
Tintoretto, Jacopo Robusti 8, 81
Tirconnel, Rory O'Donnell, first earl of 236
Titian, Vecellio Tiziano 7, 81, 269
trade routes 166
   see also piracy; silk road; *uve passe*
travel
   advice to travellers 52, 54, 60, 79–80
      Thomas Coryat 58, 66
      Fynes Moryson 52–55, 57, 58, 59, 72, 75, 80, 88, 91–92
      Thomas Palmer 52, 55, 56–57, 72

   as pilgrims 53, 82
   as Protestants 53, 57, 90, 225–26
   see also Alps, the; Coryat, Thomas; Essex, earl of; Wotton, Henry: travel
Aristotle 52
cultural difference 51, 55, 58
humanism 52
language learning *see* Florio, John; Gentili, Alberico; Moryson, Fynes; Palmer; Thomas
licences to travel 27, 51, 56, 64, 148, 227
money exchange and currency 63, 66, 79
quarantine 78
Sanità 78, 264
tolomazo (tour guide) 81
travel writing 51–53, 64–65
   Thomas Coryat 77, 78, 79, 80, 81, 86, 87
   Fynes Moryson 77, 78, 79, 85, 86, 87, 91
   see also Ascham, Roger; Elyot, Thomas; Palmer, Thomas; Sidney, Philip
Trinity College, Cambridge 43, 106
   see also individual colleges
Trinity College, Oxford 110
   see also individual colleges
Trithemius, Johannes *see Steganography*
Trento 149
Tresham, Francis 144
Troynovant 44
Tyrone, Hugh O'Neill earl of 234–36
   see also Irish campaign

uve passe 63, 166, 171

vecchi 7, 177
Vendramin, Francesco 5, 7, 8
Venice, apothecary shops *see farmacie*
Venice, barber shops 187, 188
   Borsetto's 187
Venice, churches
   Basilica San Marco 4, 81, 83, 188, 192, 202, 220
   Giovanni e Paolo (Zanipolo) 193

Venice, churches (*cont.*)
  Madonna dell'Orto 179
  Redentore, Chiesa del Santissimo
    78, 265
  San Felice 181
  San Francesco della Vigna 81
  San Giacomo di Rialto 84
  San Giovanni Elemosinario 82
  San Girolamo 176, 178–79, 181,
    187, 192, 265
  San Lorenzo 228, 252
  San Marcuola 181
  San Zulian 81
  Santa Lucia 179
  Santa Maria dell'Umiltà 178, 266
  Santo Spirito 7, 8
Venice, city
  anchorage tax 170–71, 184, 268
  Jewish Ghetto 4, 58, 82, 85, 178–79,
    181, 238, 265
  Palazzo Ducale 4, 6, 80–81, 82, 83,
    157–58, 218, 222, 265
    Bridge of Sighs 7
    Consiglio di Dieci 7
    Porta della Carta 6
    Sala del Collegio 4, 8, 157, *158*,
      159, 163, 168, 171, 187, 188,
      193, 201, 202, 203, 206, 207,
      216, 218, 220, 222, 223, 227,
      229, 231, 233, 234, 242, 246,
      252–54, 259, 262, 265, 268
    Sala delle Quattro Porte 7
    Sala del Senato 157
    Sala di Anticollegio 7, 211
    Scala dei Giganti 6
    Scala d'Oro 7, 10, 219, 222, 256,
      260
  Piazza San Marco 6, 81, 82–83, 158,
    174, 176, 179, 187, 188, 216,
    256, 260, 266, 269
    Biblioteca Marciana 80
    broglio 83, 162, 187–88, 265
    Campanile 80
    Canal Grande 6, 80, 81, 171
      gondolas 5–6, 81
    columns
      Lion of San Marco 6, 84, 157
      Teodoro 84
    Fondaco dei Tedeschi 84, 174
    Loggetta 80
    Merceria 4, 82, 84, 188, 266
    Molo 83–84
    Rialto 82, 84, 174, 187, 188
      Banco Giro 84
      bridge 84, 85, 266
      market 84
    Torre dell'Orologio 84
    Zecca 80
  La Serenissima 4, 8, 81, 87, 263, 269
  telling time in 81–82
    bells 82, 181, 186
  see also courtesans
Venice, government 2
  Church and State 164
  Collegio 5, 157–62, *160*, 163, 164,
    167, 169, 170, 172, 173, 174,
    182, 184, 185, 186, 195, 198,
    200, 203, 204, 205, 210, 212,
    213, 214, 217, 220, 224, 228,
    231, 233, 260, 263, 264, 265
    function and procedure 5,
      157–59, 162, 198
    Interdict Crisis 199, 200, 201
      202–3, 204–5, 206, 208, 210,
      212, 214, 217, 218, 220, 224
    'The King's Book' 253
    personnel 5, 188
    records
      Delle Lettere di Principi 161
      Relazione degli Ambasciatori 161
    Wotton's diplomatic
      embarrassment 254–55,
      259–60
    Wotton's resignation 266–67
    see also Scaramelli, Giovanni
      Carlo; Wotton, Henry:
      esposizioni with doge and
      Collegio
  Consiglio di Dieci 7, 162, 163, 171,
    172, 173, 204, 269
  Decime, city-wide audit 181
  doge 3, 6, 8, 80, 83, 85, 157–58,
    162, 163, 183, 191, 193, 245
    election of 195, 196
    see also Donà, Leonardo;
      Grimani, Marino; Wotton,

Henry: esposizioni with doge and Collegio
Maggior Consiglio 82, 157, 195, 213
Necrologia 85
Pregadi 157
Sanità, health authority 78, 264
Savii 8, 10, 157, *158*, 159, 163, 174, 188, 253, 254–55
Senato (Signoria, Signory) 5, 7, 8, 9, 24, 28, 56, 82, 89–90, 157, 159, 161, 164, 168, 170, 174, 175, 177, 184, 187, 196, 198, 200, 203, 236, 250, 259, 265, 269, 270
  calendars 183, 198, 223–24
  and Elizabeth I 56
  embassy 178–79, 180, 181
  function and procedure 5, 9, 82, 83, 157, 159, 168, 175, 187, 198
  Interdict Crisis 199, 202, 203, 206–14, 217, 218–19, 220, 222, 223, 242
  'The King's Book' 252–53, 254–55
  personnel 7, 8–9, 24, 83, 157, 175, 177
  Relazione degli Ambasciatori 161
  and Henry Wotton 9, 161, 163, 168, 170, 184, 200, 201, 202, 203, 206, 224, 260, 253, 255, 265
Venice, Terraferma empire
  Bassano del Grappa 77
  Padua 77, 78, 79, 87, 91, 162, 192, 193, 226, 229, 238, 246, 264, 267
    death of Julius Caesar 230–32
    fencing school 231
    Wotton's health 259
    Wotton's return to England 267
    university 6, 22, 31, 229
    see also Galilei, Galileo
  Treviso 77, 231
  Verona 52, 77, 78
  Vicenza 77
Vere, Francis 124, 125, 127
Veronese, Paolo Caliari 8, 81

Vienna 49, 64, 70, 72–75, 76, 80, 91, 101, 106, 108, 110, 119, 133, 152, 159, 161
Vinta, Belisario 147–49, 152
Virgil 20, 31
Virgin Mary 39, 251

Wales 18, 109
  Catholics, Catholicism 164, 192
  travel across 134, 137
Walsingham, Frances 49, 107
Walsingham, Francis 15, 48, 49, 56, 94, 104, 106
Walton, Izaak 17, 18, 23, 27, 33, 37, 38, 147
  The Compleat Angler 273
  'Life' of Henry Wotton 30, 148, 273
Ward, John 167, 233–34, 252, 268
Warwick, Ambrose Dudley duke of 104
Waterford 69
White, Harry 64
Willis, Simon 236–38
Wilson, Thomas 112
Winchester College 15, 18–22, 30, 33, 109, 152
  as ludus literarius 21
  see also grammar school: curriculum and pedagogy
Windsor 14, 17, 44
Woodward, Rowland 182, 187, 189–90, 200, 213
  see also Wotton, Henry: *famiglia*
Wolfe, John 35
women 68, 70, 79, 80, 85–86, 87, 89, 95
  nuns 180, 187, 192, 238, 262
  youths cross dressing as 21, 35, 36
  see also courtesans
Wotton, Edward 18–19, 48, 59, 68, 94, 106, 147, 152, 182, 280
  correspondence with brother Henry 23–24, 62, 63, 64, 65–66, 67, 69, 258
  and Philip Sidney 42, 94
Wotton, Eleanora 17
Wotton, Henry (Harry)
  adapts *La Gerusalemme liberata*
    see Torquato Tasso

311

Wotton, Henry (Harry) *(cont.)*
  achievements 267–70
  Bocton Malherbe 15–18, 23, 31, 46, 58, 95
  death 273
  diplomatic embarrassment 254–57, 259–60
  entrata 7
  esposizioni (audiences) with doge and Collegio 5, 158–59, 163, 167, 169–70, 173, 174, 183, 184, 203–5, 213, 223–24, 231, 234, 246, 256, 259, 262, 265
  and earl of Essex 13, 23, 25, 33, 43, 99, 106, 108–11, 113, 114, 117–27, *118, 129,* 130–31, 132, *135*
    Cadiz 5, 10, 23, *122,* 123–28, 132, 154, 176, 180, 194
    introduction 94
    Ireland 10, 132, 133, 134–43, 235
    rebellion 13, 23, 27, 144, 147, 272, 280–82
  'estate of Italy ... wherein I leave it' 263
  exile 3, 5, 10, 13, 23, 25, *26,* 29, 147, 149, 152, 177, 182
  famiglia 6, 39, 86, 165, 178, 182, 183, 186, 187, 188, 191, 193, 194, 244, 254, 262–63, 267
    see also spies and spying: and Wotton's network
  finances
    as ambassador 181–82, 188, 191
    as student traveller 66–67, 93, 95
  'Flight of the Earls' 234–36, 236
  and Alberico Gentili 35–43, 48, 55, 56, 90, 152, 183, 184, 225, 243, 256
  giorno d'audientia 5
  and Marino Grimani 5, 9, 85, 162, 188, 198
  gunpowder plot 198–99
  Heidelberg 64, 65, 66–67, 68, 69, 70
  illness 85, 252, 258–59
  Imperial Library, Vienna 73, 74, 161
  informant/intelligencer 57–58, 72, 90–91, 147–48 149, 152, 183, 185–86, 201–2, 203, 235
    to Edward de la Zouche 71–75, 87–90, 93, 106
    see also spies and spying: Wotton's network
  installation as ambassador 2–5, 152
  instructions from James I/VI 164
  Interdict Crisis 199–203, 204–210, 211–12, 214–21, 217–19, 220, 243
    proposes league 206, 207, 210, 222
    see also Interdict Crisis: proposed league: Cecil's rebuke; James VI/I
  introduces John Harington 227
  'The King's Book' 250, 252–55
  lectures on eyesight and optics 37, 152
  Letter from Venice 241–43, 249, 268
  and Ferdinando de' Medici 87, 94, 147–49, 150, 152, 182, 233
  mission to Scotland 149–152
  Oath of Allegiance 248–49
  piracy 167–68
  Protestant revolution, hopes of 95, 200, 209–10, 219, 222, 224, 229, 239, 241–52
  Provost at Eton College 265, *271,* 272
  religious observation/Protestantism 2, 69, 72, 92, 108, 163, 165, 180
  resignation 255, 256, 259, 260, 266–67
  return to England 258–59, 261–63, 267
  school *see* Winchester College
  sex 80, 85–86
  subsequent appointments 271
  travel in Europe 47–48, 58 59–75, 281
  travel in Italy 30, 77–87, 94–95
  travel to/in Rome 22, 64, 87–93, 177, 200
  university 3, 22, 29, 30–43

see also Oxford
   see also ambassador; diplomacy;
      embassy: English in Venice;
      spies and spying: Wotton's
      network
'war of the quill' 224, 241–44, 253–54
Wotton, James 19, 120, 127
Wotton, John 19
Wotton, Nicholas 19, 31

Wotton, Pickering 147, 186
Wotton, Thomas 15–16, 18–19, 30, 31, 49

York 15, 44, 54

Zouche, Edward de la, baron of *see* Henry Wotton: informant/ intelligencer